U0821321

pwc

普华永道

普华永道国际财务报告准则实务指引——金融工具系列（第一册）
PricewaterhouseCoopers IFRS Manual of Accounting — Financial Instruments Series (Volume One)

IFRS Manual of Accounting — Financial Instruments

Chapter 1 – Overview
Chapter 2 – Introduction
Chapter 3 – Objectives and scope of IAS 32, IAS 39 and IFRS 7
Chapter 4 – Nature and characteristics of financial instruments
Chapter 7 – Financial liabilities and equity
Chapter 11 – Presentation and disclosure

国际财务报告准则实务指引——金融工具

第一章—概览
第二章—引言
第三章—国际会计准则第 32 号、国际会计准则第 39 号及国际财务报告准则第 7 号的目标与范围
第四章—金融工具的性质和特征
第七章—金融负债和权益
第十一章—列报和披露

中英文对照

主译：陈燕华
翻译组主要成员：陈闪

中国财政经济出版社

编写本书之目的是对感兴趣的事项给予一般性的指导，而非提供专业建议。未征得具体专业意见之前，不应依据本书所述内容采取任何行动。我们不对书中所述信息是否准确或完整作出任何明示或暗示的承诺或保证。除非法律另有明文规定，普华永道不对任何个人或单位因为阅读了本书而采取或未采取某项行动的后果、或基于本书所作出的任何决定承担任何责任。

本书内容为英文本中的一个章节及其中文译文，指导概以英文为准。出版社和编译者不对英文原文及中文译文的偏差或误解承担任何责任，也不对任何个人或单位因为阅读了本书而采取或未采取某项行动所发生损失承担任何责任。

Preface

Businesses around the world are becoming more global and much of the accounting standard – setters' focus today is concerned with global harmonisation of accounting requirements. Against this backdrop, International Financial Reporting Standards (IFRS) have become increasingly important as the global business language. IFRS aims to be a comprehensive set of neutral principles that produce consistent, comparable, relevant and reliable financial information useful for investors, lenders, creditors, and those who make decisions in the capital markets. PricewaterhouseCoopers (PwC) is strongly committed to a common goal of promoting these financial reporting standards to preparers and users.

This Manual covers the complex accounting requirements of financial instruments. This aspect of accounting has become increasingly complicated in recent years and this book inclndes a wealth of practical examples and illustrations to help explain this difficult subject.

The IFRS Manual of Accounting is a comprehensive practical guide to IFRS and provides straightforward explanations of how to prepare financial statements in accordance with IFRS, with hundreds of practical examples. The Manual was developed based on the extensive experience of the PwC's global network of firms.

Due to the importance of IFRS for many companies in China and the continued convergence of China Accounting Standards and IFRS, PwC China has undertaken a significant project to translate our IFRS Manual of Accounting into Chinese. We sincerely hope that our IFRS Manual of Accounting with Chinese Translation provides practical insights and can help finance directors, accountants, auditors, analysts and other users of financial statements to bridge the gap between accounting principles and their applications.

Ernest Ip
Senior Partner
PwC China and Hong Kong

前　言

全世界的商业正变得更为全球化，且如今会计准则制定者的大部分关注点在于会计规定的全球一致化。在此背景下，国际财务报告准则（以下简称为“IFRS”）作为全球商业用语变得愈发重要。IFRS 旨在成为一套全面性、中性的原则，向投资者、借款方、债权人及其他需在资本市场中作出决策的人士提供一致的、可比较的、相关的及可靠的财务信息。普华永道致力于将这些财务准则推广给财务报表编制者及使用者这一共同目标。

这本国际财务报告准则实务指引介绍了与金融工具相关的一系列复杂的会计要求。近些年来，这方面的会计准则变得越来越复杂，而本书包括了丰富的实务案例帮助解释这一高难度的课题。

本国际财务报告准则实务指引是对 IFRS 的全面性实务指引，该指引是基于普华永道全球成员机构网络丰富的经验予以归纳而成的。对如何按照 IFRS 编制财务报表提供了简明的阐述，并附有诸多实务示例。

鉴于 IFRS 对中国的许多公司的重要性及中国会计准则与 IFRS 的持续趋同，普华永道中国已着手开始了一项具有重大意义的项目，即将国际财务报告准则实务指引译成中文。我们诚挚地希望本国际财务报告准则实务指引及其中文翻译能够提供实用的见解，并能够作为会计原则与其具体应用之间的桥梁来帮助财务总监、会计人员、审计人员、分析人员及其他财务报表使用者。

叶冠荣
首席合伙人
普华永道中国及香港

Overview/Introduction

Recent years have seen major changes in financial reporting worldwide with the single most important change being convergence around IFRS. In the wake of the global financial crisis, there has been unprecedented interest in financial instruments related accounting standards. Most of the hot topics that International Accounting Standards Board (IASB) has been discussing in the past few years are also related to financial instruments. There has also been a keen focus to improve the long term development of the CPA profession within China. As the Ministry of Finance and other regulatory bodies continue to promulgate legislation to promote the development of the Chinese CPA profession, we hope the release of our IFRS Manual of Accounting with Chinese Translation will also contribute to this effort.

The Ministry of Finance issued the Accounting Standards for Business Enterprises (hereafter referred to as "*China Accounting Standards*" or "*CAS*") in 2006. CAS incorporates all of the principles of IFRS and there has been a continued focus on convergence over the last few years. Additionally, IFRS is becoming increasingly important for many companies in China, including domestic companies seeking to raise capital overseas, as well as for foreign companies that have operations in China. With the continued convergence of CAS and IFRS, the release of our IFRS Manual of Accounting with Chinese Translation brings to China the extensive collective experience of the PwC's global network of firms in applying IFRS, especially the complex accounting requirements of financial instruments.

We hope this Manual will play a part in promoting consistent, comparable, relevant and reliable IFRS financial information and will serve as a reference tool for accounting students, academics, practitioners and users of financial statements in better understanding and implementing IFRS. More importantly, we hope the advice given in this text will assist those dealing with the many issues faced in preparing IFRS financial statements and provide helpful insight to users of such statements.

Raymund Chao
PwC Asia Pacific Assurance Leader

概述/引言

近年来全世界的财务报告发生了重大变化，其中最为重要的一项变化便是与国际财务报告准则的趋同。金融危机爆发后，各方面对金融工具相关准则的关注也上升到了一个前所未有的高度。国际会计准则委员会近几年来讨论最为热烈的议题也大多与金融工具相关。同时人们也热切地关注着中国境内注册会计师行业的长期发展。由于财政部及其他监管机构持续颁布法规以推动中国注册会计师行业的发展，我们希望本国际财务报告准则实务指引及其中文翻译的发行也能够对此作出贡献。

财政部于2006年颁布了《企业会计准则》（以下称为“*中国会计准则*”或“*CAS*”）CAS包含了IFRS中的所有原则，且在过去的几年里持续致力于两者的趋同。此外，IFRS对于中国的许多公司来说越来越重要，包括寻求筹集海外资本的国内公司以及由外国公司在中国境内投资的公司。随着CAS与IFRS的持续趋同，本国际财务报告准则实务指引及其中文翻译的发行将给中国带来普华永道全球成员机构网络在适用IFRS方面丰富的经验，尤其是金融工具复杂的会计处理。

我们希望本指引能够在推广一致的、可比的、相关的以及可靠的IFRS财务信息中起到作用，并且可以作为会计领域的学生、学者、从业人员及财务报表使用者更好地理解及运用IFRS的参考工具。更为重要的是，我们希望本指引中提出的建议能够帮助其处理在编制IFRS财务报表时遇到的问题，并向此类财务报表使用者提供有用的观点。

赵柏基
普华永道亚太区审计部主管合伙人

How to use this publication

Given the increasing importance of IFRS in China and the continued convergence of CAS and IFRS, the accounting technical team of PwC China and Hong Kong have undertaken a significant project to translate the IFRS Manual of Accounting into Chinese.

The Manual is a practical guide in applying IFRS and the views are based on the extensive experience of the PwC's global network of firms. However, IFRS is not static and is continuously developing. The views on its interpretation and application will adapt and evolve. The views expressed in this Manual are a guide to applying IFRS rather than a set of definitive interpretations. The application of IFRS requires significant judgement and specific facts and circumstances should be carefully considered.

IFRS Manual of Accounting with Chinese Translation will be released in different volumes. Depending on the topic, each release may be a chapter or a combination of a number of chapters from the Manual.

Because of the interdependencies between individual IFRS, there are many cross references between different chapters of the Manual. Although the IFRS Manual of Accounting with Chinese Translation will be released in different volumes, the cross references have been maintained. Users are encouraged to refer to those cross references in other translated chapters or to the English version of the Manual if it helps in their understanding.

This book is the first volume of IFRS Manual of Accounting – Financial Instruments 2011 Series with Chinese Translation. The content covers Chapter 1 – Overview, Chapter 2 – Introduction, Chapter 3 – Objectives and scope of IAS 32, IAS 39 and IFRS 7, Chapter 4 – Nature and characteristics of financial instruments, Chapter 7 – Financial liabilities and equity and Chapter 11 – Presentation and disclosure of the English version and its translation. While every effort has been made to ensure an accurate translation, reference should be made to the English version in the event there are any differences between the Chinese and English versions.

使用说明

鉴于 IFRS 在中国愈发重要以及 CAS 和 IFRS 的持续趋同，普华永道中国及香港的会计专业技术支持部门已着手开始了一项具有重大意义的项目，即将国际财务报告准则实务指引译成中文。

国际财务报告准则实务指引是对应用 IFRS 的实务指引，其中的观点是基于普华永道全球成员机构网络丰富的经验。然而，IFRS 不是静止的，而是持续发展的；因此，对 IFRS 的解释和适用会有所改变和发展。本指引表达的观点是对适用 IFRS 的一种指引，而非一套具有决定性的解释。IFRS 的应用需要大量的判断，还应当谨慎考虑特定的事实及所处的环境。

IFRS 实务指引及其中文翻译版将分成多册发行。根据主题，每一册可能是本指引的某一章节或是包含某几个章节。

由于各个 IFRS 准则之间的相互依存，因此本指引中不同的章节会相互参照索引。尽管 IFRS 实务指引及其中文翻译版将分成多册发行，但仍保留此类相互参照索引。如果有助于理解，我们鼓励读者阅读此类相互参照索引时参考其他已翻译的章节或指引的英文版。

本书为普华永道国际财务报告准则实务指引——金融工具系列（中英文对照）的第一册。内容为英文原版的《国际财务报告准则实务指引——金融工具》中的《第一章——概览》、《第二章——引言》、《第三章——国际会计准则第 32 号、国际会计准则第 39 号及国际财务报告准则第 7 号的目标与范围》、《第四章——金融工具的性质和特征》、《第七章——金融负债和权益》及《第十一章——列报和披露》。我们已尽最大的努力来确保翻译的准确，但中文翻译版与英文版出现不一致时，应参考英文版。

The English version of our IFRS Manual of Accounting Series includes 2 books: IFRS Manual of Accounting and IFRS Manual of Accounting – Financial Instruments with the following chapters.

IFRS Manual of Accounting

Accounting rules and principles

01 – Introduction

02 – Accounting principles and applicability of IFRS

03 – First-time adoption of IFRS

04 – Presentation of financial statements

05 – Accounting policies, accounting estimates and errors

06 – Hyper-inflation

07 – Foreign currencies

08 – Insurance contracts

Income statement and related notes

09 – Revenue and construction contracts

10 – Segment reporting

11 – Employee benefits

12 – Share-based payment

13 – Taxation

14 – Earnings per share

Balance sheet and related notes

15 – Intangible assets

16 – Property, plant and equipment

17 – Investment property

18 – Impairment of assets

19 – Lease accounting

20 – Inventories

21 – Provisions and contingencies

22 – Events after the reporting period and financial commitments

23 – Share capital and reserves

英文原版的普华永道国际财务报告准则实务指引系列包括《国际财务报告准则实务指引》和《国际财务报告准则实务指引——金融工具》两本书，其所有章节列示如下：

国际财务报告准则实务指引

会计规则和原则

01 – 引言

02 – 会计原则和国际财务报告准则的适用性

03 – 首次采用国际财务报告准则

04 – 财务报表的列报

05 – 会计政策、会计估计和差错

06 – 恶性通货膨胀

07 – 外币

08 – 保险合同

利润表及相关附注

09 – 收入与建造合同

10 – 分部报告

11 – 职工福利

12 – 以股份为基础的支付（“股份支付”）

13 – 所得税会计

14 – 每股收益

资产负债表及相关附注

15 – 无形资产

16 – 不动产、工厂和设备

17 – 投资性房地产

18 – 资产减值

19 – 租赁会计

20 – 存货

21 – 准备和或有事项

22 – 报告期后事项和财务承诺

23 – 股本和准备金

Consolidated financial statements

24 – Consolidated and separate financial statements

25 – Business combinations

26 – Disposal of subsidiaries, businesses and non-current assets

27 – Associates

28 – Joint ventures

Other subjects

29 – Related party disclosures IAS 24

30 – Statement of cash flows

31 – Interim reporting

32 – Agriculture

33 – Service concession arrangements

IFRS Manual of Accounting—Financial Instruments

01 – Overview

02 – Introduction

03 – Objectives and scope of IAS 32, IAS 39 and IFRS 7

04 – Nature and characteristics of financial instruments

05 – Embedded derivatives in host contracts

06 – Classification of financial instruments

07 – Financial liabilities and equity

08 – Recognition and derecognition

09 – Measurement of financial assets and liabilities

10 – Hedge accounting

11 – Presentation and disclosure

12 – IFRS 9, "Financial Instruments"

合并财务报表
24 – 合并财务报表和单独财务报表
25 – 业务合并
26 – 子公司、业务和非流动资产的处置
27 – 联营
28 – 合营

其他主题
29 – 关联方披露——国际会计准则第 24 号
30 – 现金流量表
31 – 中期报告
32 – 农业
33 – 服务特许权安排

国际财务报告准则实务指引——金融工具

01 – 概览
02 – 引言
03 – 国际会计准则第 32 号、国际会计准则第 39 号及国际财务报告准则第 7 号的目标与范围
04 – 金融工具的性质和特征
05 – 主合同中的嵌入衍生工具
06 – 金融工具的分类
07 – 金融负债和权益
08 – 确认和终止确认
09 – 金融资产和金融负债的计量
10 – 套期会计
11 – 列报和披露
12 – 国际财务报告准则第 9 号——金融工具

Abbreviations and terms used

Accounts	financial statements
AFS	available-for-sale
AG	Application Guidance
App	Appendix
ARC	Accounting Regulatory Committee
BC	Basis for Conclusions (to an accounting standard)
C	currency unit
Chp	Chapter
chapter (1)	'PricewaterhouseCoopers' Manual of accounting' – chapter (1)
CDO	collateralised debt obligation
CESR	Committee of European Securities Regulators
CLO	collateralised loan obligation
CPP	current purchasing power
DP	discussion paper
EBIT	earnings before interest and tax
EBITDA	earnings before interest, tax, depreciation and amortisation
ED	exposure draft
EFRAG	European Financial Reporting Advisory Group
EPS	earnings per share
EU	European Union
FASB	Financial Accounting Standards Board (US)
financial statements	Accounts
Framework	Framework for the preparation and presentation of financial statements
FVTPL	at fair value through profit or loss
GAAP	generally accepted accounting principles (and practices)

缩写及词汇对照

财务报表
可供出售
实施指南
附录
会计监管委员会
（某一准则的）结论基础
货币单位
章
第一章（普华永道《国际财务报告准则实务指引》——第一章）

担保债务凭证
欧洲证券监管委员会
担保贷款凭证
现行购买力
讨论稿
息税前收益
扣除利息、所得税、折旧和摊销之前的收益
征求意见稿
欧洲财务报告咨询组
每股收益
欧盟
（美国）财务会计准则委员会
财务报表
编报财务报表的框架

以公允价值计量且变动计入损益
公认会计原则

IAS	International Accounting Standard (see also IFRS)
IASB	International Accounting Standards Board
IFRIC	International Financial Reporting Interpretations Committee
IFRS	International Financial Reporting Standard (see also IAS)
IG	Implementation Guidance (to an accounting standard)
para(s)	paragraph(s) of Schedules to the Companies Acts, or IFRSs or IASs or FRSs, or SSAPs, or FREDs, or EDs, or DPs, or text
PPE	property, plant and equipment
US SEC	US Securities and Exchange Commission
SIC	Standing Interpretation Committee of the IASC (see IFRIC)
SPE	special purpose entity
UK	United Kingdom
US	United States of America

国际会计准则（亦请参见 IFRS）

国际会计准则理事会

国际财务报告解释委员会

国际财务报告准则（亦请参见 IAS）

（某一准则的）应用指南

段落（公司法、国际财务报告准则、国际会计准则、财务报告准则、会计实务准则、财务报告征求意见稿、征求意见稿、讨论稿或文章中的段落）

不动产、工厂和设备

美国证券交易委员会

国际会计准则委员会的常设解释委员会（参见 IFRIC）

特殊目的主体

英国

美国

Content

IFRS Manual of Accounting—Financial Instruments Series (Volume One)

Chapter 1	Overview	1001
Chapter 2	Introduction	2001
Chapter 3	Objectives and scope of IAS 32, IAS 39 and IFRS 7	3001
Chapter 4	Nature and characteristics of financial instruments	4001
Chapter 7	Financial liabilities and equity	7001
Chapter 11	Presentation and disclosure	11001

目　录

国际财务报告准则实务指引——金融工具系列（第一册）

第一章	概览	1002
第二章	引言	2002
第三章	IAS 32、IAS 39 及 IFRS 7 的目标与范围	3002
第四章	金融工具的性质和特征	4002
第七章	金融负债和权益	7002
第十一章	列报和披露	11002

Chapter 1 Overview

Content

Introduction	1001
Objectives and scope of IAS 32, IAS 39 and IFRS 7	1001
Nature and characteristics of financial instruments	1007
Embedded derivatives	1011
Classification of financial instruments	1013
Financial liabilities and equity	1017
Recognition and derecognition	1021
Measurement	1023
Hedge accounting	1029
Hedging instruments	1031
Hedge accounting criteria	1031
Hedge accounting rules	1033
Discontinuing hedge accounting	1035
Presentation and disclosure	1037
IFRS 9, 'Financial instruments'	1039

第一章　概览

目　录

引言	1002
IAS 32、IAS 39 及 IFRS 7 的目标与范围	1002
金融工具的性质和特征	1008
嵌入衍生工具	1012
金融工具的分类	1014
金融负债和权益	1018
确认和终止确认	1022
计量	1024
套期会计	1030
套期工具	1032
套期会计的条件	1032
套期会计的规定	1034
终止套期会计	1036
列报与披露	1038
国际财务报告准则第 9 号——金融工具	1040

Introduction

1.1 Current requirements for financial instruments are included in IAS 32, 'Financial instruments: Presentation', IAS 39, 'Financial instruments: Recognition and measurement', IFRS 9, 'Financial instruments', and IFRS 7, 'Financial instruments: Disclosures'.

1.2 To apply in the EU, IFRSs must be endorsed by an EU 'endorsement mechanism'. In November 2004, the European Commission adopted a 'carve-out' version of IAS 39, which deleted a limited number of words and paragraphs from IAS 39 relating to the use of the 'fair value option' for financial liabilities and certain aspects of hedge accounting. Since that time, the IASB has published an amendment to IAS 39 incorporating a revised 'fair value option' and this has been adopted for use within the EU. However, differences between the IASB's 'full IAS 39' and the EU's 'carve-out' version of the standard still remain. The IASB issued IFRS 9 in November 2009. The EU has not yet endorsed IFRS 9. The Board intends that IFRS 9 will ultimately replace IAS 39 in its entirety. However, in response to requests from interested parties that the accounting for financial instruments should be improved quickly, the Board divided its project to replace IAS 39 into three main phases. As the Board completes each phase it will delete the relevant portions of IAS 39 and create chapters in IFRS 9 that replace the requirements in IAS 39. Further discussion of the development of the financial instruments standards and of their adoption for use within the EU is provided in chapter 2.

Objectives and scope of IAS 32, IAS 39 and IFRS 7

1.3 IAS 32 establishes principles for presenting financial instruments as liabilities or equity and for offsetting financial assets and liabilities. It applies to classification of financial instruments into financial assets, financial liabilities and equity instruments from the issuer's perspective; the classification of related interest, dividends, losses and gains; and the circumstances in which financial assets and liabilities can be offset.

引言

1.1 目前对金融工具的要求包括《国际会计准则第32号——金融工具：列报》（“IAS 32”）、《国际会计准则第39号——金融工具：确认和计量》（“IAS 39”）、《国际财务报告准则第9号——金融工具》（“IFRS 9”）以及《国际财务报告准则第7号——金融工具：披露》（“IFRS 7”）。

1.2 要想在欧盟适用，国际财务报告准则（“IFRSs”）必须被欧盟的“认可机制”所认可。2004年11月，欧盟采用了IAS 39的“删减”版本，该版本删除了IAS 39中与金融负债“公允价值选择权”和套期会计某些方面相关的有限词汇和段落。之后，国际会计准则理事会（“IASB”）发布了一项有关IAS 39“公允价值选择权”的修改，这一修改已被欧盟认可并适用。但是，IASB的“IAS 39完整版”和欧盟的“删减”版本之间仍然存在差异。IASB于2009年11月发布了IFRS 9。欧盟尚未采用IFRS 9。IASB有意最终用IFRS 9替代IAS 39。然而，为响应有关各界提出的尽快改善金融工具会计处理的要求，IASB将IAS 39替代项目分成了三个主要阶段。当IASB完成一个阶段时，它将删除IAS 39中相应的部分并在IFRS 9中新增章节来替代IAS 39的要求。有关金融工具准则的改进及其被欧盟认可情况的进一步讨论请参见第2章。

IAS 32、IAS 39及IFRS 7的目标与范围

1.3 IAS 32确立金融工具作为负债或权益的列报与金融资产和负债的抵销原则。该准则规定了如何从发行人的角度将金融工具划分金融资产、金融负债和权益工具；相关利息、股利、损失和利得的分类；以及在何种情况下金融资产和负债应予以抵销。

1.4 IAS 39 is an extremely long and complex standard that establishes principles for recognising and measuring financial assets, financial liabilities and some contracts to buy or sell non-financial items. IAS 39 also deals with derecognition of financial assets and liabilities and hedge accounting.

1.5 IFRS 7 requires entities to provide disclosures that enable users to evaluate:

- the significance of financial instruments for the entity's financial position and performance; and
- the nature and extent of risks arising from financial instruments to which the entity is exposed and how the entity manages them.

1.6 The scope of the three standards is very wide ranging. The definition of a financial instrument under IFRS is "*any contract that gives rise to a financial asset of one entity and a financial liability or equity instrument of another entity*". This definition encompasses cash, debt and equity investments, trade receivables and payables, debt, certain provisions, net cash-settled commodity contracts and derivatives (including embedded derivatives). However, certain financial instruments are excluded from the scope of one or all of the standards, as summarised in the table below.

Within scope of IAS 32, IAS 39 and IFRS 7	**Within scope of IAS 32 and IFRS 7 only**	**Out of scope**
Debt and equity investments		
Contingent consideration in a business combination that is a financial instrument (Note 1).		Investments in subsidiaries, associates and joint ventures accounted for under IAS 27, IAS 28 or IAS 31. Any forward contract between an acquirer and a selling shareholder to buy or sell an acquiree that will result in a business combination at a future acquisition date (Note 2).
Loans and receivables	Lease receivables (Note 3)	
Gross amount due from customers for construction contract work		

1.4　IAS 39 是一个冗长而又复杂的准则，它对金融资产、金融负债和某些非金融项目买卖合同的确认和计量确立原则。IAS 39 还规范了金融资产和负债的终止确认以及套期会计。

1.5　IFRS 7 要求主体做出披露从而使报表使用者能对下述事项进行评估：

■ 金融工具对于主体财务状况和业绩的重要性；以及

■ 主体承受金融工具所产生的风险的性质和程度，以及主体如何管理这些风险。

1.6　这三项准则的范围十分广泛。IFRS 对金融工具的定义是"*形成一个主体的金融资产并形成另一个主体的金融负债或权益工具的合同*"。这一定义包括现金、债权和股权投资、应收和应付账款、债务、某些准备、以现金净额结算的商品合同和衍生工具（包括嵌入衍生工具）。但是，如下表所述，某些金融工具不在一个或这三个准则的范围之内。

在 IAS 32、IAS 39 和 IFRS 7 的范围之内	**仅在 IAS 32 和 IFRS 7 的范围之内**	**不在范围之内**
债权和股权投资		
属于金融工具的业务合并中的或有对价(注 1)。		采用 IAS 27, IAS 28 or IAS 31 核算的对子公司、联营和合营的投资 购买方和出售股东签订的买卖被购买方且导致在未来收购日形成业务合并的所有远期合同(注 2)
贷款和应收款项	应收租赁款(注 3)	
应向客户收取的建造合同工程款总额		

Con.

Own debt	Lease payables (Note 3) Own equity	Employee benefits Share-based payments
Cash and cash equivalents		
Derivatives-for example: ■ Interest rate swaps ■ Currency forwards/swaps ■ Purchased/written options ■ Commodity contracts (Note 4) ■ Collars/caps ■ Credit derivatives ■ Cash or net share settleable derivatives on own shares	Derivatives on own shares settled only by delivery of a fixed number of shares for a fixed amount of cash	Own use commodity contracts (Note 4)
Derivatives on subsidiaries, associates and joint ventures		
Embedded derivatives		
Weather derivatives		
Loan commitments held for trading (Note 5)	Other loan commitments	
Financial guarantees (Note 6)		Insurance contracts

Note 1 – IFRS 3 has removed the scope exemption for contingent consideration in a business combination. On adoption of IFRS 3 contingent consideration from both the acquiree and acquiror's perspective is in the scope of IAS 32, IAS 39 and IFRS 7.

Note 2 – The term of the forward contract should not exceed a reasonable period normally necessary to obtain any required approvals and to complete the transaction. Any forward contract between an acquirer and a selling shareholder to buy or sell an acquiree that will result in a business combination at a future acquisition date is within IFRS 7's scope.

Note 3 – Lease receivables are included in IAS 39's scope for derecognition and impairment purposes only. Finance lease payables are subject to the derecognition provisions. Any derivatives embedded in lease contracts are also within IAS 39's scope.

Note 4 – Contracts to buy or sell non-financial items are within IAS 32's scope, IAS 39 and IFRS 7 if they can be settled net in cash or another financial asset and they do not meet the test of being entered into and continuing to be held for the purpose of receipt or delivery of non-financial items to meet the entity's expected purchase, sale or usage requirements (known as "own use commodity contracts"). Settling net includes taking delivery of the underlying and

续表

自有负债	应付租赁款（注3） 自身权益	职工福利 以股份为基础的支付
现金及现金等价物		
衍生工具——例如： ■ 利率互换 ■ 远期货币合约/货币互换合约 ■ 购买选择权/签出期权 ■ 商品合同（注4） ■ 上下限/上限 ■ 信用衍生工具 ■ 对自身股份以现金或股份净额结算的衍生工具	只能以固定金额的现金换取固定数量的自身股份进行结算的衍生工具	自用商品合同（注4）
基于子公司、联营和合营的衍生工具		
嵌入衍生工具		
天气衍生工具		
交易性的贷款承诺（注5）	其他贷款承诺	
财务担保（注6）		保险合同

注1——IFRS 3已经删除了对企业合并中或有对价的范围豁免。采用IFRS 3后，购买方和被购买方的或有对价均在IAS 32、IAS 39和IFRS 7的范围内。

注2——远期合同的期限不应超过通常取得所有必需的批准以及完成该交易的合理期间。购买方和出售股东签订的买卖被购买方且导致在未来收购日形成业务合并的所有远期合同都属于IFRS 7的范围。

注3——应收租赁款仅在终止确认和减值测试时在IAS 39的范围之内。应付融资租赁款受终止确认条款的约束。租赁合同中所有的嵌入衍生工具均在IAS 39的范围内。

注4——买卖非金融项目的合同如果能以现金或者其他金融资产净额结算，且不能满足以获取或交付实物为目的而签订并根据主体的预期购买、出售或使用继续持有的要求（即“自用商品合同”），则属于IAS 32、IAS 39和IFRS 7的范围。净额结算包括收取相应的资产后在短期内将其出售，以从短期价格波动中获利的行为。

Con.

selling it within a short period after delivery to generate a profit from short-term fluctuations in price.
Note 5 – Loan commitments are outside IAS 39's scope if they cannot be settled net in cash or by some other financial instrument unless: they are held for trading or to generate assets of a class which the entity has a past practice of selling; or the entity chooses to include them with other derivatives under IAS 39.
Note 6 – From the issuer's perspective, financial guarantee contracts are within IAS 39's scope, unless the issuer has previously asserted explicitly that it regards such contracts as insurance contracts and has used accounting applicable to insurance contracts, in which case either IAS 39 or IFRS 4, 'Insurance contracts' may be applied.

1.7 The objectives and scope of IAS 32, IAS 39 and IFRS 7 is explained in greater detail in chapter 3.

Nature and characteristics of financial instruments

1.8 The definition of a financial instrument is set out in paragraph 1.6 above. One of the key components of the definition is that all financial instruments are defined by contracts. It follows that non-contractual obligations, such as taxation, are not financial instruments.

1.9 A financial asset is any asset that is:

- Cash.
- An equity instrument of another entity.
- A contractual right:
  - to receive cash or another financial asset from another entity; or
  - to exchange financial assets or financial liabilities with another entity under conditions that are potentially favourable to the entity.
- A contract that will or may be settled in the entity's own equity instruments and is:
  - a non-derivative for which the entity is or may be obliged to receive a variable number of the entity's own equity instruments; or

续表

注 5——贷款承诺如果不能以现金或其他金融工具净额结算，则不在 IAS 39 的范围之内，除非：它们是主体为交易所持有；或主体有出售该类资产的惯例，或主体选择将其包括在 IAS 39 的其他衍生工具中。 注 6——从财务担保合同的签发人角度看，财务担保合同在 IAS 39 的范围之内，除非该签发人以前已经明确声明将此类合同视作保险合同，并且使用了适用于保险合同的会计处理方法，即，可能是 IAS 39 或者《国际财务报告准则第 4 号——保险合同》（“IFRS 4”）。

1.7　更多涉及 IAS 32、IAS 39 和 IFRS 7 目标和范围的详细内容，请参见第 3 章。

金融工具的性质和特征

1.8　金融工具的定义，请参见上文第 1.6 段。该定义中一项重要的要素是所有金融工具均由合同确定，由此得出结论：诸如税务等的非合同义务不是金融工具。

1.9　金融资产是指下述资产：

- 现金。
- 另一主体的权益工具。
- 以下合同权利：
    - 从另一主体收取现金或另一金融资产；或者
    - 在潜在有利条件下，与另一主体交换金融资产或金融负债。

- 将以主体自身权益工具结算或可以以主体自身权益工具结算的合同，且该合同是：
    - 一项非衍生工具，使主体将获取或可能获取可变数量的自身权益工具；或者

- a derivative that will or may be settled other than by the exchange of a fixed amount of cash or another financial asset for a fixed number of the entity's own equity instruments. For this purpose the entity's own equity instruments do not include puttable financial instruments, instruments that impose on the entity an obligation to deliver to another party a *pro rata* share of the entity's net assets on liquidation and are classified as equity instruments, or instruments that are contracts for the future receipt or delivery of the entity's own equity instruments.

1.10 A financial liability is any liability that is:

- A contractual obligation:
  - to deliver cash or another financial asset from another entity; or
  - to exchange financial assets or financial liabilities with another entity under conditions that are potentially unfavourable to the entity.
- A contract that will or may be settled in the entity's own equity instruments and is:
  - a non-derivative for which the entity is or may be obliged to deliver a variable number of the entity's own equity instruments; or
  - a derivative that will or may be settled other than by the exchange of a fixed amount of cash or another financial asset for a fixed number of the entity's own equity instruments. For this purpose the entity's own equity instruments do not include puttable financial instruments, instruments that impose on the entity an obligation to deliver to another party a *pro rata* share of the entity's net assets on liquidation and are classified as equity instruments, or instruments that are contracts for the future receipt or delivery of the entity's own equity instruments.

1.10.1 The above definitions were amended to require certain puttable instruments and obligations arising on liquidation to be classified as equity, despite the contractual requirement to deliver cash or another financial asset.

1.10.2 For accounting period beginning on or after 1 February 2010, the above definition was amended to classify rights, options or warrants to acquire a fixed

- 一项衍生工具，该衍生工具将或可能按照除了以固定金额的现金或其他金融资产换取固定数量的自身权益工具以外的其他方式进行结算。其中，主体自身权益工具不包括可回售金融工具、要求主体在清算时将净资产按*比例*支付给另一方且分类为权益的工具以及本身就是在未来收取或交付主体自身权益工具的合同。

1.10　金融负债是指下述负债：

- 以下合同义务：
  - 向另一主体交付现金或其他金融资产；或者
  - 在潜在不利的条件下，与另一主体交换金融资产或金融负债。
- 将以主体自身权益工具结算或可以以主体自身权益工具结算的合同，且该合同是：
  - 一项非衍生工具，使主体承担或可能承担交付可变数量自身权益工具；或
  - 一项衍生工具，该衍生工具将或可能按照除了以固定金额的现金或其他金融资产换取固定数量的自身权益工具以外的其他方式进行结算。其中，主体自身权益工具不包括可回售金融工具、要求主体在清算时将净资产按*比例*支付给另一方且分类为权益的工具以及本身就是在未来收取或交付主体自身权益工具的合同。

1.10.1　上述定义曾被修订，要求特定可回售工具和清算产生的义务，尽管其有交付现金或其他金融资产的合同义务，仍被划分为权益。

1.10.2　对起始日在2010年2月1日或之后开始的会计期间，上述定义已被修订，将以任意货币的固定金额获取固定数量的主体自身权益工具的配股权、

number of the entity's own equity instruments for a fixed amount of any currency as equity instruments. This only applies where the entity offers the rights, options or warrants *pro rata* to all of its existing owners of the same class of its own non-derivative equity instruments.

1.11 An equity instrument is any contract that evidences a residual interest in the assets of an entity after deducting all of its liabilities. Examples of equity instruments include non-puttable ordinary shares, some types of preference shares, share warrants or written call options that allow the holder to subscribe for or purchase a fixed number of non-puttable ordinary shares in the issuing entity in exchange for a fixed amount of cash or another financial asset.

1.12 Derivatives are financial instruments that derive their value from an underlying price or index, such as an interest rate, a foreign exchange rate or commodity price. IAS 39 defines a derivative as a financial instrument or other contract with all of the following characteristics:

- Its value changes in response to the change in a specified interest rate, financial instrument price, commodity price, foreign exchange rate, index of prices or rates, credit rating or credit index, or other variable, provided in the case of a non-financial variable that the variable is not specific to a party to the contract (sometimes called the 'underlying').

- It requires no initial net investment or an initial net investment that is smaller than would be required for other types of contracts that would be expected to have a similar response to changes in market factors.

- It is settled at a future date.

1.13 The nature and characteristics of financial instruments are considered further in chapter 4.

Embedded derivatives

1.14 A derivative instrument that falls within IAS 39's scope need not be free-standing. Terms and conditions may also be embedded within another financial

期权或认股权证划分为权益工具。这仅当主体向其自身同一类别的非衍生权益工具的所有现有股东按*比例*发行配股权、期权或认股权证的情况下才适用。

1.11 权益工具是指能证明享有主体的资产在扣除所有负债后的剩余权益的合同。权益工具包括诸如不可回售普通股、某些类型的优先股及允许持有人以固定金额的现金或其他金融资产认购或购买发行主体固定数量的不可回售普通股的认股权证或签出看涨期权。

1.12 衍生工具是指由诸如利率、汇率或商品价格等相关价格或指数派生价值的金融工具。IAS 39 将衍生工具定义为具有下述特征的金融工具或其他合同:

- 其价值随特定利率、金融工具价格、商品价格、汇率、价格或利率指数、信用等级或信用指数或其他变量的变动而变动(有时称为"基础变量")。如果该变量是非金融变量,则该变量不应是合同某一方所特有的;

- 其不要求初始净投资,或要求的初始净投资小于预期对市场因素变化有类似反应的其他类型合同所要求的初始净投资;

- 其在未来某一日期进行结算。

1.13 金融工具的性质和特征,将于第 4 章中详细阐述。

嵌入衍生工具

1.14 在 IAS 39 范围内的衍生工具并不一定都是独立的,其他金融工具或非金融合同(称为"主"合同)中可能嵌入的条款也能表现得像一个独立的衍

instrument or non-financial contract (referred to as the 'host' contract) that behave like a free standing derivative. These 'embedded derivatives' should be recognised at their fair value, separately from the non-derivative host contract, when they have economic characteristics and risks that are not closely related to those of the host contract. However, an entity may designate a contract that contains one or more embedded derivative as a financial asset or financial liability at fair value through profit or loss, unless the embedded derivative does not significantly modify the cash flows required by the contract or it is clear that separation of the embedded derivative is prohibited.

1.15 Analysing non-derivative financial instruments and executory contracts for potential embedded derivatives is one of the more challenging aspects of IAS 39. This subject is considered further in chapter 5.

Classification of financial instruments

1.16 IAS 39 is a partial rather than a full fair value model. Financial assets and liabilities are measured at fair value or amortised cost depending on which defined category they fall into under the standard.

1.17 IAS 39 has four clearly defined categories of financial assets:

- A financial asset is 'at fair value through profit or loss' if it is either:
  - Held-for-trading, that is:
    - it was acquired or incurred principally for the purpose of selling or repurchasing it in the near term;
    - it forms part of a portfolio of identified financial instruments that are managed together and for which there is evidence of a recent actual pattern of short-term profit-taking; or
    - it is a derivative (except for a derivative that is a designated and effective hedging instrument).
  - Designated on initial recognition as 'at fair value through profit or loss'. The

生工具。如果它们的经济特征和风险与主合同的关系并不密切，那么，这些“嵌入衍生工具”应与非衍生工具的主合同分离并以公允价值确认。但是，主体可以将含有一个或多个衍生工具的合同整体指定为以公允价值计量且其变动计入损益的金融资产或金融负债，除非该嵌入衍生工具没有显著影响合同要求的现金流量，或者显然该嵌入衍生工具是被禁止分离的。

1.15 对非衍生金融工具和待执行的合同中潜在的嵌入衍生工具进行分析，是 IAS 39 中更具挑战性的问题之一。这一问题将在第 5 章做进一步讨论。

金融工具的分类

1.16 IAS 39 是个部分而非完全公允价值模式。金融资产和负债按其在该准则下的分类以公允价值或摊余成本计量。

1.17 IAS 39 对金融资产有明确的四分类：

- 以公允价值计量且变动计入损益的金融资产，如果其属于下述两者之一：
  - 为交易而持有，即：
    - 其主要是为近期出售或回购目的而获得或发生的；
    - 其属于集中进行管理的可辨认金融工具组合的一部分，并且有证据证明近期存在短期获利回吐；或
    - 其是一项衍生工具（被指定为有效套期工具的衍生工具除外）。
  - 在初始确认时被指定为以公允价值计量且变动计入损益。指定为以公允

conditions that are required to be met in order to designate a financial asset (or a financial liability) as 'at fair value through profit or loss' are any of the following:

- Where the designation eliminates or significantly reduces an accounting mismatch.
- When a group of financial assets, financial liabilities or both are managed and their performance is evaluated on a fair value basis in accordance with a documented risk management or investment strategy and information about this group is provided on that basis to the entity's key management personnel.
- When a contract contains an embedded derivative that meets particular conditions.

The designation is irrevocable.

- Loans and receivables are non-derivative financial assets with fixed or determinable payments that are not quoted in an active market, with the following exceptions:
  - Those that are to be sold immediately or in the near future (held-for-trading) and any others that are designated as 'at fair value through profit or loss' on initial recognition.
  - Those that are designated as available-for-sale on initial recognition.
  - Those where the entity may not recover substantially all of its original investment, other than because of credit deterioration. Such assets should be classified as available-for-sale.
- Held-to-maturity investments are non-derivative financial assets with fixed or determinable payments and fixed maturity (for example, debt securities, quoted loans and mandatory redeemable preferred shares) that an entity has the positive intention and ability to hold to maturity. Exceptions are those investments that an entity designates on initial recognition as 'at fair value through profit or loss' or as 'available-for-sale' and those that meet the definition of 'loans and receivables'. Held-to-maturity instruments must have a maturity date, so investments in equity shares cannot fall into this category. There are a number of conditions set out in

价值计量且变动计入损益的金融资产（或金融负债）需满足下述条件中任意一条：

- 该指定消除或显著减少了会计错配。
- 主体根据书面记载的风险管理或投资策略，以公允价值为基础管理一组金融资产、一组金融负债、或者一组金融资产和金融负债并以此评价其业绩，并且将该信息在此基础上提供给主体的关键管理人员；
- 合同包含满足特定条件的嵌入衍生工具。

该指定不可撤销。

- 贷款和应收款项是有固定或可确定的付款额，但没有活跃市场标价的非衍生金融资产，但下述情形除外：
  - 主体打算立即或于近期出售（为交易而持有）的贷款和应收款项，以及其他在初始确认时被指定为“以公允价值计量且变动计入损益”的贷款和应收款项。
  - 在初始确认时指定为可供出售的贷款和应收款项。
  - 因信用恶化以外的原因，主体可能无法收回几乎所有初始投资的贷款和应收款项。这些资产应当划分为可供出售的金融资产。
- 持有至到期投资是具有固定或可确定的付款额和固定到期日、且主体具有将其持有至到期的明确意图和能力的非衍生金融资产（例如债权类证券、有报价的贷款和强制可赎回优先股）。例外情况包括，主体在初始确认时指定为“以公允价值计量且变动计入损益”或“可供出售”的非衍生金融资产，以及符合“贷款和应收款项”定义的那些非衍生金融资产。持有至到期投资必须有到期日，因此，股权投资不属于该类别。IAS 39 规定了很多的限制条件，来限制主体将投资划分为持有至到期的能力。例如，如果主体在当前年度或前两个财务年度内将超过不重大金额的持有至到期投资出

IAS 39 that restrict an entity's ability to categorise investments as held-to-maturity. For example, an entity may not classify any financial assets as held-to-maturity if during the current or preceding two financial years it has sold or reclassified more than an insignificant amount of held-to maturity investments, except in certain very narrowly defined circumstances.

- Available-for-sale financial assets are non-derivative financial assets that are designated as such on initial recognition or that are not classified in any other category.

1.18 IAS 39 defines two categories of financial liabilities:

- A financial liability is 'at fair value through profit or loss' if it is either held-for-trading or designated at initial recognition as 'at fair value through profit or loss' (see the first major bullet point in para 1.17).
- All other financial liabilities fall into the other liabilities category.

1.19 The classification of financial assets and financial liabilities is considered further in chapter 6.

Financial liabilities and equity

1.20 The classification of a financial instrument as either a financial liability (debt) or equity is governed by the contractual arrangements' substance rather than its legal form. An instrument is debt when the issuer is or can be required to deliver either cash or another financial asset to the holder. This is the critical feature that distinguishes debt from equity. An instrument is classified as equity when it represents a residual interest in the issuer's net assets.

1.21 All relevant features need to be considered when classifying a financial instrument. The following are some basic examples of where an instrument will be classified as a financial liability disregarding, for the moment, the requirements for certain puttable instruments and obligations arising on liquidation:

- If the issuer can or will be forced to redeem the instrument, classification as debt is appropriate.
- If the choice of settling a financial instrument in cash or otherwise is contingent

售或重分类，除非在极有限的某些特定情形下，主体不应将任何金融资产划分为持有至到期投资。

- 可供出售的金融资产是指那些在初始确认时被指定或那些未被划分为其他类别的非衍生金融资产。

1.18 IAS 39 定义了两类金融负债：

- 以公允价值计量且变动计入损益的金融负债，如果其是为交易而持有或在初始确认时被指定为“以公允价值计量且变动计入损益”（参见第 1.17 段第一项条款）。
- 其他所有金融负债归入其他负债类。

1.19 有关金融资产和金融负债的分类将在第 6 章中做进一步的讨论。

金融负债和权益

1.20 将金融工具分类为金融负债（债务）或权益取决于合同的实质而非其法律形式。如果发行人必须或可能被要求向持有人支付现金或其他金融资产，则该金融工具是负债。这是负债与权益之间最关键的区别。如果某项金融工具代表发行人净资产的剩余权益，则其是权益。

1.21 在对金融工具进行分类时应当考虑所有相关因素。以下是一些暂时不考虑对特定可回售工具和清算产生的义务的要求的情况下，一项工具将被划分为金融负债的基本示例：

- 如果发行人可能或者将被迫赎回金融工具，将其划分为负债是恰当的。
- 如果某金融工具以现金或其他方式结算的选择取决于发行人和持有人均不

on the outcome of genuine circumstances beyond the control of both the issuer and the holder, the instrument is debt as the issuer does not have an unconditional right to avoid settlement.

- An instrument that includes an option for the holder to put the rights inherent in that instrument back to the issuer for cash or another financial instrument is debt.

1.21.1 Applying the requirements for certain puttable instruments and obligations arising on liquidation, some of the instruments in the first and third bullet points above that give the holder an equity-like return will be classified as equity, provided that all of the strict criteria in the amendment are met.

1.22 The treatment of interest, dividends, losses and gains in the income statement follows the classification of the related instrument. So, if a preference share is classified as debt, its coupon is shown as interest. But the coupon on an instrument that is treated as equity is shown as a distribution.

1.23 Not all instruments are either debt or equity. Some, known as compound instruments, contain elements of both in a single contact. Such instruments, such as bonds that are convertible into equity shares either mandatorily or at the holder's option, must be split into debt and equity components. Each is then accounted for separately. The debt element is determined first by fair valuing the cash flows excluding any equity component and the residual is assigned to equity.

1.24 Derivative contracts that only result in the delivery of a fixed amount of cash or other financial assets for a fixed number of an entity's own equity instruments are classified as equity instruments. All other derivatives on own equity are treated as derivatives and accounted for as such. This includes any that:

- can or must be settled on a net basis in cash (or other financial assets) or in shares;
- may be settled gross by delivery of a variable number of own shares; or
- may be settled by delivery of a fixed number of own shares for a variable amount of cash (or other financial assets).

Any derivative on own equity that gives either party a choice over how it is settled is a financial asset or liability, unless all of the settlement alternatives would result in equity classification.

能控制的某种现实状况的结果，该金融工具属于负债，因为发行人没有无条件避免结算的权利。

■ 如果一项工具可以使持有人有权将该金融工具内在的权利卖回给发行人以换取现金或其他金融工具，该金融工具属于负债。

1.21.1 当采用对特定可回售工具和清算产生的义务的要求时，如果满足了修订中所有的严格条件，上述第一和第三项中赋予持有人类似权益回报的某些金融工具将被划分为权益。

1.22 利润表中利息、股利、损失和利得的处理由相关金融工具的分类决定。因此，如果优先股被划分为负债，其票面利息将列示为利息。但是，被视为权益的金融工具的票面利息将作为分配列示于权益中。

1.23 并非所有的金融工具不是负债就是权益。有些被称为复合金融工具的工具，在单个合同中同时包括这两种要素。这些工具，例如可以强制或根据持有人的意愿转换成权益的债券，必须分为负债和权益部分，并分别进行会计核算。负债部分首先通过计量不包含权益部分的现金流量的公允价值来确定，剩余部分作为权益。

1.24 如果衍生工具合同仅导致支付固定金额的现金或其他金融资产以换取主体固定数量的自身权益工具，该衍生工具合同被划分为权益工具。其他所有基于自身权益的衍生工具均应视为衍生工具并以此进行会计处理。这包括诸如：

■ 可以或者必须以现金（或其他金融资产）或股份进行净额结算的衍生工具；

■ 可能通过交付可变数量的自身股份来结算的衍生工具；或者

■ 可能通过交付固定数量的自身股份以换取可变金额的现金（或其他金融资产）来结算的衍生工具。

任何基于自身权益的衍生工具，若其给予某一合同方选择结算方式的权利，则该衍生工具是一项金融资产或负债，除非所有的可选结算方式都可被分类为权益。

1.25 The classification of financial instruments as either debt or equity and the treatment of contracts that may be settled in an entity's own shares are considered further in chapter 7.

Recognition and derecognition

1.26 A financial asset or liability is recognised on the balance sheet when an entity becomes a party to the contract. IAS 39's rules for removing or 'derecognising' a financial asset or liability are far more complex.

1.27 IAS 39 includes a flow chart that summarises the criteria for derecognising a financial asset and this is reproduced below.

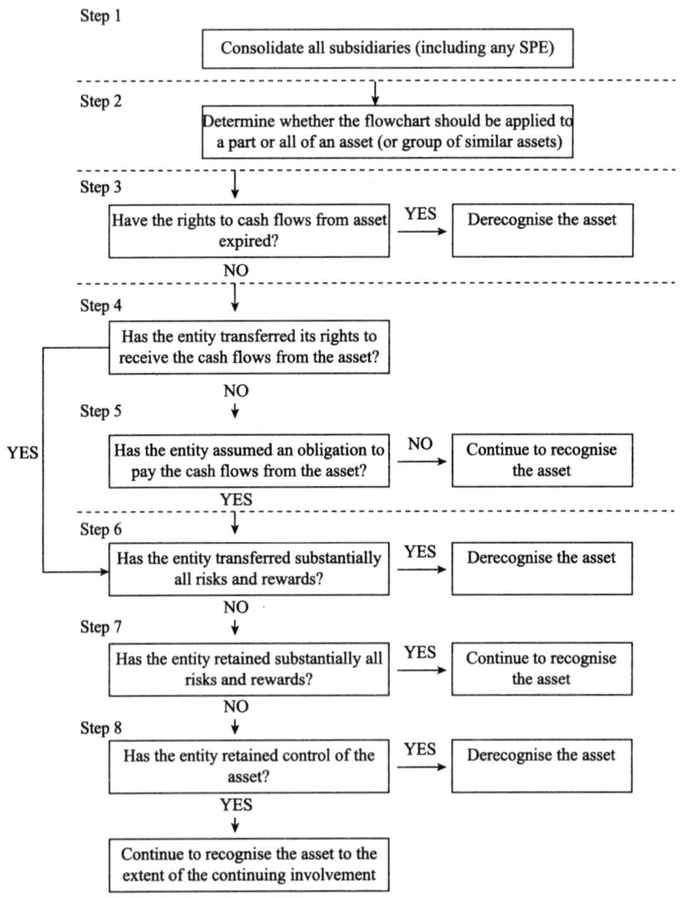

1.25　有关将金融工具划分为负债或权益及以主体自身股份结算的合同的处理方法的更多内容，请参见第 7 章。

确认和终止确认

1.26　当主体成为合同一方时，金融资产或负债就应在资产负债表中进行确认。IAS 39 对核销或“终止确认”一项金融资产或负债的规定则复杂得多。

1.27　IAS 39 包含一个流程图，汇总了终止确认一项金融资产的条件，该流程图重印如下。

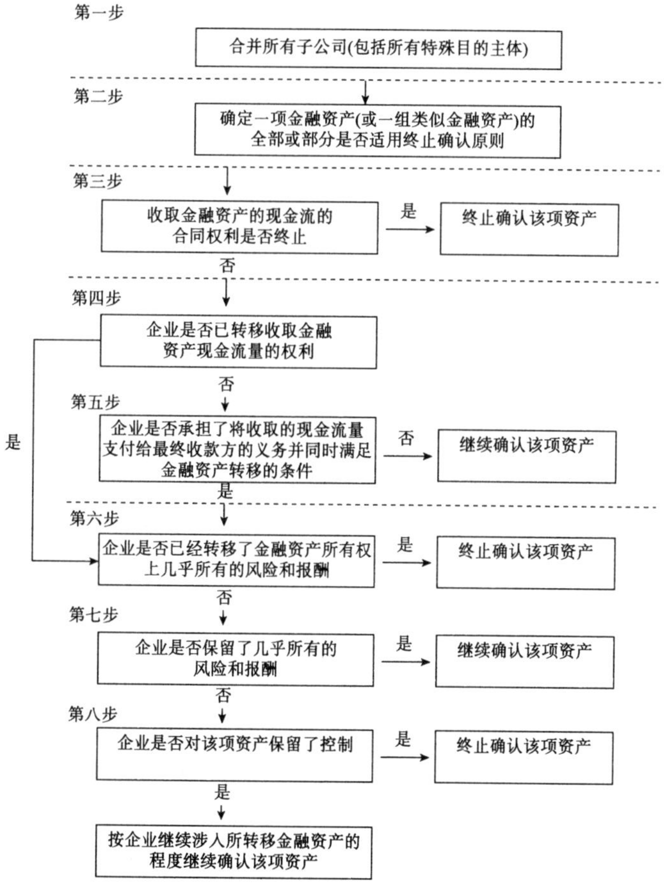

1.28 A financial liability is derecognised when it is extinguished, that is when the obligation is discharged, cancelled or expired. This condition is met when the liability is settled by paying the creditor or when the debtor is released from primary responsibility for the liability, either by process of law or by the creditor.

1.29 Entities frequently negotiate with bankers or bond-holders to cancel existing debt and replace it with new debt on different terms. For example, an entity may decide to cancel its exposure to high-interest fixed-rate debt, pay a fee or penalty on cancellation and replace it with variable-rate debt. IAS 39 provides guidance to distinguish between the settlement of debt that is replaced by new debt and the restructuring of existing debt. The distinction is based on whether or not the new debt has substantially different terms from the old debt.

1.30 Recognition and derecognition are discussed in detail in chapter 8.

Measurement

1.31 The categorisations of financial assets and financial liabilities have a significant impact on their subsequent measurement. The following table summarises the measurement principles for financial assets.

Measurement of assets		
	Measurement after initial recognition *	Changes in carrying amount
At fair value through profit or loss	Fair value	Income statement
Loans and receivables	Amortised cost	Income statement
Held-to-maturity	Amortised cost	Income statement
Available-for-sale	Fair value	Other comprehensive income (but interest, dividends, foreign exchange differences on monetary assets and changes due to impairment are taken to income statement)

1.28 当金融负债消除时，即当合同中相应的义务解除、取消或到期时，应终止确认该金融负债。当债权人得到偿付完成结算或当债务人通过法定程序或经债权人解除了负债的主要责任，即满足了上述条件。

1.29 主体经常会与银行家或债券持有人协商取消现有债务，并以不同条款的新债务替代。例如，主体可能决定取消高息固定利率债务，为该取消行为支付费用或罚金，并将其替换为可变利率债务。IAS 39 提供了相关指引以区分用新债务替代现有债务和重组现有债务。其差别在于新旧债务的条款是否存在显著差异。

1.30 确认与终止确认将在第 8 章中进行详细讨论。

计量

1.31 金融资产与金融负债的分类对其后续计量有着重要影响。下表汇总了金融资产的计量原则。

资产的计量		
	初始确认后的计量*	账面价值的变动
以公允价值计量且变动计入损益	公允价值	利润表
贷款和应收款项	摊余成本	利润表
持有至到期	摊余成本	利润表
可供出售	公允价值	其他综合收益（但是，利息、股利、货币性资产的汇兑差额以及减值产生的变动均计入利润表）

Con.

Unquoted equity investments for which fair value cannot be reliably measured	Cost	Yields and impairments are taken to income statement
* All categories of financial assets are initially measured at fair value plus transaction costs, except for assets 'at fair value through profit or loss' where transaction costs are not included. Fair value is normally the transaction price (that is, the fair value of the consideration given for the asset), but the transaction price may have to be adjusted to fair value where, for example, a non-interest bearing loan or receivable is acquired.		

1.32 An assessment should be made at each balance sheet date as to whether there is any objective evidence that a financial asset (or a group of financial assets) is impaired. IAS 39 sets out rules for accounting for impairment losses on financial assets carried at amortised cost, at cost and for available-for-sale assets.

1.33 The following table summarises the measurement principles for financial liabilities.

Measurement of liabilities		
	Measurement after initial recognition*	**Changes in carrying amount**
At fair value through profit or loss	Fair value	Income statement
Other liabilities	Amortised cost	Income statement
* Liabilities 'at fair value through profit or loss' are initially measured at fair value (transaction costs are not included). Other liabilities are initially measured at fair value less transaction costs. Fair value is generally the transaction price, but the transaction price may have to be adjusted to fair value where, for example, convertible debt is issued and it is necessary to separate out the element of proceeds that relates to the conversion right, which is an equity instrument.		

1.34 The carrying amount of a financial instrument measured at amortised cost is computed as the amount to be paid/re-paid at maturity (usually the principal amount or par/face value), plus or minus any unamortised original premium or discount, net of any origination fees and transaction costs and less principal

续表

公允价值无法可靠计量的无报价权益投资	成本	收益与减值计入利润表
*所有类别的金融资产均以公允价值加交易费用进行初始计量，除了“以公允价值计量且变动计入损益”的资产要将交易费用排除在外。公允价值通常为交易价格（即资产对价的公允价值），但交易价格可能需要调整为公允价值，例如在取得一项无息的贷款或应收款项的情况下。		

1.32　在每个资产负债表日都应当评估是否存在证明一项金融资产（或一组金融资产）发生了减值的客观证据。IAS 39 规定了以摊余成本、成本计量的金融资产及可供出售资产减值损失的会计处理。

1.33　下表汇总了金融负债的计量原则。

负债的计量		
	初始确认后的计量*	**账面价值的变动**
以公允价值计量且变动计入损益	公允价值	利润表
其他负债	摊余成本	利润表
*“以公允价值计量且变动计入损益”的负债以公允价值进行初始计量（交易费用不包括在内）。其他负债以公允价值减交易费用进行初始计量。公允价值通常为交易价格，但交易价格可能需要调整为公允价值，例如在发行可转债的情形下，有必要将与作为权益工具的转换权相关的收款部分分离出来。		

1.34　以摊余成本计量的金融工具的账面价值，是以到期日支付或偿付的金额（通常为本金或面值），加上或减去未摊销的初始溢折价，扣除启动费和交易费用，再减去已支付的本金计算得出。摊销采用实际利率法，该利率必须将金融工具在预计存续期或更短期间内（若合适）估计未来本金和利息的现

repayments. The amortisation is calculated using the effective interest method, which calculates the rate of interest that is necessary to discount the estimated stream of principal and interest cash flows (excluding any impact of credit losses) through the expected life of the financial instrument or, when appropriate, a shorter period to equal the amount at initial recognition. That rate is then applied to the carrying amount at each reporting date to determine the interest income (assets) or interest expense (liabilities) for the period. In this way, interest income or expense is recognised on a level yield to maturity basis.

1.35 Fair value is the amount for which an asset could be exchanged, or a liability settled, between knowledgeable, willing parties in an arm's length transaction. There is a general presumption that fair value can be reliably measured for all financial instruments. In looking for a reliable measure of fair value, IAS 39 provides a hierarchy to be used in determining an instrument's fair value.

- Active market – quoted market price. The existence of published price quotations in an active market is the best evidence of fair value and they must be used to measure the financial instrument. The price can be taken from the most favourable market readily available to the entity, even if that was not the market in which the transaction actually occurred. The quoted market price cannot be adjusted for 'blockage' or 'liquidity' factors. The fair value of a portfolio of financial instruments is the product of the number of units of the instrument and its quoted market prices.

- No active market – valuation technique. If the market for a financial instrument is not active, fair value is established by using a valuation technique. Valuation techniques that are well established in financial markets include recent market transactions, reference to a transaction that is substantially the same, discounted cash flows and option pricing models. An acceptable valuation technique incorporates all factors that market participants would consider in setting a price and should be consistent with accepted economic methodologies for pricing financial instruments. Normally the amount paid or received for a financial instrument is the best estimate of fair value at inception. However, where all data inputs to a valuation model are obtained from observable market transactions, the resulting calculation of fair value can be used for initial

金流（不包括信用损失的影响）折现为初始确认金额。将这一利率配上各报告日的账面价值，以确定该期间的利息收入（资产）或利息费用（负债）。这样，利息收入或费用是按至到期日同一水平的收益率确认的。

1.35 公允价值指在公平交易中，熟悉情况的当事人自愿进行资产交换或债务清偿的金额。目前普遍认为所有金融工具的公允价值均能可靠计量。为得到可靠的公允价值计量，IAS 39 对如何确定一项金融工具的公允价值提供了以下级次。

- 活跃市场——市场标价。活跃市场中存在的公开标价是公允价值的最好证据，必须用来计量金融工具。该标价可以从主体易于获得的最有利的市场取得，即便该市场并非交易实际发生的市场。市场价格不能因“大量持有”或“流动性”因素而做出调整。金融工具组合的公允价值为金融工具单位数量和其市场标价的乘积。

- 无活跃市场——评估技术。如果金融工具的市场不活跃，则公允价值以评估技术来确定。金融市场已经建立的评估技术包括近期市场交易、参照本质相同的交易、折现现金流量分析和期权定价模型。可接受的评估技术包含了市场参与者在定价时所要考虑的所有因素，且与关于金融工具定价的公认经济方法一致。通常为金融工具支付或收取的金额是在初始确认时公允价值的最好证据。但是，如果评估模型中使用的所有数据均来自可观察的市场交易，那么依此计算出来的公允价值就可以在初始确认中使用。

recognition.

- No active market – equity instruments. Normally it is possible to estimate the fair value of an equity instrument that an entity has acquired from an outside party. However, if the range of reasonable fair value estimates is significant, and no reliable estimate can be made, an entity is permitted to measure the equity instrument at cost less impairment as a last resort. A similar dispensation applies to derivative financial instruments that can only be settled by physical delivery of such unquoted equity instruments.

1.36 The principles for measuring financial assets and liabilities are considered further in chapter 9.

Hedge accounting

1.37 In simple terms, 'hedge accounting' is a technique that modifies the normal basis for recognising gains and losses (or income and expenses) on associated hedging instruments and hedged items so that both are recognised in earnings in the same accounting period.

1.38 A hedged item is an asset, liability, firm commitment, highly probable forecast transaction or net investment in a foreign operation that exposes the entity to risk of changes in fair value or future cash flows that could affect profit or loss. In particular, a hedged item could be:

- A single asset, liability, firm commitment or highly probable forecast transaction.
- A group of assets, liabilities, firm commitments or highly probable forecast transactions with similar risk characteristics.
- A portion of the risk or cash flows of a financial asset or liability.
- A non-financial asset or liability (such as inventory) for either foreign currency risk or the risk of changes in the fair value of the entire item.
- A held-to-maturity investment for either foreign currency risk or credit risk (but

■ 无活跃市场——权益工具。一般情况下，对于主体从外部某方购得的权益工具，估计其公允价值是可能的。但是，如果合理的公允价值估计数相差范围很大，且无法可靠估计，则允许主体采用成本扣除减值的这一最终手段对其进行计量。对于那些只能以这种无报价的权益工具进行实物交割来结算的衍生金融工具，给予同样的豁免。

1.36 有关金融资产和负债计量原则的更多内容，请参见第9章。

套期会计

1.37 简言之，"套期会计"是指一种改变套期工具和被套期项目相关利得和损失（或收入和费用）通常的确认基础，使得两者在同一会计期间内确认为收益的技术。

1.38 被套期项目可以是资产、负债、确定承诺、极可能发生的预期交易或对境外经营净投资，这些项目使得主体承受可能影响损益的公允价值或未来现金流量的变化风险。具体地说被套期项目可能包括：

■ 单项资产、负债、确定承诺或极可能发生的预期交易；

■ 具有相似风险特征的一组资产、负债、确定承诺和极可能发生的预期交易；

■ 金融资产或负债的部分风险或现金流量；

■ 非金融资产或负债（如存货）的外汇风险或整个项目公允价值变动的风险。

■ 持有至到期投资的外汇风险或信用风险（但非利率风险）；

not interest rate risk).

- A net investment in a foreign operation.

1.39 Generally, only assets, liabilities, firm commitments or highly probable forecast transactions that involve a party external to the entity can be designated as hedged items. However, there are exceptions to this rule for certain foreign currency intra-group transactions.

Hedging instruments

1.40 Derivatives that involve an external party may be designated as hedging instruments, except for some written options. An external non-derivative financial asset or liability may not be designated as a hedging instrument, except as a hedge of foreign currency risk.

1.41 A proportion of the entire hedging instrument, such as 50 per cent of the notional amount, may be designated as the hedging instrument. However, a hedging relationship may not be designated for only a portion of the time period during which a hedging instrument remains outstanding.

Hedge accounting criteria

1.42 In order to qualify for hedge accounting, an entity should formally designate and document the hedging relationship. This includes identifying the hedging instrument, the hedged item or transaction, the nature of the risk being hedged and how the entity will assess hedge effectiveness, together with the entity's risk management objective and strategy for undertaking the hedge.

1.43 The entity must also be able to measure and track the hedging instrument's effectiveness at the start and on an ongoing basis. IAS 39 does not require a hedge to be perfectly effective, although it is expected to be 'highly effective'. A hedge is regarded as highly effective if both of the following conditions are met:

- At the inception of the hedge and in subsequent periods, the hedge is expected to

■ 境外经营净投资。

1.39 通常情况下，只有资产、负债、确定承诺或涉及主体外合同方的极可能发生的预期交易可以被指定为被套期项目。但是，对于某些特定的集团内部外币交易，这一规则也存在着例外情况。

套期工具

1.40 除某些签出期权外，涉及主体外合同方的衍生工具可以被指定为套期工具。除非作为外汇风险套期，外部非衍生金融资产或负债不能被指定为套期工具。

1.41 套期工具整体的一定比例（比如票面金额的50%）可以被指定为套期工具。但是，不能仅仅对套期工具存续期的某一部分指定一个套期关系。

套期会计的条件

1.42 为了满足套期会计的要求，主体应当对套期关系做出正式的指定和文件记录。该文件包括套期工具的认定、被套期项目或交易、被套期风险的性质、主体如何评价套期的有效性，以及主体进行此项套期活动的风险管理目标和策略。

1.43 在套期开始时及后续期间，主体必须能够计量和跟踪套期工具的有效性。套期虽然须被预期为“高度有效”，但 IAS 39 并不要求套期完全有效。如果能同时满足下面两项条件，套期即被认为是高度有效的：

■ 在套期开始时和后续期间内，预期该套期在抵销指定套期期间内归属于被

be highly effective in achieving offsetting changes in fair value or cash flows attributable to the hedged risk during the period for which the hedge is designated.

- The actual results of the hedge are within a range of 80 – 125 per cent.

Hedge accounting rules

1.44 In order to apply hedge accounting the above criteria must be met and the hedging relationship must fall into one of three defined categories.

1.45 A 'fair value hedge' is a hedge of the exposure to changes in fair value of a recognised asset, liability or unrecognised firm commitment, or identified portion thereof, that is attributable to a particular risk and could affect profit or loss. An example is an interest rate swap hedging a fixed rate borrowing. A fair value hedge is accounted for as follows:

- The hedging instrument is measured at fair value if it is a derivative. Non-derivatives may only be designated as hedging instruments for hedges of a foreign currency risk and in that case it is only the foreign currency element of the non-derivative that is remeasured in accordance with IAS 21, 'The effects of changes in foreign exchange rates'.
- The carrying value of the hedged item is adjusted for the hedged risk only. If it is normally carried at cost, the hedged item is not adjusted to its full fair value. For example, a fixed rate borrowing is still basically measured at amortised cost and is adjusted only for the hedged risk (for example, foreign currency risk).
- All gains and losses are taken to the income statement so the result is that there is no net profit and loss effect, other than any hedge ineffectiveness. Where the hedged item is an available-for-sale financial asset, the gain or loss attributable to the hedged risk is recognised in profit or loss, rather than equity, although the remainder of any fair value gain or loss is recognised in equity.

1.46 A 'cash flow hedge' is a hedge of the exposure to variability in cash flows that is attributable to a particular risk associated with a recognised asset or liability

套期风险的公允价值变动或现金流量变动方面是高度有效的；

■ 套期的实际效果在 80% –125% 的范围之内。

套期会计的规定

1.44 为了采用套期会计，上述条件必须得到满足，同时套期关系也必须属于规定的三大类别之一。

1.45 “公允价值套期”指对已确认的金融资产、负债或未确认的确定承诺，或上述资产、负债或未确认的确定承诺的可辨认部分的公允价值变动风险的套期，即其中公允价值的变动归属于某一特定风险并能够影响损益。例如，以利率互换对一项固定利率借款进行套期。公允价值套期以如下方式进行会计处理：

■ 套期工具若为衍生工具，则以公允价值进行计量。非衍生工具只能被指定为对外汇风险套期的套期工具，在这种情形下，只需要就非衍生工具的外币因素依据《国际会计准则第 21 号——汇率变动的影响》（“IAS 21”）进行重新计量。

■ 被套期项目的账面价值仅基于被套期风险进行调整。如果被套期项目通常以成本计量，就不会将其调整为完全公允价值。例如，固定利率借款仍然基本上按照摊余成本计量，仅根据被套期风险（如，外币风险）调整其账面价值。

■ 所有的利得和损失都计入利润表，因此，除非是无效的套期，最终不会有净损益的影响。如果被套期项目是可供出售金融资产，归属于被套期风险的利得或损失被确认为损益而非权益，虽然其公允价值变动的剩余部分仍确认为权益。

1.46 “现金流量套期”是对现金流量风险的套期，其中现金流量的变动归属于与已确认资产或负债或极可能发生的预期交易有关的特定风险且能够影

or a highly probable forecast transaction and could affect profit or loss. An example is an interest rate swap hedging a variable rate borrowing. A cash flow hedge is accounted for as follows:

- The hedging instrument is measured at fair value.
- The portion of the gain or loss on the hedging instrument that is determined to be an effective hedge is recognised directly in equity. The ineffective portion of the gain or loss on the hedging instrument is recognised in profit or loss.
- The gain or loss deferred in equity is recycled to the income statement when the hedged cash flows affect income. If the hedged cash flows result in the recognition of a non-financial asset or liability on the balance sheet, the entity can choose to adjust the basis of the asset or liability by the amount deferred in equity. This choice has to be applied consistently to all such hedges.

1.47 A 'hedge of a net investment' in a foreign operation is a hedge of the reporting entity's interest in the net assets of that operation. For this purpose, net investment includes any monetary items that are accounted for as part of the net investment under IAS 21. In the consolidated financial statements, the foreign operation's net assets are retranslated with gains and losses being recognised in equity. The hedging instrument (whether a derivative or a non-derivative) is accounted for similarly to a cash flow hedge with the portion of the gain or loss on the hedging instrument that is determined to be an effective hedge being recognised directly in equity. The ineffective portion is recognised in profit or loss. The gain or loss that has been recognised in equity is recycled to profit or loss on the foreign operation's disposal.

Discontinuing hedge accounting

1.48 Hedge accounting is discontinued prospectively if any of the following occur:

- The hedge fails the effectiveness tests.
- The hedging instrument is sold, terminated or exercised.

响损益。例如，以利率互换对可变利率借款进行套期。现金流量套期以如下方式进行会计处理：

- 套期工具以公允价值计量。
- 套期工具的利得或损失中被确定为有效套期的部分，确认为权益，而无效部分计入损益。
- 当被套期现金流量影响收益时，递延在权益中的利得或损失将被转入利润表。如果被套期的现金流量导致在资产负债表中确认了一项非金融资产或负债，主体可以选择以递延在权益中的金额来调整资产与负债的确认基础。这种方式应当一致地运用于所有这样的套期。

1.47 境外经营的“净投资套期”是报告企业对该境外经营企业中净资产的套期。为此，净投资包括 IAS 21 中作为净投资的一部分核算的货币性项目。在合并财务报表中，境外经营的净资产将重新折算并且所产生的利得和损失确认为权益。套期工具（不论其为衍生工具或非衍生工具）与现金流量套期的会计处理类似，其利得或损失中被确定为有效套期的部分，确认为权益，无效部分计入损益。被确认为权益的利得或损失在处置境外经营时转入损益。

终止套期会计

1.48 如果出现下述任一事由，应采用未来适用法停止继续使用套期会计：

- 套期未能通过有效性测试。
- 套期工具被出售、终止或行使。

- The hedged item is settled.
- The entity decides to revoke the hedge relationship.
- In a cash flow hedge, the forecast transaction that is hedged is no longer expected to occur.

1.49 When a non-derivative liability has been adjusted for changes in fair value under a hedging relationship, the adjusted carrying amount becomes amortised cost. Any 'premium' or 'discount' is then amortised through the income statement over the remaining period to the liability's maturity.

1.50 If a cash flow hedge relationship ceases, the amounts accumulated in equity will be maintained in equity until the hedged item affects profit or loss. However, if the hedge accounting ceases because the forecast transaction that was hedged is no longer expected to occur, gains and losses deferred in equity are recognised in profit or loss immediately. Similarly, any amounts accumulated in equity while a hedge of net investment was effective remain in equity until the disposal of the related net investment.

1.51 Hedge accounting is considered in greater detail in chapter 10.

Presentation and disclosure

1.52 The offset principle for financial instruments is set out in IAS 32. A financial asset and a financial liability should be offset when, and only when, an entity currently has a legally enforceable right to offset the recognised amounts and intends either to settle on a net basis or to realise the asset and settle the liability simultaneously.

1.53 IFRS 7 sets out the disclosure requirements for financial instruments. The standard was developed as a response to the need for more relevant information and greater transparency about an entity's exposure arising from financial instruments, and how those risks are managed.

1.53.1 In 2008 IFRS 7 was amended effective for annual periods on or after 1 January 2009. The amendment was in response to criticisms around the quality of

- 被套期项目已经结算。
- 主体决定撤销套期关系。
- 在现金流量套期中，被套期的预期交易预计不再发生。

1.49　如果非衍生负债已经依据套期关系对公允价值变化做出了调整，那么，调整后的账面价值就成为其摊余成本。所有的“溢价”或“折价”将在至负债到期日的剩余期间内在利润表中摊销。

1.50　如果现金流量套期关系终止，直至被套期项目影响损益前，在权益中累计的金额将继续作为权益。但是，如果套期会计的终止是由于被套期的预期交易预计不再发生，递延在权益中的利得或损失将立即确认为损益。同样，直到对相关净投资进行处置，在净投资套期有效的期间累计计入权益的金额仍作为权益。

1.51　更多关于套期会计的内容，请参见第 10 章。

列报与披露

1.52　IAS 32 规定了金融工具抵销的原则。当且仅当主体拥有已确认金额的可实施法定权利并准备以净额为基础进行结算，或同时变现资产和清偿负债时，金融资产和金融负债应当互相抵销。

1.53　IFRS 7 规定了对金融工具披露的要求。作为对要求主体针对金融工具带来的风险以及如何管理这些风险提供更相关、更透明信息的回应，该准则进行了改进。

1.53.1　2008 年，IFRS 7 被修订并于起始日在 2009 年 1 月 1 日或之后的各年度期间生效。此次修订是针对金融风险披露的质量，尤其是以公允价值计量

disclosure of financial risk and particularly around financial instruments measured at fair value. This was due in part to the fact that IFRS 7 did not cover some of the disclosures that have been key as a result of the financial crisis and due to teething problems with the new standard.

1.54 IFRS 7's disclosure requirements and IAS 32's requirements for presenting financial instruments are described in chapter 11.

IFRS 9, 'Financial instruments'

1.55 IFRS 9 replaces the multiple classification and measurement models for financial assets in IAS 39 with a single model which has reduced the classification categories to amortised cost and fair value. Classification under IFRS 9 is driven by the entity's business model for managing the financial assets and the contractual characteristics of the financial assets. A financial asset is measured at amortised cost if two criteria are met: (1) the objective of the business model is to hold the financial asset for the collection of the contractual cash flows; and (2) the contractual cash flows under the instrument solely represent payments of principal and interest.

1.56 The new standard removes the requirement to separate embedded derivatives from financial asset hosts. It requires a hybrid contract to be classified in its entirety as either amortised cost or fair value. Most embedded derivatives introduce variability to cash flows, which is inconsistent with the notion that the instrument's contractual cash flows solely represent the payment of principal and interest. Most hybrid contracts with financial asset hosts are, therefore, measured at fair value in their entirety.

1.57 Two of the three fair value option criteria become obsolete under IFRS 9, as a fair value driven business model requires fair value accounting, and hybrid contracts are classified in their entity. The remaining fair value option condition in IAS 39 is carried forward to IFRS 9 – that is, management may still designate a financial asset as at fair value through profit or loss on initial recognition if this significantly reduces an accounting mismatch. The designation at fair value through

的金融工具，所提出的批评而作出的。这在某种程度上是因为 IFRS 7 并未包括导致金融危机的重要披露内容，以及此准则在运用早期所遇到的困难。

1.54 有关 IFRS 7 的披露要求和 IAS 32 的金融工具列报要求，请参见第 11 章。

国际财务报告准则第 9 号——金融工具

1.55 IFRS 9 以一个将分类类别减至摊余成本和公允价值的单一模式替代了 IAS 39 中金融资产分类和计量的多元模式。按照 IFRS 9，分类由主体管理金融资产的业务模式及金融资产的合同特征决定。如果满足以下两个条件，一项金融资产将按摊余成本计量：（1）业务模式的目标是为取得合同现金流量而持有金融资产；及（2）该工具的合同约定现金流量仅为对本金和利息的支付。

1.56 新准则删除了将嵌入衍生工具与金融资产主合同分离的要求。它要求将混合合同整体划分为以摊余成本或公允价值计量。大多数嵌入衍生工具会导致现金流量变动，这与工具的合同约定现金流量仅为对本金和利息的支付的概念是不一致的。因此，大多数有金融资产主合同的混合合同将整体以公允价值计量。

1.57 按照 IFRS 9，由于受公允价值主导的业务模式要求以公允价值核算，且混合合同以整体进行划分，原公允价值选择权三个条件中的两个已然废弃。IAS 39 中剩下的那个公允价值选择权条件仍被包括在 IFRS 9 中，即如果可以很大程度上减少会计错配，管理层仍然可以在初始确认时将一项金融资产指定为以公允价值计量且变动计入损益的金融资产。该指定仍是不可撤销的。

profit or loss continues to be irrevocable.

1.58 IFRS 9 prohibits reclassifications except in rare circumstances when the entity's business model changes. In this case, the entity is required to reclassify affected financial assets prospectively.

1.59 There is specific guidance for contractually linked instruments that create concentrations of credit risk, which is often the case with investment tranches in a securitisation. In addition to assessing the instrument itself against the IFRS 9 classification criteria, management should also 'look through' to the underlying pool of instruments that generate cash flows to assess their characteristics. To qualify for amortised cost, the investment must have equal or lower credit risk than the weighted-average credit risk in the underlying pool of instruments, and those instruments must meet certain criteria. If 'a look through' is impracticable, the tranche is classified at fair value through profit or loss.

1.60 The IFRS 9 classification principles indicate that all equity investments should be measured at fair value. However, management has an option to present in other comprehensive income unrealised and realised fair value gains and losses on equity investments that are not held for trading. Such designation is available on initial recognition on an instrument-by-instrument basis and is irrevocable. There is no subsequent recycling of fair value gains and losses to profit or loss; however, dividends from such investments continue to be recognised in profit or loss.

1.61 IFRS 9 removes the cost exemption for unquoted equities and derivatives on unquoted equities although it provides guidance on when cost may be an appropriate estimate of fair value.

1.62 The principles for IFRS 9's classification and measurement of financial assets are considered further in chapter 12.

1.58　除非在主体改变其业务模式的罕见情况下，IFRS 9 禁止重分类。在这种情况下，要求主体采用未来适用法对受影响的金融资产进行重分类。

1.59　对于产生信用风险集中的合同连结工具有特别的指引，证券化投资通常就是这种情况。除对该工具本身采用 IFRS 9 的分类条件进行评估外，管理层还应当采用“透视法”去评估产生现金流量的基础工具池的特征。若要符合按摊余成本计量，该投资的信用风险必须等于或小于基础工具池的加权平均信用风险，而且这些工具必须满足特定的条件。如果“透视”不切实可行，则该部分投资被划分为以公允价值计量且变动计入损益的金融资产。

1.60　IFRS 9 的分类原则表明所有的权益投资都应当以公允价值计量。然而，管理层可以选择将并非为交易而持有的权益投资的未实现和已实现的公允价值利得和损失都在其他综合收益中列报。这种指定在初始确认时以每个工具为基础适用，且不可撤销。期后公允价值利得或损失不得转入损益，但是，这些投资的股利将继续确认为损益。

1.61　IFRS 9 删除了针对无市场报价的权益以及基于无市场报价的权益的衍生工具以成本计量的豁免，但它提供了何时成本可能是公允价值的合理估计的指引。

1.62　IFRS 9 中有关金融资产的分类与计量原则在第 12 章中进一步阐明。

Chapter 2 Introduction

Content

Accounting for financial instruments	2001
Development of financial instruments standards	2003
EU adoption	2003
The way forward	2005
Structure of the chapters	2011

第二章　引言

目　录

金融工具的会计处理	2002
金融工具准则的制定	2004
在欧盟采用	2004
未来之路	2006
章节结构	2012

Accounting for financial instruments

2.1 Financial markets have experienced, and continue to experience, significant developments since the 1980s. As foreign exchange rates, interest rates and commodity prices became increasingly volatile, a need arose to manage the commercial risks arising from the instability of these markets. Primary financial instruments, such as bonds and shares, that comprised much of the traditional financing and risk management activities, gave way to derivative products, such as futures, options, forward contracts and swaps, in managing risks. Entities were able to change substantially their financial risk profile, virtually instantaneously, by entering into foreign exchange or interest rate swaps, or by acquiring options or forward contracts to hedge or take positions on future price movements. With the globalisation of financial markets, growth in international commerce, advancement in financial risk management and information technology, the development and use of cost effective innovative derivative products and complex financial instruments for managing risk and improving return on assets became commonplace.

2.2 However, it became apparent that this growth in the use of financial instruments had outstripped the development of guidance for their accounting. Traditional realisation and cost-based measurement concepts were no longer adequate to portray effectively their impact and risks, as some derivatives (for example, forward contracts and swaps) with no initial cost were simply not recognised until settlement, although some instruments with negative fair values were recorded as liabilities in the financial statements. Deficiencies in current accounting practices, inconsistent treatment of economically similar transactions and the lack of visibility in the financial statements caused difficulty for both preparers and users of financial statements. This resulted in an atmosphere of uncertainty, which many people believed might discourage the legitimate use of derivative instruments. Concern about inadequate accounting for derivatives was also heightened by the publicity surrounding large derivative – instrument losses at several companies. As a result, a pervasive need to develop a single, comprehensive standard for accounting and disclosure of financial instruments and hedging activities became a necessity.

金融工具的会计处理

2.1 自20世纪80年代以来，金融市场已经经历，并将继续经历巨大的发展。随着外汇汇率、利率和商品价格的波动性越来越大，出现了对这些由于市场的不稳定性而产生的商业风险进行管理的需求。在管理风险时，诸如债券和股票等构成了传统融资和风险管理活动大部分内容的主要金融工具已经被期货、期权、远期合同和互换等衍生产品所替代。主体基本上能通过签订外汇或利率互换，或通过购买期权或远期合同来对未来价格变动进行套期保值或持有敞口的方式，极大地改变其金融风险的状况。随着金融市场的全球化、国际商业的发展、金融风险管理和信息技术的进步，开发和使用高成本效益的创新型衍生产品和复杂金融工具用于管理风险及提高资产回报也变得极为常见了。

2.2 但是，使用金融工具的发展超过其会计处理指引的发展已经非常明显。传统的以实现和成本为基础的计量理念已不足以有效体现其影响和风险，因为有些没有最初成本的衍生工具（例如，远期合同和互换）仅仅直到结算时才确认，尽管一些公允价值为负数的工具在财务报表中记为负债。当前会计实务的缺陷、经济实质相似交易处理方法的不一致以及财务报表透明度不足的问题同时给财务报表的编制者和使用者带来了困难。其所带来的不确定性使很多人都认为这将阻碍衍生工具的合理使用。数家公司衍生工具重大损失的公布也加重了对衍生工具会计处理不充分问题的担忧。因此，为金融工具和套期活动的会计处理和披露制定一个单一、全面的准则的普遍需求成为必需。

Development of financial instruments standards

2.3 In 1988, the International Accounting Standards Committee (IASC), the predecessor body of the IASB, started work developing a comprehensive standard on the recognition, measurement and disclosure of financial instruments. The first standard, IAS 32, 'Financial instruments: Presentation and disclosure,' was issued in 1995 followed by IAS 39, 'Financial instruments: Recognition and measurement', in March 1999. However, when the IASB was formed in 2001, it undertook a project to improve international standards inherited from the IASC. As a result, revised versions of IAS 32 and IAS 39 were issued in December 2003. Since then further amendments have been made to these standards, the principal one being the issue of a new standard IFRS 7, 'Financial instruments: Disclosures', in August 2005. As IFRS 7 includes all the disclosure requirements relating to financial instruments, the title of IAS 32 was amended to 'Financial instruments - Presentation'.

2.3.1 The credit crisis of 2008 highlighted the complexity of both financial instruments and the accounting for them. There was pressure from the public, politicians and regulators, to re-think and simplify the accounting for financial instruments. IFRS 9, 'Financial instruments', represents the first milestone in the IASB's planned replacement of IAS 39. IFRS 9 was issued in November 2009 and replaces the multiple classification and measurement models for financial assets. The IASB continues to work on further stages of this standard as described below. IFRS 9 has been available for adoption since November 2009 but is not mandatory until periods commencing on or after 1 January 2013. The scope of the financial instrument standards is considered in chapter 3.

EU adoption

2.4 The EU Regulation required listed groups to prepare their consolidated financial statements using IFRS for periods commencing on or after 1 January 2005. For this to happen, IFRSs had to be brought into EU law through a complex

金融工具准则的制定

2.3 国际会计准则委员会（“IASC”），即 IASB 的前身，于 1988 年开始了制定有关金融工具确认、计量和披露的综合准则的工作。第一个准则 IAS 32《金融工具：列报和披露》于 1995 年发布，而 IAS 39《金融工具：确认和计量》随后于 1999 年 3 月发布。但是，当 IASB 于 2001 年成立之后，它着手于改进从 IASC 继承下来的国际准则。因此，于 2003 年 12 月发布了修订的 IAS 32 和 IAS 39。之后这些准则又被进一步地修订，主要的一个修订就是于 2005 年 8 月所发布的新准则 IFRS 7《金融工具：披露》。因为 IFRS 7 包括了金融工具所有的披露要求，所以 IAS 32 更名为《金融工具：列报》。

2.3.1 2008 年的信贷危机突显了金融工具及其会计处理两者的复杂性。公众、政客以及监管部门都施以压力以重新考虑并简化金融工具的会计处理。IFRS 9《金融工具》代表了 IASB 替代 IAS 39 计划的第一个里程碑。IFRS 9 于 2009 年 11 月发布并替代了金融资产的多重分类及计量模式。如下所述 IASB 将继续致力于该准则更多的阶段。IFRS 9 可以从 2009 年 11 月开始采用，但直到起始日在 2013 年 1 月 1 日或之后的期间才会强制实施。金融工具准则的范围在第 3 章中予以介绍。

在欧盟采用

2.4 欧盟法规要求上市集团从起始日在 2005 年 1 月 1 日或之后的期间采用国际财务报告准则编制其合并财务报表。为此，国际财务报告准则需要通过一种复杂的认可机制被引入欧盟的法规。尽管大部分 IASB 的准则已被采用，

endorsement mechanism. Although most of the IASB standards were endorsed, IAS 39 was not endorsed in full. Some aspects of IAS 39, namely the option to fair value all liabilities and certain aspects of hedge accounting that troubled banks and regulators, did not find favour with the EU and were removed. This 'carved out' version was endorsed by the EU in November 2004. The 'carve out' relating to the fair value option was removed as a result of a subsequent amendment to IAS 39 and endorsement by the EU in November 2005, but the one relating to hedge accounting remains with the result that there is still a difference between full IAS 39 and EU endorsed IAS 39. The EU has not yet endorsed IFRS 9.

The way forward

2.5 IAS 39 has been in place for over 11 years and during this time it has been amended several times. In 2008, certain clarifications and improvements were made to the standard as part of the IASB annual improvements project. However, many prepares and users of financial statements still find the requirements of IAS 39 complex. The IASB is keen to find a better accounting solution for financial instruments that will produce meaningful results without undue complexity and dependence on detailed rules.

2.6 As a first step in that process, the IASB and FASB identified three long-term projects relating to financial instruments being: derecognition; financial instruments with characteristics of equity; and replacement of IAS 39. These projects from part of the memorandum of understanding, which sets out a roadmap for convergence between IFRS and US GAAP.

2.6.1 As a result of the recent global financial crisis, the IASB has been reviewing accounting issues that have emerged, including those identified by the G20 and other international bodies such as the Financial Stability Forum. The IASB is working closely with the FASB with the aim of ensuring a globally consistent and appropriate response to the crisis. As part of this it has accelerated its project to replace IAS 39 and sub-divided it into three phases. IFRS 9, 'Financial instruments', which deals with accounting for financial assets, is part of the first stage of the project and has been finalised. The IASB is planning to

IAS 39 并未被完全认可。IAS 39 的某些方面，即对所有负债采用公允价值选择权以及困扰银行和监管部门的套期会计的特定方面，并未受到欧盟的青睐而被删除。欧盟于 2004 年 11 月采用了这个“删减”版本。对 IAS 39 的后续修订解决了与公允价值选择权相关的“删减”并被欧盟于 2005 年 11 月认可，但是与套期会计相关的删减仍然存在，因此完整版的 IAS 39 和欧盟所认可的 IAS 39 之间仍存在一个差异。欧盟仍然没有认可 IFRS 9.

未来之路

2.5 IAS 39 已经颁布了 11 年多的时间，在这期间被多次修订。在 2008 年，作为 IASB 年度改进计划的部分对该准则进行了某些澄清和改进。但是，很多财务报表的编制者及使用者仍然认为 IAS 39 的要求非常复杂。IASB 热衷于为金融工具找到一种既不过度复杂又不依赖于详细规则，并能得到有意义结果的更好会计处理方法。

2.6 作为该过程的第一步，IASB 和 FASB 确定了与金融工具相关的三个长期项目，即：终止确认、具有权益特征的金融工具和替换 IAS 39。这些项目构成 IFRS 和美国公认会计准则趋同谅解备忘录的一部分。

2.6.1 由于最近的全球金融危机，IASB 对所暴露出的、包括 G20 以及诸如金融稳定论坛等其他国际机构所发现的会计问题进行了审查。IASB 与 FASB 密切合作，旨在能够针对经济危机作出全球一致的恰当反应。作为此项工作的一部分，它已经加速了其替换 IAS 39 项目的进程并将其细分为三个阶段。IFRS 9《金融工具》规定了金融资产的会计处理，是该项目第一阶段的一部分且已完成。IASB 计划在 2011 年第二季度完成此项目的未尽部分（参见下文）。下表汇总了在理事会日程上与 IAS 32、IAS 39 和 IFRS 7 相关的大量当前项目以及预计发布日期。

finalise the remainder of the project by the second quarter of 2011 (see below). The table below summarises the large number of current projects relating to IAS 32, IAS 39 and IFRS 7 on the Boards' agenda with anticipated publication dates.

Project	**Final standard publication date**	**Notes**	**Further details**
IASB			
Exposure draft: Derecognition – disclosures	Q3 2010	1,2,3	8.4.1
Discussion paper: Financial instruments with characteristics of equity (exposure draft expected Q1 2011)	H2 2011	1,2	
Financial instruments (IAS 39 replacement)		1,2,3	
– Exposure draft: Fair value option for financial liabilities	Q2 2011		2.6.3 – 2.6.5
– Exposure draft: Amortised cost and impairment	Q2 2011		2.6.6 – 2.6.9
– Hedging (exposure draft expected Q3 2010)	Q2 2011		
– Asset and liability offsetting (exposure draft expected Q4 2010)	Q2 2011		
Exposure draft: Fair value measurement guidance	Q1 2011	1,2,3	
Exposure draft: Fair value measurement – measurement uncertainty analysis disclosure for fair value	Q1 2011		

Notes:

1 Part of the memorandum of understanding.

2 Joint project with the FASB.

3 Financial crisis related project.

2.6.2 The IASB issued IFRS 9, 'Financial instruments', in November 2009 as part of phase 1 of its accelerated project to replace IAS 39. The standard reduces the many financial assest classifications and measurement categories and their

项目	最终准则发布日期	注释	其他详细信息
IASB			
征求意见稿：终止确认－披露	2010 年第三季度	1, 2, 3	8.4.1
讨论稿：具有权益特征的金融工具（征求意见稿预期于 2011 年 1 季度发布）	2011 年下半年	1, 2	
金融工具（替换 IAS39）		1, 2, 3	
－征求意见稿：金融负债的公允价值选择权	2011 年第二季度		2.6.3－2.6.5
－征求意见稿：摊余成本及减值	2011 年第二季度		2.6.6－2.6.9
－套期保值（征求意见稿预期于 2010 年第三季度发布）	2011 年第二季度		
－资产和负债的抵消（征求意见稿预期于 2010 年第四季度发布）	2011 年第二季度		
征求意见稿：公允价值计量指引	2011 年第一季度	1, 2, 3	
征求意见稿：公允价值计量－公允价值的计量不确定性分析披露	2011 年第一季度		

注释：

1 谅解备忘录的一部分。

2 与 FASB 的联合项目。

3 与金融危机相关的项目。

2.6.2 作为加速替换 IAS 39 项目的第一阶段工作，IASB 于 2009 年 7 月发布了 IFRS 9《金融工具》。该准则减少了 IAS 39 中众多的金融工具分类和计量类别及其相关减值模型。IFRS 9 的分类和计量要求在第 12 章中进一步介绍。

associated impairment models in IAS 39. The classification and measurement requirements under IFRS 9 are considered further in chapter 12.

2.6.3 The IASB published the exposure draft 'Fair value option for financial liabilities' in May 2010. Except for the proposal below, the IASB intends to retain the existing guidance in IAS 39 regarding the classification and measurement of financial liabilities. The IASB decided not to change the accounting for liabilities substantially, as the existing requirements for liabilities generally work well. However, the main concern regarding liabilities is the impact of 'own credit' for liabilities recognised at fair value.

2.6.4 Under the proposals, entities with financial liabilities designated at FVTPL follow a two-step measurement approach. First, all changes in fair value of the financial liability are recognised in the profit or loss. Secondly, the change in value due to changes in the liability's credit risk is recognised in other comprehensive income (OCI) with an offsetting entry to profit or loss. There is no subsequent recycling of the amounts in OCI to profit or loss and the entity may transfer the cumulative gain or loss within equity.

2.6.5 Financial liabilities that are required to be measured at FVTPL (as distinct from those that the entity has designated at FVTPL) continue to have all fair value movements recognised in profit or loss, with no transfer to OCI. Derivatives (including embedded derivatives), such as foreign currency forwards and interest rate swaps, or instruments held in a trading portfolio continue to have all fair value movements recognised in profit or loss.

2.6.6 The IASB issued the exposure draft 'Financial instruments: Amortised cost and impairment' in November 2009. The IASB is proposing fundamental changes to the impairment guidance for financial assets accounted for at amortised cost. This is the second stage of the IAS 39 replacement project. The exposure draft proposes an 'effective return' approach to amortised cost measurement. For financial assets, this implies an 'expected cash flow' (ECF) impairment model.

2.6.7 The proposed approach is built on the premise that interest charged on financial instruments includes a premium for expected losses, which should not be included as part of interest revenue/income, and results in an allocation of the

2.6.3 IASB 于 2010 年 5 月发布了征求意见稿《金融负债的公允价值选择权》。除以下建议外，IASB 有意保留 IAS 39 中现有的有关金融负债的分类和计量的指引。由于现有对负债的要求总体而言仍可行，IASB 决定不对负债的会计处理做出重大改变。但是，对负债的主要顾虑在于“自身信用”对以公允价值确认的负债产生的影响。

2.6.4 在此建议下，主体对被指定为以公允价值计量且变动计入损益的金融负债采取一个两步的计量方法。首先，金融负债所有的公允价值变动确认为损益。其次，由于负债的信用风险变动而导致的价值变动计入其他综合收益（“OCI”），同时抵消损益。其他综合收益的金额后续不再转入损益，主体可以将累计利得或损失在权益内重分类。

2.6.5 按要求必须以公允价值计量且变动计入损益的金融负债（区别于那些主体指定为以公允价值计量且变动计入损益的金融负债）继续将所有的公允价值变动确认为损益，不转为其他综合收益。诸如外币期货和利率互换等衍生工具（包括嵌入衍生工具）或作为交易类组合持有的工具继续将所有的公允价值变动确认为损益。

2.6.6 IASB 于 2009 年 11 月发布了征求意见稿《金融工具：摊余成本和减值》。IASB 对以摊余成本计量的金融资产的减值指引提出了本质的改变。这是替换 IAS 39 项目的第二阶段。该征求意见稿对摊余成本计量提出了一个“实际回报”的方法。对于金融资产，这意味着“预计现金流”（“ECF”）的减值模型。

2.6.7 该方法所依据的前提条件是金融工具的利息包括预计损失的对价，此对价不应作为利息收入或收益的一部分，并将导致在金融资产的预计存续期内对预期信用损失的初始估计进行分摊。贷款人被要求于工具初始便确定代

initial estimate of expected credit losses over the expected life of the financial asset. The lender is required to identify the 'effective interest rate' (EIR) component at the inception of an instrument that represents compensation for the expected losses. Interest income is recognised over the instrument's life at the EIR, net of the expected loss component identified at inception. The premium associated with the expected losses is reflected each period as a reduction in the carrying value of the receivable (effectively a provision for bad debts).

2.6.8 Unlike the incurred loss model currently used under IAS 39, the ECF approach does not wait for evidence that an impairment has occurred; instead it requires a continuous assessment of the expected cash flows over the instrument's life. No impairment losses are recognised if the original expectations of the expected losses prove accurate. The premium associated with the initial estimate of expected losses will have reduced the receivable balance to the amount expected to be collected. However, if more losses are expected than originally estimated, an impairment charge is recognised for the decrease in the expected cash flows. If favourable changes to loss expectations occur, a credit to income is recognised for the increase in expected cash flows. The approach requires the use of an allowance account for credit losses and no direct write-offs are permitted. The exposure draft makes allowance for practical expedients in calculating amortised cost if the overall effect is immaterial. An example would be short-term trade receivables.

2.6.9 The exposure draft sets out robust presentation and disclosure requirements to ensure that users can evaluate the financial effect of interest revenue and interest expense, and the credit quality of financial assets held by the entity.

Structure of the chapters

2.7 Detailed discussion of accounting for financial instruments is structured around the following chapters:

- Objectives and scope of IAS 32, IFRS 7 and IAS 39.
- Nature and characteristics of financial instruments.

表弥补预计损失的“实际利率”（“EIR”）组成部分。利息收入按照扣除初始确认的预计损失部分的实际利率在工具存续期内确认。和预计损失相关的对价在各期反映为应收款账面余额的抵减（实际上即为坏账准备）。

2.6.8　不同于目前使用的IAS 39中的已发生损失模型，预计损失方法不会等到减值迹象的发生，而是要求在工具存续期内对预计现金流进行持续地评估。如果最初对预计损失的预期被证明准确，则不会再确认减值损失。与初始估计的预计损失相关的对价会将应收款项余额减至预期能够收回的金额。但是，当预计损失超过最初估计的金额时，则将对预计现金流的减少确认为减值。如果对预计损失发生有利的变动，则将对预计现金流的增加贷记为收益。该方法要求对信用损失采用备抵账户，不允许直接冲减。如果总体的影响不重大，该征求意见稿允许实务中使用计算摊余成本的简便方法。例如短期应收账款。

2.6.9　该征求意见稿提出了大量的列报和披露要求，以确保使用者可以对利息收入和利息成本的财务影响以及主体所持有的金融资产的信用质量做出评估。

章节结构

2.7　根据如下章节的结构，在各章中安排了有关金融工具会计处理方法的详细讨论：

- IAS 32、IFRS 7和IAS 39的目标和范围。
- 金融工具的性质和特征。

- Embedded derivatives in host contracts.
- Classification of financial instruments.
- Financial liabilities and equity.
- Recognition and derecognition of financial instruments.
- Measurement of financial instrūments.
- Hedging and hedge accounting.
- Presentation and disclosure of financial instruments.
- IFRS 9, 'Financial instruments'.

2.8 The above chapters address the requirements of IAS 32, IFRS 7, IAS 39 and IFRS 9 extant as at 31 August 2010. All four standards are supplemented by application guidance that is an integral part of the standards and, where relevant, by illustrative examples that accompany them, but that are not part of the standards. In addition, IAS 39 and IFRS 7 are also supplemented by implementation guidance that is not part of the standards. Furthermore, as IAS 39 is largely based on the US standard FAS 133, 'Accounting for derivative instruments and hedging activities', the chapters that follow draw on the guidance of that standard where it is considered appropriate and necessary to do so.

- 主合同中的嵌入衍生工具。
- 金融工具的分类。
- 金融负债和权益。
- 金融工具的确认和终止确认。
- 金融工具的计量。
- 套期和套期会计。
- 金融工具的列报和披露。
- IFRS 9《金融工具》。

2.8　上述章节中讨论了于2010年8月31日现行的IAS 32、IFRS 7、IAS 39和IFRS 9的要求。这四个准则全都有作为准则组成部分的实施指南作为补充，有的准则还有示例，不过这些示例并非准则的组成部分。此外，IAS 39和IFRS 7还有不属于准则组成部分的应用指南。另外，由于IAS 39在很大程度上基于美国准则《财务会计准则公告第133号——衍生工具和套期活动的会计处理》，接下来的章节中在适当和必要的情况下会提及该准则公告的指引。

Chapter 3 Objectives and scope of IAS 32, IAS 39 and IFRS 7

Content

Objectives 3001

Scope 3001

Interests in subsidiaries, associates and joint ventures 3003

Employee benefit plans and share-based payments 3007

Business combinations 3007

Own equity instruments 3011

Rights and obligations under lease contracts 3011

Rights and obligations under insurance contracts 3013

Contracts with discretionary participating features 3013

Derivatives embedded in insurance contracts 3015

Financial guarantee contracts 3015

Weather derivatives 3025

Loan commitments 3027

Contracts to buy or sell non-financial assets 3029

Contracts that can be settled net 3031

Written options 3035

Royalty agreements 3035

第三章 IAS 32、IAS 39 及 IFRS 7 的目标与范围

目 录

目标 3002
范围 3002
在子公司、联营和合营中的权益 3004
职工福利计划和以股份为基础的支付 3008
业务合并 3008
自身权益工具 3012
租赁合同中的权利和义务 3012
保险合同中的权利和义务 3014
具有相机参与分红特征的合同 3014
保险合同中的嵌入衍生工具 3016
财务担保合同 3016
天气衍生工具 3026
贷款承诺 3028
购买或出售非金融资产的合同 3030
可以用净额结算的合同 3032
签出期权 3036
特许权协议 3036

Objectives

3.1 IAS 32's objective is to establish principles for presenting financial instruments as financial liabilities or equity and for offsetting financial assets and financial liabilities. It applies to the classification of financial instruments into financial assets, financial liabilities and equity instruments from the perspective of the issuer. Furthermore, it deals with the classification of related interest, dividends, losses and gains; and the circumstances in which financial assets and liabilities should be offset. [IAS 32 para 2].

3.2 IAS 39's objective is to establish principles for recognising and measuring financial assets, financial liabilities and some contracts to buy or sell non-financial items. [IAS 39 para 1]. IAS 39 also deals with derecognition of financial assets and financial liabilities and hedge accounting. Requirements for presenting and disclosing information about financial instruments set out in IAS 32 and IFRS 7 are designed to complement those principles.

3.3 IFRS 7's objective is to require entities to provide disclosures that enable users to evaluate:

- The significance of financial instruments for the entity's financial position and performance.
- The nature and extent of risks arising from financial instruments to which the entity is exposed during the period at the reporting date and how the entity manages these risks.

[IFRS 7 para 1].

Scope

3.4 Generally, IAS 32, IAS 39 and IFRS 7 have to be applied by all entities preparing their financial statements in accordance with IFRS and to all types of financial instruments, except for those specifically excluded from their scope [IAS

目标

3.1　IAS 32 的目标是确立金融工具作为金融负债或权益的列报与金融资产和金融负债的抵销原则。它规定了如何从发行人的角度将金融工具划分为金融资产、金融负债和权益工具。此外，它还规定了相关利息、股利、损失和利得的分类；以及在何种情况下金融资产和负债应予以抵销。[IAS 32 第 2 段]。

3.2　IAS 39 的目标是确立金融资产、金融负债和某些购买或出售非金融项目的合同的确认和计量原则。[IAS 39 第 1 段]。IAS 39 还规范了金融资产和金融负债的终止确认及套期会计。IAS 32 和 IFRS 7 中所规定的对金融工具有关信息的列报和披露要求旨在对这些原则进行补充。

3.3　IFRS 7 的目标是要求主体做出披露从而令报表使用者能对下列事项进行评估：

- 金融工具对主体的财务状况和经营业绩的重要性。
- 主体在报告期间和报告日承受的金融工具所产生的风险的性质和程度，以及主体如何管理这些风险。

[IFRS 7 第 1 段]。

范围

3.4　一般而言，除了那些明确排除在其范围之外的项目，IAS 32、IAS 39 和 IFRS 7 适用于所有按照 IFRS 编制其财务报表的主体以及所有类型的金融工具[IAS 32 第 4 段；IAS 39 第 2 段；IFRS 7 第 3 段]。金融工具的定义很广泛，

32 para 4; IAS 39 para 2; IFRS 7 para 3]. The definition of a financial instrument is broad and is discussed in chapter 4.

3.5 The scope of the three standards is very wide-ranging, but not identical. While IAS 32 and IAS 39 only deal with recognised financial instruments, IFRS 7 applies to both recognised as well as unrecognised financial instruments. Recognised financial instruments include financial assets and financial liabilities that are within IAS 39's scope. Unrecognised financial instruments include some financial instruments, for example, loan commitments that, although scoped out of IAS 39, are within IFRS 7's scope. [IFRS 7 para 4]. In other words, all financial instruments that are scoped out of IFRS 7 are also scoped out of IAS 39, but IAS 39 contains additional scope exclusions that go beyond IFRS 7 and IAS 32. [IAS 32 para 4; IFRS 7 para 3; IAS 39 para 2]. In general, items are scoped out of all the three standards if another standard is more prescriptive.

Interests in subsidiaries, associates and joint ventures

3.6 Interests in subsidiaries, associates and joint ventures that are accounted for using the cost method prescribed in IAS 27, 'Consolidated and separate financial statements', IAS 28, 'Investment in associates', and IAS 31, 'Interest in joint ventures', or that are accounted for in accordance with IFRS 5, 'Non-current assets held-for-sale and discontinued operations', [IAS 27 para 38; IAS 28 para 14; IAS 31 para 2(a)] are outside the scope of IAS 32, IFRS 7 and IAS 39.

3.7 However, such interests fall within the scope of the financial instrument standards in either of the following circumstances:

- The parent or the investor accounts for such interests in its separate financial statements in accordance with IAS 39 either as at fair value through profit or loss or as available for sale. [IAS 27 para 38]. In that situation, the interest in a subsidiary, associate or joint venture falls within IAS 32's and IFRS 7's scope. [IAS 32 para 4(a); IFRS 7 para 3(a)]. In addition, the disclosure requirements of IAS 27, IAS 28 and IAS 31 continue to apply.
- An interest in an associate or a joint venture that is scoped out of IAS 28 or IAS

第 4 章中对其进行了讨论。

3.5　这三个准则的范围非常广泛，但并不完全相同。IAS 32 和 IAS 39 仅规范已确认的金融工具，而 IFRS 7 则适用于已确认及未确认的金融工具。已确认的金融工具包括 IAS 39 范围内的金融资产和金融负债。未确认的金融工具包括某些在 IAS 39 范围外、但在 IFRS 7 范围内的金融工具，例如贷款承诺。[IFRS 7 第 4 段]。换言之，所有不在 IFRS 7 范围内的金融工具亦不在 IAS 39 范围内，但是 IAS 39 有比 IFRS 7 和 IAS 32 更多的适用范围排除项目。[IAS 32 第 4 段；IFRS 7 第 3 段；IAS 39 第 2 段]。总体而言，如果另一个准则的规定更为细化，则这些项目即在上述三个准则的范围以外。

在子公司、联营和合营中的权益

3.6　根据《国际会计准则第 27 号——合并财务报表和单独财务报表》（“IAS 27”）、《国际会计准则第 28 号——联营中的投资》（“IAS 28”）和《国际会计准则第 31 号——合营中的权益》（“IAS 31”）中所规定的成本法进行会计处理，或根据《国际财务报告准则第 5 号——持有待售的非流动资产和终止经营》（“IFRS 5”）进行会计处理的在子公司、联营和合营中的权益不在 IAS 32、IFRS 7 和 IAS 39 的范围内。[IAS 27 第38 段；IAS 28 第 14 段；IAS 31 第 2（a）段]。

3.7　但是，这种权益在如下任何一种情况下即在金融工具准则的范围内：

- 母公司或投资人在其单独财务报表中按照 IAS 39 采用以公允价值计量且变动计入损益或可供出售的投资来对这种权益进行会计处理。[IAS 27 第 38 段]。在这种情况下，在子公司、联营或合营中的权益属于 IAS 32 和 IFRS 7 的范围。[IAS 32 第 4（a）段；IFRS 7 第 3（a）段]。此外，IAS 27、IAS 28 和 IAS 31 的披露要求继续适用。

- 由于是风险投资机构、共同基金、信托公司及包括投资连结保险基金在内的

31, because it is held by a venture capital organisation, mutual fund, unit trust and similar entity including an investment-linked insurance fund that upon initial recognition is designated as at fair value through profit or loss (so called fair value option) or categorised as held for trading. [IAS 28 para 1, IAS 31 para 1]. In that situation, the investment is accounted for in accordance with IAS 39 and the disclosure requirements of IFRS 7, as well as of paragraph 37(f) of IAS 28 and of paragraphs 55 and 56 of IAS 31, apply.

3.8 Derivatives linked to interests in subsidiaries, associates and joint ventures fall within the scope of IAS 32, IFRS 7 and IAS 39, except where the derivative meets the definition of an equity instrument of the entity in IAS 32. In that situation, it is scoped out of IAS 39 and accounted for as equity in accordance with IAS 32. [IAS 32 para 4(a); IFRS 7 para 3(a); IAS 39 para 2(a)].

3.9 An investor may, in addition to having a present ownership interest, hold share options in an investee (that is not presently a subsidiary) that, if exercised, give the investor voting power or reduce another party's voting power over the financial and operating policies of the investee (potential voting rights). Such potential voting rights that are currently exercisable and give access to the economic benefits would have been taken into account in establishing not only whether the investor has control, significant influence or joint control, but also in determining the share of the investment (economic interest) to be accounted for by consolidation, equity method or proportional consolidation. [IAS 27 paras 14, IG 4-5; IAS 28 para 8]. When instruments containing potential voting rights in substance currently give access to the economic benefits associated with an ownership interest and so affect the share of profits the investee accounts for when consolidating, proportionately consolidating or applying the equity method, the instrument is scoped out of IAS 39. [IAS 27 para IG 7]. This exclusion makes sense as it avoids double counting the same instrument twice, first by inclusion in the economic interest calculation and, secondly, by fair valuing the derivative through profit or loss. Therefore, in this situation, IAS 32 and IFRS 7 apply, but not IAS 39.

类似主体所持有且在初始确认时被指定为以公允价值计量且变动计入损益(所谓的公允价值选择权)或被分类为为交易而持有的在联营或合营中的权益不在 IAS 28 或 IAS 31 的范围内。[IAS 28 第 1 段;IAS 31 第 1 段]。在这种情况下,该投资应根据 IAS 39 进行会计处理,而 IFRS 7 的披露要求、以及 IAS 28 第 37(f)段和 IAS 31 第 55 和 56 段亦适用。

3.8　基于在子公司、联营和合营中的权益的衍生工具在 IAS 32、IFRS 7 和 IAS 39 的范围内，除非该衍生工具符合 IAS 32 中主体权益工具的定义。在这种情况下，它不在 IAS 39 的范围内，而应按照 IAS 32 作为权益进行会计处理。[IAS 32 第 4（a）段；IFRS 7 第 3（a）段；IAS 39 第 2（a）段]。

3.9　除持有当前的所有权权益外，投资人还可能持有被投资方（目前并非子公司）的股票期权，而如果行使该期权，将赋予投资人对被投资人在财务和经营政策上的表决权（潜在表决权）或减少另一方的表决权。这种当前可以行使并能够带来经济利益的潜在表决权，不仅在确定投资人是否具有控制、重大影响或共同控制时，而且在确定根据合并、权益法或比例合并进行会计处理的投资比例（经济利益）时亦需要考虑到。[IAS 27 第 14 段、IG 第 4 –5 段；IAS 28 第 8 段]。当包含潜在表决权的工具能够在当前实质上带来与所有权权益相关的经济利益，并因而影响在合并、比例合并或采用权益法时享有的被投资方利润份额时，该工具即不在 IAS 39 的范围内。[IAS 27 IG 第 7 段]。此范围排除是合理的，因为它避免了对同一工具的两次重复计算，既将其纳入经济利益的计算中，又对该衍生工具以公允价值计量且变动计入损益。因此，在这种情况下，将适用于 IAS 32 和 IFRS 7，而不适用于 IAS 39。

Employee benefit plans and share-based payments

3.10 Employee rights and obligations under employee benefit plans are financial instruments, because they are contractual rights or obligations that will result in the flow of cash to the past and present employees. However, as they are specifically accounted for under IAS 19, 'Employee benefits', they are outside the scope of IAS 32, IFRS 7 and IAS 39. [IAS 32 para 4(b); IFRS 7 para 3(b); IAS 39 para 2(c)].

3.11 Similarly, share-based payment transactions to which IFRS 2, 'Share-based payment', applies are outside the scope of IAS 32, IFRS 7 and IAS 39. However, IAS 32, IFRS 7 and IAS 39 apply to contracts to buy or sell non-financial items in share based payment transactions that can be settled net, unless they fall within the own use purchase and sale exception (see para 3.34 below). For example, if an entity enters into a contract to purchase a fixed quantity of a particular commodity in exchange for issuing a fixed number of own equity instruments that could be settled net in cash, the contract would fall within IAS 39's scope, unless it qualifies for the own use exception. [IAS 32 para 4(f)(i); IFRS 7 para 3(e); IAS 39 para 2(i)].

3.12 Furthermore, IAS 32 applies to treasury shares that are purchased, sold, issued or cancelled in connection with employee share option plans, employee share purchase plans and all other share-based payment arrangements. [IAS 32 paras 4(f)(ii), 33, 34].

Business combinations

3.13 In accordance with IFRS 3 'Business combinations', contracts for contingent consideration usually fall within the scope of IAS 32, IAS 39 and IFRS 7, provided they do not meet the definition of an equity instrument. [IFRS 3 paras 40 and 58]. However, from an acquirer's perspective only, contracts for contingent consideration in a business combination that occurred under IFRS 3 (superceded) – that is, those that occurred in annual periods starting prior to 1 July 2009, are still scoped out of IAS 32, IFRS 7 and IAS 39. From the

职工福利计划和以股份为基础的支付

3.10　根据职工福利计划所产生的职工权利和义务是金融工具，因为它们是将导致现金流向过去及当前职工的合同权利或义务。但是，由于它们专门按照《国际会计准则第 19 号——职工福利》（“IAS 19”）进行会计处理，所以不在 IAS 32、IFRS 7 和 IAS 39 的范围内。[IAS 32 第 4（b）段；IFRS 7 第 3（b）段；IAS 39 第 2（c）段]。

3.11　类似地，适用《国际财务报告准则第 2 号——以股份为基础的支付》（“IFRS 2”）的以股份为基础的支付交易也不在 IAS 32、IFRS 7 和 IAS 39 的范围内。但是 IAS 32、IFRS 7 和 IAS 39 适用于可以以净额结算的、购买或出售非金融项目的、以股份为基础的支付交易的合同，除非它们属于自用购买和出售例外情况（参见下文第 3.34 段）。例如，如果主体签订了一项可以以净额结算的，购买固定数量的特定商品来换取发行固定数量的自身权益工具的合同，除非它符合自用例外的要求，否则该合同应当在 IAS 39 的范围内，[IAS 32 第 4（f）（i）段；IFRS 7 第 3（e）段；IAS 39 第 2（i）段]。

3.12　此外，IAS 32 还适用于在职工股票期权计划、职工股票购买计划和所有其他以股份为基础的支付安排中购买、出售、发行或注销的库藏股。[IAS 32 第 4（f）（ii）、33、34 段]。

业务合并

3.13　按照《国际财务报告准则第 3 号——业务合并》（“IFRS 3”），只要或有对价合同不满足权益工具的定义，则其通常在 IAS 32、IAS 39 和 IFRS 7 的范围内。[IFRS 3 第 40、58 段]。但是从购买方的角度来看，发生在废止的 IFRS 3 下，即发生于起始日在 2009 年 7 月 1 日之前的年度期间的业务合并中的或有负债合同仍在 IAS 32、IFRS 7 和 IAS 39 范围之外。从出售方的角度来看，通常所有的或有对价合同都作为金融资产而在 IAS 39 和 IFRS 7 的范围内（也请参见 IFRS《会计实务指引》第 26 章）。

perspective of the seller, all contracts for contingent consideration normally fall within the scope of IAS 39 and IFRS 7 as a financial asset (see also IFRS Manual of Accounting chapter 26).

3.14 Forward contracts between an acquirer and a vendor in a business combination to buy or sell an acquiree at a future date are scoped out of IAS 39, but not IFRS 7. [IAS 39 para 2(g)]. The scope exemption applies to both the acquirer and the seller. The Board amended paragraph 2(g) of IAS 39 in the 2009 'Improvements to IFRSs' to clarify that:

- The scope exemption applies only to forward contracts entered into before the acquisition date (that is, before the date the acquirer obtains control of the acquiree).
- The term of the forward contract should not exceed a reasonable period normally necessary to obtain any required approvals and to complete the transaction.
- The exemption in paragraph 2(g) should not be applied by analogy to investments in associates and other similar transactions.

The amendment was effective prospectively to all unexpired contracts for annual periods beginning on or after 1 January 2010.

3.14.1 Prior to the amendment, it was unclear as to whether the paragraph 2(g) scope exemption only applied to forward contracts or also to other instruments (such as options) that, if exercised or converted, would give control of an entity to an acquirer. Significant diversity had arisen in practice as a result. The two main interpretations of the scope exemption prior to the amendment were:

- A 'narrow' interpretation under which only forward contracts between the purchaser and seller would be outside the scope of IAS 39.
- A 'broad' interpretation under which all kinds of contracts between the purchaser and seller would be outside the scope of IAS 39. This would include options (both purchased and written) that, if exercised, would give control of an entity to an acquirer.

3.14.2 If the 'broad' interpretation, referred to above, had been applied to options, these would have been remeasured from cost to fair value when the

3.14　业务合并中买卖双方签订的在未来某日购买或出售被购买方的远期合同不在 IAS 39 的范围内，但在 IFRS 7 的范围内。［IAS 39 第 2（g）段］。此范围豁免既适用于购买方也适用于出售方。理事会在 2009 年《对国际财务会计准则的改进》中修订了 IAS 39 第 2（g）段以澄清：

- 此范围豁免仅适用于购买日之前（即在购买方取得被购买方控制权之日前）签订的远期合同。
- 该远期合同的期限不得超过正常情况下获取所要求的批准和完成交易所需的合理时间。
- 第 2（g）段所述的豁免不应类推至对联营的投资和其他类似交易。

此修订以未来适用法对所有未到期的合同适用于起始日在 2010 年 1 月 1 日或之后的年度期间。

3.14.1　在此修订之前，第 2（g）段的范围豁免是否只适用于远期合同还是也适用于其他若行使或转换会将把对某主体的控制权转给购买方的工具（例如期权）尚不明确。因此实务中有很大的分歧。修订前对此范围豁免的两种主要解释为：

- 一种“狭义”的解释，即只有买卖双方之间的远期合同在 IAS 39 的范围之外。
- 一种“广义”的解释，即买卖双方之间所有类型的合同都在 IAS 39 的范围之外。这就包括若行权将把对某主体的控制权转给购买方的期权（既包括购入的又包括签出的期权）。

3.14.2　如果对期权采用了上文所述的“广义”的解释，当第一次采用修订时要将期权从成本重新计量为公允价值。此修订没有“豁免”规则。我们认为

amendment was first applied. There were no 'grandfathering' rules in the amendment. We believe that the transition guidance in the amendment suggests that the adjustment from cost to fair value that arises when the amendment is first applied should be recorded in the income statement in the year of adoption. However, the wording of the transition requirements is not clear; as a result, the adjustment could also be taken to opening retained earnings in the period of adoption (that is, no prior-year restatement).

Own equity instruments

3.15 Financial instruments issued by an entity, including options and warrants that meet the definition of an equity instrument in IAS 32 or are required to be classified as equity in accordance with paragraphs 16A, 16B, 16C and 16D of IAS 32, are outside IAS 39's but inside IAS 32's scope. Such instruments, along with other equity accounts including retained earnings, represent the residual interest of the reporting entity and are, therefore, subject to different measurement considerations to those relevant to financial assets and financial liabilities. However, the holder (but not issuer) of such an instrument should apply IAS 39 unless it meets the exceptions discussed in paragraphs 3.6 to 3.9 above. [IAS 39 para 2(d)]. IFRS 7 deals with disclosures of financial instruments in general and doesn't scope out issuers' own equity instruments, for example, disclosure about compound financial instruments in IFRS 7 para 17.

Rights and obligations under lease contracts

3.16 Finance lease contracts that give rise to financial assets for lessors and financial liabilities for lessees are financial instruments that are specially dealt within IAS 17, 'Leases'. Therefore, they fall within the scope of IAS 32 and IFRS 7, but outside of IAS 39's scope, except as follows:

- Lease receivables are included in IAS 39's scope for derecognition and impairment purposes only.
- Finance lease payables are subject to IAS 39's derecognition provisions.

修订的过渡条款建议，应在首次采用该修订时将从成本到公允价值的调整计入采用当年的利润表。但是，过渡条款的措辞并不明确，因此该调整也可能计入采用期间期初的留存收益（即不对以前年度进行重述）。

自身权益工具

3.15　主体发行的金融工具，包括符合 IAS 32 中的权益工具定义的期权和认股权证或按照 IAS 32 第 16A、16B、16C 和 16D 段的要求划分为权益的工具，在 IAS 39 的范围之外，但在 IAS 32 的范围内。这些工具和包括留存收益的其他权益账户一同代表了报告主体的剩余权益，因此和金融资产及金融负债有不同的计量考虑。但是，除非是符合上文第 3.6 到 3.9 段所讨论的例外，否则这种工具的持有人（而非发行人）应采用 IAS 39。[IAS 39 第 2（d）段]。IFRS 7 规范了对金融工具的整体披露要求，并未将发行人的自身权益工具排除在其范围之外，如 IFRS 7 第 17 段对复合金融工具的披露要求。

租赁合同中的权利和义务

3.16　为出租人带来金融资产并为承租人带来金融负债的融资租赁合同是《国际会计准则第 17 号——租赁》（“IAS 17”）中专门规范的金融工具。因此，它们在 IAS 32 和 IFRS 7 的范围内，但不在 IAS 39 的范围内，除非以下情况：

- 应收租赁款仅在终止确认和减值时在 IAS 39 的范围内。
- 应付融资租赁款应遵循 IAS 39 的终止确认条款。

■ Any derivatives embedded in lease contracts are also within IAS 39's scope. [IAS 39 para 2(b)].

Rights and obligations under insurance contracts

3.17 An insurance contract is a contract under which one party (the insurer) accepts significant insurance risk from another party (the policyholder) by agreeing to compensate the policyholder if a specified uncertain future event (the insured event) adversely affects the policyholder. [IFRS 4 App A]. Principally, rights and obligations under insurance contracts are scoped out of IAS 32, IFRS 7 and IAS 39 and are accounted for under IFRS 4, because the policyholder transfers to the insurer significant insurance rather than financial risk. [IAS 32 para 4(d); IAS 39 para 2(e)]. Financial risk is the risk of a possible future change in one or more of a specified interest rate, financial instrument price, commodity price, foreign exchange rate, index of prices or rates, credit rating or credit index or other variable, provided in the case of a non-financial variable that the variable is not specific to a party to the contract. [IFRS 4 App A]. If a financial instrument takes the form of an insurance contract, but involves the transfer of financial risks, as opposed to insurance risk, the contract would fall within the financial instrument standards. The distinction between insurance risk and other risks are set out in Appendix B to IFRS 4. [IFRS 4 App B paras 8-17]. IFRS 4 contains numerous examples of insurance contracts that fall within IFRS 4's scope and those that are not insurance contracts and may fall within the scope of IAS 32, IFRS 7 and IAS 39. [IFRS 4 App B paras 18-19] IFRS 7 provides disclosure only for those rights and obligations under insurance contracts that are also in IAS 39's scope. [IFRS 7 para 3(d)].

Contracts with discretionary participating features

3.18 Financial instruments that are within IFRS 4's scope, because they contain a discretionary participation feature are also scoped out of IAS 39. A discretionary participation feature is a contractual right to receive significant additional benefits, as a supplement to guaranteed benefits, whose amount and timing is at the issuer's

■ 任何嵌在租赁合同中的衍生工具也在 IAS 39 的范围内。

[IAS 39 第2（b）段]。

保险合同中的权利和义务

3.17　保险合同是指按照合同，一方（承保人）同意在特定的某项不确定的未来事项（保险事项）对另一方（投保人）产生不利影响时给予其赔偿从而承担投保人的重大保险风险的合同。[IFRS 4 附录 A]。从原则上讲，保险合同中的权利和义务不在 IAS 32、IFRS 7 和 IAS 39 的范围内，而应根据 IFRS 4 进行会计处理，因为投保人将重大的保险而不是金融风险转移给了承保人。[IAS 32 第4（d）段；IAS 39 第2（e）段]。金融风险是一项或多项特定利率、金融工具价格、商品价格、汇率、物价或利率指数、信用评级或信用指数或者其他变量在未来可能发生变化的风险，如果是非金融变量，该变量不与合同一方特定相关。[IFRS 4 附录 A]。如果某项金融工具以保险合同的形式出现，但转移的却是金融风险而非保险风险，那么该合同应该在金融工具准则的范围内。IFRS 4 的附录 B 给出了保险风险和其他风险之间的区别。[IFRS 4 附录 B 第8－17 段]。IFRS 4 包含多项在 IFRS 4 范围内的保险合同以及不是保险合同，因而可能在 IAS 32、IFRS 7 和 IAS 39 范围内的合同示例。[IFRS 4 附录 B 第18－19 段]。IFRS 7 中仅规定了也在 IAS 39 范围内的保险合同中的权利和义务的披露。[IFRS 7 第3（d）段]。

具有相机参与分红特征的合同

3.18　金融工具由于其具有相机参与分红特征而属于 IFRS 4 的范围，也不在 IAS 39 的范围内。相机参与分红特征是一种获得对担保利益补充重大附加利益的合同权利，其金额和时间由签发人相机抉择且基于特定合同组合的业绩、投资回报或签发该合同的公司、基金或其他主体的损益。[IFRS 4 附录 A]。但

discretion and that are contractually based on the performance of a specified pool of contracts, investment returns or profit or loss of the company, fund or other entity that issues the contract. [IFRS 4 App A]. However, these instruments are in IFRS 7's scope and subject to the requirements of IAS 32 except for those with respect to the distinction between financial liabilities and equity instruments. [IAS 32 para 4(e); IAS 39 para 2(e)].

Derivatives embedded in insurance contracts

3.19 Derivatives embedded in insurance contracts or in contracts containing discretionary participating features as discussed above are within the scope of IAS 32, IFRS 7 and IAS 39 if they require separation in accordance with IAS 39. [IAS 39 para 2(e); IFRS 4 para 34(d)]. For example, separate accounting would be required in circumstances where contractual payments embedded in a host insurance contract that is indexed to the value of equity instruments are not related to the host instrument, because the risks inherent in the host and the embedded derivative are dissimilar. [IAS 39 para AG 30(d)]. However, no separation is required if the embedded derivative itself is an insurance contract. [IAS 39 para 2(e); IFRS 4 para 7].

Financial guarantee contracts

3.20 Financial guarantee contracts (sometimes known as 'credit insurance') require the issuer to make specified payments to reimburse the holder for a loss it incurs if a specified debtor fails to make payment when due under a debt instrument's original or modified terms. [IAS 39 para 9]. That is, the holder is exposed to and has incurred a loss on the failure of the debtor to make payments. These contracts are often written by financial guarantee insurers in the form of insurance contracts, or they may be written by banks and entities that do not operate as insurance entities in other forms (for example, letter of credit, credit default contracts).

3.21 A contract that compensates the holder for more than the loss incurred does not meet the definition of a financial guarantee contract. For the definition to be

是，这些工具在 IFRS 7 的范围内，且遵循 IAS 32 除关于区分金融负债和权益工具的规定外的其他要求。[IAS 32 第4（e）段；IAS 39 第2（e）段]。

保险合同中的嵌入衍生工具

3.19　保险合同或如上所述具有相机参与分红特征的合同中的嵌入衍生工具，如果按照 IAS 39 需要分拆，则在 IAS 32、IFRS 7 和 IAS 39 的范围内。[IAS 39 第2（e）段；IFRS 4 第 34（d）段]。例如，嵌在保险合同中并与权益工具价值挂钩的合同付款与主工具不相关，因为主工具和嵌入衍生工具中内含的风险不同，在这种情况下则要求分拆。[IAS 39 AG 第 30（d）段]。但是，如果嵌入衍生工具本身是一项保险合同，则不要求分拆。[IAS 39 第 2（e）段；IFRS 4 第 7 段]。

财务担保合同

3.20　财务担保合同（有时称为“信用保险”）要求签发人当特定债务人不能按照最初的或修订的债务工具条款到期偿债，向合同持有人支付特定金额以补偿其所发生损失的合同。[IAS 39 第 9 段]。即债务人未能支付欠款时持有人所承受并已发生损失。这种合同通常是由财务担保承保人以保险合同的形式签出，或由银行和非经营保险的其他主体以其他形式（例如信用证、信用违约合同等）签出。

3.21　对持有人的补偿超过实际发生损失的合同不符合财务担保合同的定义。为符合上述定义，补偿金额必须小于或等于所发生的损失金额，以补偿持有

met, the amount of reimbursement must be either less than the amount of the loss incurred or equal to the amount incurred in order to reimburse some or all of the loss the holder suffered because the debtor defaulted.

3.22 Contracts that provide compensation if another party fails to perform a contractual obligation, such as an obligation to construct a building, are performance guarantees. They do not transfer credit risk and, therefore, do not meet the definition of a financial guarantee contract. These type of guarantees are accounted for under IFRS 4 as insurance contracts.

[The next paragraph is 3.25.]

3.25 The accounting treatment of a financial guarantee contract does not depend on its legal form nor whether it is issued by a bank, insurance company or other entity. Rather, all contracts that meet the definition of a financial guarantee fall within IAS 39's scope and are accounted for by the issuer as financial liabilities. However, an option is available to insurers to continue to account for these contracts under IFRS 4 if they had met two conditions before IAS 39 was amended to include financial guarantees in its scope. These are that the issuer has:

- previously *asserted* explicitly that it regards such contracts as insurance contracts; and
- used accounting applicable to insurance contracts.

If these two conditions are met, the issuer may elect to apply either IFRS 4 or IAS 39 to such financial guarantee contracts. The issuer can make the election on a contract by contract basis, but the election for each contract is irrevocable. [IAS 39 paras 2(e), AG4]. Assertions that the issuer regards contracts as insurance can typically be found in business documentation, contracts, accounting policies, financial statements and communication with customers and regulators. [IAS 39 para AG 4A].

3.25.1 In contrast, some credit related guarantees do not, as a precondition for payment, require that the holder is exposed to, and has incurred a loss on, the failure of the debtor to make payments on the guaranteed asset when due. Such guarantees are not financial guarantee contracts as defined in paragraph 3.20 above

人因债务人违约而遭受的部分或全部损失。

3.22 对另一方不能履行某项合同义务，如建造一座建筑物的义务，而提供补偿的合同为履约担保合同。这类担保没有转移信用风险，因此，不符合财务担保合同的定义。这种类型的担保按照 IFRS 4 作为保险合同进行会计处理。

[下一段为第 3.25 段。]

3.25 财务担保合同的会计处理并不取决于其法律形式或其是否由银行、保险公司还是其他主体签发。相反，所有符合财务担保定义的合同都在 IAS 39 的范围内，并由签发人作为金融负债处理。但是，如果在修订 IAS 39 将财务担保纳入其范围内前，承保人满足了两个条件，其有权选择继续按照 IFRS 4 对这些合同进行会计处理。这两个条件是签发人要：

- 在以前明确声明它将此类合同视作保险合同；并且
- 使用了适用于保险合同的会计处理方法。

如果满足了这两个条件，签发人可以选择采用 IFRS 4 或 IAS 39 对此类财务担保合同进行处理。签发人可就合同逐一作出选择，但对每项合同作出的选定不可撤销。[IAS 39 第 2（e）段、AG 第 4 段]。签发人将合同视为保险的声明通常出现在业务文件、合同、会计政策、财务报表和与客户和监管机构的沟通中。[IAS 39 AG 第 4A 段]。

3.25.1 相反，一些信用相关的担保，并不要求持有人承担因债务人在被担保资产到期时不能支付的风险并发生损失作为付款的前提条件。此类担保不是上文第 3.20 段所定义的财务担保合同，也不是 IFRS 4 所定义的保险合同。此类担保是必须根据 IAS 39 进行会计处理的衍生工具。［IAS 39 AG 第 4（b）

and are not insurance contracts as defined in IFRS 4. Such guarantees are derivatives that must be accounted for as such under IAS 39. [IAS 39 para AG 4(b)]. However, a contract that requires an entity to make payments when the counterparty to a derivative contract fails to make a payment when due, is considered to meet the definition of a financial guarantee contract. This is because it is not the risk inherent in the derivative that is being guaranteed; it is the counterparty's credit risk that is being guaranteed in the event the counterparty defaults.

Example 1 – Credit related guarantee

A bank issues a credit-related guarantee contract (sometimes referred to as credit derivative) that provides for payment if the credit rating of a debtor falls below a particular level.

In this situation, the credit related contract will be accounted for as a derivative financial instrument under IAS 39, because the contract holder is not required to suffer a loss on a specified debt instrument – the bank will pay for the decrease in the credit worthiness of the debtor even if the debtor does not actually default. However, if the contract provides for payment only in the event that the entity suffers loss as a result of non-payment by the debtor, the contract would be a financial guarantee contract. Holders and issuers of credit derivatives will always account for them under IAS 39.

Example 2 – Residual value guarantee

An insurer is required to make payments to the insured party based on the fair value of a non-financial asset at a future date under a residual value guarantee contract.

In this situation, the risk of changes in the fair value of the non-financial asset is not a financial risk because the fair value reflects not only changes in market prices for such assets (a financial variable), but also the condition of the specific asset held (a non-financial variable). As the change in fair value of the non-financial asset is specific to the owner, it is not a derivative instrument and, therefore, the contract will be accounted for as an insurance contract in accordance with IFRS 4. However, if the contract compensates the

段]。然而，在衍生工具合同的交易对方未能在到期付款而要求主体付款的合同，被视为符合财务担保合同的定义。这是因为所担保的并非衍生工具的内含风险；而是当交易对方违约时交易对方的信用风险。

示例 1——信用相关担保

某银行发行了一项信用相关的担保合同（有时被称为信用衍生工具），规定在某债务人的信用评级下降并低于某一特定水平时进行赔款。

在这种情况下，该信用相关合同将按照 IAS 39 作为一项衍生金融工具进行会计处理，因为并未要求合同持有人因某项特定债务工具遭受损失——即使债务人实际并未违约，银行也将因债务人的信誉下降而付款。但是，如果合同规定只有当持有人因债务人无法付款而遭受损失时才会付款，则该合同应该是一项财务担保合同。信用衍生工具的持有人和签发人应一直按照 IAS 39 对其进行会计处理。

示例 2——残值担保

根据残值担保合同，要求签发人根据某项非金融资产在未来某一日期的公允价值向投保人付款。

在这种情况下，该项非金融资产公允价值变化的风险并不是金融风险，因为该公允价值不但反映了此类资产市场价格的变化（金融变量），而且反映了所持有的特定资产的状况（非金融变量）。由于该非金融资产的公允价值变化是特别针对其所有者的，它并不是衍生工具，因此，该合同将按照 IFRS 4 作为保险合同来进行会计处理。但是，如果该合同仅根据市场价格的变化而不是所持有的特定非金融资产状况的变化对投保人进行赔偿，则该合同是一项衍生工具并在 IAS 39 的范围之内。[IFRS 4 IG

insured party only for changes in market prices and not for changes in the condition of the specific non-financial asset held, the contract is a derivative and within IAS 39's scope. [IFRS 4, IG example 1.15, IAS 39 para AG 12A].

3.26 There is no exemption under IAS 39 for financial guarantee contracts issued between members of a group or entities under common control similar to those under US GAAP FIN 45, 'Guarantor's accounting and disclosure requirements for guarantees, including direct guarantees of indebtedness to others'. Such guarantees are inter-company transactions that are eliminated on consolidation. However, in the individual financial statements of the group member issuing the guarantee, the guarantee contract will need to be accounted for in accordance with IAS 39. This is considered further in chapter 9.

Example – Parent provides a comfort letter to a subsidiary

A subsidiary of a group takes out a loan with a bank. The parent provides a comfort letter to the subsidiary such that if the subsidiary fails to repay the loan to the bank when due, the parent will pay on its behalf.

The comfort letter simply constitutes an undertaking given by the parent to its subsidiary that, in the event the subsidiary fails to repay the loan to the bank when due, the parent will step in and discharge the subsidiary's debt. This is not a financial guarantee contract as the parent has not provided any guarantee to the bank (nor would the bank be able to enforce payment under what is effectively a private arrangement between the parent and its subsidiary) to repay the loan if the subsidiary defaults.

3.27 Intra-group guarantees also frequently cover other obligations, such as pension plan contributions, lease rentals and taxes. The issue is whether, in the group members' individual financial statements, such obligations are financial guarantee contracts or insurance contracts. As noted in paragraph 3.17 above, if a financial instrument takes the form of an insurance contract, but involves the transfer of financial risks, as opposed to insurance risk, the contract would fall within the scope of the financial instrument standards. It is, therefore, necessary to determine whether the risk transferred represents insurance risk or financial risk.

示例1.15，IAS 39 AG 第12A 段］。

3.26　IAS 39 中没有与美国公认会计原则 FIN 45《担保方对担保（包括对其他方债务的直接担保）的会计处理和披露要求》类似的对在集团成员或同一控制下的主体之间所签发的财务担保合同的豁免。此类担保是在合并时要冲销的集团内部交易。但是，在签发担保的集团成员的个别财务报表中，需遵循 IAS 39 对此类担保合同进行会计处理。第9章对此进行了更多讨论。

示例——母公司向子公司提供的支持函

某集团的子公司向银行借了一笔贷款。母公司给子公司提供了一份支持函，说明如果子公司在到期时无法向银行偿还贷款，母公司将代其偿还。

此支持函仅仅构成母公司提供给子公司的一项承诺，当子公司在到期时无法向银行偿还贷款，母公司将涉入并解除子公司的债务。这不是一项财务担保合同，因为母公司并未向银行提供任何如果子公司违约将为其偿付贷款的担保（实际上这仅仅是母公司和其子公司之间的私人协议，银行并不能强制要求付款）。

3.27　集团内担保还经常涉及到诸如养老金计划提存、租金和所得税等的其他义务。问题在于，在集团成员的个别财务报表中，此类义务是财务担保合同还是保险合同。如上文第3.17 段所述，如果某项金融工具的形式是保险合同，但涉及的是金融风险而非保险风险的转移，则该合同在金融工具准则的范围内。因此，需要判定所转移的风险是保险风险还是金融风险。在养老金计划提存、经营租赁租金和所得税的担保中所转移的风险是子公司（或合营或联营）在到期时未付款的风险。未付款的原因多种多样，虽然可能包括一些金融风险变量，但是所转移的风险中很大一部分很可能与经营相关（例如，现金流困

The risk transferred in a guarantee of pension plan contributions, operating lease rentals and taxes is the risk that the subsidiary (or joint venture or associate) will not make a payment when due. The reasons for non-payment could vary widely and, whilst they might include some financial risk variables, it is likely that a significant part of the risk transferred will be operational (for example, cash flow difficulties or, at the extreme, bankruptcy). Hence, it appears that the significant risk transferred in a typical guarantee of pension plan contributions, operating lease rentals and taxes will be insurance risk. It is arguable, therefore, that guarantees of pension plan contributions, operating lease rentals and taxes should be treated as insurance contracts and accounted for accordingly.

3.28 Notwithstanding that guarantees of pension plan contributions, operating lease rentals and taxes are insurance contracts within IFRS 4's scope, it is still necessary to consider whether they meet the definition of financial guarantee contracts within IAS 39's scope. The definition of a financial guarantee contract refers specifically to the terms of a debt instrument. Although the term 'debt instrument' is not specifically defined in IFRS, it is clear from the various references made in IAS 32 that a debt instrument is a type of loan, involving a borrower and a lender. It can be concluded, therefore, that pension plan contributions and tax liabilities are not debt instruments. As regards leases, paragraph AG9 of IAS 32 states that "*a finance lease is regarded as primarily an entitlement of the lessor to receive, and an obligation of the lessee to pay, a stream of payments that are substantially the same as blended payments of principal and interest under a loan agreement. ... An operating lease, on the other hand, is regarded as primarily an uncompleted contract committing the lessor to provide the use of an asset in future periods in exchange for consideration similar to a fee for a service*". This analysis suggests that a finance lease resembles a debt instrument, while an operating lease does not. Even where operating leases do fall within the definition of a financial instrument (that is, in respect of individual payments currently due and payable), the amounts represent short-term payables, which Appendix A of IFRS 7 suggests are something other than a loan payable. Accordingly, guarantees of finance leases, but not operating leases, should be included within IAS 39's definition of a financial guarantee contract. We note that the IASB published its discussion paper 'Leases' in March 2009, which proposes

难或破产这种极端情况）。因此，通常对养老金计划提存、经营租赁租金和所得税担保中所转移的重大风险是保险风险。因此，可以据此认为对养老金计划提存、经营租赁租金和所得税的担保应被视为保险合同并相应的进行会计处理。

3.28　尽管对养老金计划提存、经营租赁租金和所得税的担保是 IFRS 4 范围内的保险合同，仍需要考虑它们是否符合 IAS 39 范围内财务担保合同的定义。财务担保合同的定义专门提及债务工具的条款。虽然“债务工具”这个词并未在 IFRS 中进行定义，但是从 IAS 32 中的各种参考中可以明确债务工具是涉及借款人和贷款人的一类的贷款。因此可以得出结论，养老金计划提存和所得税负债不是债务工具。至于租赁，IAS 32 AG 第 9 段中称“*融资租赁主要被视为出租人获取收入的权利以及承租人支付款项的义务，这一系列的支付实际上与贷款协议下本金和利息的混合付款是一致的。……另一方面，经营租赁主要被视为一项未完成的合同，该合同要求出租人在未来期间提供资产给承租方使用以换取类似劳务费的对价。*”此分析表明融资租赁与债务工具类似，而经营租赁则不然。即使在经营租赁确实符合金融工具的定义的情况下（即，对于当前已经到期且应付的单笔付款），其金额所代表的也是短期应付账款，IFRS 7 的附录 A 表明其并非应付贷款。相应地，对融资租赁而非经营租赁的担保，应被包括在 IAS 39 有关财务担保合同的定义范围内。我们注意到 IASB 于 2009 年 3 月发布了“租赁”的征求意见稿，建议删除经营租赁和融资租赁之间的区别。如果此建议最终发展为一项准则，则会有额外的担保合同被纳入 IAS 39 的范围内。

to remove the distinction between operating and finance leases. If this proposal is progressed to a standard, additional guarantee contracts will be brought into IAS 39's scope.

3.29 Financial guarantee contracts fall within the scope of IAS 32 and IFRS 7 if they are accounted for in accordance with IAS 39. However, if the issuer elects to apply IFRS 4 to those contracts, the disclosure requirements of IFRS 4 and not IFRS 7 apply. [IAS 32 para 4(d); IFRS 7 para 3(d)]. The accounting treatment of financial guarantee contracts is considered further in chapter 9.

Weather derivatives

3.30 Some contracts require a payment based on climatic variables (sometimes described as weather derivatives) or on geological or other physical variables. For such contracts, payments are sometimes made on the amount of loss suffered by the entity and sometimes not. Prior to IAS 39's revision, all such contracts were scoped out of IAS 39 and treated as insurance contracts. However, following IFRS 4's publication, such contracts are accounted for as follows:

- Contracts that require a payment only if a particular level of the underlying climatic, geological, or other physical variables adversely affects the contract holder.

  These are insurance contracts as payment is contingent on changes in a physical variable that is specific to a party to the contract.

- Contracts that require a payment based on a specified level of the underlying variable regardless of whether there is an adverse effect on the contract holder.

  These are derivatives and are within IAS 39's scope.

[IAS 39 para AG 1, IFRS 4 para BC 55].

Example – Weather derivatives

A farming entity in Punjab, a State in India, relies on the prospect of a good monsoon that would favourably impact its earnings for the season. A good monsoon in Punjab involves an average rainfall of about 400mm during the

3.29　如果财务担保协议是按照 IAS 39 进行会计处理，则其在 IAS 32 和 IFRS 7 的范围内。但是，如果发行人对这种合同选择采用 IFRS 4，则应采用 IFRS 4 而不是 IFRS 7 的披露要求。[IAS 32 第 4（d）段；IFRS 7 第 3（d）段]。在第 9 章中对财务担保合同的会计处理进行了更多讨论。

天气衍生工具

3.30　某些合同要求根据气候变量（有时被称为天气衍生工具）或地理或其他物理变量进行支付。对于此类合同，其付款有时候是根据主体所遭受损失的金额而有时候则不然。在对 IAS 39 进行修订之前，所有此类合同都在 IAS 39 的范围以外并被视为保险合同。但是，在发布了 IFRS 4 之后，此类合同按如下方式进行会计处理：

- 只在基础气候、地理或其他物理变量的特定水平对合同持有人产生不利影响时才要求进行偿付的合同。

  这些合同是保险合同，因为付款取决于合同一方特有的的某种物理变量的变化。

- 无论合同持有人是否受到不利影响，均要求以基础变量的特定水平为基础进行偿付的合同。

  这些合同是衍生工具，在 IAS 39 的范围内。

[IAS 39 AG 第 1 段；IFRS 4 BC 第 55 段]。

示例——天气衍生工具

在印度旁遮普省的一家农场主体期待对其本季收入产生有利影响的好雨季。旁遮普省的好雨季意味着在六月、七月和八月的平均降雨量约为 400 毫米。该主体与交易对方签订了一项合同，如果主体因为雨季中降雨量低

months of June, July and August. The entity enters into a contract with a counterparty that would pay a fixed sum of Rs1m if the entity suffers loss due to poor production caused by below average rainfall during the monsoon months. The premium paid on the contract is Rs50, 000.

This is an example of a highly tailored or customised policy that provides the entity protection against an adverse impact on earnings due to poor production caused by poor monsoon in Punjab, irrespective of whether the rest of India has a good monsoon or not. Hence, the contract is an insurance contract and is scoped out of IAS 39. It should be noted that even if the farming entity's loss due to poor production is less than Rs1m, the entity would receive Rs1m as stipulated in the contract. The definition of an insurance contract does not limit the payment by the insurer to an amount equal to the financial impact of the adverse event. [IFRS 4 App para B13].

If, on the other hand the sum of Rs1m was paid if the average rain fall was below 400mm during the months of June, July and August and it would be payable irrespective of fact that the farming entity in Punjab had suffered any damage, then the contract would be accounted for as a derivative instrument. This is because payment is made following the change in average rainfall which is a non-financial variable that is not specific to the holder of the contract and hence one of the variables considered in the definition of financial risk.

Loan commitments

3.31 Loan commitments are firm commitments to provide credit under pre-specified terms and conditions. [IAS 39 BC15]. They are usually entered into by financial institutions such as banks for providing loans to third parties at a specified rate of interest during a fixed period of time. Such a commitment is a derivative, since it has no initial net investment, it has an underlying variable (interest rate) and it will be settled at a future date. In effect, the lender has written an option that allows the potential borrower to obtain a loan at a specified rate.

3.32 The following loan commitments are within IAS 39's scope:

于平均降雨量导致的低产量而遭受损失时，交易对方将支付 100 万卢比的固定金额。为该合同支付的保费为 50,000 卢比。

这是一项高度定制的保险合约示例，为主体提供了因旁遮普省的差雨季所导致的低产量对收益产生的不利影响的保护，不管印度其他地方的雨季是好还是坏。因此，此合同是一项保险合同，不在 IAS 39 的范围内。值得注意的是即使该农场主体因低产量而遭受的损失在 100 万卢比以下，主体也将根据合同的规定收到 100 万卢比。保险合同的定义并没有将承保人支付的金额限定在不利事项的财务影响之内。[IFRS 4 附录第 B13 段]。

另一方面，如果因为六月、七月和八月的平均降雨量低于 400 毫米而支付 100 万卢比，且该款项无论位于旁遮普省的该农业主体是否遭受损失都要支付，那么该合同应该作为一项衍生工具来进行会计处理。这是因为款项是根据平均降雨量的变化而支付的，这是一项并非合同持有人所特有的非金融变量，因此属于金融风险的定义中所提及的变量之一。

贷款承诺

3.31 贷款承诺是根据预先确定的条款与条件提供信用贷款的确定承诺。[IAS 39 BC 第 15 段]。它们通常是由银行等金融机构所签订，用以对第三方在固定的期间提供确定利率的贷款。这种承诺是一项衍生工具，因为它没有初始净投资，它具有一个基础变量（利率）并将在未来某一日期结算。实际上，贷款人签出了一项允许潜在借款人根据确定利率获得贷款的期权。

3.32 如下贷款承诺在 IAS 39 的范围内：

- Loan commitments that the entity designates as financial liabilities at fair value through profit or loss. This may be appropriate, for example, if the entity manages risk exposures related to loan commitments on a fair value basis. [IAS 39 para 4(a)].

- An entity that has a past practice of selling the assets resulting from its loan commitments shortly after origination should apply IAS 39 to all its loan commitments in the *same class*. The term 'same class' is not explained in the standard, but we believe that a commitment to provide borrowing facilities to a corporate entity is not in the same class as a commitment to provide residential mortgage loans, because of differing risk return profiles. [IAS 39 para 4(a)].

- Loan commitments that can be settled net in cash or by delivering or issuing another financial instrument. These loan commitments are derivatives. A loan commitment is not regarded as settled net merely because the loan is paid out in instalments (for example, a mortgage construction loan that is paid out in instalments in line with the progress of construction). [IAS 39 para 4 (b)].

- Commitments to provide a loan at a below-market interest rate (see chapter 9). [IAS 39 para 4 (c)].

3.33 Loan commitments that are not within IAS 39's scope should be accounted for in accordance with IAS 37. Where events make such a loan commitment an onerous contract, the contract falls within IAS 37's scope and a liability exists that should be recognised. However, all loan commitments, whether scoped in or out of IAS 39, are subject to IAS 39's derecognition provisions and to IFRS 7's disclosure requirements. [IAS 39 para 2(h); IFRS 7 para 4].

Contracts to buy or sell non-financial assets

3.34 Contracts to buy or sell non-financial items are, in general, not financial instruments. Many commodity contracts are of this type. However, if such contracts can be settled net in cash or by exchanging another financial instrument, they fall within the scope of IAS 32, IFRS 7 and IAS 39 as if they were financial instruments (derivatives). This is so, unless the contracts were entered into and continue to be held for the purpose of receipt or delivery of non-financial items to

- 主体指定为以公允价值计量且变动计入损益的金融负债的贷款承诺。例如在主体以公允价值为基础管理贷款承诺的风险敞口时比较适宜。[IAS 39 第 4（a）段]。

- 主体有在贷款承诺签发后不久出售其所滋生资产的惯例时，应将 IAS 39 应用于*同一类别*的所有贷款承诺。该准则并未对“同一类别”一词进行解释，但是我们认为向公司提供贷款额度的承诺与提供住宅抵押贷款的承诺不属于同一类别，因为其风险回报情况不同。[IAS 39 第4（a）段]。

- 以现金净额或以交付或发行其他金融工具的方式结算的贷款承诺。这些贷款承诺是衍生工具。不能仅因为以分期付款的方式拨付贷款而将贷款承诺视为以净额结算（例如，按工程进度分期拨付的抵押建筑贷款）。[IAS 39 第 4（b）段]。

- 以低于市场利率提供贷款的承诺（请参见第 9 章）。[IAS 39 第4（c）段]。

3.33　不在 IAS 39 范围内的贷款承诺应根据 IAS 37 进行会计处理。当出现使得这种贷款承诺成为亏损合同的情形时，该合同在 IAS 37 的范围内，并应确认存在的负债。但是，所有的贷款承诺，无论其是否在 IAS 39 的范围内，均应遵守 IAS 39 的终止确认条款以及 IFRS 7 的披露要求。[IAS 39 第 2（h）段；IFRS 7 第 4 段]。

购买或出售非金融资产的合同

3.34　一般而言，购买或出售非金融资产的合同不是金融工具。许多商品合同都属于这一类别。但是，如果这种合同可以用现金或交换其他金融工具的方式以净额结算，则其在 IAS 32、IFRS 7 和 IAS 39 的范围内，就像它们是金融工具一样（衍生工具），除非该合同是根据主体的预期购买、出售或使用要求以获取或交付非金融项目为目的而签订并继续持有（经常被称为“自用”购买或出售例外）。[IAS 32 第 8 - 10 段；IFRS 7 第 5 段；IAS 39 第 5 段]。换言

meet the entity's expected purchase, sale or usage requirements (often referred to as 'own use' purchase or sale exception). [IAS 32 paras 8-10; IFRS 7 para 5; IAS 39 para 5]. In other words, if the own use exception is met, the contract must not be accounted for as a derivative (that is, the application of the own use exception is not a choice).

Contracts that can be settled net

3.35 There are various ways in which a contract to buy or sell a non-financial asset can be settled net in cash, including when:

- The terms of the contract permit either party to settle net in cash or another financial instrument or by exchanging financial instruments. Net settlement means that the entity will pay or receive cash (or an equivalent value in other financial assets) to and from the counterparty, equal to the net gain or loss on the contract on exercise or settlement.
- The ability to settle the contract net is not explicitly stated in the contract, but the entity has a practice of settling similar contracts net in cash (whether with the counterparty, by entering into offsetting contracts or by selling the contract before its exercise or lapse). For example, a futures exchange permits an entity to enter into offsetting contracts that relieves the entity of its obligation to make or receive delivery of the non-financial asset.
- For similar contracts, the entity has a practice of taking delivery of the underlying and selling it within a short period after delivery to generate a profit from short-term fluctuations in price or dealer's margin. An example is an exchange that offers a ready opportunity to sell the contract.
- The non-financial asset that is the subject of the contract is readily convertible into cash.

[IAS 32 para 9; IAS 39 para 6].

3.36 Where the second and third bullet points above apply, the entity's activities make it clear that the contracts cannot qualify for 'normal' purchase or sale exception. Accordingly, such contracts are within the scope of the financial

之，如果满足自用例外，那么合同不能被当做衍生工具进行会计处理（即，采用自用例外情况不是一个选择）。

可以用净额结算的合同

3.35 可以用净额结算的购买或出售非金融资产的合同有多种形式，包括：

- 合同条款允许合同任何一方以现金或其他金融工具进行净额结算或通过交换金融工具进行结算。净额结算意味着主体将向交易对方支付或收取等于合同行权或结算时利得或损失净额的现金（或等价的其他金融资产）。

- 合同中并未明确规定以净额结算合同的权力，但是主体有对类似合同以现金进行净额结算的惯例（不论是否通过与交易对方签订对冲合同，还是在合同行权或过期前出售合同）。例如，某项期货交易允许主体签订对冲合同，使主体免于交付或获取非金融资产的义务。

- 对于类似的合同，主体有收取交付的基础资产并在交付后的短期内将其出售，以从价格或交易商保证金的短期波动中获取利润的惯例。例如提供即时出售合同机会的交易所。

- 作为合同标的的非金融资产易于转换为现金。

[IAS 32 第 9 段；IAS 39 第 6 段]。

3.36 在适用上述第二点和第三点的情况下，主体的活动明确表明了该合同不符合“正常”的购买或出售例外。相应地，此类合同在金融工具准则的范围内。其他可以用净额结算的合同应予以评估以确定其是否符合该例外。例

instrument standards. Other contracts that can be settled net should be evaluated to determine whether they qualify for the exception. For example, to qualify for the exception, a contract's terms must be consistent with the terms of an entity's normal purchases or sales; that is, the quantity specified in the contract must be expected to be used or sold by the entity over a reasonable period in the normal course of business. Other factors that may be relevant in determining whether or not the contract qualifies for the exception may include the locations to which delivery of the items will be made, the period of time between entering into the contract and delivery and the entity's prior practices with regard to such contracts.

Example – Forward contract to purchase a commodity

Entity XYZ enters into a fixed price forward contract to purchase one million kilograms of copper in accordance with its expected usage requirements. The contract permits XYZ to take physical delivery of the copper at the end of 12 months or to pay or receive a net settlement in cash, based on the change in fair value of copper.

The above contract needs to be evaluated to determine whether it falls within the scope of the financial instruments standards. The contract is a derivative instrument because there is no initial net investment, the contract is based on the price of copper and it is to be settled at a future date. However, if XYZ intends to settle the contract by taking delivery and has no history for similar contracts of settling net in cash, or of taking delivery of the copper and selling it within a short period after delivery for the purpose of generating a profit from short-term fluctuations in price or dealer's margin, the contract is not accounted for as a derivative under IAS 39. Instead, it is accounted for as an executory contract. [IAS 39 IG A1].

In the above example, it is possible for entity XYZ and the counterparty to reach different conclusions about whether the contract falls within IAS 39's scope. For example, a 'normal' sale by the counterparty may not be a 'normal' purchase by entity XYZ that would treat the contract as a derivative. This is one of the few areas of IAS 39 where a contract may be treated as a derivative by one party, but not be treated as a derivative by the other party.

如，为了符合该例外的要求，合同条款必须与主体正常购买或出售的条款一致；即合同中所规定的数量应当预期能被主体在其正常业务流程中合理的期间内使用或出售。确定合同是否符合该例外的其他可能相关的因素可能包括项目的交货地点、签订合同和交货之间的间隔以及主体对于此类合同之前的惯例。

示例——购买商品的远期合同

主体 XYZ 根据预计的使用需求，签署了一份按固定价格购买一百万公斤铜的远期合同。该项合同允许 XYZ 在 12 个月后接受铜的实物交割，或根据铜的公允价值变化以支付或收取现金净额的方式结算。

应对上述合同进行评估以确定其是否在金融工具准则的范围内。该合同是一项衍生工具，因为没有初始净投资，合同基于铜的价格且在未来某一日期结算。但是，如果 XYZ 打算通过接受实物交割来结算此合同，并且对类似合同过去不曾以现金进行净额结算、或接受铜的交割并在交割后的较短期间内将其出售以从价格或交易商保证金的短期波动中获利的话，根据 IAS 39 此合同不作为衍生工具核算。而是作为待执行合同核算。[IAS 39 IG 第 A1 段]。

在上述示例中，主体 XYZ 和交易对方对于该合同是否在 IAS 39 的范围内可能得出不同的结论。例如，交易对方的“正常”销售对于主体 XYZ 而言并不一定属于“正常”购买，因此可能将合同视为衍生工具。这是根据 IAS 39 合同一方可能将某项合同视为衍生工具而另一方不将其视为衍生工具的少数情况之一。

Written options

3.37 A written option to buy or sell a non-financial item that can be settled net in accordance with paragraph 3.34 above cannot be considered to be entered into for the purpose of the receipt or delivery of the non-financial item in accordance with the entity's expected purchase, sale or usage requirements. This is because an option written by the entity is outside its control as to whether the holder will exercise or not. Such contracts are, therefore, always within the scope of IAS 32 and IAS 39. [IAS 32 para 10; IAS 39 para 7]. Volume adjustment features are also common, particularly within commodity and energy contracts and are discussed within chapter 5.

Royalty agreements

3.38 Although not specifically mentioned in IAS 39's scope section, the standard does not change the accounting treatment of royalty agreements which are based on the volume of sales or service revenues and that are accounted for in accordance with IAS 18, 'Revenue'. [IAS 39 para AG 2]. However, derivative contracts that are based on both sales volume and a financial variable (such as an exchange rate) are not excluded from IAS 39's scope, as set out in the example in chapter 4.

签出期权

3.37　根据上文第 3.34 段所述，根据净额结算的购买或出售非金融项目的签出期权不能被视为根据主体的预期购买、出售或使用要求以获取或交付非金融项目为目的而签订的。这是因为对于主体签出的期权，持有人是否行权不在主体的控制范围内。因此，此类合同总是在 IAS 32 和 IAS 39 的范围内。[IAS 32 第 10 段；IAS 39 第 7 段]。数量调整因素也很常见，尤其是在商品和能源合同中，在第 5 章对其进行了讨论。

特许权协议

3.38　虽然在 IAS 39 的范围部分并未明确提出，但该准则并没有改变按《国际会计准则第 18 号——收入》（"IAS 18"）核算的基于销售量或服务收入量的特许权协议的会计处理方法。[IAS 39 AG 第 2 段]。但是，同时基于销量和一个金融变量（如汇率）的衍生工具合同并未被排除在 IAS 39 的范围之外，如第 4 章中示例所示。

Chapter 4 Nature and characteristics of financial instruments

Content

Introduction	4001
Definitions relating to financial instruments	4001
Key features of the definitions	4005
Contractual basis	4005
Conditional (contingent) rights and obligations	4009
Exchange under potentially favourable or unfavourable terms	4011
Comparison with non-financial assets and liabilities	4013
Identification of financial instruments	4015
Derivative financial instruments	4021
Introduction	4021
Definition	4021
Key features of the definition	4023
Underlying	4023
Notional amounts and payment provisions	4027
Initial net investment	4029
Settlement at a future date	4039
Specific examples of derivative instruments	4041
Contracts to buy or sell non-financial items	4043
Contracts that are in substance derivatives	4043
Regular way contracts	4045
Accounting for derivatives	4045

第四章　金融工具的性质和特征

目　录

引言 4002

与金融工具相关的定义 4002

定义的关键特征 4006

以合同为基础 4006

附有条件的（或有）权利和义务 4010

在潜在有利或不利条款下的交换 4012

与非金融资产和负债的比较 4014

金融工具的识别 4016

衍生金融工具 4022

引言 4022

定义 4022

定义的关键特征 4024

基础变量 4024

名义金额和支付条款 4028

初始净投资 4030

在未来某一日期结算 4040

衍生工具的具体示例 4042

购买或出售非金融项目的合同 4044

实质上是衍生工具的合同 4044

常规合同 4046

衍生工具的会计处理 4046

Introduction

4.1 Financial instruments embrace a broad range of assets and liabilities. They include both primary financial instruments – financial assets such as cash, receivables and equity securities of another entity and financial liabilities such as debt – and derivative financial instruments such as financial options, forwards, swaps and futures. Derivative financial instruments are considered separately from paragraph 4.23 below.

Definitions relating to financial instruments

4.2 The definitions relating to financial instruments that appear in paragraph 11 of IAS 32 are common to three financial instrument standards, that is, IAS 32, IAS 39 and IFRS 7. The definitions are noted below.

4.3 A financial instrument is any contract that gives rise to a financial asset of one entity and a financial liability or equity instrument of another entity. The definitions of a financial asset and financial liability stated below include some derivative and non-derivative contracts that will or may be settled in the entity's own equity instruments. This is because a contract is not necessarily an equity instrument just because it may result in the receipt or delivery of the entity's own equity instruments, as discussed in chapter 7. [IAS 32 para 21].

4.4 A financial asset is any asset that is:

- Cash.
- An equity instrument of another entity.
- A contractual right:
  - to receive cash or another financial asset from another entity; or
  - to exchange financial assets or financial liabilities with another entity under conditions that are potentially favourable to the entity.

引言

4.1　金融工具包括广泛类别的资产和负债。它们既包括基本的金融工具——如现金、应收款和另一主体的权益证券等金融资产以及如债务等金融负债，也包括诸如金融期权、远期、互换和期货等衍生金融工具。衍生金融工具从下文第 4.23 段起进行了单独的讨论。

与金融工具相关的定义

4.2　IAS 32 第 11 段所示的与金融工具相关的定义对于三个金融工具准则，即 IAS 32、IAS 39 和 IFRS 7 均相同。如下对这些定义进行了说明。

4.3　金融工具是指形成一个主体的金融资产并形成另一个主体的金融负债或权益工具的合同。下文所述金融资产和金融负债的定义中包括一些将要或可能以主体自身的权益工具进行结算的衍生工具和非衍生工具合同。如第 7 章中所讨论的，这是因为某项合同并不仅仅因为它可能导致主体获得或交付主体自身的权益工具而成为权益工具。[IAS 32 第 21 段]。

4.4　金融资产是指下述资产：

- 现金。
- 另一主体的权益工具。
- 以下合同权利，包括：
    - 从另一主体收取现金或其他金融资产；或
    - 在潜在有利的条件下，与另一主体交换金融资产或金融负债。

- A contract that will or may be settled in the entity's own equity instruments and is:
  - a non-derivative for which the entity is or may be obliged to receive a variable number of the entity's own equity instruments; or
  - a derivative that will or may be settled other than by the exchange of a fixed amount of cash or another financial asset for a fixed number of the entity's own equity instruments. For this purpose the entity's own equity instruments do not include puttable instruments and obligations arising on liquidation that are classified as equity or instruments that are contracts for the future receipt or delivery of the entity's own equity instruments.

4.5 A financial liability is any liability that is:

- A contractual obligation:
  - to deliver cash or another financial asset to another entity; or
  - to exchange financial assets or financial liabilities with another entity under conditions that are potentially unfavourable to the entity.
- A contract that will or may be settled in the entity's own equity instruments and is:
  - a non-derivative for which the entity is or may be obliged to deliver a variable number of the entity's own equity instruments; or
  - a derivative that will or may be settled other than by the exchange of a fixed amount of cash or another financial asset for a fixed number of the entity's own equity instruments. For this purpose the entity's own equity instruments do not include puttable instruments and obligations arising on liquidation that are classified as equity or instruments that are themselves contracts for the future receipt or delivery of the entity's own equity instruments.

4.5.1 As an exception to the above, an instrument that meets the definition of a financial liability is classified as an equity instrument if it meets certain criteria set out in the February 2008 amendment to IAS 32, 'Puttable financial instruments

■ 将以主体自身权益工具结算或可以以主体自身权益工具结算的合同，且该合同是：

　■ 一项非衍生工具，使主体将获取或可能获取可变数量的主体自身权益工具；或

　■ 一项衍生工具，该衍生工具将或可能以固定金额的现金或其他金融资产换取固定数量的主体自身权益工具以外的其他方式结算。为此，主体自身的权益工具不包括划分为权益的可回售金融工具和清算时产生的义务或本身就是在未来收取或支付主体自身权益工具的合同。

4.5　金融负债是下述负债：

■ 以下合同义务，包括：

　■ 向另一主体交付现金或其他金融资产；或

　■ 在潜在不利的条件下，与另一主体交换金融资产或金融负债。

■ 将以主体自身权益工具结算或可以以主体自身权益工具结算的合同，且该合同是：

　■ 一项非衍生工具，使主体承担或可能承担交付可变数量的主体自身权益工具的义务；或

　■ 一项衍生工具，该衍生工具将或可能以固定金额的现金或其他金融资产换取固定数量的主体自身权益工具以外的其他方式结算。为此，主体自身的权益工具不包括划分为权益的可回售金融工具和清算时产生的义务或本身就是在未来收取或支付主体自身权益工具的合同。

4.5.1　作为上述定义的一个例外，对于符合金融负债定义的工具，如果满足对 IAS 32 于 2008 年 2 月的修订《可回售金融工具和清算时产生的义务》中的特定条件，则其应划分为权益工具。该修订从起始日于 2009 年 1 月 1 日或

and obligations arising on liquidation'. This amendment came into effect for accounting periods beginning on or after 1 January 2009, with earlier application permitted, and is discussed in detail in chapter 7.

4.5.2 As mentioned in chapter 7, the IASB issued an amendment to IAS 39 on the classification of rights issues. This amendment further revises the definition of a financial liability to treat certain rights issues (including rights, options and warrants), that are denominated in a currency other than the functional currency of the issuer, as equity. This amendment is mandatory for accounting periods beginning on or after 1 February 2010.

4.6 An equity instrument is any contract that evidences a residual interest in an entity's assets after deducting all of its liabilities. [IAS 32 para 11]. The term 'entity' includes individuals, partnerships, incorporated bodies and government agencies. [IAS 32 para 14]. Examples of equity instruments include non-puttable ordinary shares, some types of preference shares and share warrants or written call options that allow the holder to subscribe for or purchase a fixed number of non-puttable ordinary shares in the issuing entity in exchange for a fixed amount of cash or another financial asset.

Key features of the definitions

4.7 Some of the important concepts associated with the various terms that are included in the above definitions are considered below. An understanding of these concepts is particularly important and relevant in evaluating instruments that might qualify as financial instruments including derivatives.

Contractual basis

4.8 All financial instruments are defined by contracts. The rights or obligations that comprise financial assets or financial liabilities are derived from the contractual provisions that underlie them. The terms 'contract' and 'contractual' refer to an agreement between two or more parties that has clear economic consequences that the parties have little, if any, discretion to avoid, usually because the agreement is enforceable by law. Contracts defining financial instruments may take a variety of

之后开始的会计期间生效，允许提前实施，在第 7 章对其做了更详细的讨论。

4.5.2 如第 7 章所提及，IASB 发布了对 IAS 39 针对配股权分类的修订。该修订进一步改变了金融负债的定义，使特定的以发行人功能货币以外的货币计价的配股权（包括配股权、期权和认股权证）被视为权益。该修订从起始日于 2010 年 2 月 1 日或之后的会计期间强制实施。

4.6 权益工具指能证明享有主体的资产扣除所有负债后的剩余权益的合同。[IAS 32 第 11 段]。“主体”一词包括个人、合伙、公司和政府机构。[IAS 32 第 14 段]。权益工具的示例包括不可赎回的普通股、某些类型的优先股和使持有人可以认购或购买发行主体的固定数量的不可赎回普通股以换取固定金额的现金或其他金融资产的认股权证或签出看涨期权。

定义的关键特征

4.7 在下文讨论了与上述定义所包含的各种术语相关的一些重要概念。在对可能符合金融工具（包括衍生工具）要求的工具进行评估时，了解这些概念尤为重要。

以合同为基础

4.8 所有金融工具都是通过合同界定的。构成金融资产或金融负债的权利和义务是从其基础合同条款中得出的。术语“合同”或“合同的”是指双方或多方之间的具有明确的经济结果的协议，协议各方难以避免这种结果，因为该协议通常在法律上具有强制性。定义金融工具的合同可以有不同的形式，不一定要采用书面形式。[IAS 32 第 13 段]。主体的税收负债是一个不符合金融工具定义项目的例子，因为它并不是根据主体和税收当局之间的合同，而

forms and need not be in writing. [IAS 32 para 13]. An example of an item that would not meet the definition of a financial instrument is an entity's tax liability, as it is not based on a contract between the entity and the tax authority, but arising through statute. Similarly, constructive obligations, as defined in IAS 37, 'Provisions, contingent liabilities and contingent assets', do not arise from contracts and are not financial liabilities. [IAS 32 para AG 12]. On the other hand, a provision for an onerous contract (for example, provision for vacant leasehold property that is being sublet) is a financial liability as it arises from the unavoidable cost of meeting the obligations under the contract. Nevertheless, such provisions are scoped out of IAS 39 and are accounted for in accordance with IAS 37. [IAS 37 para 66].

4.9 A contractual right or contractual obligation to receive, deliver or exchange financial instruments is itself a financial instrument. This is evident from the definitions of financial assets and liabilities that include the terms financial assets and financial instruments within them. However, the terms are not circular. They envisage the possibility that a chain of contractual rights or contractual obligations may be established, but this chain must end ultimately with the receipt or payment of cash or to the acquisition or issue of an equity instrument. [IAS 32 para AG 7].

4.10 As the IAS 32 definitions require all financial instruments to be contracts, some question whether cash can be considered to be a contract. However, this concern is overcome because the definition of a financial asset stated in paragraph 4.4 above specifically states that cash is a financial instrument. IAS 32 application guidance also clarifies that currency (cash) is a financial asset because it represents the medium of exchange and is, therefore, the basis on which all transactions are measured and recognised in financial statements. A deposit of cash with a bank or similar financial institution is a financial asset because it represents the contractual right of the depositor to obtain cash from the institution or to draw a cheque or similar instrument against the balance in favour of a creditor in payment of a financial liability. [IAS 32 para AG 3]. On the other hand gold bullion is not a financial instrument like cash. It is a commodity. Although the bullion market is highly liquid, there is no contractual right to receive cash or another financial instrument inherent in bullion. [IAS 39 para IG B1].

是通过法律而产生的。类似地，《国际会计准则第37号－准备、或有负债和或有资产》（“IAS 37”）中定义的推定义务不是因合同而产生的义务，因而不是金融负债。[IAS 32 AG 第12段]。相反，亏损性合同的准备（例如，转租空闲租赁不动产的准备）是一项金融负债，因为它是为履行合同义务而发生的不可避免的费用。尽管如此，该准备不在 IAS 39 的范围内，而应根据 IAS 37 进行核算。[IAS 37 第66段]。

4.9　一项获取、交付或交换金融工具的合同权利或合同义务，其本身即为一项金融工具。这可以通过金融资产和负债的定义证明，此定义本身中就包括了术语金融资产和金融工具。但是这些术语并不是循环的。它们涵盖了建立一系列的合同权利或合同义务的可能性，但是这一系列必须将最终导致现金的收支或权益工具的获得或发行。[IAS 32 AG 第7段]。

4.10　因为 IAS 32 的定义要求所有的金融工具都必须是合同，有人质疑现金能否被视为合同。但是，这一问题已被解决，因为上文第4.4段中所述金融资产的定义专门提到现金是一项金融工具。IAS 32 的实施指南也澄清了货币（现金）是金融资产，因为它代表交换的媒介，并因此成为在财务报表中对所有交易进行计量和确认的基础。在银行或类似金融机构中的现金存款是金融资产，因为它代表了存款人从该机构获取现金或根据存款余额向债权人签发支票或类似工具以偿付金融负债的合同权利。[IAS 32 AG 第3段]。但是，金条和现金不一样，并不是金融工具。它是一种商品。虽然金条市场的流动性很强，但是金条本身并没有收取现金或其他金融工具的合同权利。[IAS 39 IG 第B1段]。

4.11 Some common examples of financial instruments that give rise to financial assets representing a contractual right to receive cash in the future for the holder and corresponding financial liabilities representing a contractual obligation to deliver cash in the future for the issuer are as follows:

■ Trade accounts receivable and payable.

■ Notes receivable and payable.

■ Loans receivable and payable.

■ Bonds receivable and payable.

In each case, one party's contractual right to receive (or obligation to pay) cash is matched by the other party's corresponding obligation to pay (or right to receive). [IAS 32 para AG 4].

4.12 Another type of financial instrument is one for which the economic benefit to be received or given up is a financial asset other than cash. For example, a note payable in government bonds gives the holder the contractual right to receive and the issuer the contractual obligation to deliver government bonds, not cash. The bonds are financial assets because they represent obligations of the issuing government to pay cash. The note is, therefore, a financial asset of the note holder and a financial liability of the note issuer. [IAS 32 para AG 5].

Conditional (contingent) rights and obligations

4.13 The ability to exercise a contractual right or the requirement to satisfy a contractual obligation may be absolute, or it may be contingent on the occurrence of a future event. A note receivable or payable is an unconditional promise to pay, but a financial guarantee is a conditional financial instrument as it results in a contractual right of the lender to receive cash from the guarantor and a corresponding contractual obligation of the guarantor to pay the lender, if the borrower defaults. The contractual right and obligation exist because of a past transaction or event (assumption of the guarantee), even though the lender's ability to exercise its right and the requirement for the guarantor to perform under its obligation are both contingent on a future act of default by the borrower. [IAS

4.11　以下列出了导致代表持有人在未来收取现金的合同权利的金融资产，以及相应导致代表发行人在未来支付现金的合同义务的金融负债的金融工具的常见示例：

- 贸易应收和应付账款。
- 应收和应付票据。
- 应收和应付贷款。
- 应收和应付债券。

在每种情况下，一方收取现金的合同权利（或交付现金的义务）总是与另一方相应的付款义务（或收款权利）相对应。[IAS 32 AG 第 4 段]。

4.12　另一类金融工具所获得或放弃的经济利益是非现金金融资产。例如，以政府债券结算的应付票据赋予持有人以收取政府债券而非现金的合同权利，同时要求发行人承担相应的合同义务。债券是金融资产，因为它代表了发行债券的政府支付现金的义务。因此，票据是票据持有人的一项金融资产，同时也是票据发行人的一项金融负债。[IAS 32 AG 第 5 段]。

附有条件的（或有）权利和义务

4.13　行使合同权利的能力或履行合同义务的要求可能是无条件的，也可能根据未来事项的发生与否而定。应收或应付票据是无条件付款的承诺，但财务担保则是有条件的金融工具，因为当借款人违约时，它会导致贷款人向担保人收取现金的合同权利以及担保人向贷款人支付现金的合同义务。合同权利和义务是因为过去的交易或事项（承担担保）而存在，不论贷款人是否能够行使这一权利和担保人是否必须履行这一义务都将取决于借款人未来违约行为。[IAS 32 AG 第 8 段]。

32 para AG 8].

4.14 Even though a contingent right and obligation can meet the definition of a financial asset and a financial liability, they are not always recognised in the financial statements. Some of these contingent rights and obligations may be insurance contracts within IFRS 4's scope, whilst others may be excluded from the standards' scope. [IAS 32 para AG 8].

4.15 Other contingencies that may require the payment of cash but do not as yet arise from a contract, such as a contingent receivable or payable for a court judgment, are not financial instruments. However, when those judgments become enforceable by a government or a court of law, and are thereby contractually reduced to fixed payment schedules, the judgment would be a financial instrument. When the parties agree to payment terms and those payment terms are reduced to a contract, then a financial instrument exists. Contrast this with a fine, which is not contractual.

Exchange under potentially favourable or unfavourable terms

4.16 The definitions of financial assets and financial liabilities make references to exchanges under conditions that are 'potentially favourable' or 'potentially unfavourable'. The meaning of these terms and the way they work in practice are best explained by means of an example.

Example – Exchange under potentially favourable or unfavourable terms

Entity A holds an option to purchase equity shares in a listed entity B for C5 per share at the end of a 90 day period.

The above call option gives entity A a contractual right to exchange cash of C5 for an equity share in another entity and will be exercised if the market value of the share exceeds C5 at the end of the 90 day period. This is because as the terms will be favourable to entity A at the end of term, it will exercise the call option. Since entity A stands to gain if the call option is exercised, the exchange is potentially favourable to the entity. Therefore, the option is a derivative financial asset from the time the entity becomes a party to the option

4.14 即使或有权利和义务符合金融资产和金融负债的定义，它们并不总在财务报表内予以确认。某些或有权利和义务是在 IFRS 4 范围内的保险合同，而其他的或有权利和义务则可能不在这些准则的范围内。[IAS 32 AG 第 8 段]。

4.15 其他可能要求支付现金但尚未产生于合同的或有事项，例如某项法庭判决的或有应收或应付款，不是金融工具。但是，当这些判决可由政府或法庭强制执行，并因此变为约定的固定支付计划时，该判决则应该是一项金融工具。当各方就支付条款达成协议并将这些支付条款变为合同时，则形成了一项金融工具。罚款则与此相反，它并不受合同的约束。

在潜在有利或不利条款下的交换

4.16 金融资产和金融负债的定义提到了在“潜在有利”或“潜在不利”的条件下进行交换。这些术语的含义及其在实务中的模式最好用示例予以诠释。

示例——在潜在有利或不利条款下的交换

主体 A 持有一项以每股 C5 元的价格在 90 天期间结束时购买上市主体 B 权益股票的期权。

上述看涨期权赋予了主体 A 用 C5 元的现金获取另一主体股票的合同权利，如果在 90 天期间结束时该股票的市场价值超过 C5 元则会被行使。这是因为如果在合同期末条款对主体 A 有利时，其将行使该项看涨期权。由于如果行使该期权主体 A 将获利，该交易对主体而言是潜在有利的。因此，从主体成为该期权合同的一方时该期权即是一项衍生金融资产。

contract.

On the other hand, if entity A writes an option under which the counterparty can force the entity to sell equity shares in the listed entity B for C5 per share at any time in the next 90 days, entity A has a contractual obligation to exchange equity shares in another entity for cash of C5 per share on potentially unfavourable terms if the holder exercises the option, because the market price per share exceeds the exercise price of C5 per share at the end of the 90 day period. Since entity A stands to lose if the option is exercised, the exchange is potentially unfavourable and the option is a derivative financial liability from the time the entity becomes a party to the option contract.

Comparison with non-financial assets and liabilities

4.17 As discussed above, financial instruments represent contractual rights or obligations to receive or pay cash or other financial assets. Non-financial items have a more indirect, non-contractual relationship to future cash flows.

4.18 The non-financial assets of a business (such as inventories, property, plant and equipment and intangibles) are inputs to some productive process. They are expected to contribute, along with other inputs, to the production and sale of goods or services. They must be used in a productive activity, and effectively transformed into goods or service, which must be sold, before there is any right to receive cash. Control of such physical and intangible assets creates an opportunity to generate an inflow of cash or another financial asset, but it does not give rise to a present right to receive cash or another financial asset. [IAS 32 para AG 10]. Even where physical assets, such as properties, are held as investments rather than as inventories, they are not financial instruments.

4.19 A contract to acquire or sell a non-financial asset at a specified price at a future date is not a financial instrument, because the contractual right of one party to receive a non-financial asset and the corresponding obligation of the other party do not establish a present right or obligation of either party to receive, deliver or exchange a financial asset. For example, contracts that provide for settlement only by the receipt or delivery of a non-financial item (for example, an option or

相反，如果主体A签出一项期权，根据该期权交易对方可以要求主体以每股C5元在今后90天内的任何时候出售上市主体B的权益股票，若持有人行使了该期权，则主体A有以现金每股C5元在潜在不利的条件下交付另一主体股票的合同义务，当90天期间结束时每股的市场价格超过每股C5元的行权价格。由于如果行使该期权主体A将遭受损失，该交易对主体而言是潜在不利的，从主体成为该期权合同的一方时该期权即是一项衍生金融负债。

与非金融资产和负债的比较

4.17　如上文所讨论的，金融工具代表了收取或交付现金或其他金融资产的合同权利或义务。相对而言，非金融项目与未来现金流的关系则没有那么直接，而且不基于合同。

4.18　一项业务的非金融资产（诸如存货，不动产、工厂和设备以及无形资产等）是某些生产流程的投入。它们被预期和其他投入一起投入到产品或服务的生产和销售中。它们必须用于生产活动，并有效地转换为产品或服务，而后者必须被出售才能具有收取现金的权利。控制这些有形和无形资产能创造形成现金或其他金融资产流入的机会，但并不形成收取现金或其他金融资产的现时权利。[IAS 32 AG 第10段]。即使诸如不动产等有形资产是作为投资而非存货持有时，也不是金融工具。

4.19　在未来某一日期以规定的价格购买或出售非金融资产的合同不是金融工具，因为某一方收取非金融资产的合同权益和另一方的相应义务并不形成任何一方收取、交付或交换金融资产的现时权利或义务。例如，只以非金融项目的收取或交付来结算的合同（如白银的期权或远期合同）不是金融工具。许多商品合同都属于这一类型。但是，如上文第3.33段所述，某些非金融项目的买卖合同可以以净额或通过交换金融工具来结算，或者合同中的非金融

forward contract on silver) are not financial instruments. Many commodity contracts are of this type. However, as stated in paragraph 3.33 above, contracts to buy or sell non-financial items that can be settled net or by exchanging financial instruments, or in which the non-financial item is readily convertible to cash, are treated as if they are financial instruments. [IAS 32 para AG 20]. For the same reasons as stated above, a firm commitment that involves the receipt or delivery of a physical asset is not a financial instrument. [IAS 32 para AG 21].

4.20 Another example is an operating lease to rent an office building. Under the lease, the lessor has committed to provide office space in future periods for consideration similar to a fee for a service. The contractual right of the lessee to receive the service and the corresponding obligation of the lessor do not establish a present right or obligation of either party to receive, deliver or exchange a financial asset. On the other hand, a finance lease is regarded as primarily an entitlement of the lessor to receive, and an obligation of the lessee to pay, a stream of payments that are substantially the same as a loan agreement. The lessor accounts for its investment in the amount receivable under the lease contract rather than the leased asset itself. [IAS 32 para AG 9]. Accordingly, an operating lease is not regarded as a financial instrument (except as regards individual payments currently due and payable), but a finance lease is regarded as one.

4.21 Assets (such as pre-paid expenses) for which the future economic benefit is the receipt of goods or services, rather than the right to receive cash or another financial asset, are not financial assets. Similarly, items such as deferred revenue and most warranty obligations are not financial liabilities, because the outflow of economic benefits associated with them is the delivery of goods and services, rather than a contractual obligation to pay cash or another financial asset. [IAS 32 para AG 11].

Identification of financial instruments

4.22 Paragraphs 4.8 to 4.21 considered some of the important concepts associated with the definitions relating to financial instruments supplemented, where necessary, with examples. For ease of understanding and as a practical aid,

项目可以方便地转换为现金，则这些合同被视为金融工具进行核算。[IAS 32 AG 第 20 段]。基于与上述相同的原因，涉及实物资产的收取或交付的确定承诺也不是金融工具。[IAS 32 AG 第 21 段]。

4.20 另一示例则是办公楼的经营租赁。根据该租赁，出租人承诺在未来期间提供办公场所以换取类似服务费的对价。承租人接受服务的合同权利以及出租人的相应义务并未构成任何一方收取、交付或交换金融资产的现时权利或义务。相反，融资租赁主要被视为出租人有权利收取及承租人有义务支付与贷款协议基本相同的一系列付款。出租人是对租赁合同中应收款项的投资而非租赁资产本身进行核算。[IAS 32 AG 第 9 段]。因此，经营租赁不被认为是一项金融工具（当前已到期或应付的单笔款项除外），而融资租赁则被认为是一项金融工具。

4.21 像预付费用这样的资产，其产生的未来经济利益是收取商品或劳务而不是收取现金或其他金融资产的权利，因而不是金融资产。类似地，诸如递延收入和大部分售后保证义务也不是金融负债，因为与其相关的经济利益流出是交付商品和劳务而不是交付现金或其他金融资产的合同义务。[IAS 32 AG 第 11 段]。

金融工具的识别

4.22 第 4.8 到 4.21 段讨论了和金融工具定义相关的重要概念，以及必要时所补充的示例。为了方便理解并作为实务帮助工具，下表提供了一个常见资产负债表项目清单并采用上文所讨论的概念来确定这些项目是否符合金融工

the table below provides a list of common balance sheet items and applies the concepts discussed above to determine whether the items meet the definition of a financial instrument. Paragraph references are included where applicable. The list is by no means exhaustive, but provides an aide-mémoire to help in identifying primary financial instruments. For the sake of completeness, the last two columns also establish whether the instruments so identified fall within or outside the scope of IAS 32, IFRS 7 or IAS 39 discussed in detail from paragraph 3.4 above.

Balance sheet item	**Financial instrument?** **Yes = √** **No = X**	**Included within the scope of IAS 32 and IFRS 7** **Yes = √** **No = X**	**Included within the scope of IAS 39** **Yes = √** **No = X**
Intangible assets	X – para 4.18	n/a	n/a
Property, plant and equipment	X – para 4.18	n/a	n/a
Investment property	X – para 4.18	n/a	n/a
Interests in subsidiaries, associates and joint ventures – accounted for under IAS 27, IAS 28 or IAS 31 respectively	√ – para 3.6	X – para 3.6	X – para 3.6
Interests in subsidiaries, associates and joint ventures held for sale under IFRS 5	√ – para 3.6	X – para 3.6	X – para 3.6
Interests in subsidiaries, associates and joint ventures – accounted for under IAS 39 (in accordance with IAS 27 para 37(b))	√ – para 3.6	√ – para 3.7	√ – para 3.7
Inter-company trading balances with subsidiaries, associates and joint ventures	√ – para 4.11	√	√
Investments in other entities (available-for-sale and held for trading)	√ – para 4.4	√	√
Inventories	X – para 4.18	n/a	n/a
Gross amount due from customers for construction contract work	√ – para 11.30.2	√	√
Finance lease receivables (recognised by a lessor)	√ – para 4.20	√ – para 3.16	X – para 3.16
Trade receivables	√ – para 4.11	√	√

具的定义。在适当时包括了段落索引。此清单并非绝对详尽，但为识别主要的金融工具提供了一个备忘录。为完整起见，最后两栏还确定了识别出的工具是否在如上文第 3.4 段起所详细讨论的 IAS 32、IFRS 7 或 IAS 39 的范围之内。

资产负债表项目	**金融工具？** **是 =√** **否 = X**	**在 IAS 32 和 IFRS 7 的范围内** **是 =√** **否 = X**	**在 IAS 39 的范围内** **是 =√** **否 = X**
无形资产	X – 第 4.18 段	不适用	不适用
不动产、工厂和设备	X – 第 4.18 段	不适用	不适用
投资性房地产	X – 第 4.18 段	不适用	不适用
在子公司、联营和合营中的权益——分别根据 IAS 27、IAS 28 或 IAS 31 进行会计处理	√ – 第 3.6 段	X – 第 3.6 段	X – 第 3.6 段
按照 IFRS 5 为持有待售的在子公司、联营和合营中的权益	√ – 第 3.6 段	X – 第 3.6 段	X – 第 3.6 段
在子公司、联营和合营中的权益——按照 IAS 39 进行会计处理（根据 IAS 27 第 37（b）段）	√ – 第 3.6 段	√ – 第 3.7 段	√ – 第 3.7 段
与子公司、联营和合营的公司间贸易余额	√ – 第 4.11 段	√	√
对其他主体的投资（可供出售和为交易而持有）	√ – 第 4.4 段	√	√
存货	X – 第 4.18 段	不适用	不适用
建造合同工程款总额	√ – 第 11.30.2 段	√	√
应收融资租赁款（由承租人确认）	√ – 第 4.20 段	√ – 第 3.16 段	X – 第 3.16 段
贸易应收账款	√ – 第 4.11 段	√	√

Con.

Pre-payments – goods and services	X – para 4.21	n/a	n/a
Cash and cash equivalents	√ – para 4.4	√	√
Trade payables	√ – para 4.11	√	√
Contingent consideration in a business combination	√ – para 3.13	√ – para 3.13	√ – para 3.13
Accruals – goods and services (settlement in cash)	√ – para 4.11	√	√
Deferred income	X – para 4.21	n/a	n/a
Debt instruments	√ – para 4.5	√	√
Derivative instruments	√ – para 4.1	√	√
Net settled commodity-based contracts	√ – para 3.34	√ – para 3.34	√ – para 3.34
Retirement benefit obligations	√ – para 3.10	X – para 3.10	X – para 3.10
Provisions for constructive obligations (as defined in IAS 37)	X – para 4.8	n/a	n/a
Vacant leasehold property Provision	√ – para 4.8	√	X – para 4.8
Warranty obligations (settled by delivery of goods or service)	X – para 4.21	n/a	n/a
Warranty obligations (settled by delivery of cash or other financial asset)	√ – para 4.5	√	√
Financial guarantee contracts	√ – para 4.13	√ – para 3.25 (unless IFRS 4 applied)	√ – para 3.25 (unless IFRS 4 applied)
Operating lease	X – para 4.20	n/a	n/a
Finance lease obligations	√ – para 4.20	√ – para 3.16	X – para 3.16
Dividend payable	note 1	note 1	note 1
Current and deferred tax	X – para 4.8	n/a	n/a
Redeemable preference shares (debt)	√ – para 4.5	√	√
Entity's own equity shares	√ – para 4.6	√ – para 3.15	X – para 3.15
Employee share options	√ – para 4.6	X – para 3.11	X – para 3.11
Other equity options over own equity shares	√ – para 4.6	√ – para 3.15	X – para 3.15
Non-controlling interest	√ – note 2	√ – note 2	note 2

Notes:

1 Dividend payable on the balance sheet is a financial liability when the dividend has been formally declared by the members in a general meeting and becomes a legal obligation of the entity to deliver cash to shareholders for the amount of the declared dividend. [IAS 32 para AG 13].

2 The non-controlling interest that may arise on consolidating a subsidiary is presented in the consolidated balance sheet within equity, separately from the equity of the owners of the parent. [IAS 27 (revised) para 27; IAS 32 para AG 29]. However, where the parent or any fellow subsidiary undertaking has an obligation to deliver cash or another financial asset in respect of a subsidiary's shares (for example, by virtue of a written put option), they are treated as financial liabilities in consolidated financial statements under IAS 32 and are in the scope of IAS 39. [IAS 32 para AG 29].

续表

预付款——产品和劳务	X－第4.21段	不适用	不适用
现金及现金等价物	√－第4.4段	√	√
贸易应付账款	√－第4.11段	√	√
业务合并中的或有对价	√－第3.13段	√－第3.13段	√－第3.13段
预提费用——产品和劳务（以现金结算）	√－第4.11段	√	√
递延收入	X－第4.21段	不适用	不适用
债务工具	√－第4.5段	√	√
衍生工具	√－第4.1段	√	√
以净额结算的商品合同	√－第3.34段	√－第3.34段	√－第3.34段
退休福利义务	√－第3.10段	X－第3.10段	X－第3.10段
推定义务准备（如IAS 37所定义的）	X－第4.8段	不适用	不适用
空闲租赁不动产准备	√－第4.8段	√	X－第4.8段
质量保证义务（通过提供产品或劳务来结算）	X－第4.21段	不适用	不适用
质量保证义务（通过交付现金或其他金融资产来结算）	√－第4.5段	√	√
财务担保合同	√－第4.13段	√－第3.25段（除非采用IFRS 4）	√－第3.25段（除非采用IFRS 4）
经营租赁	X－第4.20段	不适用	不适用
融资租赁义务	√－第4.20段	√－第3.16段	X－第3.16段
应付股利	附注1	附注1	附注1
当期和递延税款	X－第4.8段	不适用	不适用
可赎回的优先股（债务）	√－第4.5段	√	√
主体自身的权益股票	√－第4.6段	√－第3.15段	X－第3.15段
职工股票期权	√－第4.6段	X－第3.11段	X－第3.11段
基于自身权益股票的其他期权	√－第4.6段	√－第3.15段	X－第3.15段
非控制性权益	√－附注2	√－附注2	附注2

附注：

1 当股利已经由全体股东大会成员正式宣告发放并成为主体以现金向股东支付所宣告发放的股利金额的法定义务时，资产负债表中的应付股利即为金融负债。[IAS 32 AG第13段]。

2 在合并子公司时可能产生的非控制性权益将在合并资产负债表中的权益中列报，并与母公司所有者权益单独列示。[IAS 27（修定版）第32段；IAS 32 AG第29段]。但是，在母公司或任何同系子公司对某一子公司的股票有支付现金或其他金融资产的义务（例如，通过签出看跌期权的方式）的情况下，则需按照IAS 32在合并财务报表中将其视为在IAS 39范围内的金融负债。[IAS 32 AG第29段]。

Derivative financial instruments

Introduction

4.23 Derivatives are financial instruments that derive their value from an underlying price or index, which could be for example, an interest rate, a foreign exchange rate or commodity price. Their primary purpose is to create rights and obligations that have the effect of transferring between the parties to the instrument one or more of the financial risks inherent in an underlying primary instrument. Consequently, they may be used for trading purposes to generate profits from risk transfers or they may be used as a hedging instrument for managing risks. Generally, there is no transfer of the underlying instrument between the parties either at inception or at maturity, but there are some exceptions.

4.24 A derivative instrument gives one party a contractual right to exchange financial assets or financial liabilities with another party under conditions that are potentially favourable, or a contractual obligation to exchange financial assets or financial liabilities with another party under conditions that are potentially unfavourable. Because the terms of the exchange are determined at inception, as prices in the financial markets change, those terms may become favourable or unfavourable (see para 4.16 above). Derivative instruments may either be free-standing or embedded in a financial instrument or in a non-financial contract.

Definition

4.25 IAS 39 defines a derivative as a financial instrument or other contract with all of the following characteristics:

- its value changes in response to the change in a specified interest rate, financial instrument price, commodity price, foreign exchange rate, index of prices or rates, credit rating or credit index, or other variable, provided in the case of a non-financial variable that the variable is not specific to a party to the contract (sometimes called the 'underlying');

衍生金融工具

引言

4.23　衍生工具是其价格源自例如利率、外汇汇率或商品价格的基础价格或指数的金融工具。其主要目的是为了形成能在工具各方之间有效转移主要基础工具内含的一种或多种金融风险的效果的权利和义务。因此，可以将其用作交易目的通过转移风险来获利，或者可以将其用作套期工具来管理风险。一般而言，无论是开始还是到期均不会在各方之间转移基础工具，但也有一些例外。

4.24　衍生工具赋予一方在潜在有利的条件下与另一方交换金融资产或金融负债的合同权利，或是在潜在不利的条件下与另一方交换金融资产或金融负债的合同义务。因为交易的条款在开始时即已确定，随着金融市场价格的变动，这些条款可能会变得有利或不利（参见上文第4.16段）。衍生工具可以是独立的，也可以嵌在金融工具或非金融合同中。

定义

4.25　IAS 39将衍生工具定义为同时具有下述特征的金融工具或其他合同：

- 其价值随特定利率、金融工具价格、商品价格、汇率、价格或利率指数、信用等级或信用指数或其他变量（如果该变量是非金融变量，则该变量不应是合同某一方特有的）（有时称为“基础变量”）的变动而变动；

- it requires no initial net investment or an initial net investment that is smaller than would be required for other types of contracts that would be expected to have a similar response to changes in market factors; and
- it is settled at a future date.

[IAS 39 para 9].

Key features of the definition

4.26 The characteristics referred to above make the definition of a derivative not only complex but fairly wide. For example, many contracts such as loan commitments (see para 3.31 above), certain contracts to buy or sell a non-financial item (see para 3.34 above) and regular way trades (see para 4.41 below) meet the definition of a derivative, in addition to the more commonly used and typical derivative instruments such as forwards, swaps, futures and options. Therefore, an understanding of these characteristics is particularly important and relevant in evaluating instruments that might qualify as, or contain, a derivative instrument. The paragraphs that follow examine some of the important concepts associated with these characteristics.

Underlying

4.27 As evident from the first characteristic stated in paragraph 4.25 above, an underlying is a variable, such as:

- An interest rate (for example, LIBOR).
- A security price (for example, the price of an XYZ entity equity share listed on a regulated market).
- A commodity price (for example, the price of a bushel of wheat).
- A foreign exchange rate (for example, / $ spot rate).
- An index (for example, FTSE 100, a retail price index).
- A credit rating or a credit index (for example, Moody's credit rating).

- 不要求初始净投资，或要求的初始净投资小于预期对市场因素变化有类似反应的其他类型合同所要求的初始净投资；并且

- 在未来某一日期进行结算。

[IAS 39 第 9 段]。

定义的关键特征

4.26　上述特征使得衍生工具的定义不仅复杂而且广泛。例如，除了如远期、互换、期货和期权等较为常用且典型的衍生工具外，如贷款承诺（参见上文第 3.31 段）、特定的购买或出售非金融项目的合同（参见上文第 3.34 段）和常规交易（参见下文第 4.41 段）等许多合同都符合衍生工具的定义。因此，在对可能符合或包含衍生工具的工具进行评估时，理解这些特征尤为重要及相关。如下各段对与这些特征相关的一些重要概念进行了讨论。

基础变量

4.27　如上文第 4.25 段所述的第一个特征所示，基础变量是如下所述的一种变量：

- 利率（如伦敦同业拆借利率）。
- 证券价格（如 XYZ 主体在某规范市场上市的权益股票价格）。

- 商品价格（如一蒲式耳大麦的价格）。
- 汇率（如兑美元的即时汇率）。
- 指数（如 FTSE 100 或零售价格指数）。
- 信用等级或信用指数（如穆迪信用等级）。

- An insurance index or catastrophe-loss index.

- Other variable (for example, sales volume indices specifically created for settlement of derivatives).

- Non financial variable (for example, a climatic or geological condition such as temperature, rainfall, or earthquake severity).

4.28 Generally, an underlying may be any variable whose changes are observable or otherwise objectively verifiable. It may be the price or rate of an asset or liability that changes in response to changes in the market factors, but it is not the asset or the liability itself in most instances. Accordingly, the underlying will generally be the referenced index that determines whether or not the derivative instrument has a positive or a negative value.

4.29 If the underlying is a non-financial variable as referred to in the last bullet point in paragraph 4.27 above, it must not be specific to a party to the contract in order for the derivative definition to be met. In other words, the terms of the contract must be sufficiently generic in nature to qualify as a derivative. For example, such variables might include an index of earthquake losses in a particular region or an index of temperatures in a particular city. On the other hand, non-financial variables that are specific to a party to the contract can include the occurrence or non-occurrence of a fire that damages or destroys an asset of a party to the contract, or EBITDA or revenue. A change in the fair value of a non-financial asset is specific to the owner if the fair value reflects not only changes in market prices for such assets (a financial variable) but also the condition of the specific non-financial asset held (a non-financial variable). [IAS 39 para AG 12A]. Such contracts may fall to be treated as insurance contracts (see para 3.25 example 2 above).

4.30 A derivative instrument may have more than one underlying or variable. A typical example is a cross-currency interest rate swap that has one underlying based on a foreign exchange rate and another underlying based on an interest rate. A complex option may have two such variables, one based on an interest rate and the other based on the price of a commodity such as oil. Another example based on IAS 39's implementation guidance is given below.

- 保险指数或灾难损失指数。

- 其他变量（如特别为衍生工具的结算所设立的销售量指数）。

- 非金融变量（例如，诸如温度、降雨量或地震强度等气候或地理条件）。

4.28　一般而言，基础变量可以是变化能够被观察得到的或能够通过其他方式客观地证实的任何变量。它可以是根据市场因素的变化而变化的资产或负债的价格或费率，但是在大多数情况下并不是资产或负债本身。因此，基础变量一般都是确定衍生工具的价值是正还是负时所需参考的指数。

4.29　如果基础变量是如上文第4.27段中最后一点所提及的非金融变量，为了满足衍生工具的定义，它必须不是合同某一方所特有的。换言之，合同条款在性质上必须具有充分的普遍性才可以符合衍生工具的要求。例如，这种变量可能包括特定地区的地震损失指数或特定城市的温度指数。另一方面，合同某一方特有的非金融变量包括可能发生的会损坏或摧毁合同某一方资产的火灾，EBITDA或收入。如果非金融资产的公允价值不仅能够反映该资产市场价格（金融变量）的变化，而且能够反映所持有的特定非金融资产所处的状况（非金融变量），那么非金融资产的公允价值变化就是资产持有人所特有的。[IAS 39 AG第12A段]。这种合同可能被视为保险合同（参见上文第3.25段示例2）。

4.30　一项衍生工具可能有不止一个的基础变量或变量。一个典型的例子就是交叉货币利率互换，其中，一个基础变量基于汇率而另一个基础变量基于利率。一个复杂的期权可能有两个变量，一个基于利率而另一个基于如石油这样的商品价格。以下列出了基于IAS 39应用指南的另一示例。

Example – Foreign currency contract based on sales volume

Entity XYZ, whose functional currency is the US dollar, sells products in France denominated in euro. XYZ enters into a contract with an investment bank to convert euro to US dollars at a fixed exchange rate. The contract requires XYZ to remit euro based on its sales volume in France in exchange for US dollars at a fixed exchange rate of 1. 20.

The contract has two underlying variables (the foreign exchange rate and the volume of sales), no initial net investment or an initial net investment that is smaller than would be required for other types of contracts that would be expected to have a similar response to changes in market factors and a payment provision. If a contract has two or more underlyings, and at least one of those underlyings is not a non-financial variable specific to a party to a contract, the entire contract is accounted for as a derivative (assuming the rest of the definition of a derivative is met).

Therefore, the contact is a derivative even though one of the variables (sales volume) is a non-financial variable that is specific to a party to the contract. IAS 39 does not exclude from its scope derivatives that are based on sales volume. [IAS 39 para IG B8].

Notional amounts and payment provisions

4. 31 A derivative usually has a notional amount, which is an amount of currency, a number of shares, a number of units of weight or volume or other units specified in the contract. However, a derivative instrument does not require the holder or writer to invest or receive the notional amount at the inception of the contract. The interaction of the notional amount and the underlying determines the settlement amount under a derivative instrument. The interaction may consist of a simple multiplication (for example, price × number of shares), or it may involve a formula that has leverage factors or other constants (for example, notional amount × interest rate where interest rate = 2. 5 × LIBOR; the effect of any change in LIBOR is magnified by two and a half times).

4. 32 Alternatively, a derivative could contain a 'payment provision' specifying

示例——基于销售量的外汇合同

主体 XYZ 的功能货币为美元，在法国出售以欧元标价的产品。XYZ 与一家投资银行签订了一份合同，按固定汇率将欧元兑换成美元。合同要求 XYZ 根据其在法国的销售量划拨欧元，并按 1.20 的固定汇率换取美元。

该合同具有两个基础变量（汇率和销售量）、没有初始净投资或者初始净投资小于预计对市场因素变动有类似的反应的其他类型合同所要求的初始净投资、并且有一项支付条款。如果合同具有两个或两个以上的基础变量，并且其中至少有一个不是合同某一方所特有的非金融变量，那么整个合同应作为衍生工具核算（假定衍生工具定义中的其他条件已满足）

因此，即使其中的一个变量（销售量）是合同一方所特有的非金融变量，该合同也是一项衍生工具。IAS 39 没有从其范围中排除基于销售量的衍生工具。[IAS 39 IG 第 B8 段]。

名义金额和支付条款

4.31　衍生工具通常具有一个名义金额，它可以是一定金额的货币、一定数量的股票、一定单位的重量或数量或合同所规定的其他单位。但是，衍生工具并不要求持有人或签出人在合同开始时就投入或收取名义金额。名义金额和基础变量之间的相互作用确定了衍生工具的结算金额。这种相互作用可能是简单的乘法（如价格乘以股票数），或可能涉及到有杠杆因素或其他常数的公式（如名义金额乘以利率，而利率等于伦敦同业拆借利率的 2.5 倍；伦敦同业拆借利率任何变化的影响都将被扩大 2.5 倍）。

4.32　或者，衍生工具可能包括“支付条款”，规定了某一固定的付款额或随

a fixed payment or payment of an amount that can change (but not proportionally with a change in the underlying) as a result of some future event that is unrelated to a notional amount. For example, a contract may require a fixed payment of C1,000 if six month LIBOR increases by 100 basis points. Such a contract is a derivative even though a notional amount is not specified. [IAS 39 para AG 9]. Another example is where an entity receives C10 million if the share price of another entity decreases by more than five per cent during a six month period, but pays C10 million if the share price increases by more than five per cent during the same six month period. No payment is made if the share price is less than five per cent up or down. This is a derivative contract where there is no notional amount to determine the settlement amount. Instead, there is a payment provision that is based on changes in the underlying.

Initial net investment

4.33 The second characteristic of a derivative instrument is that it has no initial net investment, or one that is *smaller* than would be required for other types of contracts that would be expected to have a similar response to changes in market factors. Professional judgement is required in interpreting the term in italic as it does not necessarily mean insignificant in relation to the overall investment. It is a relative measure and needs to be interpreted with care. This reflects the inherent leverage features typical of derivative instruments compared to the underlying instruments.

4.34 The following examples illustrate how initial net investment is determined in various circumstances:

Example 1 – No initial net investment of the notional amount

Forward based derivative contracts such as forward foreign exchange contracts and interest rate swaps are typical derivative instruments that do not require an initial net investment. This is because they are priced at-the-money at inception, which means that the fair value of the contracts is zero. If the fair value of the contract is not zero at inception, the contract is recognised as an asset or liability.

Under a forward foreign exchange contract the two parties agree to purchase or

着与名义金额无关的某项未来事项而变化（但并非与基础变量变动成比例变化）的付款额。例如，如果6个月期的伦敦同业拆借利率增加了100个基点，则要求支付C1,000元的固定金额。即使没有明确的名义金额，此合同仍然是一项衍生工具。[IAS 39 AG 第9段]。举另一个例子，如果一个主体的股价在6个月内下跌超过5%，则另一个主体将收取C1,000万元；但是如果该股价在相同的6个月内上涨超过5%，则另一个主体将需支付C1,000万。如果该股价的涨跌不超过5%则不做任何支付。这是一个不使用名义金额来确定结算金额的衍生工具合同。但它具有基于基础变量变动的支付条款。

初始净投资

4.33　衍生工具的第二个特征是它不要求初始净投资，或要求的初始净投资小于预期对市场因素变化有类似反应的其他类型合同所要求的初始净投资。对斜体部分术语进行诠释时需要专业的判断，因为它并不一定指的是与投资总体相比不重要。它是一个相对的计量，诠释时需谨慎。这体现了衍生工具与基础工具相比特有的内在杠杆调节特征。

4.34　如下示例解释了在不同情况下如何确定初始净投资：

示例1——无名义金额初始净投资

诸如远期外汇合同和利率互换等远期结算的衍生工具合同是典型的不要求初始净投资的衍生工具。这是因为它们在开始时以平价定价，这意味着合同的公允价值为零。如果合同开始时公允价值不为零，则该合同应被确认为一项资产或负债。

在远期外汇合同下，双方同意以规定的价格购买或出售某种外币，并在

sell a foreign currency at a specified price, with delivery or settlement at a specified future date. Although the forward contract has a notional amount equal to the amount of the foreign currency, it does not require the holder or the writer to invest or receive the notional amount at the inception of the contract. Indeed, forward contracts do not have cash flows during the contract term. Settlement takes place at maturity of the contract.

Similarly, an interest rate swap may be viewed as a variation of a forward contract in which the two parties agree to exchange one set of interest cash flows calculated with reference to a fixed interest rate for another set of interest cash flows calculated with reference to a floating interest rate. No exchange of principal takes place. Typically, the rates are set so that the fair values of the fixed and floating legs are equal and opposite at inception with the result that the fair value of the swap on initial recognition is nil. As no money changes hands at inception, there is no initial net investment. Swap cash flows occur at regular intervals over the life of the swap contract based on a notional principal amount and fixed and floating rates specified in the swap.

Example 2 – Initial net investment less than the notional amount

Option contracts are derivative instruments that do require an initial net investment. An option is a contractual agreement that gives the buyer of the option the right, but not the obligation, to purchase (call) or sell (put) a specified security, currency or commodity (the underlying) at a specified price (exercise price) during a specified period of time (or on a specified date). For this right, the buyer pays a premium, which is the amount the seller requires to take on the risk involved in writing the option. Although this premium can be significant, it is often less than the amount that would be required to buy the underlying financial instrument to which the contract is linked. As such, the option fulfils the initial net investment criterion. [IAS 39 para AG 11].

On the other hand, if the option premium is so deep in-the-money that the premium paid is close to making an investment in the underlying, then the option contract will fail the initial net investment criterion. In that situation, the instrument would not be accounted for as a derivative under IAS 39, but

确定的未来日期交付或结算。虽然远期合同有等于外币金额的名义金额，但它并不要求持有人或签出人在合同开始时投入或收取该名义金额。实际上，远期合同在合同期限内没有现金流。结算将在合同到期时进行。

同样地，利率互换可被视为远期合同的变种，其合同双方协定用以固定利率计算的一套利息现金流来换取以变动利率计算的一套利息现金流。本金并不交换。一般而言，利率的设定使得在开始时固定利息部分和变动利息部分的公允价值相等并反向，因此互换在初始确认时的公允价值为零。由于在开始时没有资金交换，即没有初始净投资。在互换合同期间以固定的期间根据互换中所规定的名义本金金额和固定及变动利率而发生互换现金流。

示例 2——初始净投资小于名义金额

期权合同是要求初始净投资的衍生工具。期权是赋予买方在特定的时间内（或在特定的日期）以特定的价格（行权价格）购买（看涨）或出售（看跌）特定的证券、货币或商品（标的）的权利而非义务的合同协议。买方会为此项权利支付期权费，其金额为卖方因承担签出期权的风险所要求的金额。尽管期权费可能是重大的，它常常低于为购买与合同挂钩的标的金融工具所需的投资额。因此，期权满足初始净投资的条件。[IAS 39 AG 第 11 段]。

另一方面，如果期权费属于深度价内而使得所支付的期权费接近对标的投资，那么该期权合同不满足初始净投资的条件。在这种情况下，根据 IAS 39 该工具不应作为衍生工具核算，而是作为对标的资产本身的投资。

rather as an investment in the underlying asset itself.

Example 3 – Exchange of currencies

Some contracts may require a mutual exchange of currencies or other assets, in which case the net investment is the difference between the fair values of the assets exchanged. An example is a currency swap that requires the exchange of currencies at both inception and at maturity. The initial exchange of currencies at fair values in those arrangements (zero net investment) is not seen as an initial net investment. Instead, it is an exchange of one kind of cash for another kind of cash. [IAS 39 para AG 11].

Example 4 – Margin accounts

Many derivative instruments, such as futures contracts and exchange traded written options, require a margin payment – an initial amount that must be deposited before trading begins and which approximately equals the daily price fluctuation permitted for the contract being traded. Such payments are not part of the initial net investment. Rather, they are a form of collateral for the counterparty or clearing house to ensure that traders will perform on their contractual obligations. The initial margin may take the form of cash, securities or other specified assets, typically liquid assets. These are separate assets that are accounted for separately. [IAS 39 para IG B10]. Any variation in margin payments would be adjusted against the asset.

Example 5 – Pre-paid interest rate swap (fixed leg pre-paid)

Entity S enters into a C100m notional amount five-year pay-fixed, receive-variable interest rate swap. The interest rate of the variable part of the swap is reset on a quarterly basis to three month LIBOR. The interest rate of the fixed leg of the swap is 10% per year. At inception of the swap, Entity S pre-pays its fixed obligation of C50m (C100m × 10% × 5 years) discounted using market interest rates, while retaining the right to receive interest payments on the C100m reset quarterly based on three-month LIBOR over the life of the swap.

As stated in example 1 above at the money interest rate swap has a zero fair value at inception. Since entity S has pre-paid the fixed leg of the swap at inception at its fair value, the amount pre-paid is also equal to the fair value

示例 3——货币交换

某些合同可能要求共同交换货币或其他资产，在这种情况下净投资为所交换资产公允价值之差。例如要求在开始和到期日交换货币的货币互换。这种安排中的以公允价值进行的货币初始交换（零净投资）不被视为初始净投资。相反，这是以一种现金交换另一种现金。[IAS 39 AG 第 11 段]。

示例 4——保证金账户

许多衍生工具，例如期货合同和在交易所交易的签出期权，要求支付保证金——即在交易开始前必须缴存的初始金额，且其金额约等于进行交易的合同所允许的每日价格波动。这种付款不是初始净投资的一部分。它们是为交易对方或结算方所提供担保品的一种形式，以保证交易人会履行其合同义务。初始保证金可以表现为现金、证券或其他专门的资产，一般是流动资产。保证金账户是需要进行单独核算的独立资产。[IAS 39 IG 第 B10 段]。当保证金的支付发生变动时，资产需要被调整。

示例 5——预付的利率互换（预付固定利率款项）

主体 S 签订了一份 5 年期、名义本金为 C1.00 亿元、支付固定利率款项、收取变动利率款项的利率互换。互换中变动利率部分以 3 个月期的伦敦同业拆借利率为基础，每季度进行调整。互换中固定利率部分是每年 10%。在互换开始时，主体 S 预付了使用市场利率折现的 C5,000 万元的固定义务（C1.00 亿元 ×10% ×5 年），同时保留了在互换期内以基于 3 个月期每季度调整的伦敦同业拆借利率对 C1.00 亿元收取利息的权利。

如上文示例 1 所述，平价的利率互换在开始时公允价值为零。既然主体 S 在开始时已经预付了互换固定利率款项的公允价值，所预付的金额也等于该互换变动利率款项的公允价值。但是这一金额远远小于计算变动利率

of the variable leg of the swap. This amount is however significantly less than the notional amount (C100m) on which the variable payments under the variable leg will be calculated. In other words, the initial net investment (the amount pre-paid) is still smaller than investing in a similar primary instrument, such as a variable rate bond, that responds equally to changes in the underlying interest rate. Therefore, a pre-paid fixed leg swap fulfils the initial net investment criterion of IAS 39. Even though entity S has no future performance obligation, the ultimate settlement of the contract is at a future date and the value of the contract changes in response to changes in the LIBOR index. Accordingly, the contract is a derivative instrument.

On the other hand, if the fixed rate payment obligation is pre-paid subsequent to initial recognition, that is, during the term of the swap, then that would be regarded as a termination of the old swap and an origination of a new instrument that is evaluated under IAS 39. [IAS 39 para IG B4]. There is no explanation in the implementation guidance as to why this is so. Presumably this is because a significant fall in LIBOR between inception date and pre-payment date would cause the amount pre-paid (that is, the fair value of the fixed leg at the date of the pre-payment) to be significantly higher than the fair value of the fixed leg at date of inception. Therefore, the entity receiving the variable payments may not recover substantially all of its pre-paid investment under the contractual terms resulting in the termination of the old swap and the creation of a new instrument.

Example 6 – Pre-paid interest rate swap (floating leg pre-paid)

Entity S enters into a C100m notional amount five-year pay-variable, receive-fixed interest rate swap. The variable leg of the swap is reset on a quarterly basis to three-month LIBOR. The fixed interest payments under the swap are calculated as 10% times the swap's notional amount, that is, C10m per year. Entity S pre-pays its obligation under the variable leg of the swap at inception at current market rates, while retaining the right to receive fixed interest payments of 10% on C100m per year.

As stated in the previous example, the fair value of the fixed leg and the fair value of a floating leg are equal and offsetting so that the fair value of the

付款的名义本金（C1.00 亿元）。换言之，其初始净投资（预付金额）仍小于对基础利率的变动有着同样反应的类似主要工具投资，如变动利率债券。因此，预付固定利率款项的互换符合 IAS 39 中初始净投资的条件。即使主体 S 没有义务在未来的履约，合同的最终结算是在未来某日。且合同的价值随着伦敦同业拆借利率指数的变动而变动。因此，该合同是一项衍生工具。

相反，如果在初始确认之后，即在合同期内，预付了固定利率款项的义务，这应被视为旧互换合同的终止和一项需根据 IAS 39 进行评估的新工具的产生。[IAS 39 IG 第 B4 段]。在应用指南中并没有解释为什么这样要求。据推测这是因为在开始日和预付日之间若伦敦同业拆借利率大跌将导致所预付的金额（即，固定利率款项在预付日的公允价值）将大大高于固定利率款项在开始日的公允价值。因此，收取变动利率付款的主体不一定能够回收其按照合同条款所预付的几乎所有投资，从而导致旧互换合同的终止及新工具的产生。

示例 6——预付的利率互换（预付变动利率款项）

主体 S 签订了一份 5 年期、名义本金为 C1.00 亿元、支付变动利率款项、收取固定利率款项的利率互换。互换中变动利率部分以 3 个月期的伦敦同业拆借利率为基础，每季度进行调整。互换中固定利率部分是按 10% 乘以互换的名义本金计算得出，即每年 C1,000 万元。在互换开始时，主体 S 按照当前市场利率预付了互换变动利率款项的义务，同时保留了每年按 C1.00 亿元的 10% 收取固定利息款项的权利。

如上一示例中所述，固定利率款项的公允价值和变动利率款项的公允价值相等并相互抵销，因此利率互换在开始时公允价值为零。由于主体 S 已

interest rate swap at inception is zero. Since entity S has pre-paid the variable leg of the swap at inception at its fair value, the amount pre-paid, all else being equal, is also equal to the fair value of the fixed leg of the swap. That is, the initial net investment (the amount pre-paid) is equal to the present value of a fixed annuity of C10m per year over the swap's life. Thus, the initial net investment is equal to the investment required in a non-derivative contract that has a similar response to changes in market conditions. In other words, the amount pre-paid provides a return that is the same as that of an amortising fixed rate debt instrument of the amount of the pre-paid. For this reason, the instrument fails the initial net investment criterion of IAS 39. Therefore, the contract is not accounted for as a derivative. By discharging the obligation to pay variable interest rate payments, entity S in effect provides a loan to the counterparty. [IAS 39 para IG B5].

Example 7 – Pre-paid forward

Entity XYZ enters into a forward contract to purchase 1m entity T ordinary shares in one year. The current market price of entity T's shares is C50 per share; the one-year forward price of entity T's shares is C55 per share. XYZ is required to pre-pay the forward contract at inception with a C50m payment.

The initial investment in the forward contract of C50m is less than the notional amount applied to the underlying, 1m shares at the forward price of C55 per share, that is, C55m. However, the initial net investment *approximates* the investment that would be required for other types of contracts that would be expected to have a similar response to changes in market factors because entity T's shares could be purchased at inception for the same price of C50m. Accordingly, the pre-paid forward contract does not meet the initial net investment criterion of a derivative instrument. In this situation, the entity would record the investment itself as a non-derivative financial asset. [IAS 39 para IG B9].

It is not clear why the example in the implementation guidance uses the term 'approximate' when the initial net investment of C50m is equal to the amount that would be exchanged to acquire the asset relating to the underlying (market price of the share). Presumably the term is used to emphasise the

经在开始时预付了互换变动利率款项的公允价值，所预付的金额，在其他条件相同的情况下，也等于该项互换固定利率款项的公允价值。即，初始净投资（预付金额）等于互换期限内每年 C1, 000 万固定年金的现值。因此，初始净投资等于对市场条件变化具有类似反应的非衍生工具合同所要求的投资。换言之，预付金额提供与预付金额的摊余固定利率债务工具相同的回报。出于此原因，该工具不符合 IAS 39 的初始净投资条件。因此该合同不作为衍生工具来核算。通过履行支付变动利率付款的义务，主体 S 实际上向交易对方提供了一笔贷款。[IAS 39 IG 第 B5 段]。

示例 7——预付的远期

主体 XYZ 签订了一份远期合同，在一年后购入 1 百万股主体 T 的普通股。主体 T 股票的当前市场价格为每股 C50 元；主体 T 股票的一年期远期价格为每股 C55 元。XYZ 被要求在合同开始时为此远期合同预付 C5, 000 万元。

该远期合同 C5, 000 万元的初始投资小于将每股 C55 元的远期价格应用于标的 100 万股所得到的名义本金，即 C5, 500 万元。但是，初始净投资*近似*等于预计对市场因素变动有类似反应的其他类型合同所要求的投资，因为在合同开始时也可以按同样 C5, 000 万元的价格购买主体 T 的股票。因此，预付远期合同不符合衍生工具初始净投资条件。在这种情况下，主体应将投资本身记为一项非衍生金融资产。[IAS 39 IG 第 B9 段]。

应用指南的示例使用"近似等于"这个词的原因并不明确，因为 C5, 000 万元的初始净投资等于购买与基础变量（股票的市场价格）相关的资产所应交换的金额。据推测，该词是用以强调如上文第 4. 33 段所示述的"初始净投资测试是一个相对的计量"，如 C4, 250 万元（比初始金额小

point that the initial net investment test is a relative measure as indicated in paragraph 4. 33 above and that a pre-payment amount of, for example, C42. 5m (15% smaller than the original amount) may still meet the initial net investment criterion.

Settlement at a future date

4. 35 The final part of the definition relates to settlement at a future date. All derivatives are settled at a future date. As explained in example 1 above, forward contracts are settled at a specified date in the future, whilst for an interest rate swap settlement occurs at regular intervals over the swap's life. An option is settled upon exercise or at maturity. Therefore, even if an option is expected not to be exercised, for example, because it is out-of-the-money and no additional exchange of consideration is expected to take place, the option still meets the settlement criterion, because expiry at maturity is a form of settlement. [IAS 39 para IG B7].

4. 36 A derivative can be settled net in cash (that is, the entity has the right to receive or the obligation to pay a single net amount) or gross in cash/other financial asset (exchange of cash/other financial asset). Consider the following example:

Example – Interest rate swap with net or gross settlement

Entity ABC enters into an interest rate swap with a counterparty (XYZ) that requires ABC to pay a fixed rate of 8% and receive a variable amount based on three month LIBOR, reset on a quarterly basis. The fixed and variable amounts are determined based on a C100m notional amount. ABC and XYZ do not exchange the notional amount. ABC pays or receives a net cash amount each quarter based on the difference between 8% and three-month LIBOR. Alternatively, settlement may be on a gross basis.

As the swap contract is settled on a periodical basis, each interest payment can be viewed as a series of forward contracts to exchange and receive cash on potentially favourable or unfavourable terms. The contract meets the definition of a derivative regardless of whether each interest payment is settled net or gross, because its value changes in response to changes in an underlying variable (LIBOR). There is no initial net investment and settlements occur at

15%）的预付金额仍可能满足初始净投资的条件。

在未来某一日期结算

4.35 定义的最后部分涉及到在未来某一日期结算。所有的衍生工具都是在未来某一日期结算。如上文示例1中所解释的，远期合同在未来某一特定日期结算，而利率互换则是在互换期间内以固定的期间结算。期权在行使或到期时进行结算。因此，即使预期不会行使某项期权，例如因为其是价外期权且预计没有其他对价的交换，期权仍满足结算的条件，因为在到期时失效也是结算的一种形式。[IAS 39 IG 第 B7 段]。

4.36 衍生工具可以用现金净额结算（即，主体有收取或支付单一净额的权利或义务），或以现金或其他金融资产总额结算（交换现金和/或其他金融资产）。请看如下示例：

示例——以净额或总额结算的利率互换

主体ABC与交易对方（XYZ）签订了一项利率互换，要求ABC按8%的固定利率付款，同时按每个季度重设的3个月期伦敦同业拆借利率收取变动金额。固定和变动金额都是根据C1.00亿元的名义本金确定。ABC和XYZ不相互交换名义本金。ABC每个季度根据8%和三个月期伦敦同业拆借利率之间的差额支付或收取一笔现金净额。或者，也可以按总额进行结算。

由于互换合同是阶段性结算的，每个利率支付都可以被视为是一系列在潜在有利或不利条件下交换和收取现金的远期合同。不论是净额结算还是总额结算，此合同都符合衍生工具的定义，因为合同价值随基础变量（伦敦同业拆借利率）的变动而变动，且没有初始净投资，并且在未来某一日期结算。换言之，ABC和XYZ双方实际上是否互相支付利息（总额结算）并没有区别。[IAS 39 IG 第 B3 段]。

future dates. In other words, it makes no difference whether ABC and XYZ actually make the interest payment to each other (gross settlement). [IAS 39 para IG B3].

4.37 Settlement may also occur gross through physical delivery of the underlying financial item. An example is a forward contract to purchase C100 million of five per cent fixed rate bond at a specified fixed date in the future. In this situation, at settlement date the entity would exchange cash for physical delivery of the bond (the underlying financial item) whose nominal value is equal to the notional amount of the contract and the market interest rate is the underlying. [IAS 39 para AG10].

Specific examples of derivative instruments

4.38 The key characteristics of a derivative contract were explained and illustrated above, where relevant, with examples. The following table provides typical examples of contracts that normally qualify as derivatives together with the relevant underlying, notional and settlement amounts.

Derivative	**Underlying**	**Notional amount**	**Settlement amount**
Stock options	Market price of share	Number of shares	(Market price at settlement – Strike Price) × Number of shares
Currency forward	Currency rate	Number of currency units	(Spot rate at settlement – Forward rate) × number of currency units
Commodity future	Commodity price per unit	Number of commodity units	Net settlement occurs daily and is determined by the change in the futures price and discounted to reflect the time to maturity
Interest rate Swap	Interest rate index (receive 5% fixed and pay LIBOR)	Amounts in C's	Net settlement occurs periodically throughout the contract's term based on the formula: (Current interest rate index – fixed rate specified in the contract) × Amounts in C's
Fixed payment contract	6 month LIBOR increases by 100 points	Not specified	Settlement amount based on payment provision in the contract.

4.37　还可以通过标的金融项目实物交割的方式进行总额结算。例如在未来特定的固定日期购买 C1.00 亿元的 5% 固定利率债券的远期合同。在这种情况下，在结算日主体将以现金对票面价值等于合同名义金额而市场利率为基础变量的债券（标的金融项目）进行实物交割。[IAS 39 AG 第 10 段]。

衍生工具的具体示例

4.38　上文对衍生工具合同的关键特征进行了解释说明，并在相关的地方提供了示例。下表列出了通常符合衍生工具要求的典型合同示例及其相关基础变量、名义金额和结算金额。

衍生工具	基础变量	名义金额	结算金额
股票期权	股票的市场价格	股票数量	（结算时的市场价格 - 协议价格）×股票数量
货币远期	汇率	货币单位数量	（结算时的即期汇率 - 远期汇率）×货币单位数量
商品期货	商品单位价格	商品单位数量	根据期货价格的变化并折现以反映至到期日的时间进行每日净结算
利率互换	利率指数（收取固定利率 5% 而支付伦敦同业拆借利率）	以 C 为单位的金额	在整个合同期间根据如下公式定期净额结算：（当前利率指数 - 合同规定的固定利率）×以 C 为单位的金额
固定支付合同	6 个月期的伦敦同业拆借利率上升 100 点	未规定	结算金额根据合同中支付条款而定。

Contracts to buy or sell non-financial items

4. 39 An entity may also have a contract to buy or sell a non-financial item that can be settled net in cash or another financial instrument, or by exchanging financial instruments. Such contracts may fall within the definition of a derivative if they meet certain criteria (see further para 3. 34 of chapter 3). [IAS 39 para AG 10].

Contracts that are in substance derivatives

4. 40 It is generally inappropriate to treat two or more separate financial instruments, such as an investment in a floating rate debt instrument and a floating to fixed interest rate swap with different counter parties, as a single combined instrument ('synthetic instrument' accounting), as discussed in chapter 11. [IAS 39 para IG C6]. However, as an exception to this, non-derivative transactions should be aggregated and treated as a derivative when, in substance, the transactions result in a derivative instrument. Indicators of this would include circumstances where the transactions:

- Are entered into at the same time and in contemplation of one another.
- Have the same counterparty.
- Relate to the same risk.
- Have no substantive business purpose or there is no apparent economic need for structuring the transactions separately that could not also have been accomplished in a single transaction.

[IAS 39 para IG B6].

Example – In substance derivatives

Entity A makes a five-year fixed rate loan to entity B, while entity B at the same time makes a five-year variable rate loan for the same amount to entity A. There are no transfers of principal at inception of the two loans, since entities A and B have a netting agreement.

购买或出售非金融项目的合同

4.39　主体可能持有一个购买或出售非金融项目的合同，此合同可以用现金或其他金融工具进行净额结算，或通过交换金融工具进行结算。如果符合特定条件，该合同可能符合衍生工具的定义（进一步信息参见第 3.34 段）。[IAS 39 AG 第 10 段]。

实质上是衍生工具的合同

4.40　如在第 11 章中所讨论的，把两个或更多的独立金融工具，如一项对变动利率债务工具的投资和一项支付变动利率、收取固定利率的利率互换，作为一项单一的组合工具处理（“合成工具”会计）通常是不恰当的。[IAS 39 IG 第 C6 段]。但是，对此有一例外，如果若干非衍生工具交易在实质上形成了一项衍生工具交易，则应予以合并并作为衍生工具处理。做出这种判断的迹象包括：

- 交易同时签订并且体现在各方的计划中。
- 交易具有相同的交易对方。
- 交易与同一风险相关。
- 交易没有实质的商业目的或没有明显的经济需要将原本在单项交易中不能完成的衍生工具交易分为若干交易。

[IAS 39 IG 第 B6 段]。

示例——实质上的衍生工具

主体 A 向主体 B 提供了一笔五年期的固定利率贷款，同时主体 B 向主体 A 提供了一笔金额相同的五年期的变动利率贷款。由于主体 A 和主体 B 有互抵协议，在两笔贷款开始时没有转让本金。

The contractual effect is that the loans are, in substance, equivalent to an interest rate swap arrangement that meets the definition of a derivative – there is an underlying variable, no initial net investment and future settlement. The same answer would apply if entity A and entity B did not have a netting agreement, because the definition of a derivative instrument does not require net settlement. [IAS 39 para IG B6].

Regular way contracts

4.41 A regular way purchase or sale is a purchase or sale of a financial asset under a contract whose terms require delivery of the asset within the time frame established generally by regulation or convention in the marketplace concerned. [IAS 39 para 9]. Such contracts give rise to a fixed price commitment between trade date and settlement date that meets the definition of a derivative. However, because of the commitment's short duration, it is not recognised as a derivative financial instrument. Rather, IAS 39 provides for special accounting for such regular way contracts which is dealt with in chapter 8. [IAS 39 para AG 12].

Accounting for derivatives

4.42 The measurement requirements of IAS 39 require all derivatives to be measured at fair value on the balance sheet, with changes in fair value being accounted through profit or loss, except for derivatives that qualify as effective hedging instruments and derivatives that are linked to and must be settled by delivery of unquoted equity instruments whose fair value cannot be reliably measured. Measurement and hedging requirements are dealt with further in chapters 9 and 10 respectively.

贷款的合同后果在实质上相当于一项符合衍生工具定义的利率互换协议——存在基础变量，没有初始净投资和在未来结算。如果主体A和主体B没有互抵协议，答案也一样，因为衍生工具的定义并未要求净额结算。[IAS 39 IG第B6段]。

常规合同

4.41 常规方式购买或出售指按照合同规定购买或出售金融资产，并且该合同条款规定应根据通常由法规或市场惯例所确定的时间来交付资产。[IAS 39第9段]。这种合同在交易日和结算日之间产生了符合衍生工具定义的固定价格承诺。但是，由于承诺的时间跨度很短，这种承诺不作为衍生金融工具确认。IAS 39对这种常规方式合同另外规定了专门的会计处理方法，这在第8章中进行了讨论。[IAS 39 AG第12段]。

衍生工具的会计处理

4.42 IAS 39的计量要求规定，除了符合有效套期工具要求的衍生工具和与公允价值不能可靠计量的无报价权益工具挂钩且必须通过交付该权益工具进行结算的衍生工具以外，所有衍生工具在资产负债表中都需以公允价值计量，而公允价值的变动计入损益。在第9章和第10章中分别对计量要求和套期要求进行了进一步的讨论。

Chapter 7 Financial liabilities and equity

Content

Introduction 7001

Principles for classifying financial liabilities and equity instruments 7003

Reclassifications 7013

Contracts that are settled in cash or another financial assets 7017

Contractual obligation to settle in cash or another financial assets 7017

Restriction on the ability to satisfy contractual obligations 7025

Puttable instruments and obligations arising on liquidation 7027

Criteria to be classified as equity 7033

Transactions entered into by an instrument holder other than as owner of the entity 7041

Impact on consolidation 7041

Reclassification of puttable instruments and obligations arising on liquidation 7045

Own share buy-back programmes 7045

Absence of explicit obligations 7047

Contracts settled in cash or other financial asset that are discretionary or at the option of the issuer 7051

Payments that are discretionary or at the option of the issuer 7053

Contracts that will or may be settled in an entity's own equity instruments 7059

Contingent settlement provisions 7083

Settlement terms that are not genuine 7089

Settlements that arise only on liquidation 7093

Derivative financial instruments with settlement options 7093

Shares issued by subsidiaries 7095

Compound financial instruments 7097

Introduction 7097

Separation of a compound financial instrument on initial recognition 7099

第七章　金融负债和权益

目　录

引言 7002

金融负债和权益工具的分类原则 7004

　重分类 7014

　以现金或其他金融资产结算的合同 7018

　　以现金或其他金融资产结算的合同义务 7018

　　对履行合同义务能力的限制 7026

　　可回售金融工具和清算产生的义务 7028

　　权益划分标准 7034

　　工具持有人并非以权益所有人身份所签订的交易 7042

　　对合并的影响 7042

　　可回售金融工具和清算产生的义务的重分类 7046

　　自身股票赎回计划 7046

　　明确义务的缺失 7048

　由发行人自主决定或其有权选择以现金或其他金融资产结算的合同 7052

　　由发行人自主决定或其有权选择的支付 7054

　将要或可能以主体自身的权益工具结算的合同 7060

　或有结算条款 7084

　　不现实的结算条款 7090

　　仅在清算时产生的结算 7094

　　具有结算选择权的衍生金融工具 7094

　　子公司发行的股份 7096

　复合金融工具 7098

　　引言 7098

　　初始确认时对复合金融工具的分拆 7100

Separation of a compound instrument containing non-equity derivatives 7107
Conversion at or before maturity 7117
Mandatorily convertible instruments 7119
Early redemption or repurchase 7127
Modification of terms to induce early conversion 7131
Settlement options 7135
Convertible bond denominated in a foreign currency 7137
Preference shares with various rights 7147
Derivatives over own equity instruments 7153
Contracts accounted for as equity instruments 7153
Contracts accounted for as financial liabilities 7165
Contracts accounted for as derivative assets or liabilities 7175
Issuer or holder's settlement options 7185
Treatment of interest, dividends, gains and losses 7185
Treatment of transaction costs of equity instruments 7189
Treasury shares 7193

对含有非权益性衍生工具的复合工具的分拆 7108
到期日或之前的转换 7118
强制性可转换工具 7120
提前赎回或回购 7128
为促使提前转换而更改条款 7132
结算选择权 7136
以外币计价的可转换债券 7138
具有各种不同权利的优先股 7148
基于自身权益工具的衍生工具 7154
作为权益工具核算的合同 7154
作为金融负债核算的合同 7166
作为衍生工具资产或负债核算的合同 7176
发行人或持有人的结算选择权 7186
利息、股利、利得和损失的处理 7186
权益工具交易费用的处理 7190
库藏股 7194

Introduction

7.1 IAS 32, 'Financial instruments: presentation', contains the principles for distinguishing between liabilities and equity issued by an entity. The substance of the contractual arrangement of a financial instrument, rather than its legal form, governs its classification. The overriding criterion is that if an entity does not have an unconditional right to avoid delivering cash or another financial asset to settle a contractual obligation, the contract is not an equity instrument.

7.1.1 IAS 32 should be applied by all entities to all types of financial instruments except those outside the standard's scope. The scope exemptions to IAS 32 are discussed in chapter 3. In practice one of the more common and complex scope exemptions relates to contracts that fall within the scope of IFRS 2, 'Share-based payment', IAS 19, 'Employee benefits', or IFRS 4, 'Insurance contracts'. Where the holder is an employee, director or provider of service to the entity, the contract should be carefully analysed to determine whether it is within the scope of IFRS 2, (see chapter 12 of the IFRS Manual of Accounting) or IAS 19 (see chapter 11 of the IFRS Manual of Accounting) or IAS 32.

7.2 The IASB published an amendment to IAS 32 on the classification of rights issues on 8 October 2009. The amendment addresses the accounting for rights issues (including rights, options and warrants) that are denominated in a currency other than the functional currency of the issuer (see para 7.40). The amendment is effective for annual periods beginning on or after 1 February 2010, with early adoption permitted.

7.2.1 The IASB published IFRIC 19, 'Extinguishing financial liabilities with equity instruments', in November 2009. This interpretation clarifies the accounting when an entity renegotiates the terms of its debt with the result that the liability is extinguished by the debtor issuing its own equity instruments to the creditor. The interpretation is effective for annual periods beginning on or after 1 July 2010, with early adoption permitted. Refer to chapter 8 for further guidance on IFRIC 19.

7.3 Classifying liability and equity instruments in accordance with IAS 32's rules

引言

7.1 IAS 32 规定了区分主体所发行的负债和权益的原则。金融工具的分类取决于其合同的实质，而不是其法律形式。最重要的标准是，如果一个主体不能无条件地避免以交付现金或其他金融资产来履行一项合同义务，那么该合同就不是一项权益工具。

7.1.1 所有主体对所有类型的金融工具均应采用 IAS 32，除非这种金融工具在该准则的范围之外。IAS 32 的豁免范围在第 3 章中进行了讨论。实务中更为常见、更为复杂的豁免范围之一是《国际财务报告准则第 2 号——以股份为基础的支付》（“IFRS 2”）、《国际会计准则第 19 号——职工福利》（“IAS 19”）或《国际财务报告准则第 4 号——保险合同》（“IFRS 4”）范围内的合同。在持有人为职工、董事或主体的服务提供人的情况下，应仔细地对合同进行分析以确定其属于 IFRS 2（参见《国际财务报告准则会计实务指引》第 12 章）、IAS 19（参见《国际财务报告准则会计实务指引》第 11 章），还是 IAS 32 的范围。

7.2 IASB 于 2009 年 8 月 10 日针对配股权的分类对 IAS 32 发布了一项修订。此修订针对的是以发行人功能货币以外的货币计价的配股权（包括配股权、期权和认股权证）的会计处理（参见第 7.40 段）。此修订于起始日在 2010 年 2 月 1 日或之后的年度期间生效，允许提前实施。

7.2.1 IASB 于 2009 年 11 月发布了《国际财务报告解释公告第 19 号——以权益工具解除金融负债》（“IFRIC 19”）。此解释公告对主体通过重新协商其债务条款，以债务人向债权人发行其自身权益工具来解除负债的会计处理进行了澄清。此解释公告于起始日在 2010 年 7 月 1 日或之后的年度期间生效，允许提前实施。有关 IFRIC 19 的更多指引请参见第 8 章。

7.3 按照 IAS 32 的规定来划分负债和权益工具很复杂，需要对工具合同条款

is complex and requires the assessment of each component of an instrument's contractual terms. The impact of an incorrect classification on such issues as borrowings and other ratios (including debt covenants) and reported earnings can be highly significant to investors and other users of financial statements.

[The next paragraph is 7.6.]

Principles for classifying financial liabilities and equity instruments

7.6 Before considering IAS 32's general principles for classifying a financial instrument as a financial liability or equity, it is appropriate to set out the standard's basic definitions of a financial liability and an equity instrument.

7.7 IAS 32 defines a financial liability as any liability that is:

- A contractual obligation:
  - to deliver cash or another financial asset to another entity; or
  - to exchange financial assets or financial liabilities with another entity under conditions that are potentially unfavourable to the entity.
- A contract that will or may be settled in the entity's own equity instruments and is:
  - a non-derivative for which the entity is or may be obliged to deliver a variable number of the entity's own equity instruments; or
  - a derivative that will or may be settled other than by the exchange of a fixed amount of cash or another financial asset for a fixed number of the entity's own equity instruments. For this purpose the entity's own equity instruments do not include puttable instruments and obligations arising on liquidation that are classified as equity (as explained in para 7.7.1), rights issues denominated in a currency other than the functional currency of the issuer if they meet certain conditions (as explained in para. 7.40) or instruments that

中的每一项内容进行评估。对于投资人以及财务报表的其他使用者而言，不正确的分类可能对诸如借款及其他比率（包括债务契约）和列示的收益等方面产生重大影响。

[下一段为第 7.6 段。]

金融负债和权益工具的分类原则

7.6　在讨论 IAS 32 中将金融工具划分为金融负债或权益的一般原则之前，应当首先阐明一下该准则对金融负债和权益工具的基本定义。

7.7　IAS 32 将金融负债定义为下述负债：

- 以下合同义务：
  - 向另一主体交付现金或其他金融资产；或者
  - 在潜在不利的条件下，与另一主体交换金融资产或金融负债。
- 将以主体自身权益工具结算或可以以主体自身权益工具结算的合同，且该合同是：
  - 一项非衍生工具，使主体承担或可能承担交付可变数量自身权益工具的义务；或
  - 一项衍生工具，该衍生工具将或可能以固定金额的现金或其他金融资产换取固定数量的主体自身权益工具以外的其他方式结算。为此，主体自身的权益工具不包括被划分为权益的可回售金融工具和清算产生的义务（如第 7.7.1 段所说明的）、符合一定条件的以发行人功能货币以外的货币计价的配股权（如第 7.40 段所说明的）或那些本身就是在未来收取或交付主体自身权益工具的合同。

are contracts for the future receipt or delivery of the entity's own equity instruments.

[IAS 32 para 11].

7.7.1 An exception is built in to the above general definition to the effect that an instrument that meets the definition of a financial liability is classified as an equity instrument if it has all the features and meets the conditions in the February 2008 amendment to IAS 32, 'Puttable financial instruments and obligations arising on liquidation' (see para 7.24.5). This amendment came into effect for accounting periods beginning on or after 1 January 2009.

7.8 IAS 32 defines an equity instrument as any contract that evidences a residual interest in an entity's assets after deducting all of its liabilities. [IAS 32 para 11]. A residual interest is not necessarily a proportionate interest ranking *pari passu* with all other residual interests, for example, it may be an interest in a fixed amount of the entity's shares that may rank first in preference. For the purposes of determining whether a financial instrument is an equity instrument rather than a financial liability, the standard requires an issuer to apply the following expanded definition of an equity instrument that is essentially a converse of the above definition of a financial liability. Accordingly, an instrument is an equity instrument if, and only if, both of the conditions below are met:

- The instrument includes no contractual obligation:
  - to deliver cash or another financial asset to another entity; or
  - to exchange financial assets or financial liabilities with another entity under conditions that are potentially unfavourable to the entity.
- If the instrument will or may be settled in the issuer's own equity instruments, it is:
  - a non-derivative that includes no contractual obligation for the issuer to deliver a variable number of its own equity instruments; or
  - a derivative that will be settled only by the issuer exchanging a fixed amount of cash or another financial asset for a fixed number of its own equity instruments. For this purpose the issuer's own equity instruments do not

［IAS 32 第 11 段］。

7.7.1 上述基本定义存在一个例外，即如果某个符合金融负债定义的工具具有 IAS 32 于 2008 年 2 月的修订《可回售金融工具和清算产生的义务》中所述的所有特征并符合其条件，就应将其划分为一项权益工具（参见第 7.24.5 段）。此项修订于起始日在 2009 年 1 月 1 日或之后的会计期间生效。

7.8 IAS 32 将权益工具定义为能证明享有主体的资产扣除所有负债后的剩余权益的合同。［IAS 32 第 11 段］。剩余权益并不一定与所有其他的剩余权益具有相同级别的*权益比例*，例如，它可以是对主体股票的固定金额所享有的优先级别可能是最高的权益。在确定一项金融工具是权益工具而不是金融负债时，该准则要求发行人采用如下与上述金融负债定义基本相反的扩展的权益工具定义。相应地，当且仅当下述两个条件同时被满足时，一项工具属于权益工具：

- 这一工具不包括下述合同义务：
  - 向其他主体交付现金或其他金融资产；或
  - 在对主体潜在不利的条件下与另一主体交换金融资产或金融负债。
- 如果这一工具将要或可能以发行人自身的权益工具结算，那么这一工具需是：
  - 一项非衍生工具，且该非衍生工具对发行人来说不含交付可变数量的自身权益工具的合同义务；或
  - 一项衍生工具，且该衍生工具将通过发行人以固定金额的现金或其他金融资产换取固定数量的自身权益工具的方式进行结算。为此，主体自身权益工具不包括被划分为权益的可回售金融工具和清算产生的义务或那

include puttable instruments and obligations arising on liquidation that are classified as equity or instruments that are contracts for the future receipt or delivery of the issuer's own equity instruments.

A contractual obligation, including one arising from a derivative financial instrument, that will or may result in the future receipt or delivery of the issuer's own equity instruments, but does not meet both conditions above, is not an equity instrument. As an exception, an instrument that meets the definition of a financial liability is classified as an equity instrument if it has all the features and meets the conditions in the February 2008 amendment to IAS 32, 'Puttable financial instruments and obligations arising on liquidation' (see para 7.24.5).

[IAS 32 para 16].

7.9 IAS 32 is a contract-based standard. 'Contract' or 'contractual' refers to an agreement between two or more parties that has clear economic consequences that the parties have little, if any, discretion to avoid, usually because the agreement is enforceable by law. Contracts, and thus financial instruments, may take a variety of forms and need not be in writing. [IAS 32 para 13]. Liabilities or assets that are not contractual (for example obligations established from local law or statute, such as income taxes) are not financial liabilities or financial assets. Similarly, constructive obligations, as defined in IAS 37, do not arise from contracts and are not financial liabilities. [IAS 32 para AG 12].

7.10 IAS 32 states that an issuer of a financial instrument should classify a financial instrument, or *its component parts*, on initial recognition as a financial liability, a financial asset or an equity instrument in accordance with the contractual arrangement's substance and the definitions of a financial liability, a financial asset and an equity instrument. [IAS 32 para 15]. The role of 'substance' in the classification of financial instrument should be restricted to considering the instrument's contractual terms. Anything that falls outside the contractual terms should not be considered for the purpose of assessing whether an instrument should be classified as a liability under IAS 32. Furthermore, in assessing the substance of the terms and conditions of a financial instrument, the impact of relevant local laws, regulations and the entity's governing charter in effect at the date of classification on those terms should also be considered as noted in paragraph 7.21,

些本身就是在未来收取或交付主体自身权益工具的合同。

一项将导致或可能导致未来收取或是交付发行人自身权益工具的合同义务，包括因衍生金融工具而产生的合同义务，如果不能同时满足上述两个条件，即不属于权益工具。对此有个例外，如果某个符合金融负债定义的工具具有IAS 32于2008年2月修订的《可回售金融工具和清算产生的义务》中所述的所有特征并符合其条件，就应将其划分为一项权益工具（参见第7.24.5段）。

[IAS 32第16段]。

7.9　IAS 32是一个基于合同的准则。“合同”或“合同的”是指双方或多方之间的具有明确经济结果的协议，因为该协议通常在法律上具有强制性，协议各方难以避免这种结果。合同，亦即金融工具，可以有不同形式，不一定采用书面形式。[IAS 32第13段]。非合同性的负债或资产（诸如所得税等因地方法律或法规而形成的义务）不是金融负债或金融资产。类似地，IAS 37中定义的推定义务不是因合同产生的义务，因而也不是金融负债。[IAS 32 AG第12段]。

7.10　IAS 32规定，金融工具的发行人应在初始确认时根据合同安排的实质以及金融负债、金融资产和权益工具的定义将该金融工具或*其组成部分*划分为金融负债、金融资产或权益工具。[IAS 32第15段]。“实质”在金融工具分类中应局限于该工具的合同条款。在按照IAS 32评估一项工具是否应被划分为一项负债时，合同条款以外的任何因素都不应予以考虑。此外，如第7.21段所述，在评估一项金融工具条款和条件的实质时，还应考虑在分类日有效的相关当地法律、法规以及主体的管理章程，但不包括对这些法律、法规及章程的未来修改对这些条款的影响。[IFRIC 2第5段]。

but not expected future amendments to those laws, regulations and charter. [IFRIC 2 para 5].

7.11 A contractual financial obligation is necessary to classify a financial instrument as a liability. Such a contractual obligation could be established explicitly or could be indirectly established (see para 7.27). However, the obligation must be established through the terms and conditions of the financial instrument. As the IFRIC agreed in March 2006, economic compulsion, by itself, does not result in a financial instrument being classified as a liability.

Example 1 – 'Step-up' instrument

An entity issues a non-redeemable callable bond where the fixed dividend of 5% can be deferred at the issuer's option. The instrument includes a 'step-up' dividend clause that would increase the dividend to 25% at a pre-determined date in the future unless the instrument had previously been called by the issuer.

This instrument includes no contractual obligation to pay the dividends or to call the instrument. Although there is an economic compulsion for the issuer to call the instrument on the date the dividend payment 'steps-up', there is no contractual obligation to do so. Therefore, the instrument would be classified as an equity instrument.

Example 2 – Discretionary dividends that have historically been paid each year

An entity issues a non-redeemable callable subordinated bond with a fixed 6% coupon. The coupon can be deferred in perpetuity at the issuer's option. The issuer has a history of paying the coupon each year and the current bond price is predicated on the holders expectation that the coupon will continue to be paid each year. In addition the stated policy of the issuer is that the coupon will be paid each year, which has been publicly communicated.

Although there is both pressure on the issuer to pay the coupon, to maintain the bond price, and a constructive obligation to pay the coupon, there is no contractual obligation to do so. Therefore the bond is classified as an equity

7.11　合同义务是将一项金融工具划分为负债的必要条件。这种合同义务可以明确地确立，也可以间接地形成（参见第7.27段）。但是，这种义务必需由该金融工具的条款和条件来确立。如国际财务报告解释委员会（“IFRIC”）于2006年3月所议定的，经济压力自身并不会导致一项金融工具被划分为负债。

示例1——“股利递增”工具

某主体发行了一项发行人可赎回、但持有人不可要求赎回的债券，发行人有权将其5%的固定股利递延。该工具包括一个股利“递增”条款，规定除非发行人在事先确定的某个未来日期之前已经将此工具回购，否则该日期之后的股利增加为25%。

该工具不存在支付股利或赎回的合同义务。虽然有经济压力促使发行人在股利“递增”之日将其赎回，但发行人并没有这样做的合同义务。因此，该工具应当被划分为一项权益工具。

示例2——历史上每年均支付的任意股利

某主体发行了一项票面固定利率为6%的发行人可赎回、但持有人不可要求赎回的次级债券。发行人有权永久地递延票面利息。之前发行人每年都支付利息，而且目前债券的价格是按照持有者预期该利息仍将于每年支付来确定的。此外，发行人每年支付利息的政策已经公布。

尽管发行人有压力支付利息以维持债券价格，又有支付利息的推定义务，但其并没有这样做的合同义务。因此，该债券被划分为一项权益工具。

instrument.

7.12 Examining a financial instrument's component parts is key to correct classification. This is because debt instruments and shares come in many forms. They may be redeemable or non-redeemable. The returns may be mandatory or discretionary or may combine elements of both. Sometimes they may contain features (such as put and call options) that may or may not oblige the issuer to settle the instrument in cash or other financial assets. Consequently, it is necessary to examine the contractual terms of each component carefully, bearing in mind the definitions of a financial liability and an equity instrument, to determine whether they exhibit characteristics of a financial liability or equity. Once the characteristics of the individual components are determined, they can be combined to arrive at the overall assessment of whether the entire instrument is classified as a financial liability, or an equity instrument, or a compound instrument containing both liability and equity components.

[The next paragraph is 7.14.]

7.14 Where an entity issues two or more instruments at (or nearly at) the same time to the same counterparty, the indicators outlined in IAS 39 must be considered when determining whether the contracts are linked and viewed as a single arrangement or as two separate contracts. Indicators that contracts are linked include:

- they are entered into at the same time and in contemplation of one another;
- they have the same counterparty;
- they relate to the same risk;
- there is no apparent economic need or substantive business purpose for structuring the transaction separately that would not also have been accomplished in a single transaction; and
- they cannot be transferred or redeemed separately.

[IAS 39 paras AG 51(e) and IG B.6].

7.14.1 The general classification principles described above appear to be relatively

7.12 检查某项金融工具的组成部分是进行正确分类的关键。这是因为债务工具和股票有很多种形式。他们可能是可赎回的也可能是不可赎回的。其回报可能是强制的也可能是任意的，或者同时包括这两种因素。有时他们还可能包括可能使发行人有义务以现金或其他金融资产对该工具进行结算的特征（例如看涨和看跌期权）。因此，必须仔细地检查各组成部分的合同条款，并谨记金融负债和权益工具的定义，以判定其显示的是金融负债还是权益的特征。确定好各组成部分的特征后，要将他们综合起来进行整体评估，以判定整个工具应划分为金融负债、权益工具，还是既包括负债部分又包括权益部分的复合工具。

[下一段为第7.14段。]

7.14 当某主体同时（或几乎同时）向同一交易对方发行了两种或以上的工具时，须考虑IAS 39中所列出的迹象以确定这些合同是否相互关联及其是否应被视为一个交易还是两个单独的合同。表明这些合同相互关联的迹象包括：

- 同时签订并且体现在各方的计划中；
- 具有相同的交易对方；
- 与同一风险有关；
- 没有明显的经济需要或实质的商业目的将原本在一个单项交易中不能完成的交易分立为若干交易；以及
- 无法单独转移或赎回。

[IAS 39 AG第51（e）段及IG第B.6段]。

7.14.1 上文所述的原则看起来相对简单，但在实际应用中常常会构成困难。

simple, but the application in practice often presents difficulties. The contractual arrangement's substance and its legal form are commonly consistent, but not always. Since the contractual arrangement's substance rather than its legal form takes precedence, there could be situations where instruments that qualify as equity for regulatory or legal purposes are, on closer examination, liabilities for financial reporting purposes.

Reclassifications

7.15 Equity or liability classification is made by the entity on initial recognition in accordance with paragraph 15 of IAS 32. However, if the contractual terms and conditions are subsequently changed, it may result in derecognising the original instrument (equity or liability) and the recognising of a new instrument (liability or equity). The accounting treatment for modifications of the contractual terms of financial liabilities, that may result in derecognising the liability and recognition of an equity instrument is dealt with in chapter 8.

7.15.1 The IFRIC issued rejection wording in November 2006 that clarified the accounting treatment for transfers from equity to liability when the transfer is a result of a change in the instrument's contractual terms. This might be, for example a change in the contractual terms to require a coupon, which was previously at the discretion of the issuer, to be paid on the occurrence of a genuine contingent settlement event. The IFRIC clarified that a financial liability is initially recognised at the time when the contractual terms are changed, irrespective of whether the change affects the contractual cash flows. The new liability is measured at fair value in accordance with paragraph 43 of IAS 39.

7.15.2 The IFRIC also observed that the change in the instrument's terms gives rise to derecognising the original equity instrument. Paragraph 33 of IAS 32 states that no gain or loss is recognised in profit and loss on the purchase, sale, issue or cancellation of an entity's own equity instruments. The difference between the carrying amount of the equity instrument and the fair value of the newly-recognised financial liability is recorded in equity at the time the terms are changed. This applies even if the change in terms has no impact on the instrument's expected cash

合同安排的实质与其法律形式通常是一致的，但也并非总是如此。因为合同安排的实质比其法律形式更为重要，有可能出现从监管和法律的角度作为权益的工具，在经过更仔细的检查后发现，从财务报告的角度应将其作为负债的情况。

重分类

7.15　主体在初始确认时按照 IAS 32 第 15 段的规定进行权益或负债分类。但是，如果之后合同的条款和条件发生了变化，可能会导致终止确认原有工具（权益或负债）并确认一项新的工具（负债或权益）。对有关可能导致终止确认负债并确认一项权益工具的金融负债合同条款变更的会计处理在第 8 章中进行讨论。

7.15.1　IFRIC 于 2006 年 11 月发布了无须解释性指引的说明，并澄清了工具的合同条款变化导致其从权益变为负债时的会计处理。例如这可能是由于合同条款的变化，使得原本由发行人自主决定支付的利息变更为将在发生某一现实的或有结算事项时支付。IFRIC 澄清，不论是否影响合同现金流，当合同条款变化时，主体都将初始确认一项新的金融负债。新负债根据 IAS 39 第 43 段以公允价值计量。

7.15.2　IFRIC 也注意到工具条款的变化会导致原权益工具的终止确认。IAS 32 第 33 段规定在购回、出售、发行或取消主体的自身权益工具时不应在损益中确认任何利得或损失。权益工具的账面金额与新确认金融负债的公允价值之间的差额在条款变化时确认为权益。即便条款变化不影响工具的预计现金流量时也是如此。

flows.

7.15.3 As far as reclassifications from financial liability to equity are concerned absent any modifications to the instrument's contractual terms and conditions, the guidance where the instrument's contractual terms and conditions have not changed is less clear than the case where the instrument's contractual terms and conditions have changed. IAS 32 is silent on whether a re-assessment is required after initial recognition as paragraph 15 of IAS 32 only prescribes that an entity should classify the instrument, or its component parts, on initial recognition. Therefore, it is possible to argue that an instrument should not be reclassified after inception. On the other hand, paragraph 39 of IAS 39 states that an entity should remove a financial liability (or a part of a financial liability) from its balance sheet when, and only when, it is extinguished; that is when the obligation specified in the contract is discharged or cancelled or expires. Therefore, one could argue that if the contractual obligation that triggered liability classification terminates, then reclassification is appropriate because the obligation has been discharged or cancelled. Because of the lack of clarity in the literature, we believe that both treatments can be supported, and as a result an entity should determine an appropriate accounting policy and apply it consistently.

7.15.4 Consider the following example: An entity issues a 5 year convertible bond where the holder has the option to convert it into the issuers's equity shares after the first year, but where the conversion ratio is only fixed at the end of the first year at the lower of CU5 and 130 per cent of the equity share price. As the number of shares the bond could be converted into is variable, on initial recognition the conversion option is recognised as a separate embedded derivative liability. However, at the end of year one, under the contract's original terms, the conversion ratio is fixed and, therefore, no longer meets the definition of a financial liability. In considering the guidance in IAS 32 above, the change in the conversion ratio from variable to fixed at the end of year 1 would not result in reclassification because the assessment would be based only on the terms at inception of the contract. Alternatively, in considering the guidance in IAS 39, the conversion option would be reclassified from a derivative liability to equity, because the obligation to deliver a variable number of shares upon conversion expires and the obligation to then deliver a fixed number of shares meets the

7.15.3　对从金融负债重分类为权益来说，对工具合同条款和条件没有变化的情形的指引不如对工具合同条款和条件变化的情形的指引明确。IAS 32 并没有规定在初始确认之后是否需要进行重新评价，IAS 32 第 15 段只是规定了主体应在初始确认时对金融工具或其组成部分进行分类。因此，一方面可以这样来理解，即在初始日后就不应再对金融工具进行重分类。而另一方面，IAS 39 第 39 段中提到，当且仅当金融负债（或金融负债的一部分）消除时（即：当合同中规定的义务解除、取消或到期时），主体应当将其从资产负债表内转出。因此，也可以理解为如果导致负债分类的合同义务已经终止，由于该项义务已经被解除或取消，那么重分类是恰当的。因为准则的不明确，我们认为两种处理方法均有理可依，因此主体应确定一个恰当的会计政策并一贯地应用该项政策。

7.15.4　请看如下示例：某主体发行了一个 5 年期可转换债券，持有人有权选择在第一年后将其转换为发行人的股票，但是转换率只能在第一年年末才能确定为 CU5 元和股票价格的 130% 两者之中的较低者。因为在初始确认时该债券所能转换的股票数量是可变的，可转换期权被单独确认为一项嵌入衍生工具负债。但在第一年年末，转换率根据合同的初始条款已固定，因此它便不再符合金融负债的定义。考虑到上文所述 IAS 32 的指引，在第一年年末转换率从可变变为固定并不会导致重分类，因为该分类评估是仅仅依据合同在初始日的条款进行的。或者，考虑到 IAS 39 的指引，可以将该可转换期权从衍生工具负债重分类为权益，因为在转换时交付可变数量股票的义务已到期，而之后交付固定数量股票的义务符合权益的定义。

definition of equity.

7. 15. 5 Reclassifications of puttable instruments and obligations arising on liquidation are dealt with from paragraph 7. 24. 8.

[The next paragraph is 7. 17.]

Contracts that are settled in cash or another financial assets

Contractual obligation to settle in cash or another financial assets

7. 17 It is apparent from the above IAS 32 definitions of liability and equity instrument that the critical feature that distinguishes a liability from an equity instrument is the existence of a contractual obligation to deliver cash or another financial asset to the holder or to exchange a financial asset or financial liability with the holder under conditions that are potentially unfavourable to the issuer. In other words, if the issuer does not have an unconditional right to avoid delivering cash or another financial asset to settle a contractual obligation, the obligation meets the definition of a liability, with the limited exception of puttable instruments and obligations arising on liquidation that meet the strict criteria set out from paragraph 7. 23.

7. 18 An instrument that an issuer may be obliged to settle in cash or another financial instrument is a liability regardless of the manner in which it otherwise could be settled. For example, the obligation to deliver cash may cover the basic obligation either to repay the principal or interest/dividends or both. Also, the obligation need not be discharged in cash or another financial asset; it could be discharged by transfer of other kinds of assets in certain circumstances (for example, a property) as illustrated in paragraph 7. 27 below. Indeed, in some circumstances it can even be settled by the issuer's own equity instruments. As long as the instrument involves a contractual unconditional obligation to deliver cash or another financial asset, that instrument (or component of the instrument) should be classified and accounted for as a liability (with the exception of certain puttable instruments and obligations arising on liquidation). Some examples of instruments that contain an obligation to transfer cash are considered below:

7.15.5　可回售工具和清算产生的义务的重分类在第 7.24.8 段及其下文中讨论。

［下一段为第 7.17 段。］

以现金或其他金融资产结算的合同

以现金或其他金融资产结算的合同义务

7.17　从上文 IAS 32 对负债和权益工具的定义中可以明显看出，将负债与权益工具区分开来的关键特征是存在向持有人支付现金或其他金融资产，或在对发行人潜在不利的条件下，与持有人交换金融资产或金融负债的合同义务。换言之，如果发行人不能无条件地避免支付现金或其他金融资产来结算合同义务，则该项义务符合负债的定义，一个有限例外为符合第 7.23 段及下文中所述严格标准的可回售金融工具和清算产生的义务。

7.18　发行人可能被要求以现金或其他金融工具结算的工具是一项负债，不论其是否可以通过其他方式结算。例如，支付现金的义务可能包括偿付本金或利息/股利或两者的基本义务。并且，该义务并不一定要以现金或其他金融资产来解除；如下文第 7.27 段所示，在某些特定条件下可以通过转移其他类型的资产（如不动产）的方式来解除。实际上，在某些情况下甚至可以用发行人自身的权益工具进行结算。只要金融工具含有无条件支付现金或其他金融资产的合同义务，该工具（或该工具的组成部分）即应被划分为负债并据以进行会计处理（某些特定的可回售金融工具和清算产生的义务除外）。以下对一些含有支付现金义务的工具示例进行了讨论：

Example 1 – 6% mandatorily redeemable preference shares with mandatory fixed dividends

Preference share is the name given to any share that has some preferential rights in relation to other classes of shares, particularly in relation to ordinary shares. These preferential rights are of great variety, but refer normally to the right to a *fixed dividend*, although they could also refer to the right on winding up to receive a fixed part of the *capital* or otherwise to participate in the distribution of the company's assets (shares with such rights are often known as participating preference shares).

In determining whether a mandatorily redeemable preference share is a financial liability or an equity instrument, it is necessary to examine the particular contractual rights attaching to the instrument's principal and return components.

The instrument, in this example, provides for mandatory periodic fixed dividend payments and mandatory redemption by the issuer for a fixed amount at a fixed future date. Since there is a contractual obligation to deliver cash (for both dividends and repayment of principal) to the shareholder that cannot be avoided, the instrument is a financial liability in its entirety.

Example 2 – Non-redeemable preference shares with mandatory fixed dividends

When preference shares are non-redeemable, the appropriate classification is determined by the other rights that attach to them. Classification is based on an assessment of the contractual arrangement's substance and the definitions of a financial liability and an equity instrument. [IAS 32 para AG 26].

It is necessary to examine the particular contractual rights attaching to the instrument's principal and return components. In this example, the shares are non-redeemable and thus the amount of the principal has equity characteristics, but the entity has a contractual obligation to pay dividends that provides the shareholders with a lender's return. This obligation is not negated if the entity is unable to pay the dividends because of lack of funds or

示例1——具有6%强制性固定股利的强制性可赎回优先股

优先股是任何与其他类型的股票（尤其是普通股）相比较具有某些优先权利的股票。优先权利种类繁多，通常情况下指收取*固定股利*的权利，虽然也可以指在清盘时收取固定比例的资本或参与公司资产分配的权利（具有此类权利的股票通常称为参与优先股）。

在确定一项强制性可赎回优先股是金融负债还是权益工具时，必须要检查附着在该工具上的本金和回报部分的具体合同权利。

本示例中的工具规定有强制性定期固定股利的支付且发行人在未来某一固定日期以固定的金额强制赎回。因为向股东支付现金（股利和本金的偿付）的合同义务不可避免，此项工具完全是一项金融负债。

示例2——具有强制性固定股利的不可赎回优先股

如果优先股是不可赎回的，应根据附着在其上的其他权利确定适当的分类。对优先股的分类应根据对合同实质的评估以及金融负债和权益工具的定义来进行。[IAS 32 AG 第26段]。

必须要检查附着在该工具本金和回报部分的特定合同权利。在本示例中，股票不可赎回，因此其本金金额具有权益的特征，但是主体有向股东以支付股利的形式提供贷款人回报的合同义务。即使主体因为资金短缺或可分配利润不充足而不能支付股利，也不能使本项义务无效。因此，支付股利的义务符合金融负债的定义。总体分类上来说，该股票可能是一项复合工具，并可能要求对各个组成部分单独地进行会计处理（参见下文第

insufficient distributable profits. Therefore, the obligation to pay the dividends meets the definition of a financial liability. The overall classification is that the shares may be a compound instrument, which may require each component to be accounted for separately (see further para 7.65 below). It would be a compound instrument if the coupon was initially set at a rate other than the prevailing market rate (an 'off-market' rate) or the terms specified payment of discretionary dividends in addition to the fixed coupon. If the coupon on the preference shares was set at market rates at the date of issue and there were no provisions for the payment of discretionary dividends, the entire instrument would be classified as a financial liability, because the stream of cash flows is in perpetuity.

Example 3 – Perpetual debt

'Perpetual' debt instruments (such as 'perpetual' bonds, debentures and capital notes) normally provide the holder with the contractual right to receive payments on account of interest at fixed dates extending into the indefinite future. The holder either has no right to receive a return of principal or a right to a return of principal under terms that make it very unlikely or very far in the future.

In this example, the instrument is perpetual and non-redeemable, but the entity has a contractual obligation to deliver cash in the form of interest payments to perpetuity. The obligation to pay interest meets the definition of a financial liability. For example, an entity may issue a financial instrument requiring it to make annual payments in perpetuity equal to a stated interest rate of 8% applied to a stated par or principal amount of C1m. Assuming 8% to be the market rate of interest for the instrument when issued, the instrument is classified as a liability in its entirety at the net present value of the interest payments. In this situation, the instrument's holder and issuer have a financial asset and a financial liability, respectively. [IAS 32 para AG 6].

Example 4 – Zero coupon bond

A zero coupon bond is an instrument where no interest is payable during the instrument's life and that is normally issued at a deep discount to the value at

7.65段）。如果票面利率最初并非是按照市场利率（一个“低于市场”的利率水平）设定或者条款规定除了固定的票面利率之外还需支付任意股利，则该股票为一项复合工具。如果优先股的票面利率是按照发行日的市场利率设定且没有支付任意股利的条款，则整个工具将被划分为金融负债，因为其现金流量是永续的。

示例3——永续债务

“永续”债务工具（如“永续”债券、信用债券和资本票据）通常赋予持有人按固定的日期在未来无限期收取利息的合同权利。持有人无权收回本金或有权收回本金但其条件使得收回不大可能或在极其遥远的未来才能收回。

在本示例中，该工具是永续和不可赎回的，但是主体有永远以利息的形式支付现金的合同义务。支付利息的义务符合金融负债的定义。例如，主体可能发行一项金融工具，该工具按面值或本金C100万元、以8%的利率按年永续支付利息。假设8%是该工具发行时的市场利率，则该工具整体以其利息付款的净现值被划分为一项负债。在这种情况下，该项工具的持有人和发行人分别拥有一项金融资产和一项金融负债。[IAS 32 AG第6段]。

示例4——零息债券

零息债券是一种在存续期内不用支付利息的工具，通常情况下以其赎回价值很低的折扣折价发行。虽然没有定期的强制利息付款，该项工具要由

which it will be redeemed. Although there are no mandatory periodic interest payments, the instrument provides for mandatory redemption by the issuer for a determinable amount at a fixed or determinable future date. Since there is a contractual obligation to deliver cash for the value at which the bond will be redeemed, the instrument is classified as a financial liability.

7.18.1 Paragraph 19 of IAS 32 states that a contractual obligation does not give rise to a financial liability if the entity has an unconditional right to avoid delivering cash or another financial asset in settlement of that obligation. Shareholders as a collective body make key decisions affecting an entity's financial position and performance over its life (for example regarding the distribution of dividends). Hence, their decisions have to be analysed from an accounting perspective. Shareholders can make decisions as part of the entity (as members of the entity's corporate governance structure) or they can be separate and distinct from the entity itself when making these decisions (as holders of a particular instrument). In light of the accounting principles under IAS 32, the role of shareholders – that is whether they are viewed as 'part of the entity' or as 'separate and distinct from the entity' – is critical in determining the classification of financial instruments where the entity's shareholders decide whether the entity delivers cash or another financial asset under those instruments.

7.18.2 Shares usually have voting rights leading to a two-fold role for a shareholder: (1) a holder of a financial instrument issued by the entity and (2) a member of the corporate governance structure of the entity. In other words, in addition to the contractual rights to cash flows (for example, dividends), the shareholder has a contractual right to participate in the decision-making process of the entity's governing body. Shareholder rights in relation to the entity's decision making process are generally exercised collectively in a general shareholder meeting (GSM). In many jurisdictions, corporate law stipulates that the GSM is one of the governing bodies of the entity and prescribes a specific process regarding how a GSM is to be held, who is entitled to propose an agenda item and how decisions are to be taken. In order to determine whether collective decisions of shareholders are decisions of the entity, it is necessary to determine whether these decisions are made as part of the entity's normal decision making process for similar transactions.

发行人在未来某一既定日期或某一可确定的日期以某一可确定的金额强制赎回。因为具有按债券赎回的价值支付现金的合同义务，所以该工具划分为一项金融负债。

7.18.1　IAS 32 第 19 段规定，如果主体能无条件地避免交付现金或其他金融资产以结算某项合同义务，则该项合同义务不是一项金融负债。股东们作为一个集体在主体存续期间制定影响主体财务状况和业绩的关键决策（如分配股利），因此需要从会计角度对其决策进行分析。股东们可以作为主体的一部分来作出决策（作为主体公司治理机构的成员），或者他们在作出决策时是独立的且区别于主体本身（作为某一工具的持有人）。根据 IAS 32 所规定的会计原则，在由主体的股东决定主体是否为这些工具交付现金或其他金融资产的情况下，股东的角色——即他们是被视为“主体的一部分”还是被视为“独立的且区别于主体”——对于确定金融工具的分类非常关键。

7.18.2　股票通常具有投票权使得股东具有双重角色：（1）主体所发行的金融工具的持有人和（2）主体公司治理机构的成员。换言之，除了对现金流（如股利）的合同权利以外，股东还具有参与主体管理机构决策制定过程的合同权利。股东与主体决策制定过程相关的权利一般都是通过股东大会（GSM）共同行使的。在很多管辖区内，公司法规定股东大会为主体的管理机构之一，并规定了召开股东大会的具体流程、谁有资格来提请议程项目以及如何作出决策。为确定股东们的集体决策是否是主体的决策，需要确定作出这些决策是否是作为主体在对类似交易的正常决策制定过程的一部分所作出。

7.18.3 If the decisions are made as part of the entity's normal decision-making process for similar transactions, the shareholders are considered to be part of the entity. For example, if an entity's equity instruments embody a contractual obligation to pay cash, but the shareholders can as part of their normal decision making process for this type of transaction refuse to make such a cash payment, the shares would be classified as equity. The entity in this case has an unconditional right to avoid the payment of cash. [IAS 32 para 19].

7.18.4 If the decisions are not made as part of the entity's normal decision making process for similar transactions (for example, one shareholder or a class of shareholders can make the decision and this is not the process the entity generally follows to make financial decisions), the shareholders are viewed as separate and distinct from the entity. For example, if a single shareholder can make a decision that creates a contractual obligation for the issuer to pay cash for the entity's shares and such decisions normally require a majority of the shareholder votes, these shares would be classified as a liability. The entity in this case does not have an unconditional right to avoid payment of cash. See paragraph 7.51 for more examples.

Restriction on the ability to satisfy contractual obligations

7.19 A restriction on the ability of an entity to satisfy a contractual obligation, such as lack of access to foreign currency or the need to obtain approval for payment from a regulatory authority, does not negate the entity's contractual obligation or the holder's contractual right under the instrument. [IAS 32 para 19(a)]. For example, an obligation is not negated even if the instrument's terms are such that the amount payable on redemption is dependent on the company having sufficient distributable profits or reserves. A type of income bond where the bond is not redeemable by the issuer, but interest is payable only in the event that the issuer has sufficient distributable profits, is such an instrument. The bond would be classified as a liability because of the obligation to pay interest. The fact that the obligation to pay is dependent on the existence of profits makes the obligation contingent, but it does not remove the obligation (see further chapter 4).

7.18.3 如果决策是作为主体在对类似交易的正常决策制定过程的一部分所作出，则股东被视为主体的一部分。例如，如果主体的权益工具包括支付现金的合同义务，但是股东可以通过对此类交易的正常决策制定过程拒绝现金支付，那么这些股票应该划分为权益。在这种情况下，主体有无条件避免现金支付的权利。[IAS 32 第 19 段]。

7.18.4 如果决策不是作为主体在对类似交易的正常决策制定过程的一部分所作出（例如，某位股东或某一类股东可以作出决策，而且这并不是主体在制定财务决策时所一般遵循的流程），那么股东被视为独立的且区别于主体。例如，如果某一位股东能够作出令发行人为其股票支付现金的合同义务的决定，且该决定通常需要半数以上的股东投票赞成，那么这些股票应该划分为负债。在这种情况下，主体不具有无条件避免现金支付的权利。更多示例参见第 7.51 段。

对履行合同义务能力的限制

7.19 存在对主体履行合同义务的能力的限制，如不能获得外币或需要得到有关监管部门的批准才能支付等，并不能否定在该金融工具中主体所承担的合同义务或持有人所享有的合同权利。[IAS 32 第 19（a）段]。例如，即使是工具的条款规定在赎回时应支付的金额取决于公司是否具有充足的可分配利润或准备时，也不能取消此项义务。有一种收入债券就是这种工具，该债券不能由发行人赎回，利息只在发行人具有充足的可分配利润时方可支付。因为有支付利息的义务，该债券应该划分为一项负债。付款义务取决于是否具有利润的事实使得该项义务成为或有义务，但是并不能解除该项义务（参见第 4 章）。

Puttable instruments and obligations arising on liquidation

7.20 Other than those instruments that meet the criteria set out from paragraph 7.24.5 below, financial instruments that give the holder the right to put them back to the issuer for cash or another financial asset (a 'puttable instrument') are financial liabilities. For example, an entity that issues a preference share that is puttable by the holder at some future date would recognise a financial liability. The holder has a put option that requires the issuer to redeem the instrument for cash or another financial asset at some future date. Since the existence of an option for the holder to put the instrument back to the issuer for cash or another financial asset means that the issuer does not have an unconditional right to avoid delivering cash or cash equivalent, the puttable instrument meets the definition of a financial liability. This is so whether or not the amount of cash or other financial assets to be delivered to the holder is fixed. For example it may be determined on the basis of an index or other item that has the potential to increase or decrease the final amount payable. [IAS 32 para 18(b)]. In these situations, from the issuer's perspective, the embedded put option is a written option that may need to be separated from the host contract, unless the whole instrument is accounted for at fair value through profit or loss. Embedded derivatives are discussed in chapter 5. Puttable instruments can also arise in finite life entities, as noted in the example below.

Example – Obligation arising on the liquidation of the issuer

A limited partnership has a finite life of 25 years. The partnership's equity will be redeemed at the end of its term.

In this situation, unless the criteria in paragraph 7.24.5 are met, the partnership's equity will be presented as a liability because the amount is payable only on liquidation and liquidation is certain (that is, not contingent) as the entity has a finite life.

Even where a partnership has an indefinite life, if a partner's equity interest is redeemable upon a partner's death, that partner's equity interest should be classified as a liability, unless the criteria applicable to puttable financial instruments in paragraph 7.24.5 are met. This is because the redemption is

可回售金融工具和清算产生的义务

7.20 除了那些符合第 7.24.5 段及下文规定标准的工具之外，如果一项金融工具的持有人有权将其卖回给发行人以获取现金或其他金融资产（“可回售工具”），则该金融工具是一项金融负债。例如，主体发行了一种可由持有人在未来某一日期卖回的优先股，则其应该确认一项金融负债。持有人具有一项看跌期权，要求发行人在未来某一日期以现金或其他金融资产赎回该项工具。持有人有权将该工具卖回给发行人以换取现金或其他金融资产，这就意味着发行人没有无条件避免交付现金或现金等价物的权利，因此这一可回售工具符合金融负债的定义。无论需要交付给持有人的现金或其他金融资产的金额是否固定，这个结论不会改变。例如该金额可能取决于可能导致最终应付金额发生增减的某一指数或其他事项［IAS 32 第 18（b）段］。在这些情况下，从发行人的角度来看，除非整个工具按照以公允价值计量且变动计入损益进行会计处理，其嵌入看跌期权是一项可能需要从主合同中分离出的签出期权。对嵌入衍生工具的讨论参见第 5 章。如下例所示，约定经营期限的主体也可能产生可回售工具。

示例——因发行人清算而产生的义务

某有限合伙关系经营期限为 25 年。在到期日该合伙关系的权益将被赎回。

在这种情况下，除非符合第 7.24.5 段中所述的条件，该合伙关系的权益将被列报为一项负债，因为权益只在清算时支付，而因为该主体有约定的经营期限，清算是确定的（即非或有事项）。

即使在合伙关系没有确定的经营期限的情况下，除非符合第 7.24.5 段中所述的适用于可回售金融工具的各条件，如某一合伙人的权益在某一合伙人死亡之时可以被赎回，该合伙人的权益也应划分为一项负债。这是因为虽然合伙关系本身没有清算，但是这种赎回基于一种肯定会发生的事

based on an event that is certain to occur, although the partnership itself is not being liquidated.

7.21 Financial instruments that would be classified as equity if the holders did not have the right to request redemption are equity if the entity has the unconditional right to refuse redemption of the instrument. This is the case even if, in practice, the entity rarely does refuse a holder's request for redemption or if the unconditional right to refuse redemption arises from local law, regulation or the entity's governing charter rather than the terms of the instrument itself. Sometimes redemption is prohibited only if conditions, such as liquidity constraints, are met (or not met). In such cases, the entity still has an obligation in respect of the holder's redemption rights, as the conditions merely defer the payment of a liability already incurred. Alternatively, an unconditional prohibition may be partial. For example, a co-operative entity may be prohibited from redeeming its members' shares if redemption would cause the number of shares to fall below a specified level. In such circumstances, only members' shares in excess of the prohibition against redemption are liabilities. The number of shares or the amount of paid-in capital subject to a redemption prohibition may change over time. Such a change in the redemption prohibition leads to a transfer between financial liabilities and equity. The amount, timing and reason for the transfer should be separately disclosed. [IFRIC 2 paras 5-13].

[The next paragraph is 7.23.]

7.23 In February 2008 the IASB published 'Amendments to IAS 32 and IAS 1, 'Puttable financial instruments and obligations arising on liquidation' (the amendment). Some financial instruments, commonly issued by open-ended mutual funds, unit trusts, partnerships and some co-operative entities, allow the holder to 'put' the instrument – that is, require the issuer to redeem the instrument for cash or another financial asset – on terms that give the holder an equity-like return. Before the amendment, such financial instruments were classified as financial liabilities rather than equity, because of the contractual obligation for the issuer to deliver cash if the put is exercised by the holder, as discussed above.

7.24 The amendment introduces a limited exception to this rule. It requires financial instruments that would otherwise meet the definition of a financial liability

件。

7.21　如果主体拥有无条件拒绝赎回金融工具的权利，而持有人亦没有要求赎回的权利，该金融工具应该被划分为权益。在实务中，即使主体很少拒绝持有人的赎回要求，或这种无条件拒绝赎回的权利源于当地法律、法规或主体管理章程而非该工具本身的条款时也是如此。有的时候，仅在满足（或不满足）特定条件下（如流动性限制），赎回是被禁止的。在这种情况下，主体仍负有满足持有人赎回权的义务，因为这些条件仅仅是延迟已经发生债务的付款。或者，无条件禁止可能是部分的。例如，如果赎回将导致股份的数量降至特定水平之下，则禁止合作主体赎回成员股份。在这种情况下，成员股份超过禁止赎回的部分是一项负债。受到禁止赎回约束的股份数量或实收资本金额可能会随时间而变动。这种变动将导致金融负债和权益之间的划转。对划转的金额、时间和原因应进行单独披露。[IFRIC 2 第5-13 段]。

[下一段为第 7.23 段。]

7.23　IASB 于 2008 年 2 月发布了《对 IAS 32 和 IAS 1 的修订——可回售金融工具和清算产生的义务》（“修订”）。一些通常由开放型共同基金、信托公司、合伙关系和一些合作主体所发行的金融工具，允许持有人按照与权益类似回报的条件“卖回”工具——即，要求发行人以现金或其他金融资产赎回该工具。在此修订之前，这种金融工具被划分为金融负债而不是权益，因为如上所述，如果持有人行权，发行人就有交付现金的合同义务。

7.24　该修订中引入了限定在一定范围内的例外规定。它要求在符合第 7.24.5 段中所规定的某些特定严格条件的情况下，将本符合金融负债定义的

to be classified as equity where certain strict criteria are met, as set out in paragraph 7.24.5. Those instruments addressed by the amendment are:

- Puttable financial instruments. A puttable instrument is defined as a financial instrument that gives the holder the right to put the instrument back to the issuer for cash or another financial asset or is automatically put back to the issuer on the occurrence of an uncertain future event or the death or retirement of the instrument holder. [IAS 32 para 11].

- Instruments, or components of instruments, that impose on the entity an obligation to deliver to another party a *pro rata* share of the entity's net assets only on liquidation. The obligation arises because liquidation is either certain to occur (such as in limited life entities) or is uncertain to occur but is at the option of the instrument holder. [IAS 32 para 16C].

7.24.1 The amendment's scope is limited to non-derivative contracts. Derivative contracts (such as warrants) to be settled by the issue of a fixed number of financial instruments classified as equity under the amendment for a fixed amount of cash or other financial asset cannot be equity themselves. [IAS 32 para 11].

7.24.2 The amendment should not be used by analogy. [IAS 32 para 96B]. Furthermore, the classification of instruments under this exception should be restricted to the accounting for such an instrument under IAS 32, IAS 39, IFRS 7 and IAS 1. The instruments should not be considered an equity instrument under other guidance, in particular IFRS 2, 'Share-based payments'. [IAS 32 para 96C].

7.24.3 Entities should apply the amendment for accounting periods beginning on or after 1 January 2009. The amendment is applied retrospectively if applicable.

7.24.4 The concurrent amendment to IAS 1 requires disclosures about financial instruments classified as equity as a result of the amendment to IAS 32. Detail about these disclosures is given in chapter 23 of the IFRS Manual of Accounting.

金融工具划分为权益。该修订所涉及的工具包括：

- 可回售金融工具。可回售工具定义为给予持有人将该工具卖回给发行人以换取现金或其他金融资产，或在某些未来不确定性事件发生时或在工具持有人死亡或退休时自动卖回给发行人的权利的金融工具。[IAS 32 第 11 段]。

- 仅在清算时才会使主体有按*比例*向另一方交付该主体净资产的义务的工具或工具的组成部分。这种义务之所以形成是因为清算肯定会发生（如约定经营期限的主体）或虽然清算不一定会发生但工具持有人有权进行清算。[IAS 32 第 16C 段]。

7.24.1　该修订的范围仅限于非衍生工具合同。通过发行固定数量的按该修订可被划分为权益的金融工具以换取固定金额的现金或其他金融资产的衍生工具合同（如认股权证）本身不能作为权益。[IAS 32 第 11 段]。

7.24.2　该修订不可被类推。[IAS 32 第 96B 段]。此外，根据此项例外对工具进行分类时应仅限于按照 IAS 32、IAS 39、IFRS 7 和 IAS 1 对这种工具进行会计处理时。在运用其他指南时，尤其是《国际财务报告准则第 2 号——以股份为基础的支付》时，不能将这种工具视为权益工具。[IAS 32 第 96C 段]。

7.24.3　主体应从起始日在 2009 年 1 月 1 日或之后的会计期间采用该修订。如果适用，应追溯调整。

7.24.4　对 IAS 1 的并行修订要求对因 IAS 32 的修订而被划分为权益的金融工具进行披露。在《国际财务报告准则实务指引》第 23 章中对该披露要求进行了详细介绍。

Criteria to be classified as equity

7.24.5 A non-derivative puttable instrument or obligation on liquidation (for example, arising in a limited life entity) is classified as equity only if all of the following criteria are met:

Criteria	Comment
1 The financial instrument is in the most subordinated class of instruments. That is, it:	The instrument's claim on liquidation is assessed as if the entity were to liquidate on the date of classification. [IAS 32 para AG14B].
■ has no priority over other claims to the entity's assets on liquidation; and	If an entity has two equally subordinated classes of instrument with different terms, neither can be classified as equity under the amendment.
■ does not need to be converted to another instrument before it is in the most subordinated class. [IAS 32 paras 16A(b) and 16C(b)].	Additionally, if an open-ended investment fund has a small class of non-redeemable voting management shares that are the most subordinated, and a large class of non-voting investor shares that are puttable at fair value at the option of the holder, the investor shares are not the most subordinated class of instrument. Therefore, the non-voting investor shares cannot be classified as equity, regardless of the value or number of the management shares.
2 For puttable instruments, all instruments in its class should have identical features. [IAS 32 para 16A(c)].	To be identical, all puttable instruments in a class should:

权益划分标准

7.24.5　只有满足以下所有条件，非衍生可回售工具或清算产生的义务（例如产生于某一具有约定经营期限的主体）才可以划分为权益：

条件	备注
1. 该金融工具属于最次级的工具。即：	该工具在清算时的清偿权是假设主体在分类日即清算的情况下评估的。[IAS 32 AG 第 14B 段]。
■ 清算时相比其他对主体资产的清偿权没有优先；且	如果主体拥有级别相等但条款不同的两类次级工具，根据该修订两者均不能划分为权益。
■ 在属于最次级的工具之前不需要转换为另一种工具。[IAS 32 第 16A(b) 和 16C(b)段]。	此外，如果一个开放型投资基金有一小类不可赎回的、有表决权的管理股份是最次级的，以及一大类持有人有权按照公允价值卖回的无表决权的投资人股票，则这些投资人股票不是最次级的工具。无论管理股票的价值或数量有多少，无表决权的投资人股票均不能划分为权益。
2. 对于可回售工具而言，所有此类工具均应具有完全相同的特征。[IAS 32 第 16A(c)段]。	如要完全相同，所有该类的可回售工具均应：

Con.

Criteria	Comment
For obligations arising on liquidation, only the obligation on liquidation should be identical for all instruments in that class. [IAS 32 para 16C(c)].	■ have the same formula or other method to calculate the redemption price; ■ rank equally on liquidation; ■ have identical voting rights; and ■ have all other features identical (for example, calls, management fees, currency of denomination). For example, an open-ended fund has two sub-funds – sub-fund A and sub-fund B – and two classes of puttable share – A shares and B shares – whose returns are based on the performance of sub-funds A and B respectively. The A and B shares are both the most subordinated class of shares in the fund's consolidated financial statements. However, neither are equity, as they do not have identical features because they carry rights to different sub-funds.
3 The instrument should entitle the holder to a *pro rata* share of the entity's net assets on liquidation. [IAS 32 paras 16A(a) and 16C(a)].	An instrument with a preferential right on liquidation is not an instrument with an entitlement to a *pro rata* share of the entity's net assets. So if a puttable instrument has a right to a fixed dividend on liquidation in addition to a share of the entity's net assets, but the other instruments in the class do not have the same right on liquidation, none of the shares in that class are equity. [IAS 32 para AG14C].
4 For puttable instruments only, the total expected cash flows attributable to the instrument over the instrument's life should be based substantially on the profit or loss, the change in recognised	Profit or loss and the change in recognised net assets should be measured in accordance with the relevant IFRSs and not any other GAAP. [IAS 32 para AG14E]. Cash flows attributable to the instrument over

续表

条件	备注
对清算产生的义务而言，该类所有工具只需清算义务完全相同即可。[IAS 32 第 16C(c) 段]。	■ 在计算赎回价格时采用相同的公式或其他方法； ■ 在清算时级别相等； ■ 具有相同的表决权； ■ 所有其他的特征都相同（如看涨期权、管理费、计价货币）。 例如，一个开放型基金有两个子基金，子基金 A 和子基金 B，以及两类可回售股份，股份 A 和股份 B，其回报分别根据子基金 A 和子基金 B 的业绩而定。在基金的合并财务报表里，股份 A 和股份 B 都是最次级的股份。但是，两者均不是权益，因为它们拥有不同子基金的权利而不具备完全相同的特征。
3. 该项工具应使持有人在清算时按比例获得该主体净资产。[IAS 32 第 16A(a) 和 16C(a)段]。	清算时具有优先权的工具不是有权按*比例*获得主体净资产的工具。所以，如果一个可回售工具在清算时除了有权获得主体净资产之外还有权获得固定股利，而同类的其他工具在清算时不具有相同的权利，那么该类别的股份均不属于权益。[IAS 32 AG 第 14C 段]。
4. 仅就可回售工具而言，在其存续期内预计归属于该工具的总现金流应在很大程度上取决于该工具存续期内主体的损益、已确认净资产的变动、或公允价值的变化(不包括任何由该工具本身所导致	损益及已确认净资产的变动应按照相关的国际财务报告准则来计量，而非其他任何一般公认会计准则。[IAS 32 AG 第 14E 段]。 在其存续期内归属于该工具的现金流应取

Con.

Criteria	Comment
net assets, or the change in the fair value of entity over the instrument's life (excluding any effects of the instrument). [IAS 32 para 16A(e)].	its life should be based on the profit or loss or change in the entity's net assets as a whole, not just part of the entity's business. This condition would be met where the put is for cash equivalent to the entity's: ■ fair value; ■ IFRS book value of assets; or ■ approximation to fair value using a formula based on net profit, for example, multiples of EBITDA, provided that the formula (for example, the multiple used) is reviewed regularly to ensure that it results in an approximate of fair value.
5 There are no other instruments that: ■ substantially restrict or fix the return earned by the instrument holder; and ■ have cash flows based substantially on profit or loss; the change in recognised net assets; or the change in the fair value of the entity over the instrument's life (excluding any effects of the instrument). [IAS 32 paras 16B and 16D].	If an instrument provides a fixed or limited return because of the interaction with other instruments issued by the entity (for example, another instrument is participating in the share of net assets), it is not equity. Non-financial contracts with the holder of the instrument should be ignored if those contracts have similar terms and conditions to an equivalent contract that might occur between a non-instrument holder and the entity. However, if the entity cannot determine that the non-financial contract with the puttable instrument holder is similar to an equivalent contract that might occur between a non-instrument holder and the issuing entity, it should not classify the puttable instrument as an equity instrument. Examples of contracts entered into on normal commercial terms with unrelated parties that are unlikely to prevent puttable instruments from being classified as equity include:

续表

条件	备注
的影响)。[IAS 32 第 16A(e)段]。	决于主体整体的损益或净资产变化,而非主体业务的一部分。 在回售义务是获取主体如下项目的等价现金的情况下,此条件即满足: ■ 公允价值; ■ 资产在国际财务报告准则下的账面价值;或 ■ 采用一种基于净利润的公式所得的公允价值近似值,例如扣除利息、税项、折旧和摊销之前的盈利(EBITDA)的倍数,但前提条件是需定期对该公式(如所使用的倍数)进行审核以确保其能得到公允价值近似值。
5. 没有其他符合下述情况的工具: ■ 能很大程度上限制或固定工具持有人所获得的回报;和 ■ 现金流在很大程度上取决于该工具存续期内主体的损益、已确认净资产的变动、或公允价值的变化(不包括任何由该工具本身所导致的影响)。 [IAS 32 第 16B 和 16D 段]。	如果一项工具因为与主体所发行的其他工具之间的相互作用而提供固定或有限的回报(例如另一工具参与净资产分配),则不是权益。 对于与工具持有人所签订的非金融合同,如果其条款和条件与由非工具持有人和主体签订的同等合同类似,则可以忽略该非金融合同。但是,如果主体不能够判定与可回售工具持有人所签订的非金融合同是否与某非工具持有人和主体可能签订的同等合同类似,则不应将该可回售工具划分为权益工具。 不太可能妨碍可回售工具划分为权益、与非关联方按照正常商务条款签订的合同例子包括:

Con.

	Criteria	Comment
		■ Instruments with cash flows substantially based on individual assets of the entity or on a percentage of revenue, such as commission arrangements. ■ Employee profit-related performance bonuses. ■ Contracts requiring the payment of an insignificant percentage of profit for services rendered or goods provided. [IAS 32 para AG14J].
6	For puttable instruments only, the instrument should not contain any liability features, other than the put itself. [IAS 32 para 16A(d)].	For instruments containing obligations arising on liquidation there is no requirement for there to be no other contractual obligations, so the instrument may be compound (for example, a compound instrument where the liability component is extinguished over the instrument's life). However, a puttable instrument cannot have another contractual obligation apart from the put itself and, hence, can never be a compound instrument. For example, a puttable financial instrument that contains an obligation to either: ■ distribute current period profits on the demand of each holder based on a *pro rata* share of the entity's profits; or ■ distribute all taxable income as a requirement of the entity's constitution cannot be classed as an equity instrument.

续表

条件	备注
	■ 基本上依据主体单项资产或收入百分比的现金流的工具,例如佣金协议。 ■ 与利润相关的员工业绩奖。 ■ 所提供的服务或货物收取的服务费占利润比例不重大的合同。 [IAS 32 AG 第 14J 段]。
6. 仅对于可回售工具而言，除了回售义务本身之外，工具不应包括任何负债特征。[IAS 32 第 16A(d)段]。	对于含有因清算产生的义务的工具而言，并没有要求其不能具有其他合同义务，因此这种工具可能是复合工具（例如，其债务部分在工具存续期内逐渐消除的复合工具)。但是可回售工具除了回售义务外不能有其他的合同义务，因此，它永远不会是复合工具。 例如某项可回售金融工具具有下述义务: ■ 应各个持有人的要求按*比例*分配主体当期利润；或 ■ 应主体章程的要求分配所有应税所得 则其不能被划分为权益工具。

Transactions entered into by an instrument holder other than as owner of the entity

7.24.6 In certain situations the holder of a puttable instrument may enter into transactions with the entity in a role other than that of an owner. For example, a partner in a partnership may also provide management services to the entity or be remunerated for providing a financial guarantee for the partnership's debts. In other cases, rebates are given to the instrument holders based on their services rendered or business generated during the current and previous years. Such cash flows and contractual terms and conditions should be disregarded for the purposes of determining the classification of an instrument under all the criteria above, as long as they are similar to an equivalent transaction that might occur between a non-instrument holder and the issuing entity, that is, at arm's length. [IAS 32 para AG14I]. This is because such cash flows and contractual features are separate and distinct from the cash flows and contractual features of the puttable financial instrument.

Impact on consolidation

7.24.7 Instruments issued by a subsidiary that meet the criteria outlined above, and are, therefore, within the scope of the amendment at a separate or individual financial statements level, are not considered to be the most subordinated class from the group's perspective. [IAS 32 para BC 48]. Furthermore, the total expected cash flows over the life of a puttable financial instrument issued by a subsidiary will not be substantially based on the profit or loss or change in net assets of the whole group, but rather will be a subset of that group, being that of the subsidiary. Consequently, a puttable non-controlling interest is always classified as a liability on consolidation, even if it is classified as an equity interest in the subsidiary's own financial statements. [IAS 32 para AG 29A].

7.24.7.1 Instruments issued by the parent that meet the criteria outlined above, and are, therefore, within the scope of the amendment at a separate financial statements level, in most cases will continue to be classified as equity at a

工具持有人并非以权益所有人身份所签订的交易

7.24.6　在某些特定情况下，可回售工具的持有人可能以非所有人的角色与主体进行交易。例如，合伙关系的合伙人还可能为主体提供管理服务或为合伙关系的债务提供财务担保而获得酬劳。在其他情况下，可能根据工具持有人在当年或之前年度所提供的服务或所进行的业务向其提供回扣。在根据上文所述所有条件确定工具的分类时，只要这种回扣的现金流及合同条款和条件与非工具持有人和发行主体之间可能发生的同等交易类似，即是公平交易时，应不予以考虑。[IAS 32 AG 第 14I 段]。这是因为这种现金流和合同特征是独立且有别于可回售金融工具的现金流和合同特征的。

对合并的影响

7.24.7　对于由子公司发行的符合上文所述条件，因而在单独或个别的财务报表层面适用于该修订的工具而言，从集团的角度来看不应被视为最次级类别。[IAS 32 BC 第 48 段]。此外，由子公司发行的可回售金融工具在其存续期内的总预计现金流将不是在很大程度上取决于整个集团的损益或净资产的变动，而是取决于该集团的一个子集，即其属于该子公司的那部分。因此，即使在子公司自己的财务报表中被划分为权益，可回售非控制性权益在合并时总是被划分为负债。[IAS 32 AG 第 29A 段]。

7.24.7.1　由母公司发行的符合上文所述条件的工具，在单独财务报表层面是在此修订范围内，大多数情况下其在合并报表层面也将继续被划分为权益。集团层面反映出的任何非控制性权益通常不满足 IAS 32 第 16B 段的条件，因

consolidated financial statements level. Any non-controlling interest reflected at the group level does not generally meet the conditions in paragraph 16B of IAS 32 and, therefore, will generally not prevent such parent puttable instruments from being classified as equity on consolidation. This is because:

- cash flows attributable to the non-controlling interest are based on a subset of the consolidated net assets, that is, net assets of the respective subsidiary, rather than consolidated net assets; and
- in most cases the non-controlling interest will not have the effect of substantially restricting or fixing the residual return attributable to holders of the parent's puttable instruments.

[IAS 32 paras 16B, AG14J(a)].

7.24.7.2 If, however, the non-controlling interest meets the conditions in paragraph 16B of IAS 32 the parent's puttable instruments that meet the conditions for equity classification at a separate financial statements level are classified as a liability on consolidation. This will be the case when:

- the subsidiary's net assets represent substantially all of the consolidated net assets such that the cash flows attributable to the non-controlling interest are substantially based on consolidated net assets; and
- the non-controlling interest in the respective subsidiary is so significant that combined with the condition above it has the effect of substantially restricting or fixing the residual return attributable to holders of the parent's puttable instruments.

Judgement is applied to determine whether the subsidiary's net assets and the non-controlling interest in the respective subsidiary are so significant that the parent's puttable instruments classified as equity at a separate financial statements level are classified as a liability on consolidation.

7.24.7.3 The evaluation of instruments, or components of instruments, that impose on the entity an obligation to deliver to another party a *pro rata* share of the net assets of the entity only on liquidation will follow the criteria above as the requirements of paragraph 16D of IAS 32 are consistent with paragraph 16B.

此，通常不会妨碍将那些母公司的可回售工具在合并时划分为权益工具。这是因为：

■ 属于非控制性权益的现金流是基于合并净资产的一个子集，即各个子公司的净资产，而非合并净资产；并且

■ 在大多数情况下非控制性权益不会在很大程度上限制或固定母公司可回售工具持有人所属的剩余回报。

[IAS 32 第 16B 段,AG 第 14J(a)段]。

7.24.7.2 但是，如果非控制性权益满足了 IAS 32 第 16B 段的条件，在母公司单独财务报表层面满足权益分类条件的可回售工具在合并时应划分为负债。在下述情况下即如此：

■ 子公司的净资产代表了几乎所有的合并净资产，以至于非控制性权益所属的现金流几乎全部基于合并净资产。

■ 相关子公司的非控制性权益非常重大，在和以上条件综合在一起时，它会在很大程度上限制或固定母公司可回售工具持有人所属的剩余回报。

在确定子公司的净资产和相关子公司的非控制性权益是否非常重大到以至于母公司将单独财务报表层面分类为权益的可回售工具在合并时分类为负债时，要进行判断。

7.24.7.3 由于 IAS 32 第 16D 段的要求和第 16B 段是一致的，对使主体仅在清算时有义务向另一方按*比例*交付净资产的工具或工具的组成部分的评估将遵从上述条件。

Reclassification of puttable instruments and obligations arising on liquidation

7.24.8 Instruments will be in the scope of the amendment from the date when the instrument has all the features and meets the criteria set out above. This may not occur at the date of issue of the instrument, so it is necessary to reassess the classification if there is a change in relevant circumstances. For example, an entity may issue or redeem other instruments that change the most subordinated class of shares, which may require reclassification of some financial instruments from debt to equity or vice versa. [IAS 32 para 16E]. See chapter 23 of the IFRS Manual of Accounting for specific disclosure requirements on such a reclassification.

7.24.9 An entity should reclassify a financial instrument when appropriate, as follows:

- Reclassify an equity instrument to a financial liability from the date the instrument ceases to have all the features required by the amendment. The financial liability is measured at the instrument's fair value at the date of reclassification. Any difference between the carrying value of the equity instrument and liability's fair value on the date of reclassification is recognised in equity.
- Reclassify a financial liability as equity from the date the instrument has all the features required by the amendment. The equity instrument should be measured at the carrying value of the financial liability at the date of reclassification. [IAS 32 para 16F].

Own share buy-back programmes

7.25 During certain times of the year (for example, before an entity releases its results), listed companies are prohibited by certain local listing rules from buying their own shares in the market. The local listing rules may permit other arrangements to be entered into with independent third parties that result in the listed entity's shares being purchased on behalf of the listed entity for example, by a bank. The contract requires the company to buy the shares the bank has purchased immediately after the prohibition period. For further details on own share buy-back programmes see chapter 23 of the IFRS Manual of Accounting.

可回售金融工具和清算产生的义务的重分类

7.24.8　当工具具有所有特征且符合上述规定条件之日起开始适用该修订。这种情况可能在工具发行日尚未发生，所以如果相关情况发生变化则需要对其分类进行重新评估。例如，主体可能发行或赎回其他工具使最次级股份发生变更，这可能会要求将某些金融工具从负债重分类为权益，反之亦然。[IAS 32 第 16E 段]。有关对这种重分类的具体披露要求，请参见《国际财务报告准则实务指引》第 23 章。

7.24.9　在适当情况下主体应对金融工具进行重分类，具体如下：

- 在某项权益工具不再具有该修订所要求的所有特征之日起将该权益工具重分类为金融负债。金融负债应在重分类之日按照该工具的公允价值进行计量。在重分类之日权益工具的账面价值和负债的公允价值之间的任何差额均确认为权益。

- 从工具具有该修订所要求的所有特征之日起将金融负债重分类为一项权益。在重分类之日应按照金融负债的账面价值对权益工具进行计量。[IAS 32 第 16F 段]。

自身股票赎回计划

7.25　在一年中的某些特定时间（例如，在主体公布其经营结果之前），某些当地上市规则会禁止上市公司在市场上购买其自身股票。当地上市规则可能会允许上市公司与独立第三方，如银行，签订其他协议，从而代上市主体购买其股票。合同要求公司在禁买期结束之后立即购买银行所购买的股票。有关自身股票赎回计划的详细信息，请参见《国际财务报告准则实务指引》第 23 章。

7.26 Own share buy-back programmes contain an obligation for an entity to purchase its own equity instruments for cash or another financial asset from the third party. This, therefore, gives rise to a financial liability for the present value of the redemption amount (for example, the present value of the forward repurchase price, option exercise price or other redemption amount). [IAS 32 para 23].

Absence of explicit obligations

7.27 IAS 32 states that the obligation to deliver cash or another financial asset need not be explicitly stated in the instrument. It may be established indirectly. However, the indirect obligation must be established through the terms and conditions of the financial instrument. [IAS 32 para 20]. IAS 32 clarifies the notion that an instrument may establish an obligation indirectly through its terms and conditions in two specific situations that are considered below.

7.28 First, a financial instrument may contain a non-financial obligation that must be settled if, and only if, the entity fails to make distributions or to redeem the instrument. If the entity can avoid a transfer of cash or another financial asset only by settling the non-financial obligation, the financial instrument is a financial liability. [IAS 32 para 20(a)].

Example – Settlement of obligation by transfer of non-cash asset

A property company raises C150m for constructing a number of properties. The loan has a maturity period of 5 years. The loan agreement stipulates that the property company must transfer to the lender one of its investment properties if it is unable to settle the loan for cash at maturity.

In this agreement, if the property company is unable to settle the loan at maturity for cash, it is obliged to settle the obligation by transferring to the lender one of its other investment properties that, at the time of the settlement, may well be in excess of C150m. Therefore, an indirect financial obligation arises as the agreement contains a non-financial obligation that can be avoided only by making a transfer of cash. Hence, it is a financial liability.

7.26　自身股票赎回计划包括主体以现金或其他金融资产从第三方购买其自身权益工具的义务。因此，这将导致按照赎回金额现值（例如，远期回购价格的现值、期权行权价格或其他赎回金额）确认一项金融负债。[IAS 32 第 23 段]。

明确义务的缺失

7.27　IAS 32 规定交付现金或其他金融资产的义务无需在工具中明确标明，可以通过间接的方式形成。但是，这种间接义务必须由该金融工具的条款和条件来确立。[IAS 32 第 20 段]。IAS 32 通过如下所述两种具体情况，对工具可以通过其条款和条件间接形成义务的概念进行了阐述。

7.28　首先，一项金融工具中可能包括一项非金融义务，这项义务当且仅当主体不能进行股利分配或赎回该工具时必须被履行。如果主体只能以履行非金融义务来避免交付现金或其他金融资产，则该金融工具是一项金融负债。[IAS 32 第20(a)段]。

示例——通过交付非现金资产来结算义务

一家房地产公司为建造数项不动产筹集了 C1.5 亿元的资金。此贷款的期限为 5 年，且贷款协议规定，如果该房地产公司到期不能用现金清偿贷款，则必须向贷方交付其某处投资物业。

在此协议中，如果该房地产公司到期不能用现金清偿贷款，则其有义务向贷方交付其某处投资物业，该投资物业在结算时很可能价值远大于 C1.5 亿元。因此就产生了一项间接金融义务，因为该协议包括一项只能通过交付现金来避免的非金融义务。因此，这是一项金融负债。

7.29 The second situation is where a financial instrument is a financial liability if it provides that on settlement the entity will deliver either:

- cash or another financial asset; or
- its own shares whose value is determined to exceed substantially the value of the cash or other financial asset.

Although the entity does not have an explicit contractual obligation to deliver cash or another financial asset, the value of the share settlement alternative is such that the entity will have little choice but to redeem the obligation in cash. In any event, the holder has been guaranteed, in substance, receipt of an amount that is at least equal to the cash settlement option. Hence, the instrument is a financial liability.

[IAS 32 para 20(b)].

7.30 The IFRIC clarified in March 2006 that where an instrument (the 'base' instrument) contains a clause that requires cash or other financial assets to be delivered on that base instrument if there is a contractual obligation to make payment on another (the 'linked') instrument, then the inclusion of this linker clause would establish an indirect obligation to deliver cash or another financial assets on the base instrument. As a result the IFRIC agreed that the base instrument would be classified as a financial liability.

Example – Financial instrument ('base' instrument) linked to another (the 'linked') instrument

An entity issues non-redeemable callable preference shares (the 'base' instrument) with dividends that must be paid if interest is paid on another (the 'linked') instrument. The issuer must pay the interest on the 'linked' instrument that is also perpetual.

In this example, the linkage to the linked instrument, on which there is a contractual obligation to pay interest, results in an indirect contractual obligation to pay dividends on the base instrument. If the linked instrument is callable by the issuer at any time, the issuer could avoid paying the dividends on the base instrument. Therefore, until the linked instrument is called, a contractual obligation to pay dividends on the base instrument exists. If the

7.29 第二种情况是如果一项金融工具在结算时主体将交付：

- 现金或其他金融资产；或
- 主体自身的股票，且这些股票的价值显著地超出现金或其他金融资产的价值，则该金融工具是一项金融负债。

尽管主体没有明确地承担交付现金或其他金融资产的合同义务，但是可选的股票结算方式对主体如此不利，因而主体没有什么选择而只能使用现金清偿该项义务。在任何情况下，实质上持有人可以确保至少获得以现金结算所能得到的金额。因此，该工具是一项金融负债。

[IAS 32 第20(b)段]。

7.30 IFRIC 于 2006 年 3 月澄清，如果一项工具（“基础”工具）包括了如下条款，要求如果有向另一项（“关联”）工具付款的合同义务，则该基础工具需交付现金或其他金融资产，那么加入该关联条款即会形成一项为该项基础工具支付现金或其他金融资产的间接义务。因此，IFRIC 同意该基础工具应该划分为金融负债。

示例——与另一项（“关联”）工具相关联的金融工具（“基础”工具）

某主体发行了不可赎回的可回购优先股（“基础”工具），如果支付了另一（“关联”）工具的利息则必须支付其股利。发行人必须为同样是永续的“关联”工具支付利息。

在本示例中，与具有支付利息合同义务的关联工具相关联导致了一项为基础工具支付股利的间接合同义务。如果发行人可以在任何时候回购该关联工具，发行人即可避免为该基础工具支付股利。因此，在关联工具被回购之前，都会存在一项为基础工具支付股利的合同义务。如果预计的永续股利的现值等于该金融工具的全部本金，则整个工具应该划分为一项负债。另一方面，如果预计股利的现值不等于该金融工具的全部本金，则剩

present value of the expected dividend stream to perpetuity is equal to the whole principal of the financial instrument, the entire instrument would be classified as a liability. On the other hand, if the present value of the expected dividend stream is not equal to the whole principal of the financial instrument, the residual amount is attributable to the equity component.

7.30.1 Indirect obligations are considered part of the terms and conditions of a contract. A change to the indirect obligations of an instrument, which would include the repurchase by the entity of the 'linked' instrument in the above example, is, therefore, considered a change to the contract's contractual terms and conditions.

7.30.2 Whether changes to the terms of a 'base' liability that remove any contractual obligation to pay cash or transfer another financial asset result in extinguishment accounting is a matter of accounting policy choice as such changes are not specifically addressed in IAS 32 and such a transaction is not within IFRIC 19's scope. An entity can apply the same accounting treatment as when convertible debt is converted into shares (see para 7.70 below) where the existing debt's carrying value is transferred to equity and no gain or loss arises on conversion. Alternatively, the entity applies the extinguishment principles in chapter 8 where the existing instrument is derecognised and the new equity instruments issued are recognised at fair value. The difference would be recognised in profit or loss. [IAS 39 para 41].

Contracts settled in cash or other financial asset that are discretionary or at the option of the issuer

7.31 An equity instrument is any contract that evidences a residual interest in an entity's assets after deducting all of its liabilities. Therefore, only those instruments (or components of instruments) that do not meet the definition of a liability will be classified as equity. In other words, the entity must have an unconditional right to avoid delivery of cash or another financial asset. A typical example is an entity's non-puttable ordinary shares. The exception to this principle is when a puttable instrument or an obligation arising on liquidation meets the strict criteria in the February 2008 amendment to IAS 32 to be classified as equity (see para 7.24.5).

余金额应被分配至权益部分。

7.30.1 间接义务被视为合同条件和条款的一部分。因此，某项工具间接义务的变化，包括上述示例中主体回购“关联”工具，可被视为合同条款与条件的变化。

7.30.2 改变“基础”负债条款的变动来消除所有支付现金或交付其他金融资产的合同义务是否会导致会计上的债务解除是一个会计政策选择的问题，因为这种变动在 IAS 32 中并未专门提及，而且这种交易也不在 IFRIC 19 的范围内。主体可以采用和可转换债券转换为股票同样的会计处理（参见下文第 7.70 段）将现有负债的账面金额转入权益，在转换时不会产生利得或损失。或者，主体采用第 8 章的债务解除原则终止确认现有工具并按照公允价值确认新发行的权益工具。差异应该确认为损益。[IAS 39 第 41 段]。

由发行人自主决定或其有权选择以现金或其他金融资产结算的合同

7.31 权益工具是能证明享有主体的资产扣除所有负债后的剩余权益的合同。因此，只有那些不符合负债定义的工具（或工具的组成部分）才可以被划分为权益。换言之，主体必须具有无条件避免支付现金或其他金融资产的权利。一个典型的例子是主体的不可回售普通股。该原则的例外是当可回售工具或清算产生的义务符合 IAS 32 于 2008 年 2 月的修订中所规定的严格条件时应划分为权益（参见第 7.24.5 段）。

Payments that are discretionary or at the option of the issuer

7.32 If an instrument does not have a contractual (including contingent) obligation to deliver cash or another financial asset, it is classified as an equity instrument. Therefore, where payments of interest/dividends or the principal amount or both are discretionary in nature, equity treatment is appropriate for some or all of the instrument. For example, dividends payable on non-puttable ordinary shares depend on the entity's profitability. However, there is no compulsion on the directors to declare a dividend even though a past pattern of dividend payments may have created an expectation on the shareholders that a dividend will be declared and payable. Such discretionary payments do not create contractual obligations, because the directors cannot be required to deliver cash or another financial asset to the shareholders. Nevertheless, a liability must be recognised in respect of such non-puttable ordinary shares where the directors formally act to make a distribution and become legally obligated to the shareholders to do so. This may be the case following the declaration of a dividend, or when the entity is being wound up and any assets remaining after the satisfaction of liabilities become distributable to shareholders. [IAS 32 para AG 13]. Chapter 23 of the IFRS Manual of Accounting provides further guidance on the accounting for dividends.

Example – Non-redeemable preference shares with dividend payments linked to ordinary shares

An entity issues an non-redeemable preference shares on which dividends are payable only if the entity also pays a dividend on its ordinary shares ('dividend pusher').

In this example, the dividend payments on the preference shares are discretionary and not contractual, because no dividends can be paid if no dividends are paid on the ordinary shares, which are an equity instrument. As the perpetual preference shares contain no contractual obligation ever to pay dividends and there is no obligation to repay the principal, they should be classified as equity in their entirety.

Where the dividend payments are also cumulative, that is, if no dividends are

由发行人自主决定或其有权选择的支付

7.32　如果一项工具不具有支付现金或其他金融资产的合同（包括或有）义务，则其应被划分为一项权益工具。因此，当利息/股利或本金或两者的支付都是由公司自主决定的，则该工具部分或者全部应作为权益。例如，不可回售普通股的股利取决于主体的盈利能力。但是，即便过往的股利支付可能已经让股东们期望将宣告并发放股利，对董事而言并无强制要求其发放股利。这种自主决定的支付并不会形成合同义务，因为不能要求董事向股东交付现金或其他金融资产。尽管如此，在董事正式地进行利润分配且对股东具有这样做的法定义务的情形下，则必须将该不可回售普通股确认一项负债。在宣告发放股利之后或者当主体结束业务之后，清偿完负债的剩余资产应向股东支付就属于这样的例子。[IAS 32 AG 第 13 段]。《国际财务报告准则实务指引》第 23 章中对股利的会计处理提供了进一步的指引。

示例——股利的支付与普通股关联的不可赎回优先股

某主体发行了一种不可赎回优先股，其股利只有在主体同时为其普通股支付股利时得以支付（“股利保付机制”）。

在本示例中，对优先股的股利支付是自主决定的而不是合同要求，因为如果不对作为权益工具的普通股支付股利则不用支付其股利。由于永续优先股中没有任何支付股利的合同义务且没有义务偿还本金，其作为一个整体应被划分为权益。

在股利是累计的，即如果不支付普通股的股利，优先股的股利会被递延

paid on the ordinary shares, the preference dividends are deferred, the perpetual shares will be classified as equity only if the dividends can be deferred indefinitely and the entity does not have any contractual obligations whatsoever to pay those dividends.

A liability for the dividend payable would be recognised once the dividend is declared.

7.33 The classification of a preference share as an equity instrument or a financial liability would not be impacted by, for example:

- A history of making distributions.
- An intention to make distributions in the future.
- A possible negative impact on price of the issuer's ordinary shares if distributions are not made (because of restrictions on paying dividends on the ordinary shares if dividends are not paid on the preference shares).
- The amount of the issuer's reserves.
- An issuer's expectation of a profit or loss for a period.
- An ability or inability of the issuer to influence the amount of its profit or loss for the period.

[IAS 32 para AG 26].

7.34 As explained in paragraph 7.20 unless, exceptionally, the criteria to be treated as equity in the February 2008 amendment to IAS 32 are met, where the holder has a put option that requires the issuer to redeem equity shares at some future date, the instrument (that is the equity shares and the put) is treated as a liability; the issuer cannot avoid settling the principal in cash. On the other hand, as discussed in chapter 5, if the issuer has an option to call or redeem what would be otherwise equity shares for cash at some future date, the instrument does not satisfy the definition of a financial liability as the issuer can avoid settling the principal in cash. This is because the issuer does not have a present obligation to transfer financial assets to the shareholders. In this case, redemption of the shares is solely at the issuer's discretion. An obligation may arise, however, when the issuer of the shares exercises its option, usually by formally notifying the

的情况下，只有股利能被无限期地递延且主体没有任何合同义务支付这些股利时，永续优先股才会被划分为权益。

在宣告股利后应该将应付股利确认为一项负债。

7.33 将一项优先股划分为权益工具还是金融负债，不受下列因素影响：

- 以前发放股利的情况；
- 未来发放股利的意向；
- 没有发放优先股股利对发行人普通股的价格可能产生的负面影响（因为不向优先股支付股利限制了向普通股支付股利）；
- 发行人各种准备金的金额；
- 发行人对某一期间内损益的预期；
- 发行人能否影响当期损益。

[IAS 32 AG 第 26 段]。

7.34 如第 7.20 段所述，除非符合 2008 年 2 月对 IAS 32 的修订中所规定的作为权益的条件这一例外，否则当持有人具有要求发行人在未来某一日期赎回股票的看跌期权时，该工具（即股票及看跌期权）是一项负债；发行人无法避免以现金的形式结算本金。另一方面，如第 5 章中所讨论的，如果发行人有权在未来某一日期以现金召回或赎回应为权益的工具，该项工具不符合金融负债的定义，因为发行人可以避免以现金的形式结算本金。这是因为发行人没有向股东交付金融资产的现时义务。在这种情况下，是否赎回股份完全取决于发行人的意愿。但是，当股票发行人行使其期权后——通常是在将赎回股票的意向正式通告股东时，这时将会产生一项义务。[IAS 32 AG 第 25 段]。

shareholders of an intention to redeem the shares. [IAS 32 para AG 25].

7.34.1 The accounting treatment becomes more complex when the issuer has the option to avoid settling an instrument in cash through exercising an option to convert the instrument into a fixed number of equity shares, as illustrated below.

Example – Instrument convertible only at the option of issuer

An entity issues an instrument with the following terms:

- The instrument has a stated 5% coupon that is mandatory.
- The issuer has an option to convert the instrument into a fixed number of its own shares at any time. The holder has no conversion option.
- The issuer has an option to redeem the instrument in cash at any time. The redemption price is the fair value of the fixed number of shares into which the instrument would have converted if it had been converted. The holder has no redemption option.
- The instrument has a 30 year stated maturity and, if not converted or redeemed previously, will be repaid in cash at maturity for its par value plus accrued but unpaid interest.

There are two valid views regarding the classification of the instrument by the issuer depending on analysis of the host contract (that is, liability host versus equity host). Therefore, we consider that an issuer has a policy choice between the following two treatments:

(1) The host contract can be viewed as an equity instrument, as the issuer has the ability to convert the instrument into a fixed number of its own shares at any time. It, therefore, has the ability to avoid making a cash payment or settling the instrument in a variable number of its own shares. Any feature that may have been considered to be an embedded derivative would not meet the definition of a derivative on a stand-alone basis given the ability to avoid payment. Hence, the issuer's conversion and redemption options would not be separated and the entire instrument would be classified as equity.

7.34.1 如下所述，当发行人有权通过行权将工具转换为固定数量的股票以避免用现金结算工具时，其会计处理会更为复杂。

示例——只有发行人有权决定的可转换工具

某主体发行了具有如下条款的工具：

- 该工具的票面利率为5%且强制支付。
- 发行人有权在任何时间将该项工具转换为固定数量的自身股票。持有人没有转股权。
- 发行人有权在任何时间以现金赎回该项工具。赎回价格为如果工具转股其所能转换的固定数量的股票的公允价值。持有人无权要求赎回。
- 该工具的票面期限为30年，如未提前转股或赎回，则将在到期日按面值加应计未付的利息以现金偿还。

根据对主合同（即负债主合同还是权益主合同）的分析，从发行人的角度对该工具进行分类有两种有效的观点。因此，我们认为发行人有权选择下述两种政策之一：

（1）该主合同可被视为一项权益工具，因为发行人可以在任何时间将其转换为固定数量的自身股份。因此，发行人能够避免支付现金或以可变数量的自身股票结算该工具。因为可以避免付款，任何可能被视为嵌入衍生工具的特征自身均不符合衍生工具的定义。因此，发行人的转股权和赎回权不应被分离出来，整个工具应划分为权益。

(2) The issuer can classify this instrument as a liability, being a hybrid instrument comprised of:

(a) a host liability component for the obligation to pay the mandatory coupons and to repay the instrument at maturity; and

(b) an embedded derivative component for the entity's option to settle the instrument early in either a fixed number of its own shares or cash of an equivalent value. As these two early settlement mechanisms are interdependent, they are viewed as part of a single embedded derivative rather than as two separate embedded derivatives.

If option 2 is taken as a policy choice then the issuer has a second decision to make with regards measurement. On initial recognition either the fair value option can be taken in accordance with IAS 39 (as there is a significant embedded derivative) and the entire contract will be measured at fair value through profit or loss, or the issuer can value the host liability contract at amortised cost and separate the embedded derivative.

7.35 Where a financial instrument only results in a contractual obligation for the issuer to deliver cash or other financial assets upon the occurrence of an uncertain future event, the instrument may still need to be classified as a financial liability from initial recognition if it meets the definition of a contingent settlement event. See paragraph 7.50 for more details.

Contracts that will or may be settled in an entity's own equity instruments

7.36 A contract is not an equity instrument solely because it may result in the receipt or delivery of the entity's own equity instruments. [IAS 32 para 21]. The classification of contracts that will or may be settled in the entity's own equity instruments is dependent on whether there is variability in either the number of own equity instruments delivered and/or variability in the amount of cash or other financial assets received, or whether both are fixed.

（2）发行人可将此工具划分为一项负债，它是一项包括下述项目的混合工具：

（a）主合同负债部分为支付强制性票面利息及到期偿还该工具的义务；和

（b）嵌入衍生工具部分为主体可以用固定数量的自身股票或相等价值的现金提前结算该项工具的期权。因为这两种提前结算机制具有相互依赖性，所以将其视为单一嵌入衍生工具的一部分而不是两个单独的嵌入衍生工具。

如果发行人选择了第二种处理方法作为其会计政策，其还需要在计量方面再作出决定。初始确认时，可以按照 IAS 39 的规定采用公允价值选择权（因为有一个重大的嵌入衍生工具）而将整个合同以公允价值计量且变动计入损益，或者发行人可以将嵌入衍生工具分离出来，而主负债合同则按照摊余成本计量。

7.35　当金融工具只有在某些未来不确定性事件发生时才会使发行人有支付现金或其他金融资产的合同义务时，如果符合或有结算事件的定义，那么该工具可能还是需要在初始确认时划分为一项金融负债。更详细的信息参见第 7.50 段。

将要或可能以主体自身的权益工具结算的合同

7.36　某项合同并不仅仅因为它可能导致主体获得或交付其自身的权益工具而成为权益工具。[IAS 32 第 21 段]。将会或可能以主体自身的权益工具结算的合同，其分类取决于所交付权益工具的数量是否可变，以及/或者所收取的现金或其他金融资产的金额是否可变，或两者是否都是固定的。

7.37 A contract that will be settled by the entity receiving (or delivering) a fixed number of its own equity instruments in exchange for a fixed amount of cash or another financial asset is an equity instrument [IAS 32 para 22]. This is commonly referred to as the 'fixed for fixed' requirement. For example, an entity receives C100 upfront from the holder to issue 100 of the entity's own equity in three years time. This would meet the 'fixed for fixed' requirement as both the number of own equity shares delivered and the cash received is fixed when the financial instrument is initially recognised. The instrument would meet the definition of an equity instrument as the holder gets a residual interest in the entity. By fixing upfront the amount paid and the number of shares received the holder benefits from any upside and suffers the loss from any fall in the residual value of the entity.

7.38 However, an entity may have a contractual right or obligation to receive or deliver a number of its own shares or other equity instruments that varies so that the fair value of the entity's own equity instrument to be received or delivered equals the amount of the contractual right or obligation. Such a contract may be for a fixed amount or an amount that fluctuates in part or in full in response to changes in a variable. [IAS 32 para 21]. It would be inappropriate to account for such contracts as an equity instrument when an entity's own equity instruments are used 'as currency' as such a contract represents a right or obligation for a specified amount rather than a specified residual equity interest. Therefore, such a contract would be classified as a financial liability. The underlying variable can include the entity's own share price. [IAS 32 para AG 27(d)].

Example 1 – Own shares to the value of C1 million

An entity receives C1m in exchange for its promise that it will deliver its own equity shares in an amount sufficient to equal a value of C1m at a future date. If the share price at the date on delivery of the contract is C5, the entity would be required to issue 200,000 shares ie a total value of C1m.

On the day the issuer delivers its own equity, the holder would be indifferent whether it received cash of C1m or shares to the value of C1m which it could sell and receive C1m in cash. Therefore, the entity is using its own equity as currency and as such the holder does not get a full residual interest. Hence the

7.37　主体通过收取（或交付）固定数量的自身权益工具以交换固定金额的现金或其他金融资产来结算的合同是一项权益工具［IAS 32 第 22 段］。这通常被称为“固定换固定”要求。例如，某主体要在三年内发行 100 股而从持有人处收取了 C100 元的预付款。这就符合“固定换固定”的要求，因为在金融工具初始确认时对所交付的自身权益股票的数量以及所收取的现金都已固定。由于持有人获得了主体的剩余权益，该工具应当符合权益工具的定义。通过预先固定下来所支付的金额和所收取的股票数，持有人可因主体剩余价值的任何上涨而受益或因其任何下降而遭受损失。

7.38　但是，主体可能拥有收取或交付某一可变数量的自身股票或其他权益工具的合同权利或义务，其中可获取或需支付的主体自身权益工具的公允价值等于该合同权利或义务的金额。该合同的金额可以是固定的，也可以完全或部分地基于变量的变化而变化。［IAS 32 第 21 段］。当主体自身的权益工具被用作“货币”时将这种合同作为权益工具进行会计处理就不合适了，因为这种合同所代表的是某一指定金额的权利或义务而不是指定的主体剩余权益。因此，这种合同应当划分为金融负债。基础变量可包括主体自身股票的价格。［IAS 32 AG 第 27(d)段］。

示例 1——价值为 C100 万元的自身股票

某主体收取了 C100 万元，并承诺其在未来某日交付价值足以等同于 C100 万元的自身权益股票。如果该合同交付日股票价格为 C5 元，那么主体应当发行 200,000 股股票，即总价值为 C100 万元。

在发行人交付其自身权益之日，不管是收到 C100 万元的现金还是价值为 C100 万元的股票（持有人可以将其出售并收取 C100 万元）对于持有人来说没有区别。因此主体将其自身权益用作了货币，而持有人并未获得完全的剩余权益。因此，该金融工具是一项负债。

financial instrument is a liability.

Example 2 – Bermudan option with fixed but different strike prices

An entity issues an option to sell a fixed number of its own equity shares at a specified exercise price. The terms of the option state that the specified exercise price varies with the share price of the entity such that:

Share price	Conversion ratio
0-10C	10 shares at 1C per share
11-20C	10 shares at 1.5C per share

The variability in the exercise price, as a function of share price of the entity, results in a variable amount of cash for a fixed number of shares. The 'fixed for fixed' requirement is therefore violated. The option is, therefore, classified as a derivative financial liability and not as an equity instrument.

Example 3 – Call options where the underlying is an exchange ratio

Entities A, B and X are all listed companies. Entity A purchases an option to buy 5% of the share capital of entity X from entity B in return for entity A delivering its own equity shares to entity B. The exchange ratio is fixed when the option is written (for example, entity A pays 0.8 of entity A's own shares for the purchase of an option over 1 share of entity X).

This exchange ratio will violate the 'fixed for fixed' requirement. The fixed number of entity A's shares that entity A may issue is not equal to a fixed amount of cash, as the value of each share acquired in exchange can vary. Therefore, entity A must treat its purchased option as a derivative instrument under IAS 39.

7.39 The IASB was concerned that restricting the definition of an underlying variable could lead to structuring opportunities and abuse. Therefore, the standard requires that all forms of variability in either the own shares received or delivered, or the cash or another financial asset delivered or received, would result in financial asset or financial liability classification.

7.40 A contract that will be settled by an entity delivering a fixed number of its

示例2——具有固定但不同行权价格的百慕大期权

某主体发行期权，以指定的行权价格出售其固定数量的自身权益股份。该期权的条款规定特定的行权价格将随着主体股票的价格变化而变化，具体如下：

股票价格	转换比率
C0 至 10 元	10 股，每股 C1 元
C11 至 20 元	10 股，每股 C1.5 元

以主体股票价格为机制的行权价格的可变性导致以可变金额的现金换取固定数量的股票，因而违背了"固定换固定"的要求。因此，该期权划分为一项金融负债衍生工具而非权益工具。

示例3——基础变量为交换率的看涨期权

主体 A、B 和 X 均为上市公司。主体 A 认购了一个从主体 B 购买主体 X 的 5% 股份的期权，作为回报，主体 A 向主体 B 交付其自身权益股票。在该期权签出日交换率就已经固定（例如，主体 A 支付 0.8 个其自身股票换取主体 X 1 个股份的期权）。

这个交换率违背了"固定换固定"的要求。主体 A 可能发行的固定数量的其自身股票并不等于固定金额的现金，因为通过交换所获得的各个股份的价值均可能发生变化。因此，主体 A 必须将其所购买的期权视为 IAS 39 的衍生工具进行处理。

7.39　IASB 担心限制基础变量的定义可能导致对合同的设计和滥用。因此，该准则要求所有类型的可变性，无论是收取或交付的自身股票还是交付或收取的现金或其他金融资产，都将导致金融资产或金融负债的分类。

7.40　将通过主体交付固定数量的自身权益工具以换取固定金额的外币（即

own equity instruments in exchange for a fixed amount of foreign currency (that is a currency other than the functional currency of the entity) is a financial liability. The exception to this rule, in relation to rights issues, applicable to accounting periods beginning on or after 1 February 2010 is discussed in paragraph 7.41. This is a liability because an obligation denominated in a foreign currency represents a variable amount of cash in the entity's functional currency. A foreign currency convertible bond (see example at para 7.79) is, therefore a financial liability made up of two components. These components are: (1) a host bond denominated in the foreign currency (whose foreign exchange risk is accounted for under IAS 21, 'The effects of changes in foreign exchange rates') and (2) an embedded derivative which is a written option for the holder to exchange the foreign currency bond for a fixed number of functional currency denominated shares.

7.41 The IASB published an amendment to IAS 32, 'Financial instruments: Presentation' on the classification of rights issues on 8 October 2009. The amendment addresses the accounting for rights issues (including rights, options and warrants) that are denominated in a currency other than the functional currency of the issuer. The amendment states that, if such rights are issued pro rata to an entity's existing shareholders for a fixed amount of any currency, they should be classified as equity, regardless of the currency in which the exercise price is denominated. This is a narrow amendment and should not be extended to other instruments by analogy (for example, warrants or rights issues on other than a *pro rata* basis and foreign currency denominated convertible bonds-see paragraph 7.79). The amendment is effective for annual periods beginning on or after 1 February 2010, with early adoption permitted. If an entity applies the amendment to an earlier period it shall disclose that fact. An example of an entity that has applied the amendment is shown in Table 7.1 below.

主体功能货币以外的其他货币）进行结算的合同为金融负债。在第 7.41 段讨论了上述原则对有关配股权的一个例外情况，此例外在起始日为 2010 年 2 月 1 日或以后的会计期间生效。这是一个负债，因为以外币计价的义务代表了以主体功能货币计价的可变金额的现金。因此，外币可转换债券（参见第 7.79 段的示例）是由两个组成部分所组成的一个金融负债。这两个组成部分为：（1）以功能货币计价的主合同债券（其外汇风险遵循《国际会计准则第 21 号——汇率变动的影响》进行会计处理和（2）一个嵌入衍生工具，即持有人以外币债券换取固定数量的以功能货币计价的股份的签出期权。

7.41　IASB 于 2009 年 10 月 8 日就配股权的分类发布了对《国际会计准则第 32 号——金融工具：列报》的一项修订。该修订规定了以发行人功能货币之外的货币计价的配股权（包括权利、期权和认股权证）的会计处理方法。该修订指出，如果这种权利是按比例发行给主体现有的股东并将收取固定金额的任何货币，则无论其行权价以何种货币计价，都应将其划分为权益。这是一项范围很窄的修订，不能以类推的方式适用于其他工具（例如并非按*比例*发行的认股权证或配股权以及以外币计价的可转换债券——参见第 7.79 段）。该修订于起始日在 2010 年 2 月 1 日或之后开始的年度期间生效，允许提前实施。如果主体在较早期间采用了该修订，则应披露这一事实。下表 7.1 中列示了一个主体采用此修订的示例。

Table 7. 1 – classification of rights issues

HSBC Holdings plc – Annual report – 31 December 2009

1 Basis of preparation (extract)

(a) Compliance with International Financial Reporting Standards (extract)
During 2009, HSBC adopted the following significant standards and amendments to standards:

- 'Classification of Rights Issues-Amendment to IAS 32', ('the amendment') which is effective for annual periods beginning on or after 1 February 2010, with early adoption permitted. HSBC has elected to adopt the amendment in advance of the effective date and, as required by IAS 8, has applied the amendment retrospectively. The amendment requires that rights issues, options or warrants to acquire a fixed number of the entity's own equity instruments for a fixed amount of any currency are equity instruments if the entity offers the rights issues, options or warrants pro rata to all of its existing owners of the same class of its own non-derivative equity instruments. The offer of rights by HSBC Holdings plc to its shareholders on 20 March 2009 was accounted for as an equity instrument, as required by the amendment, in the consolidated financial statements of HSBC and the separate financial statements of HSBC Holdings.

2 Summary of significant accounting policies (extract)
(ac) Rights issues
Rights issues to acquire a fixed number of the entity's own equity instruments for a fixed amount of any currency are equity instruments if the entity offers the rights issues pro rata to all of its existing owners of the same class of its own non-derivative equity instruments. On initial recognition, these rights are recognised in shareholders' equity and are not subsequently re-measured during the offer period. Following the exercise of the rights and the allotment of new shares, the cash proceeds of the rights issue are recognised in shareholders' equity. Incremental costs directly attributable to the rights issue are shown as a deduction from the proceeds, net of tax.

41 Rights issue (extract)
On 2 March 2009, HSBC Holdings announced its proposal to raise £12.5 billion (US$17.8 billion), net of expenses, by way of a fully underwritten rights issue. Under the proposal, HSBC offered its shareholders the opportunity to acquire 5 new ordinary shares for every 12 ordinary shares at a price of 254 pence per new ordinary share. For shareholders on the Hong Kong and Bermuda Overseas Branch Registers this offer was expressed in Hong Kong dollars and US dollars, respectively, fixed at published exchange rates on 27 February 2009. The proposal was subject to authorisation by the shareholders which was obtained at a general meeting held on 19 March 2009. The offer period commenced on 20 March 2009 and closed for acceptance on 3 April 2009. Dealing in the new shares began on 6 April 2009.

For details of called-up share capital and other equity instruments see Note 37.

表 7.1—配股权的分类

HSBC Holdings plc—年报—2009 年 12 月 31 日

1. 编报基础（节选）

（a）遵循国际财务报告准则（节选）
在 2009 年，HSBC 采用了如下重大的准则以及对准则的修订：

《配股权的分类——对 IAS 32 的修订》（“此修订”）适用于起始日在 2010 年 2 月 1 日或之后开始的年度期间，允许提前实施。HSBC 选择在生效日之前采用此修订并按照 IAS 8 的规定追溯适用。此修订规定如果主体按比例将配股权、期权和认股权证发行给其自身同一类非衍生权益工具的所有现有股东，这些以固定金额的任何货币获取固定数量的主体自身权益工具的配股权、期权和认股权证是权益工具。按照此修订的规定，HSBC Holdings plc 于 2009 年 3 月 20 日发行给其股东的配股权在 HSBC 的合并财务报表和 HSBC Holdings 的单独财务报表中作为权益工具核算。

2. 重大会计政策汇总（节选）
（ac）配股权
如果主体按比例将配股权、期权和认股权证发行给其自身同一类非衍生权益工具的所有现有股东，这些以固定金额的任何货币获取固定数量的主体自身权益工具的配股权、期权和认股权证是权益工具。在初始确认时，这些配股权在股东权益中确认并且在其有效期内不做期后重新计量。在配股权行权及分配新股票后，配股权的现金收款确认在股东权益中。直接归属于配股权的增量费用扣税后列示为收款的抵减。

41. 配股权（节选）
HSBC Holdings 于 2009 年 3 月 2 日宣布了其通过全额配股在扣除费用后筹资 125 亿英镑（178 亿美元）的提案。在此提案下，HSBC 向其股东提供每 12 股普通股可以用每股 254 便士购买 5 股新普通股的机会。对于在香港和百慕大海外分支机构注册处的股东，此报价分别以 2009 年 2 月 27 日公布的汇率固定为港币和美元表示。此提案须由股东授权，并于 2009 年 3 月 19 日的股东大会通过。报价有效期从 2009 年 3 月 20 日开始至 2009 年 4 月 3 日结束。新股发行于 2009 年 4 月 6 日开始。

对于已缴股本和其他权益工具的详细信息请参见附注 37。

7.42 Some financial instruments (denominated in the same currency as the issuer's functional currency) may be settled in a variable number of own equity instruments but also include a cap or floor or both (that is, a collar) that limits that variability. The existence of the cap, floor or collar does not change the instruments classification from being a financial liability, as it is settled in a variable number of shares. However, it is necessary to determine whether the cap, floor or collar represents an embedded derivative and, if so, whether it is required to be separated out from the host instrument, as discussed in the examples below.

Example 1 – Instruments that are settled in a variable number of shares but subject to a cap

An entity issues an instrument that is settled at the end of the year by delivering equity shares to the value of C100. The fair value of the shares at the date of issue is C10. The instrument also contains a cap that limits the number of shares that the entity is required to deliver to 20 shares in order to prevent excessive dilution of the existing shareholders through the issue of new shares.

There are two acceptable views on how the cap should be accounted for. Therefore, the issuer has an accounting policy choice between the following two treatments.

View 1 – The contract is a non-derivative liability for a fixed monetary amount

The host contract is an obligation to issue a variable number of shares whose *value equals100* (that is, a fixed monetary amount). The entire instrument is a liability on the grounds that the 'fixed for fixed' requirement in paragraph 16(b)(ii) of IAS 32 is not met for the instrument as a whole (that is, the instrument is settled in a variable number of shares).

The cap itself is scoped out of IAS 39 because it meets the definition of equity under IAS 32 since it results in the exchange of a fixed amount of cash (that is, the fixed monetary amount of 100) for a fixed number of shares of 20. However, it is not recognised separately as an equity component under IAS 32 because paragraph 16(b)(i) is applied to the whole instrument (rather than only the cap), and the whole instrument results in the delivery of a variable

7.42 有些金融工具（以发行人的功能货币计价）可以用可变数量的自身权益工具结算，但是也包括上限或下限或上下限以限制可变性。存在上限、下限或上下限的情形并不能改变该工具作为金融负债的分类，因为它是以可变数量的股票来结算的。然而，必须确定这种上限、下限或上下限是否是嵌入衍生工具，如果是，如下文所述示例中所讨论的，则要确定是否要求将其从主工具中分离出来。

示例1——以可变数量的股票结算但有上限的工具

某主体发行了一个将在年末通过交付价值为C100元的权益股票来结算的工具。其股票在发行日的公允价值为C10元。该工具还包括一个上限，将要求主体交付的股票数量限制在20股以内，以防止新股发行对现有股东过度稀释。

如何对此上限进行会计处理有两种可以接受的观点。因此，发行人可以选择如下两种处理方式之一作为其会计政策。

观点1——该合同是一项固定货币金额的非衍生工具负债

该主合同是一项发行价值等于*100*（即，固定货币金额）的可变数量股票的义务。整个工具是一项负债，因为该工具作为一个整体不符合IAS 32第16（b）（ii）段所述的“固定换固定”要求（即，该工具以可变数量的股票结算）。

此上限本身不在IAS 39的范围内，由于它导致以固定金额的现金（即固定货币金额100）交换固定数量的20股股票，满足了IAS 32中对权益的定义。但是，它并未按照IAS 32被单独确认为一项权益组成部分，是因为第16（b）（i）段适用于工具整体（而不仅仅是上限），而工具整体导致交付可变数量的股票。IAS 32第25段中进一步支持了这一观点，因为决定按合同所需交付的股票数量（即，直至100的固定货币金额）的股

number of shares. Paragraph 25 of IAS 32 further supports this view because the movement in share price that determines the number of shares to be delivered under the contract (that is, to the fixed monetary amount of 100) is outside the control of the issuer and the holder.

View 2 – Contract contains a debt host with a purchased put

The host instrument is an obligation to deliver a *variable number of shares* which is a liability. The instrument also contains an embedded derivative whose effect is to cap the amount of shares the entity will have to deliver according to the debt host, so that, overall, the issuer does not deliver shares in excess of the cap. This embedded derivative can be viewed as a purchased put that will be net share settled (that is, the number of shares to be delivered under the put will vary depending on the share price so that the overall contract results in the delivery of the capped number of shares).

As the cap is not closely related to the debt host (it is linked to movements in the share price), the embedded cap would need to be bifurcated and accounted for at fair value through profit and loss (assuming the fair value option is not used for the entire contract).

Example 2 – Instruments that are settled in a variable number of shares but subject to a cap and floor (that is, a collar)

An entity issues an instrument that is settled at the end of the year by delivering equity shares to the value of C100. The fair value of the shares at the date of issue is C10. The instrument also contains:

- A cap that limits the number of shares that the entity is required to deliver to 20 shares.
- A floor that requires the entity to deliver a minimum of 5 shares.

The host instrument can be viewed as an obligation to deliver a variable number of shares to the value of C100 which is a liability. The instrument also contains two embedded derivatives: a cap and a floor. Because the cap and floor are linked to the same risk exposure (that is, the share price) and are

票价格变动不在发行人和持有人的控制范围之内。

观点2——含有买入看跌期权的主债务的合同

此工具主体是一项需要交付*可变数量股票*的义务，即一项负债。该工具还含有一项嵌入衍生工具，使得主体按照主债务不得不交付的股票数量有个上限，即总体而言发行人不会交付超过该上限的股票。该项嵌入衍生工具可被视为一项将以股票净额结算的购入看跌期权（即根据该看跌期权所应交付的股票数量将根据股票价格而变化，使得合同整体而言所交付的股票数量在上限以内）。

因为此上限与主债务并不密切相关（它与股票价格的变动相关联），所以嵌入上限应当被分离出来，并以公允价值计量且其变动计入损益来进行会计处理（假设并未对整个合同采用公允价值选择权）。

示例2——以可变数量的股份结算但有上限和下限（即上下限）的工具

某主体发行了一个将在年末通过交付价值为C100元的权益股票来结算的工具。其股票在发行日的公允价值为C10元。该工具还包括：

- 要求该主体交付的股票数量限制在20股以内的上限。

- 要求该主体最少交付5股的下限。

此工具主体可被视为一项需要交付价值为C100元的可变数量股份的义务，即一项负债。该工具还包含两个嵌入衍生工具：上限和下限。因为该上限和下限与相同的风险（即，股份价格）相关联并且相互依存，所以不能将其作为两个单独的工具进行分析。该上限和下限必须捆绑在一起并

interdependent, they cannot be analysed as two separate instruments. The cap and floor need to be bundled together and treated as a single compound embedded derivative [IAS 39 para AG 29]. This compound embedded derivative is within IAS 39's scope because it does not result in the delivery of a fixed amount of cash for a fixed number of shares and, therefore, needs to be assessed for bifurcation. However, note that even if was considered that the cap and floor were individually scoped out of IAS 39 as described in view 1 of example 1 for the instrument with a cap only the instrument as a whole would still be a liability on the basis that paragraph 16(b)(i) of IAS 32 results in the delivery of a variable number of shares. Assuming that the fair value option is not used for the entire contract, the cap and floor should be bifurcated as a single compound derivative that is not closely related to the debt host (the underlying of the compound derivative is the share price).

Alternatively if the instrument is viewed as a host instrument with an obligation to deliver a *variable number of shares* (as described in view 2 of example 1 for the instrument with a cap only), this debt host would contain both a purchased put for the cap that is net share settled as well as a written call for the floor that is net share settled. The cap and floor need to be bundled together and treated as a single embedded derivative as noted above. [IAS 39 para AG29].

As a result, under both approaches the instrument would be accounted for as a debt host with a compound embedded derivative that should be accounted for separately.

7.43 A single instrument should not be separated into a number of different instruments in order to satisfy the 'fixed for fixed' requirement where otherwise it would result in variability in either own equity, cash or another financial asset, if accounted for as a single instrument. For example, variability resulting from interdependent profit levels.

Example – Contingent consideration varies with time and performance conditions

Entity A acquires entity B and the contingent consideration payable to the seller is based on the following terms:

视为一个单一的复合嵌入衍生工具［IAS 39 AG 第 29 段］。由于此复合嵌入衍生工具不会导致为固定数量的股票交付固定金额的现金，它在 IAS 39 的范围之内，因此需要评估是否分离出来。但值得注意的是，即使像示例 1 仅有上限的工具观点 1 所描述的那样，认为就上限和下限单独而言均不在 IAS 39 的范围之内，按照 IAS 32 第 16（b）（i）段由于导致交付可变数量的股票，工具整体仍然应该是一项负债。假设未对合同整体采用公允价值选择权，该上限和下限应被分离出来作为一个与主债务并不是密切相关的单一的复合衍生工具（复合衍生工具的基础变量为股票价格）。

或者如果该工具被视为一项需要交付*可变数量股票*义务的工具（如示例 1 仅有上限的工具观点 2 所描述的那样），此债务主合同应该既包含一个针对上限的以股票净额结算的购入看跌期权，又包含一个针对下限的以股票净额结算的签出看涨期权。如上所述该上限和下限必须捆绑在一起并视为一个单一的嵌入衍生工具。［IAS 39 AG 第 29 段］。

因此，在这两种方法下该工具都应作为债务主合同及一个应当单独核算的复合嵌入衍生工具来进行会计处理。

7.43　如果将某工具作为一个单项工具进行会计处理将导致自身权益、现金或其他金融资产为可变的，则不能为了满足“固定换固定”的要求而将其分为数项不同的工具。例如，因互相依赖的利润水平而引起的变动。

示例——随时间和业绩条件变动的或有对价

主体 A 收购了主体 B，其应付给卖方的或有对价基于如下条款：

- If a performance target of profits of C100m is achieved by entity B in year 1, 100 additional shares will be issued to the seller.
- If a performance target of profits of C200m is achieved by entity B by the end of year 2 (cumulative of year 1 and year 2), 150 more shares will be issued to the seller.
- Entity B must meet the performance target in year 1 in order to be eligible to earn the additional shares in year 2 (that is, it is not possible to only receive 150 shares)

Where there are multiple contingent events it must be determined whether the unit of account is the overall contract or separate contracts within that overall contract. In order to be assessed as separate contracts they must be readily separable and independent of each other and relate to different risk exposures. In this example the periods are not readily separable or independent of each other as the delivery of shares in year 2 depends on the profits and delivery of shares in year 1. This is considered as one overall contract that results in a variable number of shares. It fails the 'fixed for fixed' requirement and is classified as a liability not equity.

7.43.1 In November 2009 the IFRIC discussed whether a type of instrument where the exercise price is pre-determined at inception and only varies over time met the fixed for fixed condition and would, therefore, be classified as equity. The IFRIC acknowledged there is diversity in practice in accounting for such instruments, but rejected issuing interpretive guidance due to the longer term debt-equity project (Financial instruments with characteristics of equity – 'FICE') that is in progress.

7.43.2 In the light of the IFRIC discussions and diversity in practice, our view is that an entity may determine that such an instrument, where the exercise price is pre-determined at inception and only varies over time, meets the fixed for fixed condition and is classified as equity. If the strike price is not pre-determined at inception but determinable based on variables, such as the share price for example, the fixed for fixed condition would not be met. An entity may also determine that such an instrument where the exercise price is pre-determined at inception and only

- 如果主体 B 在第一年利润业绩目标达到 C1 亿元，将另发行 100 股股票给卖方；
- 如果主体 B 在第二年年底（第一、二年累计）利润业绩目标达到 C2 亿元，将再发行 150 股股票给卖方；
- 主体 B 必须满足第一年的业绩目标卖方才有资格在第二年获取另外的股票（即不可能只获得 150 股股票）。

在出现多重或有事项的情况下，必须确定核算单位到底是合同总体还是合同总体中的单独合同。要作为单独合同，它们必须随时可拆分、相互独立以及涉及不同的风险。在此示例中，各期间并非随时可拆分或相互独立，因为第二年股票的交付取决于第一年的利润及股票交付。这被视为一个合同总体并导致可变数量的股票。它不符合“固定换固定”的要求，应划分为负债而非权益。

7.43.1　IFRIC 在 2009 年 11 月讨论了一种工具，如果其行权价在初始即以预先确定并仅随时间的变动而变动，则其是否满足固定换固定的要求并因此应划分为权益。IFRIC 承认在实务中对这种工具会计处理的多样性，但由于债务—权益长期项目（具有权益特征的金融工具——“FICE”）尚未完成而拒绝发布解释性指引。

7.43.2　鉴于 IFRIC 的讨论及实务中的多样性，我们的观点是主体可以认为这种行权价在初始即予以预先确定并仅随时间的变动而变动的工具满足固定换固定的要求并将其划分为权益。如果行权价不是在初始即予以预先确定而是根据诸如股票价格这样的变量确定的，固定换固定的条件将不能满足。主体也可以认为这种行权价在初始即予以预先确定并仅随时间的变动而变动的工具是一项金融负债，由于预先确定的行权价引入的变量并不满足固定换固定的条件。

varies over time is a financial liability on the basis that the pre-determination of the exercise price introduces some variability that fails the fixed for fixed criterion.

7.43.3 An entity's decision as to whether the fixed for fixed condition is met when the strike price is pre-determined at inception and only varies over time is an accounting policy decision that should be applied consistently and disclosed appropriately.

7.43.4 An entity that previously considered that the fixed for fixed condition was not met may continue with its existing policy or may change its policy by following the guidance for changes in accounting policy as discussed in chapter 5 of the IFRS Manual of Accounting.

Example – Variation in the cash received due to step-up adjustments

Entity A (US dollar functional currency) writes an option to entity B (not an employee) that enables entity B to buy 1 share of entity A on the following terms:

- If the option is exercised in year 1 the strike price is $1.
- If the option is exercised in year 2 the strike price is $2.
- If the option is exercised in year 3 the strike price is $3.

Entity A has a policy choice, which should be applied consistently.

Entity may consider that the instrument is an equity instrument, because the exercise price is pre-determined and varies only with time. It, therefore, can be considered as meeting the condition that a fixed number of equity instruments will be issued for a fixed price.

On the other hand, entity A may consider that the instrument is a derivative financial liability. Entity A may consider that the different strike prices introduce variability such that a fixed number of shares will not be issued for a fixed amount of cash.

7.44 Complexity arises in practice when applying the principles for settlement in an entity's own equity instruments. Although IAS 32 states that variability in either the entity's own equity delivered or cash or another financial asset received results

7.43.3 当行权价在初始即予以预先确定并仅随时间的变动而变动时，主体对于其是否满足了固定换固定条件的决定是一个会计政策的选择，应当一致地运用并适当披露。

7.43.4 主体若在以前认为没有满足固定换固定条件的，可以继续采用现有政策，或按照《国际财务报告准则实务指引》第5章中所讨论的变更会计政策的指引来变更其会计政策。

示例——因递增调整而使所收到的现金发生的变化

主体A（以美元为功能货币）向主体B（非员工）签出一项期权使得主体B能够按照如下条件购买主体A的1股股票：

- 如果期权在第1年行使其履约价格为1美元。
- 如果期权在第2年行使其履约价格为2美元。
- 如果期权在第3年行使其履约价格为3美元。

主体A有会计政策的选择，并应当一致地采用。

主体可以认为该工具是一项权益工具，因为行权价在初始即予以预先确定并仅随时间的变动而变动。因此，该工具可被认为满足了以固定数量的权益工具按照固定价格发行的条件。

另一方面，主体A可以认为该工具是一项衍生金融负债。主体A可以认为不同的行权价引入了变量，因此固定数量的股票将不以固定金额的现金发行。

7.44 实务中，对以主体自身权益工具结算的原则的应用很复杂。虽然IAS 32指出不论变动来自于所交付的主体自身权益还是所收到的现金或其他金融资产均将导致一项金融负债，但实际上并非所有形式的变动都会违背“固定换

in a financial liability, not all forms of variability do in fact violate the 'fixed for fixed' requirement, including the example of a pre-determined price that only varies over time in paragraph 7.43.4 above. Another example is an adjustment to the conversion ratio of a convertible bond triggered by a stock split. For example the original conversion ratio is 1 share for every £1 (with a notional value of £2), however, upon a stock split each share now has a notional value of £1. It would, therefore, be necessary to adjust the conversion ratio to 2 shares for every £1 in order to maintain the relative economic rights of the shareholders and bondholders. Although the adjustment results in variability in the number of own equity delivered, the fact that this variability serves to maintain the relative economic rights of the shareholders and bondholders results in no violation of the 'fixed for fixed' requirement.

7.45 Where variability is caused by the inclusion of an anti-dilution clause, such as the stock split clause outlined above, this will not result in a violation of the 'fixed for fixed' requirement provided, firstly the relative rights of the shareholders and bondholders are maintained, and secondly the instrument would otherwise meet the 'fixed for fixed' requirement. Other examples of anti-dilutive clauses are adjustments made for the payment of dividends and bonus issues, where new shares are issued to the entity's shareholders for no additional consideration through a capitalisation of reserves.

7.46 A common adjustment in convertible bonds is the inclusion of a change of control clause. The clause adjusts the otherwise fixed for fixed conversion ratio upon a change of control event. The purpose of the adjustment is to compensate the bondholder for the loss of optionality either through a stated compensation amount or via a formula. As this change in control adjustment is not compensation that relates to the issuance of the equity shares but rather is compensation for the loss of optionality, it does not affect the relative rights of the shareholders and bondholders and does not result in a violation of the 'fixed for fixed' requirement.

7.47 The table below sets out the classification in various scenarios where a fixed or variable monetary obligation (not indexed to the entity's own share price) is settled in a fixed number or variable number of the entity's own shares. Instruments classified as financial liabilities under IAS 32, will require further analysis under

固定”的要求，包括上文第7.43.4段中预先确定的价格仅随时间的变动而变动的例子。另一个例子就是由股票分割所引起的对可转换债券转股率的调整。例如初始转股率为每英镑1股（票面值为2英镑），但是在股票分割后每股现在的票面值为1英镑。因此，应该需要把转股率调整为每英镑2股以维持股东和债券持有人的相对经济权利。虽然这种调整导致所交付的自身权益的数量发生变化，但是这种变化是为了维持股东和债券持有人的相对经济权利的事实使其并未违背“固定换固定”的要求。

7.45 当变动是由于引入了某项反稀释条款而导致的情形下，例如上文所述的股票分割条款，其并不会违背“固定换固定”要求，但前提条件是首先要维持股东和债券持有人的相对权利，其次是该项工具要符合“固定换固定”的要求。反稀释条款的其他例子有针对股利支付和红利股而作出的调整，其中红利股是通过准备金的资本化以无对价的方式向主体的股东发行新股。

7.46 可转换债券的一种常见调整是控制权变更条款的情况。该条款在发生控制权变更事件时对本已属于固定换固定的转股率进行调整。这种调整的目的是通过规定的补偿金额或是某一公式来补偿债券持有人丧失的选择权。因为这种控制权变更的调整并非是对发行股票的补偿而是对丧失选择权的补偿，所以不会影响股东和债券持有人的相对权利，也不会违背“固定换固定”的要求。

7.47 下表列出了以固定或可变数量的主体自身股票对固定或可变的货币性义务（并非与主体的自身股票价格变动挂钩）进行结算的各种情况下的分类。按照IAS 32划分为金融负债的工具将需要按照IAS 39进一步分析，以确定是否需要将任何嵌入衍生工具分离出来。

IAS 39 to determine whether any embedded derivatives require to be bifurcated.

Contract settled in the equity's own shares	**Monetary value of consideration**[1]	**Number of equity shares**	**Classification**
Scenario 1	Fixed	Variable	Financial liability
Scenario 2	Variable	Variable	Financial liability
Scenario 3	Variable	Fixed	Financial liability
Scenario 4	Fixed in a currency other than the entity's functional currency[2]	Fixed	Financial liability
Scenario 5	Fixed	Fixed	Equity

1 in the functional currency of the issuer.

2 subject to the exception discussed from paragraph 7. 41.

7. 48 IAS 32 does not deal with the option to exchange a fixed number of one kind of the entity's own equity for a fixed number of a different kind of equity. An example is an option for a minority shareholder to exchange its holding of shares in a subsidiary for a fixed number of equity shares in the parent. Both legs of the contract are a fixed number of shares and in both cases the shares are a residual interest in some or all of the entity, that is equity. The contract does not violate the part of the definition of a financial liability in paragraph 11 (b) (i) of IAS 32 because, although it is a non-derivative contract, it does not oblige the entity to deliver a variable number of its own equity instruments and hence the entity is not using its own equity instruments as 'currency'. From the perspective of the parent in preparing its separate financial statements, the contract is a derivative as it is over an asset (investment in its subsidiary), rather than an equity instrument.

7. 49 A contract that will be settled in cash or another financial asset as opposed to the delivery of shares is a financial asset or financial liability even if the amount of cash or another financial asset that will be received or delivered is based on changes in the market price of the entity's own equity. An example is a net cash-settled share option. [IAS 32 para AG 27 (c)]. Derivatives on own shares are considered further from paragraph 7. 89 below.

以主体自身股票结算的合同	对价的货币价值[1]	权益股票数量	分类
第 1 种情况	固定	可变	金融负债
第 2 种情况	可变	可变	金融负债
第 3 种情况	可变	固定	金融负债
第 4 种情况	以主体功能货币以外的另一种货币固定[2]	固定	金融负债
第 5 种情况	固定	固定	权益

1. 以发行人的功能货币计价。
2. 第 7.41 段及其下文中讨论的例外除外。

7.48　IAS 32 并未规范主体用固定数量的一种自身权益换取固定数量的另一种权益的期权。比如少数股东用其持有的子公司的股票换取母公司固定数量的权益股票的期权。该合同所交换的双方均为固定数量的股票，且这两种股票均为主体的部分或全部的剩余权益，即权益。该合同并未违背 IAS 32 第 11（b）（i）段中金融负债的定义，虽然其是一项非衍生工具合同，但并未要求主体交付可变数量的自身权益工具，因此主体并非将其自身权益工具用作“货币”。从母公司编制其单独财务报表的角度来看，该合同是一项衍生工具，因为它涉及的是一项资产（其对子公司的投资）而非权益工具。

7.49　如果一项合同将以现金或其他金融资产结算而非交付股票，即使将收取或交付的现金或其他金融资产的金额取决于主体自身权益的市场价格的变动，该合同仍是一项金融资产或金融负债。如以现金进行净额结算的股票期权。[IAS 32 AG 第27（c）段]。第 7.89 段及其下文对标的为自身股票的衍生工具做了进一步讨论。

Contingent settlement provisions

7.50 The obligation to deliver cash or financial assets need not be certain of occurring, it may be contingent on the occurrence or non-occurrence of uncertain future events (or on the outcome of uncertain circumstances) that are beyond the control of both the issuer or the holder of the instrument. Examples of such uncertain future events may include, but are not limited to:

- Changes in stock market index or consumer price index.
- Changes in interest rates or exchange rates.
- Changes in tax laws or other regulatory requirements.
- Changes in the issuer's key performance indicators such as revenue, net income or debt-to-equity ratios.

7.51 In accordance with IAS 32 paragraph 25, the instrument is a financial liability in the circumstances specified above. This is because at the time of the initial recognition, the issuer does not have an unconditional right to avoid delivering cash or another financial asset (or otherwise to settle it in such a way that it would be a financial liability) as it does not control the final outcome. A transfer of economic benefits as a result of a past event (the issue of the instrument) cannot be avoided depending on the outcome of the future event. Such financial instruments should, therefore, be classified as a financial liability.

Example 1 – Change of control events

A contract between entity A and a third party contains a requirement for entity A to make payments to the third party on a change of control of entity A. For example, where entity A may be taken over by entity B and where entity B is not connected to entity A.

The change of control event is outside the control of both the entity and the third party provided that it needs not to be agreed by the entity at a general meeting, as discussed in paragraphs 7.18.1-7.18.4. This will be the case if a purchaser could approach individual shareholders and buy their shares. Payments to a third party that are contingent on a change of control event are,

或有结算条款

7.50 交付现金或其他金融资产的义务并不要求确定会发生，其也可能视工具的发行人或持有人均不能控制的未来不确定事项的发生与否（或某种不确定性状况的结果）而定。这些未来不确定事项的例子包括但不限于：

- 股票市场指数或消费者价格指数的变动；
- 利率或汇率的变动；
- 税收法律或其他法规要求的变动；
- 发行人如收入、净收益或债务权益比率等关键业绩指标的变动。

7.51 按照 IAS 32 第 25 段的规定，符合上述规定的工具是一项金融负债。这是因为在初始确认时，发行人不具有无条件避免交付现金或其他金融资产（或者通过形成主体的一项金融负债来结算这一合同）的权利，因为其不能控制最终结果。取决于未来事项的结果，由过去事项（该工具的发行）所导致的经济利益的转移无法避免。因此，这种金融工具应该划分为金融负债。

示例 1——控制权变更事项

主体 A 和某第三方之间所签订的合同要求主体 A 在其控制权发生变更时向该第三方支付款项。例如，当主体 A 被主体 B 所接管且主体 B 与主体 A 并无关联时。

如第 7.18.1 到第 7.18.4 段所讨论的，控制权变更的事项如果不需要由主体在股东大会中同意即不在主体和该第三方的控制范围之内。在购买方联络各股东并购买其股份的情况下即会发生这种情况。因此，如果不要求股东大会通过，那么根据控制权变更事项向第三方支付的或有付款就是金融负债。

therefore, financial liabilities when no agreement by a general meeting is required.

Example 2 – Shares with an obligation to pay out a percentage of profits

A bond includes an obligation to pay out a fixed 10% of profits each year and is mandatorily redeemable at par after 20 years.

The instrument has two liability components, a contractual obligation to redeem the instrument at par after 20 years and a contractual obligation to pay 10% of profits until redemption. The latter is a financial liability because, although the payment depends on the entity making profits (an uncertain future event), the future profits are outside the control of both the issuer and holder, but if profits are made the issuer cannot avoid making the payment, hence it meets the definition of a contingent settlement event. The 10% obligation does not meet the definition of an embedded derivative as the entity's profit is a non-financial variable that is specific to a party to the contract. [IAS 39 para 9].

Example 3 – mandatorily redeemable where an IPO does not occur

An undated cumulative bond, whose interest payments are at the discretion of the entity absent an IPO, contains a clause that states that the instrument (including all unpaid cumulative interest) will become mandatorily payable if there is not an IPO by the end of three years from the instrument's issuance date. Although it may be within the entity's control to determine whether the IPO is attempted, market and regulatory forces determine whether any attempt is successful (that is, whether the market will accept an IPO and whether all regulatory approvals will be obtained). These forces are beyond the control of the entity, therefore redemption upon an IPO event not occurring meets the definition of a contingent settlement event and results in the bond being classified as a financial liability from inception.

7.52 Where the event is within the control of the issuer but not the holder, it is possible for the issuer to avoid the event occurring and hence avoid settling the instrument, hence the event would not meet the definition of a contingent settlement event. For example an undated cumulative bond whose interest payments

示例 2——具有支付一定比例利润的义务的股份

某债券具有每年固定支付利润的 10% 并在 20 年后按票面价值强制赎回的义务。

该工具有两个负债组成部分，一个是在 20 年后按票面价值赎回该工具的合同义务，另一个是在赎回前支付利润的 10% 的合同义务。后者是一项金融负债，因为虽然该付款取决于主体盈利（一项未来不确定事项），未来利润不受发行人或持有人的控制，只要有利润发行人就不能避免此项支付，因此它符合或有结算事项的定义。该项 10% 的义务不符合嵌入衍生工具的定义，因为主体的利润是一项合同一方所特有的非金融变量。[IAS 39 第 9 段]。

示例 3——当首次公开募股（"IPO"）未能进行时将强制赎回

某项期限不定的累积债券，在未发生 IPO 的情况下，其利息支付由主体自行决定，另外有一项条款规定如果在该工具发行日后三年内未完成 IPO，则该工具（包括所有未支付的累计利息）将变为一项强制性应付款项。虽然决定是否尝试 IPO 属于主体的控制范围，但是该尝试是否能够成功取决于市场及监管（即，市场是否接受 IPO 以及是否能够获得监管批准）。这些效力不属于主体的控制范围，因此当 IPO 未发生时赎回符合或有结算事项的定义，从而使该债券在最初即被划分为一项金融负债。

7.52　当事项在发行人而不是持有人的控制范围内时，发行人能够避免事项的发生从而能够避免结算工具，因此该事项不符合或有结算事项的定义。例如，某项期限不定的累积债券，其利息由主体自主决定，其中有一条款规定该工具（包括所有未支付累计利息）将在成功完成 IPO 时变为强制性应付款

are at the discretion of the entity that contains a clause that states that the instrument (including all unpaid cumulative interest) will become mandatorily payable if a successful IPO occurs. As outlined in example 3 above, it is within an entity's control to determine whether an IPO is attempted and, hence, the entity can avoid a successful IPO taking place. Therefore, the clause does not meet the definition of a contingent settlement provision and results in the bond being classified as an equity instrument from inception.

7.52.1 Contingent settlement provisions sometimes exist within the terms of convertible loan instruments. If a convertible instrument must be settled in cash on the occurrence of a contingent settlement event (for example, a change in tax law; default on the instrument) that is, outside the control of both issuer and holder, the whole instrument, including the option to convert, is treated as a financial liability.

7.52.2 Cash settlement of one financial instrument can be contingent upon the default of another financial instrument as discussed below.

Example – Instruments that are redeemable on default on another instrument('cross default clauses')

An entity has issued two instruments. The first instrument is mandatorily redeemable and pays a mandatory fixed coupon and is therefore classified as a financial liability in accordance with IAS 32. The second instrument has no mandatory payments other than it is mandatorily redeemable if there is an event of default on the first instrument.

The event of default on the first instrument is a contingent settlement provision that makes the second instrument a financial liability of the issuer under paragraph 25 of IAS 32. Whether or not an entity defaults on the payment related to an instrument depends, in part, on whether it has adequate resources to make the payments when contractually due. The availability of adequate resources depends primarily on the future revenue and income of the entity. Paragraph 25 of IAS 32 is clear that revenues and net income are not within the entity's control. Therefore, mandatory redemption in the event of default meets the definition of a genuine

项。如上文示例3中所述，是否尝试进行IPO属于主体的控制范围，因此，主体可避免成功地完成IPO。因此，该条款不符合或有结算条款的定义，从而使得该债券从最初即被划分为权益。

7.52.1　有时在可转换贷款工具的条款中也有或有结算条款。如果某项可转换工具在发行人和持有人的控制范围外的某或有结算事项发生时（如税收法律的变动；对该工具的违约）必须以现金结算，则包括转股权在内的整个工具要作为金融负债来处理。

7.52.2　如下所述，一项金融工具的现金结算可能视另一项金融工具的违约情况而定。

示例——在另一项工具违约时可赎回的工具（交叉违约条款）

某主体发行了两项工具。第一项工具强制可赎回且支付固定金额的强制票面利息，因此根据IAS 32划分为金融负债。第二项工具除了在第一项工具违约的情况下需强制赎回之外没有其他强制性付款。

第一项工具的违约事项是一个或有结算条款，它使得第二项工具根据IAS 32第25段的要求作为发行人的一项金融负债。主体是否对与工具相关的付款违约部分取决于当合同规定到期时其是否有足够的资金来源来完成付款。是否有足够的资金来源主要取决于主体的未来收入和收益。IAS 32第25段明确指出收入和净收益不在主体的控制范围内。因此，在有违约事件时的强制性赎回符合现实的或有结算条款的定义，从而使第二项工具划分为金融负债。

contingent settlement provision, which results in the second instrument being classified as a financial liability.

7.53 There are three exceptions where uncertain events outside the control of the issuer would not meet the definition of a contingent settlement event. These are where:

- The part of the contingent settlement provision that could require settlement in cash or another financial asset (or otherwise in such a way that it would be a financial liability) is not *genuine* (see para 7.54). [IAS 32 para 25].
- The issuer can be required to settle the obligation in cash or another financial asset (or otherwise to settle it in such a way that it would be a financial liability) only in the event of liquidation of the issuer (see para 7.56). [IAS 32 para 25].
- A third exception is introduced by the amendment to IAS 32 for puttable instruments and obligations arising on liquidation, as discussed from paragraph 7.20. This is effective for accounting periods beginning on or after 1 January 2009.

Settlement terms that are not genuine

7.54 The standard explains that a contingent settlement provision in a contract is not genuine if it requires settlement in cash only on the occurrence of an event that is extremely rare, highly abnormal and very unlikely to occur. In that situation, the contingent settlement provisions are not taken into account in the instrument's classification. Thus, a contract that requires settlement in cash or a variable number of the entity's own shares only on the occurrence of an event that is extremely rare, highly abnormal and very unlikely to occur is an equity instrument. Similarly, if settlement in a fixed number of an entity's own shares may be contractually precluded in circumstances that are outside the control of the entity, those circumstances can be ignored if there is no genuine possibility that they will occur. In that situation, the instrument continues to be classified as an equity instrument and not as a financial liability. [IAS 32 para AG 28].

7.53　不在发行人控制范围内的不确定事项里有三个例外不符合或有结算事项的定义。它们是：

- 能够要求以现金或其他金融资产（或者通过形成一项金融负债）进行结算的或有结算条款部分是不现实的（参见第 7.54 段）。[IAS 32 第 25 段]。

- 只有在发行人清算时才能够要求发行人履行交付现金或其他金融资产的义务（或者通过形成一项金融负债来结算这一合同）（参见第 7.56 段）。[IAS 32 第 25 段]。

- 如第 7.20 段及其下文所讨论的，第三个例外是由 IAS 32 针对可回售工具和清算产生的义务的修订引入的。该修订从起始日在 2009 年 1 月 1 日或之后开始的会计期间生效。

不现实的结算条款

7.54　该准则说明如果一个合同的或有结算条款要求只有在发生了极端罕见、严重异常和几乎不可能发生的事件后才能以现金结算，那么这是一个非现实的条款。在这种情形下，这些或有结算条款在对工具进行分类时并不予以考虑。因此，如果一项合同只有在发生了极端罕见、严重异常和几乎不可能发生的事件时才能以现金或可变数量的主体自身股票进行结算，则该合同是一项权益工具。类似地，合同可能规定在某种主体无法控制的情况下，不以固定数量的主体自身股票进行结算，但是只要这些情况的发生不具有现实可能性，则可以忽略。在这种情形下，该工具将继续划分为权益工具而非金融负债。[IAS 32 AG 第 28 段]。

7.55 In practice, terms are included in a contract for a purpose that is likely to have commercial effect. Therefore, it would be unusual to include settlement terms in a contract that are contingent on an event that is extremely rare, highly abnormal and very unlikely to occur. If such ineffective terms are included, it should be concluded that the terms are not genuine and should be ignored in determining the instrument's classification. However, 'not genuine' should not be equated to 'remote'. The IASB makes it clear in the Basis for conclusions to IAS 32 that it is not appropriate to disregard events that are merely 'remote'. The specific facts and circumstances would need to be considered.

Example 1 – Settlement terms based on increase in an index

An entity issues an instrument that is redeemable in cash if the FTSE 100 triples within a two month period.

In general, it is not for the entity to speculate whether an index will behave in a certain manner that may or may not trigger redemption of the instrument. As the entity will be unable to avoid a settlement in cash if the index reaches that level, the instrument should be treated as a financial liability.

However, in this situation, the tripling of the FTSE 100 within such a short period of time is extremely rare, highly abnormal and unlikely to occur. Furthermore, in practice, an investor is highly unlikely to advance funds on such redemption terms. Clearly the terms are artificial and not genuine and should be ignored for classification purposes.

Example 2 – Settlement terms based on changes in regulation

A bank issues an instrument that is redeemable in cash if the banking regulator changes the instrument's current classification from tier 1 capital to tier 2 capital in the future.

Whether the contingency in this example is genuine would depend upon the specific facts and circumstances. In some jurisdictions, the industry regulator has a history of applying such changes always prospectively and grandfathering existing instruments under their original classification. In that situation, a regulatory change would not affect the classification of an

7.55 在实务中，合同所包含的条款都可能有商业目的。因此，在合同中加入取决于极端罕见、严重异常和几乎不可能发生的事件的结算条款应该很少见。如果加入了这种无效条款，应断定这些条款是非现实的，在确定工具的分类时应将其忽略。但是，“非现实”不应等同于“可能性极小”。IASB 在 IAS 32 的《结论基础》中明确澄清道，不应忽视那些仅仅是“可能性极小”的事件，需要考虑具体的事实和情况。

示例 1——基于某项指标增长的结算条款

某主体发行了一项工具，如果 FTSE 100 指数在两个月内翻三倍该工具就将以现金赎回。

通常情况下，主体无法推测某项指数是否按照某种可能触发工具赎回的特定的方式变动。由于如果该指数达到了所述水平主体将无法避免以现金结算，该工具应作为一项金融负债。

但是，在此示例中，FTSE 100 指数在如此短暂的期间内翻三倍的情况是极端罕见、严重异常和几乎不可能发生的。此外，在实务中，投资人基本不可能为这种赎回条款预付款项。很明显该条款是虚假的，并不现实，在分类时应将其忽略。

示例 2——基于法规变动的结算条款

某银行发行了一项工具，如果银行监管机构未来将该工具从当前的 1 类资本变为 2 类资本就将以现金赎回。

本示例中的或有事项是否现实应该取决于具体的事实和情况。在某些管辖区域内，行业监管机构总是在未来适用这些变动，不去追溯现有工具的初始分类。在这种情形下，法规的变动应该不会影响某项已发行在外的工具的分类，因此，该或有事项将被视为不现实的。

instrument that is currently outstanding and, consequently, the contingency would be regarded as not genuine.

Settlements that arise only on liquidation

7.56 Obligations to deliver cash or other financial assets that are contingent only on the issuer's liquidation should be ignored. This is rather obvious because different rights and obligations associated with the instruments come into effect at liquidation that would not otherwise be triggered during the ordinary course of business and, hence, would be inconsistent with the going concern assumption. A contingent settlement provision that provides for payment in cash or another financial asset only on the entity's liquidation is similar to an equity instrument that has priority in liquidation. Such a provision should, therefore, be ignored in classifying the instrument. However, if the instrument is redeemable on the occurrence of an event that may ultimately lead to eventual liquidation (for example, the entity becomes insolvent, goes into receivership or administration which is beyond the control of the entity), the instrument should still be classified as a financial liability.

Derivative financial instruments with settlement options

7.57 Sometimes a derivative contract may contain settlement options that give either party a choice over how it is settled (for example, the issuer or the holder can choose to settle the contract net in cash, or by exchanging shares for cash). IAS 32 states that when a derivative financial instrument gives one party a choice over how it is settled, it is a financial asset or a financial liability, unless all of the settlement alternatives would result in it being an equity instrument. [IAS 32 para 26].

7.58 An example of a derivative financial instrument with a settlement option that is a financial liability is an option for an entity to buy its own shares from a third party that the entity can decide to settle net in cash or by exchanging its own shares for cash. Forward and option contracts to buy or sell an entity's own equity instruments that contain settlement options are discussed in paragraph 7.97 below.

仅在清算时产生的结算

7.56 仅在发行人清算时才要交付现金或其他金融资产的义务，应予以忽略。这相当显而易见，因为这些工具相关的不同权利和义务在清算时才生效，而在正常的业务流程中不会发生，因此，与持续经营的假设不一致。只有在主体清算时才会支付现金或其他金融资产的或有结算条款与在清算时具有优先权的权益工具类似。因此，在对工具分类时应将其忽略。但是，如果对工具的赎回是在可能最后导致清算的事项发生时（例如，主体在其无法控制的情况下资不抵债、被接管或管理），则仍应将该工具划分为一项金融负债。

具有结算选择权的衍生金融工具

7.57 有时衍生工具合同可能会包含给予任意一方选择结算方式的结算选择权（例如，发行人或持有人可以选择以现金进行净额结算，或以股票交换现金的方式结算）。IAS 32 规定如果一项衍生金融工具给予合同某一方选择结算方式的权利，则该衍生工具是一项金融资产或金融负债，除非所有的可选结算方式都将使其成为一项权益工具。[IAS 32 第 26 段]。

7.58 包含结算选择权的衍生金融工具作为金融负债的一个例子是：主体从第三方购买其自身股票的股票期权，且主体可以决定以现金进行净额结算或以股票交换现金的方式结算。在下文第 7.97 段中讨论了有关含有结算选择权的购买或出售主体自身权益工具的远期合同和期权合同。同时，某些以非金融项目（并非“自用”）与主体自身权益工具交换的合同，如果可以通过交付

Also, some contracts to buy or sell a non-financial item (not for 'own use') in exchange for the entity's own equity instruments are financial assets or financial liabilities and not equity instruments, if they can be settled either by delivery of the non financial item or net in cash or another financial instrument. [IAS 32 para 27]. Where the settlement option is contingent on a future event occurring, it will still fall under the settlement option accounting in accordance with paragraph 26 of IAS 32 from initial recognition, as discussed in paragraph 7.76.

Shares issued by subsidiaries

7.59 Normally equity shares issued by subsidiaries to persons outside the group are classified as non-controlling interests in the consolidated financial statements in accordance with IAS 1, 'Presentation of financial statements', and IAS 27, 'Consolidated and separate financial statements'. When classifying a financial instrument (or a component of it) in consolidated financial statements, an entity should consider all the terms and conditions agreed between group members and the instrument holders in determining whether the group as a whole has an obligation to deliver cash or another financial asset in respect of the instrument, or to settle it in a manner that results in liability classification.

7.60 For example, a member of the group might give a guarantee to pay amounts in respect of those shares, such as dividends or amounts due on their redemption; or another group member might undertake to purchase the shares in the event that the subsidiary issuing them fails to make the expected payments. Where this is so, the outside shareholders will look to the guarantor if the subsidiary has defaulted.

7.61 Consequently, in such a situation, the subsidiary may appropriately classify the instrument without regard to these additional terms in its separate financial statements. However, in the consolidated financial statements, the effect of other agreements between group members and the instrument holders means that the group as a whole is unable to avoid the transfer of economic benefits. Therefore, where such an obligation or settlement provision exists from the perspective of the group, the instrument (or the component of it that is subject to the obligation) is classified as a financial liability in the consolidated financial statements. [IAS 32 para AG 29].

[The next paragraph is 7.63.]

非金融项目或使用现金或其他金融工具进行净额结算，则其是金融资产或金融负债，而非权益工具。[IAS 32 第 27 段]。如第 7.76 段所讨论的，在结算选择权取决于某项未来事件的发生的情况下，其初始确认仍需遵照 IAS 32 第 26 段规定的结算选择权的会计处理方法。

子公司发行的股份

7.59　通常由子公司发行给集团外投资人的权益股票根据《国际会计准则第 1 号——财务报表的列报》和《国际会计准则第 27 号——合并财务报表和单独财务报表》的规定在合并财务报表中划分为非控制性权益。在合并财务报表中对金融工具（或其组成部分）进行分类时，主体应考虑集团成员和工具持有人之间形成的协议条款，以确定集团作为一个整体是否由于该工具而承担了交付现金或其他金融资产的义务，或承担了以导致该工具划分为金融负债的方式结算的义务。

7.60　例如，某集团成员可能对股份相关的支付金额作出担保，诸如股利，赎回时应付的金额；或者另一集团成员可能承诺在发行股份的子公司不能支付预期款项的情况下购买这些股份。在这种情况下，如果子公司违约则外部股东将会诉诸担保人。

7.61　因此，在这种情形下，子公司在没有考虑这些附加协议的情况下也可能在其单独财务报表中对这一工具进行适当的分类。但是，在合并财务报表中，集团成员与工具持有人之间的附加协议的影响意味着集团作为一个整体无法避免经济利益的转移。因此，从集团的角度，只要存在这样的义务或结算条款，该工具（或其中与上述义务相关的部分）在合并财务报表中将要被划分为金融负债。[IAS 32 AG 第 29 段]。

[下一段为第 7.63 段。]

Compound financial instruments

Introduction

7.63 Not all financial instruments are either liability or equity. Some, known as compound instruments contain elements of both in a single contact. A compound financial instrument is a non-derivative financial instrument that, from the issuer's perspective, contains both a liability and an equity component. [IAS 32 paras 28, AG 30]. Typical examples of such instruments are:

- A bond that is convertible into a fixed number of equity shares at the holder's option. From the issuer's perspective, such an instrument comprises two components: a financial liability (issuer's contractual obligation to deliver cash or another financial asset for payment of interest and principal, if not converted) and an equity instrument (a written call option granting the holder the right, for a specified period of time, to convert it into a fixed number of the entity's ordinary shares). The economic effect of issuing such an instrument is substantially the same as issuing simultaneously a debt instrument with an early settlement provision and warrants to purchase ordinary shares, or issuing a debt instrument with detachable share purchase warrants. [IAS 32 para 29]. If the issuer call option is contingent on a future event, it should still be for accounted for as a call option from initial recognition. For example:

Example 1 – Provisional issuer call option to redeem at par

Company A issues a convertible bond that, if converted, converts into a fixed number of equity shares. The bond also contains a provisional call option that gives the issuer the option to redeem the bond at par if the shares price is 130% of the conversion price for at least 20 days.

The convertible bond is a compound financial instrument with a debt host and equity conversion option. As the issuer call option is to redeem the bonds at par, it does not result in the conversion option having a cash settlement alternative. The conversion option is not, therefore, accounted for as an

复合金融工具

引言

7.63 并非所有金融工具不是负债就是权益。有些被称为复合工具的工具，就在单一的合同中包含两种成分。复合金融工具是从发行人的角度而言同时包含负债和权益部分的非衍生金融工具。[IAS 32 第 28 段、AG 第 30 段]。这种工具的典型例子包括：

- 持有人有权选择转换为固定数量的权益股票的债券。从发行人的角度看，这种工具由两部分组成：一项金融负债（发行人交付现金或其他金融资产以支付利息和本金（如果未转换）的合同义务）和一项权益工具（一项签出看涨期权，授予持有人在特定时期内将负债转换为主体固定数量的普通股的权利）。发行这种工具的经济效果实质上与以下做法一样：同时发行一项可提前偿付的债务工具和一项购买普通股的认股权证，或是发行一项附可单独出售的认股权证的债务工具。[IAS 32 第 29 段]。如果发行人的看涨期权取决于某个未来事件，在初始确认时仍需将其作为一项看涨期权来进行会计处理。例如：

示例 1——有条件的按照票面价值赎回的发行人看涨期权

A 公司发行了一个可转换债券，若转股，则转换为固定数量的权益股票。该债券还包含一项有条件的看涨期权，使发行人有权在股票价格为转换价的 130% 的天数至少达到 20 天时按票面价值赎回该债券。

此可转换债券是一项具有主债务和转股权的复合金融工具。由于发行人的看涨期权是按照票面价值赎回债券，并不会使得转股权有现金结算的选择。因此，该转股权不用按照 IAS 32 第 26 段作为一项嵌入衍生工具进行会计处理。

embedded derivative in accordance with paragraph 26 of IAS 32.

In respect of the issuer call option, the value of any derivative feature (such as a call option) embedded in a compound financial instrument, (other than the equity component) is included in the liability component. [IAS 32 para 31]. The call option is, therefore, considered part of the liability and not the equity component. The assessment of whether the call or put option is closely related to the host debt contract from the issuer's perspective is made before separating the equity element under IAS 32. [IAS 39 para AG 30(g)].

- A mandatorily redeemable preference shares with dividend payments made at the issuer's discretion before the redemption date. Such an instrument contains a liability component (issuer's contractual obligation to deliver cash or another financial asset for payment of the redemption amount) and an equity component (the holder's right to receive dividends, if declared). [IAS 32 para AG 37].

Separation of a compound financial instrument on initial recognition

7.64 The issuer of a non-derivative financial instrument should first evaluate the financial instrument's terms to determine whether it contains both a liability and an equity component. This evaluation should be done in accordance with the contractual arrangement's substance and the definition of a financial liability, financial asset and an equity component. If such components are identified, the issuer should account for the components separately as financial liabilities, financial assets or equity instruments. [IAS 32 para 28]. The liability and the equity components must be presented separately on the balance sheet. [IAS 32 para 29].

7.65 The above approach is often described as 'split accounting'. Split accounting is applied by the issuer of the financial instruments to measure the liability and the equity components upon initial recognition of the instrument. The method, illustrated by reference to a convertible bond that is a most common form of a compound financial instrument, but which is equally applicable to other forms of compound financial instruments, allocates the fair value of the consideration for the compound instrument into its liability and equity components, as follows:

对于发行人的看涨期权，复合金融工具中除权益部分以外的任何嵌入衍生工具（如看涨期权）的价值包括在负债组成部分中。[IAS 32 第 31 段]。因此，该看涨期权被视为负债而非权益的一部分。从发行人的角度判定看涨期权或看跌期权是否与主债务合同密切相关而进行的评估要在按照 IAS 32 对权益成分进行分离之前进行。[IAS 39 AG 第 30（g）段]。

- 强制性可赎回优先股，其赎回日前的股利支付由发行人自主决定。这种工具包含负债部分（发行人交付现金或其他金融资产以支付赎回金额的合同义务）以及权益部分（如果宣告发放股利，持有人收取股利的权利）。[IAS 32 AG 第 37 段]。

初始确认时对复合金融工具的分拆

7.64　非衍生金融工具的发行人应首先对金融工具的条款进行评估以确定其是否同时包含负债和权益部分。这种评估应该按照合同安排的实质以及金融负债、金融资产和权益部分的定义来进行。一旦确定了各组成部分，发行人应将这些组成部分单独作为金融负债、金融资产或权益工具进行会计处理。[IAS 32 第 28 段]。在资产负债表中负债部分和权益部分必须单独列报。[IAS 32 第 29 段]。

7.65　上述方法经常被称为"分割会计法"。财务报表的编制者会在工具初始确认时采用分割会计法对其负债和权益部分进行计量。如下所述，这种方法将复合工具对价的公允价值分配至其负债和权益部分，在此以最常见的一种复合金融工具形式——可转换债券进行举例说明，但它同样也适用于其他形式的复合金融工具。

- The fair value of the consideration in respect of the liability component is measured first, at the fair value of a similar liability (including any embedded non-equity derivative features such as an issuer's call option to redeem the bond early) that does not have any associated equity conversion option. This becomes the liability component's carrying amount at initial recognition.

  In practice, the liability component's initial carrying value is determined by discounting the contractual stream of future cash flows (interest and principal) to the present value at the current rate of interest applicable to instruments of comparable credit status and providing substantially the same cash flows on the same terms, but without the equity component (the equity conversion option).

  The value of any embedded non-equity derivative features is separately determined and included in the liability component.

- The equity component (the equity conversion option) is assigned the residual amount after deducting from the fair value of the instrument as a whole the amount separately determined for the liability component.

  The equity component is excluded from IAS 39's scope and is never remeasured after initial recognition.

Since the sum of the carrying amounts assigned to the liability and equity components on initial recognition is always equal to the consideration received, which, in most circumstances is equal to the fair value of the instrument as a whole, no gain or loss arises from initially recognising the instrument's components separately in the above manner.

[IAS 32 paras 31, AG 31].

7.66 The requirement to separate the liability and the equity components of a single compound financial instrument in the above manner is consistent with the requirements for initial measurement of a financial liability in IAS 39 and the definitions in IAS 32 and the Framework of an equity instrument as a residual interest. Furthermore, the approach removes the need to estimate inputs to, and apply, complex option pricing models to measure the equity component of some compound financial instruments. [IAS 32 paras BC 29 – 30].

- 首先根据不包含任何转股权的类似负债（包括诸如发行人可提前赎回债券的看涨期权等任何非权益性的嵌入衍生工具）的公允价值对相关负债部分对价的公允价值进行计量。这就是负债部分初始确认时的账面价值。

  实务中，负债部分的初始账面价值是由合同规定的未来现金流量（利息和本金）折现的现值来确定，其中利率为具有可比信用等级并在相同条件下提供几乎相同的现金流量但不具有权益部分（转股权）的工具的当前适用利率。

  任何非权益的嵌入衍生工具的价值均需单独确定并包含在负债部分中。

- 从工具整体的公允价值中扣除单独确定的负债部分的金额，其余额作为权益部分（转股权）的价值。

  权益部分不在 IAS 39 的范围内，初始确认后不再重新计量。

由于初始确认时分配给负债部分和权益部分的账面价值之和总是等于所收到的对价，而后者在大多数情况下都等于工具整体的公允价值，按照上述方式对工具的各组成部分进行初始确认不产生利得或损失。

[IAS 32 第 31 段、AG 第 31 段]。

7.66　以上述方式分拆单个复合金融工具的负债和权益部分的要求符合 IAS 39 中关于金融负债初始计量的规定，并符合 IAS 32 和《框架》中对权益工具的定义，即其是一种剩余权益。另外，这种方法无需通过估计某些参数值并使用复杂的期权定价模型来计量某些复合金融工具的权益部分。[IAS 32 BC 第 29 - 30 段]。

7.67 Once a compound financial instrument has been separated into its liability and equity components on initial recognition, the classification of the liability and equity components is not revised as a result of a change in the likelihood that a conversion option will be exercised, even when the option's exercise may appear to have become economically advantageous to some holders. This is because the entity's contractual obligation to make future payments remains outstanding until it is extinguished through conversion, the instrument's maturity or some other transaction. [IAS 32 para 30].

Example – Separation of a convertible bond

An entity issues 600,000 convertible bonds at the start of year 1. The bonds have a 3-year term, and are issued at par with a face value of C100 per bond, resulting in total proceeds of C60m, which is also the fair value of the bonds. Interest is payable annually in arrears at a nominal annual interest rate of 6%. Each C100 nominal bond is convertible at any time up to maturity into 25 ordinary shares. When the bonds are issued, the prevailing market interest rate for similar debt without conversion options is 9%. The entity incurs an issue cost of 1% on the nominal value of the bond amounting to C600,000.

As explained in paragraph 7.65 above, the liability component is measured first by discounting the contractually determined stream of future cash flows (interest and principal) to present value using a discount rate of 9%, the market interest rate for similar bonds having no conversion rights, as shown below.

	C
PV of interest payable at the end of year 1 – 3,600,000/1.09	3,302,752
PV of interest payable at the end of year 2 – 3,600,000/$(1.09)^2$	3,030,048
PV of interest payable at the end of year 3 – 3,600,000/$(1.09)^3$	2,779,861
PV of principal of C60,000,000 payable at the end of three years – 60,000,000/$(1.09)^3$	46,331,009

7.67 复合金融工具一旦在初始确认时被分拆为负债和权益部分后，负债和权益部分的分类不应因行使转股权的可能性发生变化而改变，即使行使转股权对某些持有人来说有利可图。这是因为主体未来支付的合同义务只有在发生转换、工具到期或其他某些交易发生的情况下才能得以解除。[IAS 32 第 30 段]。

示例——可转换债券的分拆

某主体在第 1 年年初发行了 600,000 份可转换债券。该债券期限为三年，按每份面值 C100 元发行，取得总收入 C6,000 万元，这也是该债券的公允价值。利息按 6% 的名义利率在借款期每年年末支付。每份面值 C100 元的债券都可以在到期之前的任何时间转换为 25 股普通股。在债券发行时，不具备转股权的类似债券的市场利率为 9%。主体发生了占债券名义价值 1% 的发行成本，金额为 C600,000 元。

如上文第 7.65 段所解释的，负债部分首先按照由合同规定的未来现金流量（利息和本金）折现的现值来计量，其中利率为不具有转股权的类似债券的市场利率 9%。如下所示。

	C
第 1 年年末应付利息的现值——3,600,000/1.09	3,302,752
第 2 年年末应付利息的现值——3,600,000/$(1.09)^2$	3,030,048
第 3 年年末应付利息的现值——3,600,000/$(1.09)^3$	2,779,861
C60,000,000 元的本金在第 3 年年末的现值——60,000,000/$(1.09)^3$	46,331,009

Total liability component	55, 443, 670
Total equity component (residual) *	4, 556, 330
Fair value of bonds	60, 000, 000

* The equity component is a written call option that allows the holder to call for the shares on exercise of the conversion option at any time before maturity (American option). Since equity is a residual, application of complex option pricing models are not necessary to determine the equity component. Instead, the difference between the bond's proceeds and the liability component's fair value of the liability component as computed above – the residual – is assigned to the equity component.

In accordance with IAS 32, the issue cost of C600, 000 will need to be allocated between the liability and the equity components in proportion to the allocation of the proceeds as shown below:

	Equity component	**Liability component**	**Total**
	C	**C**	**C**
Gross proceeds allocated as above	4, 556, 330	55, 443, 670	60, 000, 000
Issue cost	(45, 563)	(554, 437)	(600, 000)
Net proceeds	4, 510, 767	54, 889, 233	59, 400, 000

The amount credited to equity of C4, 510, 767 is not subsequently remeasured.

The liability component will be classified under IAS 39 either as a financial liability at fair value through profit or loss or as another liability measured at amortised cost using the effective interest rate method. If classified as a financial liability at fair value through profit or loss, the liability component will be initially recognised at C55, 443, 670 and the issue cost of C554, 437 allocated to the liability component will be immediately expensed to the income statement. However, under the latter classification, the liability

负债部分总额	55, 443, 670
权益部分总额(剩余值)*	4, 556, 330
债券的公允价值	60, 000, 000

* 权益部分是一项允许持有人在到期日前的任何时间行使转股权以取得股票的签出看涨期权(美式期权)。因为权益是剩余部分,在确定权益部分时无需采用复杂的期权定价模型,而只是将债券收入和如上所计算的负债部分公允价值之间的差额——即余额——分配给权益部分。

根据 IAS 32 的规定，C600, 000 元的发行成本需要按照如下所示收入分配比例在负债和权益部分之间进行分配。

	权益部分	负债部分	合计
	C	C	C
如上所述所分配的总收入	4, 556, 330	55, 443, 670	60, 000, 000
发行成本	(45, 563)	(554, 437)	(600, 000)
净收入	4, 510, 767	54, 889, 233	59, 400, 000

贷记权益的金额 C4, 510, 767 元期后不再重新计量。

负债部分将按照 IAS 39 分类为以公允价值计量且变动计入损益的金融负债或是按实际利率法计算的以摊余成本计量的其他负债。如果分类为以公允价值计量且变动计入损益的金融负债，该负债部分将以 C55, 443, 670 元的金额初始确认，而分配至负债部分、金额为 C554, 437 的发行成本将立即计入利润表。但是，按照后一种方式进行分类时，该负债部分将以扣除发行成本后的 C54, 889, 233 元初始确认。［IAS 39 第 43 段］。如下所示，其将按照 9. 38837% 的实际利率增至第 3 年年末的最终赎回金额

component will be initially recognised net of issue cost at C54, 889, 233. [IAS 39 para 43]. It will accrete to its final redemption amount of C60, 000, 000 at the end of year 3 at an effective interest rate of 9. 38837% as shown below:

Year	Opening liability	Interest @ 9.38837%	Cash paid	Closing liability
	C	C	C	C
1	54, 889, 233	5, 153, 205	(3, 600, 000)	56, 442, 438
2	56, 442, 438	5, 299, 025	(3, 600, 000)	58, 141, 464
3	58, 141, 464	5, 458, 536	(63, 600, 000)	-
Total finance cost		15, 910, 767		
Total finance cost consists of:				
Interest payments		10, 800, 000		
Issue cost allocated to liability component		554, 437		
Discount (representing gross proceeds allocated to equity component)		4, 556, 330		
		15, 910, 767		

Separation of a compound instrument containing non-equity derivatives

7.68 As explained above, a non-derivative compound financial instrument must be separated into its equity and liability components. In a convertible bond, the equity component arises from the embedded option to convert the liability into the issuer's equity. However, a convertible bond may also contain other non-equity derivative features such as a call, put or pre-payment option. The way in which a compound financial instrument with multiple derivative features is separated into its constituent parts is indicated below:

C60,000,000 元。

年份	期初负债	按照 9.38837% 计算的利息	已付现金	期末负债
	C	C	C	C
1	54,889,233	5,153,205	(3,600,000)	56,442,438
2	56,442,438	5,299,025	(3,600,000)	58,141,464
3	58,141,464	5,458,536	(63,600,000)	–
财务费用合计		15,910,767		
财务费用合计中包括：				
利息		10,800,000		
分配至负债部分的发行成本		554,437		
折现（代表总收入中分配至权益部分的金额）		4,556,330		
		15,910,767		

对含有非权益性衍生工具的复合工具的分拆

7.68 如上文所解释的，非衍生复合金融工具必须分拆为权益和负债部分。在可转换债券中，权益部分产生于将负债转换为发行人权益的嵌入期权。但是，可转换债券可能还会包含其他非权益的衍生工具，例如看涨期权、看跌期权或提前偿付选择权。将包含多项衍生工具的复合金融工具分拆成各个部分的方法说明如下：

- First, the value of non-equity derivatives must be included in the liability component. [IAS 32 para 31]. This means that the liability component is established by measuring a bond's fair value with similar terms, credit status and containing similar non-equity derivative features, but without the equity conversion feature.

- Secondly, the equity component is then arrived at by deducting the fair value attributable to the bond as determined above from the compound instrument's fair value.

- Thirdly, given that the liability component contains the non-equity derivative features, it is necessary to assess whether such embedded derivative features are closely related to the host debt contract. This assessment is made before separating the equity element as determined above (see chapter 5). [IAS 39 para AG 30 (g)]. In a convertible bond, that assessment will involve determining whether the call option's exercise price is approximately equal to the sum of the debt and the equity components, which is equal to the convertible bond's par value. If the bond is callable at par, the embedded call option is closely related to the host debt instrument. The embedded call option is not bifurcated (split out) and the liability component is determined as indicated above. If, on the other hand, the bond is callable at the carrying value of the liability component, the embedded call option is not closely related to the debt host. In that situation, the embedded call option is separated out of the liability component and accounted for separately. Separating the embedded derivative from the liability component does not affect the amount determined for the equity component as noted in bullet point two above.

Example – Convertible debt with embedded puts and calls

A company issues a convertible debt instrument that contains both an equity conversion option and embedded written puts and purchased calls. The debt component is initially measured at the fair value of a plain vanilla debt with the same contractual maturity plus the value of the written puts less value of the purchased calls, in accordance with paragraph 31 of IAS 32 and as illustrated in paragraphs IE 37 and IE 38 (example 10) of IAS 32.

■ 首先，非权益衍生工具的价值必须包含在负债部分中。[IAS 32 第 31 段]。这意味着负债部分是通过计量具有类似条款、信誉等级且包含类似非权益衍生工具但没有转股权的债券的公允价值来确定的。

■ 第二步，通过将如上所确定的分配至该债券的公允价值从复合工具的公允价值中扣除，从而得到权益部分。

■ 第三步，由于负债部分包含非权益衍生工具，需要评估这些嵌入衍生工具是否与主债务合同紧密相关。该评估是在根据上述方法对权益部分进行分拆之前进行的（参见第 5 章）。[IAS 39 AG 第 30（g）段]。在可转换债券中，该评估将涉及到确定看涨期权的行权价格是否大致等于负债和权益部分之和，即等于该可转换债券的票面价值。如果该债券可按照票面价值赎回，则这种嵌入看涨期权与主债务工具紧密相关。这种嵌入看涨期权不必分拆（分割），负债部分按照上文所述方法来确定。而另一方面，如果该债券可按照负债部分的账面价值赎回，则这种嵌入看涨期权不与主债务工具紧密相关。在这种情形下，这种嵌入看涨期权应从负债部分中分拆出来并单独进行会计处理。将嵌入衍生工具从负债部分中分拆出来并不影响如上文第 2 点所述确定为权益部分的金额。

示例——包含嵌入看跌和看涨期权的可转换债务

某公司发行了一项可转换债务工具，其既含有转股权又含有嵌入的签出看跌期权和购入看涨期权。负债部分是按照 IAS 32 第 31 段以及 IE 第 37 和 38 段（示例 10）中所述，根据具有相同合同期限的纯债务的公允价值加上签出看跌期权的价值减去购入看涨期权的价值来进行初始计量的。

Where the puts and calls are not required to be separated from the debt host, the debt component is measured at amortised cost using the effective interest rate method as defined in paragraph 9 of IAS 39 and discussed in chapter 9. The puts and calls are considered in determining the expected future life of the instrument and, therefore, the expected interest rate.

- Finally, the sum of the carrying amounts assigned to the various components as indicated above on initial recognition must always be equal to the compound instrument's fair value as a whole. No gain or loss should arise from initially recognising the instrument's components separately. [IAS 32 para 31].

7.69 The ability to convert the host instrument into own equity of the entity may be contingent on an uncertain future event. Where the uncertain future event meets the definition of a contingent settlement event as defined as in paragraph 7.50, the classification of the conversion option on initial recognition would depend on whether the conversion option meets or violates the 'fixed for fixed' requirement if the uncertain future event occurs.

Example 1 – Contingently convertible bond

Entity A issues a contingently convertible bond; the debt host becomes convertible into common shares of entity A at a fixed ratio of 1:1.25 only if the contingent event occurs. The contingent event meets the definition of a contingent settlement event in accordance with paragraph 25 of IAS 32 and is 'genuine' – for example, a change in control event. There are no adjustments to the conversion ratio upon the contingent event occurring, and there are no other put or call options.

The instrument is first separated into its component parts, namely a debt host and equity conversion option. The fact that the option is only contingently convertible will not cause liability classification of the conversion option under paragraph 25 of IAS 32 provided that, upon occurrence of the contingent event, it would be settled in such a way as to require classification as equity. If the contingent event were to occur in the example above, the conversion to own shares would still satisfy the 'fixed for fixed' requirement in paragraph

在不要求将看跌期权和看涨期权从主债务中分拆出来的情况下，负债部分需采用 IAS 39 第 9 段中所规定并在第 9 章中所讨论的按实际利率法得到的摊余成本进行计量。在确定工具的预计未来寿命，进而确定预计利率时要考虑这些看跌期权和看涨期权。

■ 最后，在初始确认时按以上步骤分配至各个组成部分的账面价值之和必须等于复合工具整体的公允价值。分别对工具的各组成部分进行初始确认不应产生利得或损失。[IAS 32 第 31 段]。

7.69　将主工具转换为主体自身权益的能力可能取决于某项未来不确定事项。在未来不确定事项符合第 7.50 段中或有结算事项定义的情况下，转股权在初始确认时的分类应该取决于该转股权在未来不确定事项发生时是否符合“固定换固定”的要求。

示例 1——或有可转换债券

主体 A 发行了一项或有可转换债券，只有在或有事项发生时，主债务才可以按 1∶1.25 的固定比率转换为主体 A 的普通股。该或有事项符合 IAS 32 第 25 段中或有结算事项的定义并且是“现实的”——如控制权变更事项。在发生该或有事项时不会调整转换率，也没有其他看涨或看跌期权。

首先将该工具分拆为其组成部分，即主债务和转股权。若转股权在或有事项发生时导致可转换债券以权益分类的方式结算，该转股权是或有事项的情况，并不会导致其按照 IAS 32 第 25 段的规定被划分为一项负债。如果上文示例中的或有事项发生的话，转换为自身股票仍能满足 IAS 32 第 16（b）（ii）段中所规定的“固定换固定”要求。该转股权应该被划分为权益部分，该债券从而成为一项复合金融工具。

16(b)(ii) of IAS 32. The conversion option would be classified as an equity component, resulting in a compound financial instrument.

Example 2 – Separation of a callable convertible bond

An entity issues 600, 000 callable convertible bonds at the beginning of year 1. The bonds are issued at par with a face value of C100 per bond, giving total proceeds of C60m, which is also the bond's fair value. The bonds are convertible by the holder into a fixed number of shares at any time after the first anniversary of its issue. Furthermore, the bonds do not have a fixed maturity; instead the issuer can call/redeem the bond at any time at the fixed stated principal amount of the bond.

The following information is relevant:

	Cm
Value of a straight bond without a call or equity conversion feature (plain vanilla)	57
Value of issuer call option in a similar bond without an equity conversion option based on an option pricing model (derivative asset)	2

As explained above, the value of the call option (the non-equity derivative) of C2m must be included in the liability component. In this situation, the inclusion results in the value of a callable bond without the equity conversion feature (the liability component) to be less than the value of a plain vanilla bond. This is because the issuer's right to call the bond in the event that interest rates go up and bond price increases makes the value of a callable bond less attractive to the holder than a plain vanilla bond.

Value of callable bond (the liability component)	55
Value of equity component (the conversion option) = residual	5
Fair value of bond = consideration received	60

As the liability component contains the call option, it is now necessary to assess whether the call option is closely related to the host debt instrument. In this situation, the call option's exercise price is set at C60m, the fixed stated

示例 2——可赎回可转换债券的分拆

某主体在第 1 年年初发行了 600, 000 份可赎回可转换债券。该债券按每份 C100 元的面值发行，所得总收入为 C6, 000 万元，亦为该债券的公允价值。该债券的持有人可以在其发行一年后的任何时间将其转换为固定数量的股份。此外，该债券没有固定的到期日；但发行人可以在任何时间将其以债券固定的本金金额召回/赎回。

相关信息如下：

	C 百万元
不具备赎回或转股特征的普通债券（基本型）的价值	57
根据期权定价模型所确定的无转股权的类似债券中发行人看涨期权的价值（衍生工具资产）	2

如上文所述，金额为 C200 万元的看涨期权（非权益衍生工具）的价值必须包含在负债部分中。在这种情形下，这会使得没有转股特征的可赎回债券（负债部分）的价值低于基本型纯债券的价值。这是因为发行人在利率上涨和债券价格上升时有权赎回债券使得可赎回债券与基本型纯债券相比对持有人的吸引力更低。

可赎回债券的价值（负债部分）	55
权益部分的价值（转股权）＝剩余值	5
债券的公允价值 ＝ 所收到的对价	60

由于负债部分包含看涨期权，因此现在需要评估判定看涨期权是否与主债务工具紧密相关。在本示例中，看涨期权的行权价格规定为 C6, 000 万元，即债券固定的票面本金。因此，在每个行权日，该期权的行权价格

principal of the bond. Therefore, at each exercise date, the option's exercise price of C60m is likely to be approximately equal to the amortised carrying amount of the bond plus the equity conversion option. Therefore, the call option is closely related to the host debt instrument. As a result, the call option is not separately accounted for, but remains part of the liability component. [IAS 39 AG 30(g)(i)].

The liability component of C55m will be subsequently measured in accordance with its classification under IAS 39 either as a financial liability at fair value through profit or loss or as another liability measured at amortised cost using the effective interest rate method. Although, in this situation, the bond can be called by the issuer at any time or converted by the holder at any time after the first anniversary of its issue, the liability component of C55m is not automatically accreted to its redemption amount of C60m by the end of year 1. This is because the effective interest rate method requires the entity to discount the cash flows over the instrument's expected life, taking into account all the financial instrument's contractual terms including pre-payment, call and similar options [IAS 39 para 9]. This period may well be a period greater than one year.

On the other hand, if the call option's exercise price were set at an amount that is not approximately equal to the debt instrument's amortised carrying amount or not set to reimburse the lender for the approximate present value of lost interest for the remaining terms of the host contract, the call option would fall to be accounted for separately. [IAS 39 AG 30(g)]. In that situation, the proceeds of the converted bond would be allocated as follows:

	Dr	Cr
	Cm	**Cm**
Cash	60	
Derivative asset (issuer call option)	2	
Host debt instrument		57
Equity component (written equity call option)		5

C6,000 万元可能与该债券的摊余账面价值加转股权大致相等。即该看涨期权与主债务工具紧密相关。因此该看涨期权不用单独进行会计处理，而是作为负债部分的一部分。[IAS 39 AG 第 30（g）（i）段]。

金额为 C5,500 万元的负债部分将按照其根据 IAS 39 的分类进行后续计量，即以公允价值计量且变动计入损益的金融负债或是按实际利率法计算的摊余成本计量的其他负债。虽然在本示例中，该债券可能被发行人在任何时间赎回或是由持有人在发行一年以后任何时间转换为股票，金额为 C5,500 万元的负债部分并不会自动地在第一年年末增加至 C6,000 万元的赎回金额。这是因为实际利率法要求主体在工具的预计寿命期间对现金流进行折现，并需要考虑到所有的金融工具合同条款，包括提前偿付选择权、看涨期权和类似期权。[IAS 39 第 9 段]。此期间很可能会大于一年。

另一方面，如果看涨期权的行权价格设置为一个与债务工具的摊余账面价值并不大致相等的金额，或者未被设定为补偿借款人在主合同剩余期间利息损失现值的近似值，则该看涨期权应单独进行会计处理。[IAS 39 AG 第 30（g）段]。在这种情形下，可转换债券的收入将按如下方式分配：

	借	贷
	C 百万元	C 百万元
现金	60	
衍生工具资产（发行人看涨期权）	2	
主债务工具		57
权益部分（签出权益看涨期权）		5

As can be seen from the above, the separation of the call option asset affects the value of the liability and not the equity component. The derivative asset will be fair valued at each subsequent balance sheet date until the option is exercised. The liability component would be amortised over its expected life (determined without reference to the call option to avoid double counting) under the effective interest method as stated above.

Conversion at or before maturity

7.70 The terms of a convertible instrument may require the instrument to be converted into the entity's ordinary shares either at or any time before maturity. IAS 32 states that on conversion of a convertible instrument at maturity, the entity derecognises the liability component and recognises it as equity. The original equity component remains in equity. There is no gain or loss on conversion at maturity. [IAS 32 para AG 32].

Example – Conversion at maturity

The facts are the same as the example in paragraph 7.67 above, except that the bond is converted at the end of its three-year term.

The amortised cost of the bond will be stated at C60m at maturity after the last payment of interest has been made. As the bond is converted, the entity will issue 15m (600,000 × 25) of C1 nominal value. The liability component will be derecognised and transferred to equity. The accounting entries would be as follows:

	Dr	Cr
	Cm	Cm
Liability	60	
Share capital		15
Reserves (a component of equity)		45

The amount that was previously recognised in equity, that is, C5m remains in equity.

由上所述，看涨期权资产的分拆会影响到负债而不是权益部分的价值。该衍生工具资产将在期后的每个资产负债表日评估其公允价值，直至被行权。负债部分应当在其预计存续期（确定时不考虑看涨期权以避免重复计算）内按上文所述的实际利率法进行摊销。

到期日或之前的转换

7.70　可转换工具的条款可能要求该工具在到期日或之前任何时间转换为主体的普通股。IAS 32 指出在可转换工具到期转换时，主体应终止确认其负债部分并将其确认为权益。原来的权益部分仍保留为权益。可转换工具到期转换时不产生利得或损失。[IAS 32 AG 第 32 段]。

示例——到期转换

其事实情况与上文第 7.67 段所述示例相同，只是债券在三年期满时进行了转换。

在到期日支付了最后一笔利息后，该项债券的摊余成本为 C6,000 万元。由于债券已被转股，主体将发行 1,500 万（600,000 × 25）面值为 C1 元的股票。其负债部分将被终止确认并转入权益。如下为其会计分录：

	借	贷
	C 百万元	C 百万元
负债	60	
股本		15
准备（权益的一项组成部分）		45

之前在权益中所确认的金额，即 C500 万元，仍保留在权益中。

7.71 The guidance included in paragraph AG 32 of IAS 32 as discussed above deals with conversion at maturity. However, the contractual terms of some convertible instruments allow for the conversion before the instrument's final maturity date. There is no specific guidance in IAS 32 as to what should be the accounting treatment if the holder elects to convert the bond early. However, as the instrument 'matures' on the date that the holder converts in accordance with the instrument's contractual terms, the guidance in IAS 32 paragraph AG 32 is relevant. Therefore, where a convertible debt is converted before maturity, the amount recognised in equity in respect of the shares issued should be the amount at which the liability for the debt is stated as at the date of conversion.

Example – Before maturity conversion of a convertible bond with an American conversion option

Convertible bonds with American options (those that give the holder the right to exercise the option at any time) are regularly converted before the loan's original maturity. To the extent that the carrying amount at the conversion date is not equal to the principal amount converted this should be accounted for in accordance with paragraph AG 32 of IAS 32, as the word 'maturity' means any date when the holder converts in accordance with the instrument's contractual terms. As an American option allows for conversion at any time before the expiry date, the conversion date will be the maturity date. As such, there is no gain or loss on conversion with American options. During the life of the host bond, expectations about early conversion should not be taken into account when estimating the cash flows used to apply the effective interest rate. The early conversion option is a characteristic of the equity component (the conversion option) not of the host liability. The estimated cash flows used to apply the effective interest rate method are, therefore, the contractual cash flows based on the contractual final maturity of the host liability (assuming there are no other puts or calls).

Mandatorily convertible instruments

7.72 A convertible bond may contain terms that *compel* the holder to convert the

7.71 如上所述，IAS 32 AG 第32段中的指引讨论了在到期日进行转换的情况。然而，有些可转换工具的合同条款允许工具在最终到期日之前进行转换。在 IAS 32 中并没有明确规定如果持有人选择提前转换债券应采取的会计处理方法。但是，因为在持有人根据工具的合同条款将其转换的那一天该工具即“到期”，所以 IAS 32 AG 第32段中的指引也是相关的。因此，在可转换债券在到期日前转换的情况下，所发行股票在权益中所确认的金额应该是转换日该债务所列报的金额。

示例——具有美式转股权的可转换债券在到期日之前的转换

具有美式期权（即那些给予持有人在任何时间行使权利的期权）的可转换债券一般都会在贷款的原有到期日之前转换。尽管转换日的账面价值并不等于所转换的本金金额，还是应按照 IAS 32 AG 第32段规定对其进行会计处理，因为“到期”一词指持有人按照该工具的合同条款进行转换的任意一天。由于美式期权允许在到期日之前的任何时间转换，转换日即为到期日。因此，美式期权的转换不会有利得或损失。在主债券的存续期间，在采用实际利率估计现金流时不应考虑对提前转换的预期。这种提前转换的选择权是权益部分（转股权）而不是主负债的特征。因此，应用实际利率法时估计现金流是根据主负债的合同最终到期日而确定的合同现金流（假设没有其他看跌期权或看涨期权）。

强制性可转换工具

7.72 可转换债券中可能包含*强制*持有人而不是由持有人选择转换债券的条

bond rather than being at the holder's option. Depending on the terms, the number of shares issued on conversion may be either variable or fixed. To the extent that the mandatorily convertible bond can only be settled by the issue of a variable amount of ordinary shares calculated to equal a fixed amount in the issuer's functional currency (that is, there is a repayment of principal), the instrument is a liability. To the extent that the mandatorily convertible bond can only be settled by the issue of a fixed number of ordinary shares, that part of the instrument is an equity component. Some mandatorily convertible instruments pay no interest or pay interest only if an ordinary dividend is paid (discretionary). This type of instrument has no liability component. Others pay interest until the bond is converted, in which case the issuer allocates part of the consideration received equal to the liability component. This is measured at the present value of the interest payments, discounted at the market rate of interest for a similar instrument with a similar credit status that has no conversion option. The balance of the consideration is allocated to the equity component as illustrated below.

Example – Mandatorily convertible bonds

An entity issues 600,000 convertible bonds at the start of year 1. The bonds have a 3-year term, and are issued at par with a face value of C100 per bond, resulting in total proceeds of C60m, which is also the bond's fair value. Interest is payable annually in arrears at a nominal annual interest rate of 6%. Each C100 nominal bond is mandatorily convertible at the end of the 3 year term into 25 ordinary shares. When the bonds are issued, the prevailing market interest rate for similar debt without conversion options is 9%. The entity incurs issue cost of 1% on the nominal value of the bond amounting to C600,000.

As explained in the above paragraph, the liability component is measured first by discounting the contractually determined stream of future cash flows (interest only) to present value using a discount rate of 9%, the market interest rate for similar bonds having no conversion rights, as shown below.

款。根据条款的规定，在转换时所需发行的股票数量可能是可变的也可能是固定的。如果强制性可转换债券只能够通过发行相当于以发行人功能货币计量的固定金额（即，偿付本金）的可变数量普通股的形式进行结算，则该工具是一项负债。如果该强制性可转换债券只能通过发行固定数量的普通股的方式进行结算，则该工具的这一部分是权益部分。有些强制性可转换债券不支付利息或只在支付普通股股利时才会支付利息（可任意选择）。这种类型的工具没有负债部分。而其他工具在债券被转换之前会支付利息，在这种情形下发行人要把所收到的对价分配一部分作为负债。即采用具有类似信用等级但无转股权的类似工具的市场利率将利息付款折为现值来进行计量。如下所示，对价的余额被分配至权益部分。

示例——强制性可转换债券

某主体在第 1 年年初发行了 600, 000 份可转换债券。该债券的期限为 3 年，按每份 C100 元的面值发行，所得总收入为 C6, 000 万元，亦为该债券的公允价值。利息按照票面利率 6% 每年年末支付。在 3 年期限结束时每个面值为 C100 元的债券将被强制转换为 25 股普通股。债券发行时，没有转股权的类似债务的市场利率为 9%。该主体发生了占债券票面价值 1% 的发行成本，金额为 C600, 000 元。

如上文所解释的，首先采用 9% 的折现率，即没有转股权的类似债务的市场利率，将合同规定的未来现金流（只有利息）折为现值来对负债部分进行计量，如下所示：

	C
PV of interest payable at the end of year 1 – C3, 600, 000/ 1.09	3, 302, 752
PV of interest payable at the end of year 2 – C3, 600, 000/ $(1.09)^2$	3, 030, 048
PV of interest payable at the end of year 3 – C3, 600, 000/ $(1.09)^3$	2, 779, 860
Total liability component	9, 112, 660
Total equity component (residual) *	50, 887, 340
Total proceeds of the bond issue	60, 000, 000

* The difference between the proceeds of the bond and the fair value of the liability component as computed above (the residual) is assigned to the equity component.

In accordance with IAS 32, the issue cost of C600, 000 will need to be allocated between the liability and the equity components in proportion to the allocation of the proceeds as shown below:

	Equity component	Liability component	Total
	C	C	C
Gross proceeds allocated as above	50, 887, 340	9, 112, 660	60, 000, 000
Issue cost	(508, 873)	(91, 127)	(600, 000)
Net proceeds	50, 378, 467	9, 021, 533	59, 400, 000

The amount credited to equity of C50, 378, 467 is not subsequently remeasured.

The liability component of C9, 021, 533 will be measured subsequently at

	C
第 1 年年末应付利息的现值——3, 600, 000/1. 09	3, 302, 752
第 2 年年末应付利息的现值——3, 600, 000/（1. 09）^{2}	3, 030, 048
第 3 年年末应付利息的现值——3, 600, 000/（1. 09）^{3}	2, 779, 860
负债部分合计	9, 112, 660
权益部分合计（余额）*	50, 887, 340
发行债券的总收入	60, 000, 000

* 将债券收入和如上所计算的负债部分的公允价值之间的差额（即余额）分配给权益部分。

如下所示，根据 IAS 32 的规定，C600, 000 元的发行成本需要按收入分配的比例在负债和权益部分之间分配：

	权益部分	**负债部分**	**合计**
	C	**C**	**C**
如上所述分配的总收入	50, 887, 340	9, 112, 660	60, 000, 000
发行成本	(508, 873)	(91, 127)	(600, 000)
净收入	50, 378, 467	9, 021, 533	59, 400, 000

分配至权益的金额 C50, 378, 467 元在期后不用重新计量。

金额为 C9, 021, 533 元的负债部分将采用实际利率法以摊余成本进行后续计

amortised cost using the effective interest rate method. As the interest payments on the bonds will reduce the liability component to zero, the effective interest rate in this situation is that rate of interest which discounts the three interest payments of C3, 600, 000 per year to its present value of C9, 021, 533. This rate amounts to 9. 5659% as shown below:

Year	Opening liability	Interest @ 9. 5659%	Cash paid	Closing liability
	C	C	C	C
1	9, 021, 533	862, 990	(3, 600, 000)	6, 284, 523
2	6, 284, 523	601, 171	(3, 600, 000)	3, 285, 694
3	3, 285, 694	314, 306	(3, 600, 000)	–
Total finance cost		1, 778, 467		

When the bond is converted, the entity issues 15 million shares of C1 each. The original equity component of C50, 378, 467 effectively becomes the consideration for these shares where relevant, this amount would be allocated between share capital and share premium as follows:

	C
Share capital – 15 million shares of C1 each	15, 000, 000
Share premium	35, 378, 467
Original equity component	50, 378, 467

In other words, a mandatorily convertible instrument issued in the functional currency of the issuer is effectively a forward contract to issue or to deliver a fixed number of shares for which the consideration has been received in advance. Contrast this with the situation of an instrument that is convertible at any time before maturity (a written call option) discussed in paragraph 7. 67 above.

量。由于债券利息的支付将使负债部分降低至零，在此情况下的实际利率是将每年 C3,600,000 元的三笔利息付款折现至 C9,021,533 元现值的利率。如下所示，此利率为 9.5659%：

年份	期初负债	按 9.5659% 计算的利息	已付现金	期末负债
	C	C	C	C
1	9,021,533	862,990	(3,600,000)	6,284,523
2	6,284,523	601,171	(3,600,000)	3,285,694
3	3,285,694	314,306	(3,600,000)	–
财务费用合计		1,778,467		

当债券转换时，该主体将发行 1,500 万 C1 元的股票。金额为 C50,378,467 元的初始权益部分实际上是这些股票的相关对价，此金额将按照如下方式在股本和股本溢价之间分配：

	C
股本——1,500 万面值为 C1 元股份	15,000,000
股本溢价	35,378,467
初始权益部分	50,378,467

换言之，以发行人的功能货币计价发行的强制性可转换工具实际上是一个发行或交付固定数量股票的远期合同，其对价已经预先支付。与此截然不同的是在上文第 7.67 段所讨论的可以在到期日之前任何时间转换的工具（签出看涨期权）。

Early redemption or repurchase

7. 73 An entity may redeem or repurchase a convertible instrument before maturity, for example through negotiations with the bondholders, without affecting the conversion rights. When an entity extinguishes a convertible instrument before maturity through an early redemption or repurchase in which the original conversion privileges are unchanged, the entity should allocate the redemption consideration paid (including any transaction costs) to the instrument's liability and equity components at the date of repurchase or redemption. In making this allocation, the entity should use the same methodology (using current market data) that was used in the original allocation of proceeds received from the convertible instrument's issue between the separate components on initial recognition. [IAS 32 para AG 33].

7. 74 Once the allocation of the consideration has been made, any resulting gain or loss is treated in accordance with accounting principles applicable to the related component, as follows:

- The difference between the consideration allocated to the liability component and its carrying value is recognised in profit or loss.
- The amount of consideration relating to the equity component is recognised in equity.

[IAS 32 para AG 34] .

Example – Early redemption of a convertible bond

The facts are the same as the example in paragraph 7. 67 above, except that on the first day of year 2, the entity makes a tender offer to the bondholders to repurchase the bond for its fair value at that date of C63m, which the bondholders accept. At the date of repurchase, the entity could have issued a non-convertible bond with a two-year term bearing an interest rate of 7%. The transaction cost of redeeming the bonds amounted to C200, 000.

The carrying value of the liability component prior to redemption at the end of year 1 as calculated previously amounts to C56, 442, 438. The original equity

提前赎回或回购

7.73 主体可以在不影响转股权的情况下，如通过与债券持有人进行协商的方式在某项可转换工具到期之前就将其赎回或回购。如果主体通过在到期日前赎回或回购而终止一项初始转股权未发生变化的可转换工具，则主体应在回购或赎回日将所支付的赎回对价（包括任何交易费用）分配至该工具的负债和权益部分。在进行分配时，主体应采用与在初始确认时将发行该可转换工具所收到的收入分配至不同部分时一致的方法（使用当前的市场数据）。[IAS 32 AG 第 33 段]。

7.74 对价分配后，所产生的利得或损失应分别根据相关部分适用的会计原则进行处理，具体如下：

- 分配至负债部分的对价和其账面价值之间的差额确认为损益。

- 与权益部分相关的对价金额在权益中确认。

[IAS 32 AG 第 34 段]。

示例——可转换债券的提前赎回

其事实情况与上文第 7.67 段所述示例相同，只是在第 2 年的第一天，该主体向债券持有人提出以债券在该日的公允价值 C6300 万的价格回购该债券，债券持有人接受了该条件。在回购当日，主体也可以发行两年期、利率为 7% 的不可转换债券。赎回债券的交易成本金额为 C200, 000 元。

赎回之前负债部分于第 1 年年末的账面价值为之前计算的 C56, 442, 438 元。初始权益部分的金额为 C4, 510, 767 元。

component amounts to C4, 510, 767.

As explained above, the repurchase price is allocated between the liability component and the equity component on the same basis used in the original allocation process. This means the fair value of the liability component is measured first by discounting the remaining stream of future cash flows (interest and principal) to present value at the beginning of year 2, using a discount rate of 7%, the market interest rate for similar bonds having no conversion rights, as shown below.

	C
PV of interest payable at the end of year 2 – C3, 600, 000/ 1.07	3, 364, 486
PV of interest payable at the end of year 3 – C3, 600, 000/ $(1.07)^2$	3, 144, 379
PV of principal of C60, 000, 000 payable at the end year 3 – C60, 000, 000/ $(1.07)^2$	52, 406, 324
Total liability component	58, 915, 189
Total equity component (residual) *	4, 084, 811
Total consideration payable on repurchase of bonds	63, 000, 000

* The difference between the consideration payable and the liability component's fair value as computed above is assigned to the equity component.

In accordance with IAS 32, the redemption cost of C200, 000 will need to be allocated between the liability and the equity components in proportion to the allocation of the consideration as shown below:

如上文所解释的，回购价格应该按照与初始分配流程相同的方法在负债和权益部分之间分配。这就意味着，首先采用 7% 的折现率将剩余的未来现金流（利息和本金）折为第 2 年年初的现值来对负债部分的公允价值进行计量，该折现率为没有转股权的类似债券的市场利率，如下所示：

	C
第 2 年年末应付利息的现值——C3, 600, 000/1. 07	3, 364, 486
第 3 年年末应付利息的现值——C3, 600, 000/（1. 07）^{2}	3, 144, 379
第 3 年年末应付本金 C60, 000, 000 的现值——C60, 000, 000/（1. 07）^{2}	52, 406, 324
负债部分合计	58, 915, 189
权益部分合计（余额）*	4, 084, 811
回购债券的应付对价合计	63, 000, 000

* 如上所计算的应付对价和负债部分的公允价值之间的差额分配至权益部分。

如下所示，根据 IAS 32 的规定，将需要把 C200, 000 元的赎回成本按对价分配比例在负债和权益部分之间分配：

	Equity component	Liability component	Total
	C	C	C
Consideration allocated as above	4, 084, 811	58, 915, 189	63, 000, 000
Redemption cost	12, 968	187, 032	200, 000
Total	4, 097, 779	59, 102, 221	63, 200, 000
Difference arising on repurchase is as follows:			
Consideration inclusive of costs as above	4, 097, 779	59, 102, 221	63, 200, 000
Carrying value prior to redemption as stated above	4, 510, 767	56, 442, 438	60, 953, 205
	412, 988	(2, 659, 783)	(2, 246, 795)

The accounting entries in respect of the repurchase of the bond are as follows:

	Dr	Cr
	C	C
Bond Liability	56, 442, 438	
Debt Settlement expense (income statement)	2, 659, 783	
Cash		59, 102, 221
To record the repurchase of the liability component and the loss arising thereon		
Equity	4, 097, 779	
Cash		4, 097, 779

To record the cash paid on the repurchase of the equity component

The resulting balance of C412, 988 relating to the equity component can be transferred to a different line item in equity, for example, retained earnings.

Modification of terms to induce early conversion

7.75 An entity may amend the terms of a convertible instrument to induce early

	权益部分	负债部分	合计
	C	C	C
如上所分配的对价	4,084,811	58,915,189	63,000,000
赎回成本	12,968	187,032	200,000
合计	4,097,779	59,102,221	63,200,000
回购时产生差额如下：			
如上包括成本的对价	4,097,779	59,102,221	63,200,000
如上所述赎回前的账面价值	4,510,767	56,442,438	60,953,205
	412,988	(2,659,783)	(2,246,795)

有关债券回购的会计分录如下：

	借	贷
	C	C
债券负债	56,442,438	
债务结算费用（利润表）	2,659,783	
现金		59,102,221
确认负债部分的回购及其相关损失		
权益	4,097,779	
现金		4,097,779

确认回购权益部分所支付的现金

权益部分所剩余额 C412,988 元可转到权益不同项目中，如留存收益。

为促使提前转换而更改条款

7.75　主体可能修改可转换工具的条款以促使持有人提前转换，例如提供更

conversion, for example by offering a more favourable conversion ratio or paying other additional consideration in the event of conversion before a specified date. In that situation, the entity should recognise a loss, at the date the terms are amended, calculated as the difference between:

- the fair value of the consideration the holder receives on the instrument's conversion under the revised terms; and
- the fair value of the consideration the holder would have received under the original terms.

[IAS 32 para AG 35].

Example – Early conversion of a convertible bond

The facts are the same as the example in paragraph 7.67 above, except that on the first day of year 2, the entity modifies the convertible instrument's terms to induce the bondholders to convert the bond within 60 days. Each C100 nominal bond is now convertible into 30 ordinary shares rather than the 25 ordinary shares under the original terms. The market value of the entity's shares at the date of the amendment is C5 per share.

As explained above, the loss arising on increasing the conversion ratio is calculated as follow:

	Cm
Fair value of consideration receivable under the new terms:	
Number of bonds (600,000) × Conversion ratio (30) × C5	90
Fair value of consideration receivable under the original terms:	
Number of bonds (600,000) × Conversion ratio (25) × C5	75
Value of additional shares issuable on conversion recognised in profit or loss	15

On the date of conversion, the entity issues 18m shares instead of 15m under the original conversion terms. Therefore, the consideration received for the 18m shares comprises the carrying value of the bond of C56,442,438 plus C15m (the market value of 3m shares @ C5 per share).

The accounting entries to record the early conversion are as follows:

有利的转换率或在特定日期前转换将获得额外的对价。在这种情形下，主体应在条款修改日按以下两者之差确认一项损失：

- 持有人根据修订后的条款转换工具所能获得对价的公允价值；和
- 持有人根据原有条款所能获得对价的公允价值。

［IAS 32 AG 第 35 段］。

示例——可转换债券的提前转换

其事实情况与上文第 7.67 段所述示例相同，只是在第 2 年的第一天，该主体更改了可转换工具的条款以促使债券持有人在 60 天内转换该债券。现在面值每 C100 元的债券可转换为 30 股普通股而不是原来条款中所规定的 25 股普通股。该主体的股票在修订日的市场价值为每股 C5 元。

如上文所解释的，因提高转换率而导致的损失计算如下：

	C 百万元
根据新条款应收到对价的公允价值：	
债券数（600,000）× 转换率（30）× C5	90
根据原来条款应收到对价的公允价值：	
债券数（600,000）× 转换率（25）× C5	75
转换时额外发行股票的价值确认为损益	15

在转换日，主体发行了 1800 万股，而不是根据原来转换条款的 1500 万股。因此，这 1800 万股股票收到的对价包括债券账面价值 C56, 442, 438 元及 C1500 万（300 万股股票按每股 C5 元计算的市场价值）。

确认提前转换的会计分录如下文所述：

	Dr	Cr
Bond liability	56, 442, 438	
Profit or loss (fair value of 3m shares @ C5 per share)	15, 000, 000	
Equity (issue of 18m shares)		71, 442, 438

Settlement options

7. 76 In some instances, a convertible instrument may contain a settlement option that allows the issuer either to deliver a fixed number of shares when the bondholders exercise their rights to convert or deliver cash equal to the fair value of those shares at the date of conversion. Consistent with paragraph 7. 57, where a convertible instrument contains such a cash settlement option, the conversion option is not an equity instrument, even though it is indexed to the market price of the entity's shares. Rather, it is an embedded derivative (effectively a written call option issued by the entity over its own shares) that is not closely related to the debt host. This means that instead of accounting for the conversion right as an equity instrument, the entity would account for the conversion right as a financial liability (a derivative) at fair value, with changes in fair value recognised in profit or loss. The effect of fair valuing the derivative means that gains and losses based on the entity's own share price would be reported in the profit or loss. This is also the case where the cash settlement option is contingent on a future event happening.

Example – Contingent settlement options

An entity has issued convertible bonds whose terms include a clause giving the issuer the option to redeem in cash the bonds at their fair market value in the event of the occurrence of an uncertain future event instead of issuing a fixed number of equity shares.

The conversion option is a derivative. The terms of the convertible bond give the issuer the option to redeem the bonds for cash at their fair market value

	借	贷
债券负债	56,442,438	
损益(每股C5元的300万股股票的公允价值)	15,000,000	
权益(发行1800万股股票)		71,442,438

结算选择权

7.76　在某些情况下，可转换工具中可能包含结算选择权，允许发行人在债券持有人行使转股权时交付固定数量的股票或支付这些股票在转换日公允价值的等值现金。与第7.57段一致，在可转换工具包含这种现金结算选择权的情况下，即使它与主体股票的市场价格挂钩，转股权也不是一项权益工具。相反，它是一项与主债务不紧密相关的嵌入衍生工具（实际上是主体对其自身股票所发行的一项签出看涨期权）。这就意味着，主体应当将该转股权作为一项以公允价值计量且变动计入损益的金融负债（衍生工具）来核算，而不是作为权益工具。对衍生工具进行估价的结果意味着根据主体自身股票价格而产生的利得和损失应该计入损益。在现金结算选择权取决于某项未来事件发生的情况下亦然。

示例——或有结算选择权

某主体发行了一项可转换债券，其条款中的一条授予发行人一个选择权，使其在某个未来不确定事项发生时可以根据债券的市场公允价值以现金赎回债券而不是发行固定数量的权益股份。

此转股权是一项衍生工具。该可转换债券的条款使发行人有权在某项未来或有事项发生时按照债券的市场公允价值以现金将其赎回。在未来不确定

contingent upon a future event. On the occurrence of the uncertain future event there is a settlement alternative for the equity conversion option, as it can be settled at fair value, either in shares or in cash – that is, there is a net cash settlement option. An equity conversion option for which either party has a choice of settlement in cash or shares is a financial liability. [IAS 32 para 26]. Paragraph 26 of IAS 32 overturns the usual principle that something that is in the control of an issuer is not an obligation. This right of choice of settlement is contingent upon a future event in the example above, but the equity conversion option must still be accounted for as an embedded derivative in accordance with paragraph 26 of IAS 32.

7.77 When the holder exercises its right to convert and the entity chooses to settle its obligation by issuing a fixed number of shares, then the liability's carrying value together with the derivative's fair value would be derecognised and transferred to equity as the share issue is treated as an equity transaction. Alternatively, the entity may record the shares at fair value and the difference between the fair value of the shares and the carrying value of the liability plus the fair value of the derivative is recognised in profit or loss. The same accounting treatment is achieved if the entity chooses the cash alternative as the amount of the cash consideration that is equal to the fair value of the shares at the date of conversion will be applied to extinguish the liability and the derivative instruments with any difference taken to profit or loss. Either method is acceptable, but it is an accounting policy choice that should be disclosed and applied consistently.

Convertible bond denominated in a foreign currency

7.78 It is not uncommon for an entity to issue a convertible bond that is denominated in a currency other than its functional currency, as discussed in paragraph 7.40. For example, an entity whose functional currency is the Swiss franc may issue a euro denominated convertible bond that can be converted into a fixed number of its own Swiss franc denominated equity instruments. In this case, the instrument comprises a host debt instrument denominated in a foreign currency and a written option to exchange a fixed number of the entity's own equity instruments for a fixed amount of cash that is denominated in a foreign currency.

事项发生时，该转股权即具有结算选择，其可以以股票或现金按照公允价值结算——即，净现金结算选择权。任何一方可以选择以现金或是股票结算的转股权是一项金融负债。[IAS 32 第26 段]。IAS 32 第26 段颠覆了在发行人控制范围内的事项不是一项义务的常规原则。尽管在如上示例中这种选择结算方式的权利取决于某项未来事件，但是该转股权仍必须遵循 IAS 32 第26 段作为一项嵌入衍生工具核算。

7.77 当持有人行使其转股权且主体选择通过发行固定数量的股票的方式来结算其义务时，负债的账面价值以及衍生工具的公允价值应该一起被终止确认并转入到权益中，因为发行股份是作为一项权益交易进行处理。或者，主体也可以按公允价值确认股票，并将股票的公允价值和负债的账面价值与衍生工具的公允价值之和的差额确认为损益。如果主体选择了现金结算也会得到相同的会计处理，因为转换日现金对价等于股票的公允价值，用该金额清偿负债和衍生工具，而产生的任何差额均将计入损益。这两种方法均可以采用，但是会计政策的选择应予以披露并一致地实施。

以外币计价的可转换债券

7.78 如第 7.40 段所述，主体发行以功能货币以外的货币计价的可转换债券的情况并不少见。例如，功能货币为瑞士法郎的主体可能发行以欧元计价的可转换债券，该债券可能被转换为固定数量的以瑞士法郎计价的自身权益工具。在这种情况下，该工具包含一个以外币计价的主债务工具和一个以固定数量的主体自身权益工具交换固定金额外币现金的签出期权。

7.79 In April 2005, the IFRIC considered the accounting for a foreign currency convertible bond and stated that a fixed amount of foreign currency constitutes a variable amount of cash in the entity's functional currency. This position has not changed as a result of the IAS 32 amendment for the classification of rights issues discussed in paragraph 7.41 Therefore, foreign-currency-denominated-convertible bonds that will be settled by an entity delivering a fixed number of its own equity instruments in exchange for a fixed amount of foreign currency fail the 'fixed for fixed' requirement. The whole of the convertible bond is classified as a financial liability under IAS 32 and is subject to IAS 39 for recognition and measurement. The embedded written option's value changes in response to changes in the values of entity's equity and foreign exchange movements. Therefore, it is not a closely related embedded derivative, because the risks inherent in the derivative (equity risk) and in the debt host are dissimilar. [IAS 39 para AG 30(d)]. If the host debt is carried at amortised cost, it will be subject to the translation rules of IAS 21, 'The effect of changes in foreign exchange rates', and the embedded derivative liability will be separated and fair valued through profit or loss.

Example – Convertible debt denominated in a foreign currency

On 1 January 20X5 a company with C functional currency issued 36,000 convertible bonds at par with a face value of US$1,000 per bond, giving total proceeds of US$36m. The bonds carry a coupon rate of 4% per annum payable in arrears. Each $1,000 bond is convertible, at the holder's discretion, at any time prior to maturity on 31 December 20X9, into 100 ordinary shares of C1 nominal.

The following information is relevant:

	Spot rate	Fair value of embedded derivative*
1 January 20X5	C1 = US$1.80	C3m
31 December 20X5	C1 = US$1.75	C4m
Average rate for the year	C1 = US$1.775	

* In accordance with paragraph AG 28 of IAS 39, the embedded derivative's

7.79　在 2005 年 4 月，IFRIC 讨论了外币可转换债券的核算并声明固定金额的外币构成了以主体功能货币计价的可变金额的现金。此立场并未因如第 7.41 段所讨论的有关配股权的分类对 IAS 32 的修订而改变。因此，主体通过交付固定数量的自身权益工具来换取固定金额的外币来结算的外币可转换债券并不符合“固定换固定”的要求。根据 IAS 32 的规定，该可转换债券整体被划分为金融负债并需遵循 IAS 39 进行确认和计量。该嵌入签出期权的价值会随着主体的权益及外汇汇率的变动而变动。因此，它不是一个紧密相关的嵌入衍生工具，因为其固有风险（权益风险）与主债务中的固有风险不同。[IAS 39 AG 第 30（d）段]。如果主债务以摊余成本计量，则需要遵循《国际会计准则第 21 号——汇率变动的影响》中的折算规则，而且需要将嵌入衍生工具负债分拆出来并以公允价值核算，且公允价值的变动计入损益。

示例——以外币计价的可转换债务

某功能货币为 C 的公司在 20X5 年 1 月 1 日按每份债券面值 1,000 美元发行了 36,000 份可转换债券，共获得了 3600 万美元的收入。该债券的票面年利率为 4%，每年年末支付。持有人可自行决定在到期日 20X9 年 12 月 31 日前的任何时间将每 1,000 美元的债券转换为 100 股面值为 C1 元的普通股。

相关信息如下：

	即期汇率	**嵌入衍生工具的公允价值***
20X5 年 1 月 1 日	C1 = 1.80 美元	C3 百万元
20X5 年 12 月 31 日	C1 = 1.75 美元	C4 百万元
年平均汇率	C1 = 1.775 美元	

* 根据 IAS 39 AG 第 28 段规定，嵌入衍生工具（签出期权）的公允价

fair value (the written option) must be determined first at inception of the contract. In this instance, the embedded derivative is indexed to both the share price denominated in C and the C/US$ exchange rate. Generally, where the derivatives relate to different risk exposures and are readily separable and independent of each other, they should be valued and accounted for separately. [IAS 39 para AG 29]. However, in this case, the exercise price of the equity conversion option is denominated in US$, but the underlying share is traded in C. Therefore, it is not possible to separate the equity price risk from the foreign currency risk and value each component separately, because the two are interdependent. In that situation, they should be bundled together and treated as a single compound derivative. [IAS 39 para AG 29]. On this basis, the fair value of the embedded derivative, calculated using an option pricing model, amounted to C3m and C4m respectively at 1 January 20X5 and 31 December 20X5.

As explained above, as the issuer's functional currency is C and the convertible bonds are denominated in US dollars, the conversion option is not an equity instrument, but an embedded derivative that is not closely related to the host debt instrument, because the risks inherent in the derivative (equity risk) and the host are dissimilar. Therefore, the conversion option should be separated and classified as a derivative liability.

The carrying value of the host contract at initial recognition is the difference between the consideration received of C20m ((US$36m @ 1.8) and the fair value of the embedded derivative of C3m, that is, C17m or US$30.6m (C17m @1.8).

The host foreign currency debt of US$30.6m will be measured subsequently at amortised cost using the effective interest rate method and then retranslated at each subsequent reporting date at the closing US$/C exchange rate. The company will pay 4% interest per annum on US$36m, that is, US$1.44m each year for the next 4 years and a principal amount of US$36m at the end of year 4, if the debt is not converted. The effective interest rate that discounts the interest and principal payments to its present value of US$30.6m is 8.5883% as shown below:

值必须在合同开始时首先确定。在本示例中，嵌入衍生工具与以 C 计价的股票和 C 兑美元的汇率均有关系。通常，如果多个嵌入衍生工具有不同的风险敞口，容易分拆且相互独立，应对其分别进行估价和核算。[IAS 39 AG 第 29 段]。但是，在本示例中，转股权的行权价格的面值为美元，但是其相应的股票则是以 C 来交易的。因此，不可能将权益价格风险与外币风险分拆开来并对每项组成成分单独进行估价，因为这两项因素是相互依存的。在这种情形下，应将其合并在一起视为一项混合嵌入衍生工具。[IAS 39 AG 第 29 段]。在此基础上，嵌入衍生工具根据期权定价模型所计算的于 20X5 年 1 月 1 日和 20X5 年 12 月 31 日的公允价值分别为 C300 万元和 C400 万元。

如上文所解释的，因为发行人的功能货币为 C 而可转换债券以美元计价，所以该转股权不是一项权益工具，而是一项与主债务工具不紧密相关的嵌入衍生工具——因为衍生工具的固有风险（权益风险）与主债务不同。因此，应将该转股权分拆出来并划分为一项金融负债。

在初始确认时主合同的账面价值为所收到的对价 C2,000 万元（3,600 万美元 × 1.8）与嵌入衍生工具的公允价值 C300 万元之间的差额，即 C1,700 万元或 3,060 万美元（C1,700 万元 × 1.8）。

3,060 万美元的外币主负债将按照实际利率法采用摊余成本进行后续计量，且在每个后续报告日按照期末美元兑 C 的汇率重新折算。如果该债务未被转换，公司将在随后的 4 年按照年利率 4% 为 3,600 万美元本金支付利息，即每年 144 万美元，并在第 4 年年末偿付 3,600 万美元的本金。如下所示，将利息和本金付款折为 3,060 万美元现值的实际利率为 8.5883%：

	Opening liability	Interest @ 8.5883%	Cash paid	Closing liability
	$'000	$'000	$'000	$'000
Year 1	30,600	2,628	(1,440)	31,788
Year 2	31,788	2,730	(1,440)	33,078
Year 3	33,078	2,841	(1,440)	34,479
Year 4	34,479	2,961	(37,440)	0

The interest payable in US$ would be recorded in profit or loss at the average rate ruling during the year. The closing liability would be translated at the spot rate at the balance sheet. Any exchange difference arising is recognised in profit or loss as part of finance cost. Therefore, the amortised cost of the host foreign currency debt instrument at 31 December 20X5 would be calculated as follows:

		C'000
Opening liability	US$30,600,000 @ 1.8	17,000
Interest cost (profit or loss)	US$2,628,000 @ 1.775	1,481
Cash paid	US$1,440,000 @ 1.75	(823)
Exchange difference (profit or loss)*		507
Closing liability	US$31,788 @ 1.75	18,165

* The exchange difference comprises the exchange difference on the opening liability of C486 (US$30,600 @ [1.75 – 1.8] and the exchange difference on the interest cost between closing rate and average rate of C21 (US$2,628 @ [1.775 – 1.8]).

At 31 December 20X5, the fair value of the embedded derivative liability is C4m. The increase in fair value results in a loss of C1m, which is recognised in profit or loss.

The foreign currency convertible bond would be reported and presented in the financial statements as follows:

	期初负债	按 8.5883% 计算的利息	已付现金	期末负债
	美元千元	美元千元	美元千元	美元千元
第 1 年	30,600	2,628	(1,440)	31,788
第 2 年	31,788	2,730	(1,440)	33,078
第 3 年	33,078	2,841	(1,440)	34,479
第 4 年	34,479	2,961	(37,440)	0

以美元支付的利息应当按照当年的平均汇率确认为损益。期末负债应当按照资产负债表日的即期汇率进行折算。所产生的任何汇兑差额均作为财务费用的一部分确认为损益。因此，外币主债务工具在 20X5 年 12 月 31 日的摊余成本将按如下方式进行计算：

		C'000
期初负债	US$30,600,000 × 1.8	17,000
利息费用（损益）	US$2,628,000 × 1.775	1,481
已付现金	US$1,440,000 × 1.75	(823)
汇兑差额（损益）*		507
期末负债	US$31,788 × 1.75	18,165

* 汇兑差额包括期初负债的汇兑差额 C486 元（US$30,600 × [1.75 − 1.8]）和利息费用期末汇率和平均汇率之间的汇兑差额 C21 元（US$2,628 × [1.775 − 1.8]）。

于 20X5 年 12 月 31 日，该嵌入衍生工具负债的公允价值为 C400 万元。公允价值的增加导致了 C100 万元的损失，确认为损益。

该外币可转换债券应该按如下方式在财务报表中进行报告和列报：

Income statement for the year ended 31 December 20X5	**C'000**
Other gains and (losses)	
Derivative instrument	(1,000)
Finance cost	
Interest expense	(1,481)
Foreign exchange difference	(507)
	(1,988)

Balance sheet	**31 Dec 20X5**	**1 Jan 20X5**
	C'000	**C'000**
Current liabilities		
Borrowings	18,165	17,000
Derivative on convertible bond	4,000	3,000
	22,165	20,000

Alternatively, the foreign exchange difference may be presented in other gains and (losses). Similarly, the bond and the derivative can be presented as a single number on the balance sheet.

7.79.1 If a subsidiary issues a convertible bond that (if converted) converts into the parent's shares, the currency that should be looked to in determining whether the 'fixed for fixed' requirement in IAS 32 is met depends on the specific circumstances. For the purposes of the group's consolidated financial statements, a group should look to either the functional currency of the parent (whose shares the bond is convertible into), or that of the subsidiary (whose liability will be extinguished if the bond is converted). The choice to look to the functional currency of the subsidiary or the parent is a policy choice and should be applied on a consistent basis to all similar instruments. The IFRIC decided to give no guidance on this issue. In the subsidiary's individual financial statements, the convertible is classified as a financial liability in its entirety, as the conversion option relates to the parent's shares and not the subsidiary's equity. In the subsidiary's individual financial statements, under IAS 39 the conversion option is an embedded derivative, which should be separated, as it is not closely related to the debt host.

截至 20X5 年 12 月 31 日止年度利润表	**C'000**
其他利得和（损失）	
衍生工具	(1,000)
财务费用	
利息费用	(1,481)
外币折算差额	(507)
	(1,988)

资产负债表	**20X5 年 12 月 31 日**	**20X5 年 1 月 1 日**
	C'000	**C'000**
流动负债		
借款	18,165	17,000
可转换债券中的衍生工具	4,000	3,000
	22,165	20,000

或者，外币折算差额也可以在其他利得和（损失）中进行列报。同样，债券和衍生工具可以在资产负债表中按照单一数值列报。

7.79.1 如果某子公司发行了可转换为母公司股票的可转换债券，在确定是否符合 IAS 32 中所规定的“固定换固定”要求时所采用的货币应视具体情况而定。在集团的合并财务报表中，集团应采用母公司（债券将转换为该公司的股票）或子公司（债券转换后其负债将被清偿）的功能货币。采用子公司还是母公司的功能货币是一个会计政策的选择，应该一致地应用于所有类似的工具。IFRIC 决定不就这一问题提供任何指南。在子公司的个别财务报表中，因为转股权与母公司的股票而不是子公司的权益相关，该可转换债券整个地划分为金融负债。在子公司的个别财务报表中，根据 IAS 39 的规定该转股权是一项嵌入衍生工具，因为其与主负债不紧密相关，应将其分拆出来。

Preference shares with various rights

7.80 Preference shares come with various rights. They may be redeemable at the option of the holder or the issuer, mandatorily redeemable or non-redeemable. Dividends on such shares may be either fixed or payable at the issuer's discretion or their payments may be linked to payments on another instrument. IAS 32 requires the classification of preference shares to be based on an assessment of the contractual arrangement's substance and the definitions of a financial liability and an equity instrument. [IAS 32 paras AG 25, AG 26].

7.81 Because preference shares are relatively common, we summarise below, for ease of understanding and as a practical aid, the appropriate classification of preference shares for various combinations of redemption and dividend rights. It is assumed that the criteria for equity classification in the 2008 amendment to IAS 32 for puttable financial instruments and obligations arising on liquidation summarised in paragraph 7.24.5 have not been met.

Classification of preference shares

Terms		Classification	
Redemption of principal	Payment of dividends (assume all at market rates)	Type of Instrument	Reasons
Non-redeemable	Discretionary	Equity	There is no contractual obligation to pay cash. Any dividends paid would be recognised in equity (see para 7.56).
	Non-discretionary	Liability	Liability component is equal to the present value of the dividend payments to perpetuity. As the dividends are set at market rates, the proceeds will be equivalent to the fair value (at the date of issue) of the dividends payable to perpetuity. Therefore, the entire proceeds would be classified as a liability.

具有各种不同权利的优先股

7.80 优先股可附带各种不同的权利。它们可能由持有人或发行人选择赎回、强制赎回或是不可赎回。这种股票的股利可以是固定的也可以由发行人决定是否支付或是其支付可能与另一个工具的支付相关联。IAS 32 要求优先股的分类应根据对合同安排实质的评估以及金融负债和权益工具的定义而作出。[IAS 32 AG 第 25、AG 26 段]。

7.81 因为优先股相对较为常见，为了便于理解及提供实务应用的帮助，我们在下表中总结了优先股在各种赎回和股利权利组合下的适当分类。在此假定以下优先股并不满足总结于第 7.24.5 段的于 2008 年对 IAS 32 针对可回售金融工具和清算产生的义务的修订中所规定的权益分类标准。

优先股的分类

条款		分类	
本金的赎回	股利的支付（假定所有都是根据市场费率而定）	工具类型	原因
不可赎回	自主决定	权益	没有支付现金的合同义务。所支付的任何股利都将确认在权益中（参见第 7.56 段）。
	非自主决定	负债	负债部分等于支付的永续股利的现值。因为股利是根据市场费率设定的，所以发行收入将等同于支付的永续股利（在发行之日）的公允价值。因此，发行收入将整体划分为负债。

Con.

Redeemable at the issuer's option at some future date.	Discretionary	Equity	There is no contractual obligation to pay cash. An option to redeem the shares for cash does not satisfy the definition of a financial liability. Any dividends paid would be recognised in equity (see para 7.33).
	Non-discretionary	Liability with an embedded call option derivative	Liability component equal to the present value of the dividend payments to perpetuity. As the dividends are set at market rates, the proceeds will be equivalent to the fair value (at the date of issue) of the dividends payable to perpetuity. Therefore, the entire proceeds would be classified as a liability. In addition, because the entire instrument is classified as a liability, the issuer call option to redeem the shares for cash is an embedded derivative (an asset). The embedded derivative may have to be accounted for separately, unless the option's exercise price is approximately equal on each exercise date to the instrument's amortised cost (see para 7.65).
Mandatorily redeemable at a fixed or determinable amount at a fixed or future date	Discretionary	Compound	Liability component equal to the present value of the redemption amount. Equity component is equal to proceeds less liability component. Any dividends paid are related to the equity component and would be recognised in equity (see para 7.103).

续表

可由发行人选择在某一未来日期赎回。	自主决定	权益	没有支付现金的合同义务。以现金赎回股票的选择权不满足金融负债的定义。所支付的任何股利都将确认在权益中（参见第7.33段）。
	非自主决定	含有嵌入看涨期权衍生工具的负债	负债部分等于支付的永续股利的现值。因为股利是根据市场费率设定的，所以发行收入将等同于支付的永续股利（在发行之日）的公允价值。因此，发行收入将整体划分为负债。 此外，因为工具整体被划分为一项负债，发行人以现金赎回股票的看涨期权是一项嵌入衍生工具（资产）。除非期权在每个行权日的行权价格大致等于工具的摊余成本，嵌入衍生工具可能必须单独核算（参见第7.65段）。
可在某固定或未来日期按照固定或可确定的金额强制赎回	自主决定	复合	负债部分等于赎回金额的现值。权益部分等于发行收入减去负债部分。所支付的任何股利都与权益部分相关并将确认在权益中（参见第7.103段）。

Con.

			It should be noted, however, that if any unpaid dividends are added to the redemption amount, then the whole instrument is a financial liability. [IAS 32 para AG 37].
	Non-discretionary	Liability	The entity has an obligation to pay cash in respect of both principal and dividends.
Redeemable at the holder's option at some future date.	Discretionary	Compound	Liability component equal to the present value of the redemption amount (on the basis that the criteria in the 2008 amendment to IAS 32 have not been met (see para 7.24.5). Equity component is equal to proceeds less liability component (see para 7.53). Any dividends paid are related to the equity component and would be recognised in equity (see para 7.103). It should be noted, however, that if any unpaid dividends are added to the redemption amount, then the whole instrument is a financial liability. [IAS 32 para AG 37].
	Non-discretionary	Liability with an embedded put option derivative	There is a contractual obligation to pay cash in respect of both the principal and dividend. In addition, because the entire instrument is classified as a liability, the embedded put option to redeem the shares for cash is an embedded derivative. The embedded derivative may have to be accounted for separately unless the option's exercise price is approximately equal on each exercise date to the instrument's amortised cost (see chapter 5).

续表

			但值得注意的是，如果赎回时所需支付的金额还包括未支付的股利，则整个工具是一项金融负债。[IAS 32 AG 第 37 段]。
	非自主决定	负债	主体有为本金和股利支付现金的义务。
可由持有人选择在某一未来日期赎回。	自主决定	复合	负债部分等于赎回金额的现值（如果不符合 2008 年对 IAS 32 的修订中所规定的标准（参见第 7.24.5 段））。 权益部分等于发行收入减去负债部分（参见第 7.53 段）。所支付的任何股利都与权益部分相关并将确认在权益中（参见第 7.103 段）。 但值得注意的是，如果赎回时所需支付的金额还包括未支付的股利，则整个工具是一项金融负债。[IAS 32 AG 第 37 段]。
	非自主决定	具有嵌入看跌期权衍生工具的负债	主体有为本金和股利支付现金的合同义务。此外，因为工具整体被划分为一项负债，以现金赎回股票的嵌入看跌期权是一项嵌入衍生工具。除非期权在每个行权日的行权价格大致等于工具的摊余成本，嵌入衍生工具可能必须单独核算（参见第 5 章）。

7.82 In the above table, dividend payments need not be a fixed percentage of the preference shares' nominal value. In some circumstances, the payment of dividends may be based on a fixed percentage of profits, for example, ten per cent of profits made each year. Such dividends would not be an embedded derivative because they are based on a non-financial variable that is specific to one party to the contract (see further chapter 4). To the extent that the distribution based on a percentage of profits, is non-discretionary and cannot be avoided, such payments would give rise to a liability treatment, even though the payments are contingent on the issuer making profits (see para 7.50 above).

[The next paragraph is 7.89.]

Derivatives over own equity instruments

7.89 An entity may enter into a derivative contract for the purchase or sale of its own equity instruments. Depending upon the nature of the contract (forward based or option based) and the settlement terms (for example, gross or net in cash) in particular, such contracts may be accounted for as equity instruments, financial liabilities or as derivative assets and liabilities.

Contracts accounted for as equity instruments

7.90 A derivative contract that will be settled by the entity receiving or delivering a fixed number of its own equity instruments in exchange for a fixed amount of cash or another financial asset is an equity instrument. [IAS 32 paras 22, AG 27 (a)]. An example is an issued share option that gives the counterparty a right to buy a fixed number of the entity's shares for a fixed price. The contract's fair value may change due to variation in the share price and market interest rates. However, provided that such changes in the contract's fair value do not affect the amount of cash or other financial assets to be paid or received, or the number of equity instruments to be received or delivered, on the contract's settlement, the contract is treated as an equity instrument. [IAS 32 para 22].

7.91 Any consideration received (such as the premium received for a written option or warrant on the entity's own shares) on a derivative contract that is an

7.82　在上表中，股利支付并不一定需要按照优先股面值的固定百分比而定。在某些情况下，股利的支付可能会根据利润的固定百分比而定，例如每年赚取利润的百分之十。这种股利不构成一个嵌入衍生工具，因为它们基于合同一方特定的非金融变量（更多讨论参见第4章）。在根据利润百分比进行的分配不能自主决定且不可避免的情况下，即使这种付款取决于发行人的获利情况，也应当将其作为负债核算（参见上文第7.50段）。

[下一段为第7.89段。]

基于自身权益工具的衍生工具

7.89　主体可能签订一项衍生工具合同以购买或出售其自身权益工具。根据合同的性质（远期合同还是期权合同），尤其是结算条款（如总额还是净现金），这种合同可能被当做权益工具、金融负债或衍生工具资产和负债来进行核算。

作为权益工具核算的合同

7.90　如果一个衍生工具合同由主体通过收取或交付固定数量的自身权益工具以交换固定金额的现金或其他金融资产来结算，则该合同是一项权益工具。[IAS 32第22段、AG第27（a）段]。例如，发行在外的股票期权赋予了交易对方以固定价格购买固定数量的主体股票的权利。该合同的公允价值可能会随着股票价格以及市场利率的波动而变动。但是，只要该合同的公允价值变动不影响结算时需要支付或可收到的现金或其他金融资产的金额或需交付或可收取的权益工具的数量，则其应作为一项权益工具处理。[IAS 32第22段]。

7.91　因属于权益工具的衍生工具合同而收到的所有款项（诸如基于主体自身股票的签出期权或认股权的对价）直接增加权益。支付的所有款项（诸如

equity instrument is added directly to equity. Any consideration paid (such as the premium paid for a purchased option) is deducted directly from equity. Changes in an equity instrument's fair value are not recognised in the financial statements. [IAS 32 para 22].

7.92 The following examples illustrate the accounting treatment discussed above where an entity enters into derivative contracts to receive or deliver a fixed amount of its own shares in exchange for a fixed amount of cash at some future date.

Example 1 – Purchased call option to receive a fixed number of own shares for a fixed sum[IAS 32 para IE 15]

On 1 February 20X5, an entity purchases a call option for C5,000 under which it has the right but not the obligation to acquire 1,000 of its own shares for cash at the option's exercise of C102 per share. The option will be gross settled in that the entity will take delivery of the shares and pay the exercise price of C102,000 (C102 × 1,000) on the fixed maturity date of 31 January 20X6.

The following information is given:	**Market price per share**	**Fair value of option**
	C	**C**
At 1 February 20X5	100	5,000
At 31 December 20X5	104	3,000
At 31 January 20X6	104	2,000

The accounting entries from inception to settlement of the contract are as follows:

At 1 February 20X5	**Dr**	**Cr**
Equity	C5,000	
Cash		C5,000

At inception of the contract, the entity would record the premium paid for the right to receive a fixed amount of its own shares in one year for a fixed price. As the contract meets the definition of an equity instrument, the premium is

购入期权所支付的对价）直接从权益中扣减。权益工具公允价值的变动不在财务报表中确认。[IAS 32 第 22 段]。

7.92　如下示例说明了上文所述的当主体签订了于未来某一日期收取或交付固定数量的自身股票以换取固定金额的现金的衍生工具合同时应采用的会计处理。

示例 1——收取固定数量的自身股票以换取固定金额的现金的购入看涨期权［IAS 32 IE 第 15 段］

20X5 年 2 月 1 日，某主体以 C5,000 元购买了一项看涨期权，根据该期权主体有权利但无义务在行使期权时以现金按每股 C102 元的价格购买 1,000 股其自身股票。该期权将以主体在固定到期日 20X6 年 1 月 31 日收取股票并支付行权价格 C102,000 元（C102 元 × 1,000）的方式总额结算。

相关信息如下：	**每股市场价格**	**期权的公允价值**
	C	**C**
20X5 年 2 月 1 日	100	5,000
20X5 年 12 月 31 日	104	3,000
20X6 年 1 月 31 日	104	2,000

从合同开始到结算的会计分录如下所述：

20X5 年 2 月 1 日	**借**	**贷**
权益	C5,000	
现金		C5,000

在合同开始时，主体应当记录为换取在一年后以固定的价格收取固定数量的其自身股票的权利所支付的对价。因为该合同符合权益工具的定义，所以对价按照如上讨论直接计入权益。

charged directly to equity as discussed above.

At 31 December 20X5

No entry is made on 31 December because no cash is paid or received. As the option contract meets the definition of an equity instrument, it is not subsequently re-measured as explained in paragraph 7. 91. Therefore, the option's fair value is not relevant.

At 31 January 20X6	**Dr**	**Cr**
Equity	C102, 000	
Cash		C102, 000

The entity exercises the call option on the exercise date as it is in the money (exercise price of C102 per share < market price of C104 per share). As the contract is settled gross, the entity takes delivery of 1, 000 of its own shares and pays a fixed amount of C102, 000 to the counterparty that is recognised directly in equity. Hence, the total amount debited to equity in relation to the purchase is C107, 000.

Example 2 – Written call option to deliver a fixed number of own shares for a fixed sum [IAS 32 para IE 20]

On 1 February 20X5, an entity writes a call option for C5, 000 under which it has an obligation to sell 1, 000 of its own shares for cash at a fixed price of C102 per share, if the counterparty exercises the option. The option will be gross settled in shares in that the entity will deliver its own shares and receive the exercise price of C102, 000 (C102 × 1, 000) on the fixed maturity date of 31 January 20X6.

The following information is given:	**Market price per share**	**Fair value of option**
	C	**C**
At 1 February 20X5	100	5, 000
At 31 December 20X5	104	3, 000
At 31 January 20X6	104	2, 000

20X5 年 12 月 31 日

12 月 31 日不作分录，因为没有支付或收到现金。因为该期权合同符合权益工具的定义，如上文第 7.91 段所解释的，无需进行后续的重新计量。因此，该期权的公允价值并不相关。

20X6 年 1 月 31 日	**借**	**贷**
权益	C102, 000	
现金		C102, 000

由于看涨期权是价内期权（行权价格每股 C102 元小于市场价格每股 C104 元），主体在行权日行使了该期权。该合同以总额进行结算，所以主体收取了 1, 000 股其自身股票并向交易对方支付了 C102, 000 元的固定金额，并将其直接确认在权益中。因此，与购买相关而借计权益的总额为 C107, 000 元。

示例 2——交付固定数量的自身权益以换取固定金额的现金的签出看涨期权［IAS 32 IE 第 20 段］

20X5 年 2 月 1 日，某主体以 C5, 000 元签出了一项看涨期权，如果交易对方行使该期权，主体有以现金按每股 C102 元的固定价格出售 1, 000 股其自身股票的义务。该期权将以股票的形式进行总额结算，主体在固定到期日 20X6 年 1 月 31 日交付其自身股票并收取行权价格 C102, 000 元（C102 × 1, 000）。

相关信息如下：	**每股市场价格**	**期权的公允价值**
	C	**C**
20X5 年 2 月 1 日	100	5, 000
20X5 年 12 月 31 日	104	3, 000
20X6 年 1 月 31 日	104	2, 000

The accounting entries from inception to settlement of the contract are as follows:

At 1 February 20X5	Dr	Cr
Cash	C5, 000	
Equity		C5, 000

At inception of the contract, the entity would record the premium received in exchange for the obligation to deliver a fixed amount of its own shares in one year for a fixed price. As the contract meets the definition of an equity instrument, the premium is credited directly to equity as discussed above.

At 31 December 20X5

No entry is made on 31 December because no cash is paid or received. As the option contract meets the definition of an equity instrument, it is not subsequently re-measured as explained in paragraph 7. 91. Therefore, the option's fair value is not relevant.

At 31 January 20X6	Dr	Cr
Cash	C102, 000	
Equity		C102, 000

The counterparty exercises the call option on the exercise date as it is in the money (exercise price of C102 per share < market price of C104 per share). Therefore, the entity is obliged to deliver 1, 000 of its own shares in exchange for C102, 000 in cash. Hence, the total amount credited to equity in relation to the sale is C107, 000.

Example 3 – Purchase put option to deliver a fixed number of own shares for a fixed sum [IAS 32 para IE 25]

On 1 February 20X5, an entity purchases a put option for C5, 000 under which it has the right to sell 1, 000 of its own shares for cash at a fixed price of C98 per share, if the entity exercises the put option. The option will be

从合同开始到结算的会计分录如下所述：

20X5 年 2 月 1 日	**借**	**贷**
现金	C5, 000	
权益		C5, 000

在合同开始时，主体应当记录为换取一年后以固定的价格交付固定数量的其自身股票的义务所收到的对价。因为该合同符合权益工具的定义，所以对价按照如上讨论直接计入权益。

20X5 年 12 月 31 日

12 月 31 日不作分录，因为没有支付或收到现金。因为该期权合同符合权益工具的定义，如上文第 7.91 段所解释的，无需进行后续的重新计量。因此，该期权的公允价值并不相关。

20X6 年 1 月 31 日	**借**	**贷**
现金	C102, 000	
权益		C102, 000

由于看涨期权是价内期权（行权价格每股 C102 元小于市场价格每股 C104 元），交易对方在行权日行使了该期权，为此主体需要交付 1, 000 股其自身股票以换取 C102, 000 元的现金。因此，与出售相关而贷计权益的总额为 C107, 000 元。

示例 3——交付固定数量的自身股票以换取固定金额的现金的购入看跌期权［IAS 32 IE 第 25 段］

20X5 年 2 月 1 日，某主体以 C5, 000 元购买了一项看跌期权，如果主体行使了该期权，主体有以现金按每股 C98 元的固定价格出售 1, 000 股其自身股票的权利。该期权将以主体在固定到期日 20X6 年 1 月 31 日交付股

gross settled in that the entity will deliver its own shares and receive the exercise price of C98, 000 (C98 × 1, 000) on the fixed maturity date of 31 January 20X6.

The following information is given:	Market price per share	Fair value of option
	C	C
At 1 February 20X5	100	5, 000
At 31 December 20X5	95	4, 000
At 31 January 20X6	95	3, 000

The accounting entries from inception to settlement of the contract are as follows:

At 1 February 20X5	Dr	Cr
Equity	C5, 000	
Cash		C5, 000

At inception of the contract, the entity would record the premium paid in exchange for the right to deliver a fixed amount of its own shares in one year for a fixed price. As the contract meets the definition of an equity instrument, the premium is credited directly to equity as discussed above.

At 31 December 20X5

No entry is made on 31 December because no cash is paid or received. As the option contract meets the definition of an equity instrument, it is not subsequently re-measured as explained in paragraph 7. 91. Therefore, the option's fair value is not relevant.

At 31 January 20X6	Dr	Cr
Cash	C98, 000	
Equity		C98, 000

票并收取行权价格 C98, 000 元（C98 元 ×1, 000）的方式总额结算。

相关信息如下：	每股市场价格	期权的公允价值
	C	C
20X5 年 2 月 1 日	100	5, 000
20X5 年 12 月 31 日	95	4, 000
20X6 年 1 月 31 日	95	3, 000

从合同开始到结算的会计分录如下所述：

20X5 年 2 月 1 日	**借**	**贷**
权益	C5, 000	
现金		C5, 000

在合同开始时，主体应当记录为换取一年后以固定的价格交付固定数量的其自身股票的权利所支付的对价。因为该合同符合权益工具的定义，所以对价按照如上讨论直接贷记权益。

20X5 年 12 月 31 日

12 月 31 日不作分录，因为没有支付或收到现金。因为该期权合同符合权益工具的定义，如上文第 7. 91 段所解释的，无需进行后续的重新计量。因此，该期权的公允价值并不相关。

20X6 年 1 月 31 日	**借**	**贷**
现金	C98, 000	
权益		C98, 000

The entity exercises the put option on the exercise date as it is in the money (exercise price of C98 per share > market price of C95 per share). Therefore, the counterparty is obliged to deliver C98,000 in cash to the entity in exchange for 1,000 shares. Hence, the total amount credited to equity is C93,000.

Example 4 – Forward contract to sell a fixed number of own shares for a fixed sum [IAS 32 para IE 10]

On 1 February 20X5, an entity enters into a forward sale contract under which it has an obligation to sell 1,000 of its own shares for cash at a fixed price of C104 per share on 31 January 20X6.

For simplicity, it is assumed that no dividends are paid on the underlying shares (that is the 'carry return' is zero) so that the present value of the forward price equals the spot price when the fair value of the forward contract is zero. The fair value of the forward has been computed as the difference between the market share price and the present value of the fixed forward price.

The following information is given:	**Market price per share**	**Fair value of forward**
	C	**C**
At 1 February 20X5	100	Nil
At 31 December 20X5	110	(6,300)
At 31 January 20X6	106	(2,000)

The present value of the forward price on 1 February 20X5 is C100 per share.

The accounting entries from inception to settlement of the contract are as follows:

At 1 February 20X5

At inception of the contract, no entries are made as no cash is paid or received for the forward contract – it has an initial fair value of zero. As the entity enters into a forward contract to deliver a fixed number of its own shares in exchange for a fixed amount of cash or another financial asset, the forward

由于看跌期权是价内期权（行权价格每股 C98 元大于市场价格每股 C95 元），主体在行权日行使了该期权，为此交易对方有义务向主体交付 C98,000 元的现金以换取其 1,000 股股票。因此，贷记权益的总额为 C93,000 元。

示例 4——出售固定数量的自身股票以换取固定金额的现金的远期合同
［IAS 32 IE 第 10 段］

20X5 年 2 月 1 日，某主体签订了一项远期销售合同，根据该合同其具有在 20X6 年 1 月 31 日以现金按每股 C104 元的固定价格出售 1,000 股其自身股票的义务。

为简便起见，假定对标的股票不支付任何股利（即“套息交易回报/持有回报”为零），使得当远期合同的公允价值为零时远期价格的现值等于即期价格。该远期合同的公允价值按照股票市场价格和固定远期价格的现值之间的差额计算。

相关信息如下：	每股市场价格 C	远期的公允价值 C
20X5 年 2 月 1 日	100	0
20X5 年 12 月 31 日	110	(6,300)
20X6 年 1 月 31 日	106	(2,000)

20X5 年 2 月 1 日时远期价格的现值为每股 C100 元。

从合同开始到结算的会计分录如下所述：

20X5 年 2 月 1 日

在合同开始时不作分录，因为针对远期合同没有支付或收到现金——其初始公允价值为零。由于主体签订的远期合同将交付固定数量的自身股票以换取固定金额的现金或其他金融资产，该远期合同符合权益工具的定义，因为它不能够以除了交付股票以换取现金之外的其他方式结算。

contract meets the definition of an equity instrument because it cannot be settled otherwise than through the delivery of shares in exchange for cash.

At 31 December 20X5

No entry is made on 31 December because no cash is paid or received. As the forward contract meets the definition of an equity instrument, it is not subsequently re-measured as explained in paragraph 7. 91. Therefore, the contract's fair value is not relevant.

At 31 January 20X6	**Dr**	**Cr**
Cash	C104, 000	
Equity		C104, 000

The entity settles the forward contract by delivery of 1, 000 of its own shares and receives cash of C104 ,000 in exchange.

Contracts accounted for as financial liabilities

7. 93 The above circumstances deal with derivative contracts that require gross physical settlement in shares for a fixed amount of cash at some future date. These physically settled contracts are treated as equity instruments. However, a contract that contains an obligation for an entity to purchase its own equity instruments for cash or another financial asset gives rise to a financial liability for the present value of the redemption amount (for example, for the present value of the forward repurchase price, option exercise price or other redemption amount). This is the case even if the contract itself is an equity instrument. When the financial liability is recognised initially under IAS 39, its fair value (the present value of the redemption amount) is reclassified from equity. Subsequently, the financial liability is measured in accordance with IAS 39. If thc contract expires without delivery, the carrying amount of the financial liability is reclassified to equity. [IAS 32 para 23] .

Example 1 – Forward contract to purchase a fixed number of own shares for a fixed sum [IAS 32 para IE 5]

On 1 February 20X5, an entity enters into a forward purchase contract under

20X5 年 12 月 31 日

12 月 31 日不作分录，因为没有支付或收到现金。因为该远期合同符合权益工具的定义，如上文第 7.91 段所解释的，无需进行后续的重新计量。因此，该合同的公允价值并不相关。

20X6 年 1 月 31 日	**借**	**贷**
现金	C104,000	
权益		C104,000

主体通过交付 1,000 股其自身股票以换取 C104,000 元现金的方式对该项远期合同进行结算。

作为金融负债核算的合同

7.93 以上情况是关于要求在某一未来日期以固定金额的现金换取股票的总额实物结算的衍生工具合同的。这些以实物结算的合同被视为权益工具。但是，如果一项合同使主体承担以现金或其他金融资产回购自身权益工具的义务，则该合同形成主体的一项金融负债，其金额等于赎回时所需支付金额的现值（例如，远期回购价格、期权行权价格或其他赎回金额等的现值）。即使合同本身是一项权益工具时也是如此。当这项金融负债根据 IAS 39 进行初始确认时，其公允价值（赎回价格的现值）应从权益中扣除并重新分类。随后，应根据 IAS 39 对该金融负债进行计量。如果合同到期没有发生支付，则该金融负债的账面价值重新划分为权益。[IAS 32 第 23 段]。

示例 1——购买固定数量的自身股票以换取固定金额的现金的远期合同
[IAS 32 IE 第 5 段]

20X5 年 2 月 1 日，某主体签订了一项远期购买合同，根据该合同其具有

which it has the obligation to acquire 1,000 of its own shares for cash at a fixed price of C104 per share on 31 January 20X6.

For simplicity, it is assumed that no dividends are paid on the underlying shares (that is the 'carry return' is zero) so that the present value of the forward price equals the spot price of the entity's shares when the fair value of the forward contract is zero. The fair value of the forward has been computed as the difference between the market share price and the present value of the fixed forward price.

The following information is given:	**Market price per share**	**Fair value of forward**
	C	**C**
At 1 February 20X5	100	Nil
At 31 December 20X5	110	6,300
At 31 January 20X6	106	2,000

The present value of the forward price on 1 February 20X5 is C100 per share.

The accounting entries from inception to settlement of the contract are as follows:

At 1 February 20X5	**Dr**	**Cr**
Equity	C100,000	
Liability		C100,000

As the entity enters into a forward contract to purchase a fixed number of its own shares in exchange for a fixed amount of cash or another financial asset, the forward contract meets the definition of an equity instrument, because it cannot be settled otherwise than through the delivery of shares in exchange for cash. Furthermore, at inception of the contract the entity has an obligation to pay C104,000 in cash in one year's time. Therefore, in accordance with paragraph 7.93, the entity recognises a liability for the redemption amount of

在 20X6 年 1 月 31 日以现金按每股 C104 元的固定价格购买 1,000 股其自身股票的义务。

为简便起见，假定对标的股票不支付任何股利（即“息差交易回报/持有回报”为零），使得当远期合同的公允价值为零时远期价格的现值等于即期价格。该远期合同的公允价值按照股票市场价格和固定远期价格的现值之间的差额计算。

相关信息如下：	**每股市场价格**	**远期的公允价值**
	C	**C**
20X5 年 2 月 1 日	100	0
20X5 年 12 月 31 日	110	6,300
20X6 年 1 月 31 日	106	2,000

20X5 年 2 月 1 日，远期价格的现值为每股 C100 元。

从合同开始到结算的会计分录如下所述：

20X5 年 2 月 1 日	**借**	**贷**
权益	C100,000	
负债		C100,000

由于主体签订的远期合同将以固定金额的现金或其他金融资产换取固定数量的自身股票，该远期合同符合权益工具的定义，因为它不能够以除了交付股票以换取现金之外的其他方式结算。此外，在合同开始时主体具有一年以后以现金支付 C104,000 元的义务。因此，根据第 7.93 段所述，该主体针对该项一年后应付的赎回金额 C104,000 元按照其现值 C100,000 元确认一项负债。

C104, 000 payable in one year at its present value of C100, 000.

At 31 December 20X5	Dr	Cr
Interest expense	C3, 660	
Liability		C3, 660

As the liability needs to be accreted to its final redemption amount of C104, 000, the entity recognises interest expense to 31 December in accordance with the effective interest rate method.

At 31 January 20X6	Dr	Cr
Interest expense	C340	
Liability		C340

The entity recognises interest expense to 31 January with the result that the liability is stated at its redemption amount.

	Dr	Cr
Liability	C104, 000	
Cash		C104, 000

The entity settles its obligation under the forward contract to purchase its own shares for cash of C104, 000.

It should be noted that whilst an entity is required to recognise a liability at inception for a forward purchase of its own shares, there is no equivalent requirement to recognise an asset for a forward sale of its own shares, even though the two contracts are economically the 'mirror image' of each other (see example 4 in para 7. 92 above). This is because in the former situation the shares that are the subject of a forward purchase cease to be equity until acquired as the entity has an obligation to pay cash. In a forward sale, the equity shares continue to be equity until sold.

20X5 年 12 月 31 日	**借**	**贷**
利息费用	C3, 660	
负债		C3, 660

由于需要将该项负债增加至最终赎回金额 C104, 000，主体按照实际利率法确认截至 12 月 31 日的利息费用。

20X6 年 1 月 31 日	**借**	**贷**
利息费用	C340	
负债		C340

主体确认截至 1 月 31 日的利息费用，其结果是该项负债以赎回金额列报。

	借	**贷**
负债	C104, 000	
现金		C104, 000

主体结算了该远期合同下以 C104, 000 元的现金购买其自身股票的义务。

需要注意的是，在要求主体一开始即针对远期购买其自身股票的事项确认一项负债的同时，并没有要求其针对远期销售其自身股票的事项确认一项资产的相同要求，尽管这两种合同从经济角度来看互为“镜像”（参见上文第 7. 92 段中示例 4）。这是因为在前一种情况下作为远期购买的股票直至购买前不是一项权益，因为主体具有支付现金的义务。在远期销售中，权益股票直至出售前仍是权益。

7.94 An entity's contractual obligation to purchase its own equity instruments gives rise to a financial liability for the present value of the redemption amount even if the obligation to purchase is conditional on the counterparty exercising a right to redeem. An example is a written put option that gives the counterparty the right to sell an entity's own equity instruments to the entity for a fixed or variable price. See also chapter 24 of the IFRS Manual of Accounting concerning obligations to acquire a minority interest.

Example 2 – Written put option to purchase a fixed number of own shares for a fixed sum [IAS 32 para IE 30]

On 1 February 20X5, an entity writes a put option for C5, 000 under which it has the obligation to purchase 1, 000 of its own shares for cash at a fixed price of C98 per share, if the counterparty exercises the put option. The option will be gross settled in that the entity will purchase its own shares and pay the exercise price of C98, 000 (C98 × 1, 000) on the fixed maturity date of 31 January 20X6.

The following information is given:	**Market price per share**	**Fair value of option**
	C	**C**
At 1 February 20X5	100	5, 000
At 31 December 20X5	95	4, 000
At 31 January 20X6	95	3, 000

The present value of the option's exercise price on 1 February 20X5 is C95 per share.

The accounting entries from inception to settlement of the contract are as follows:

At 1 February 20X5	**Dr**	**Cr**
Cash	C5, 000	
Equity		C5, 000

At inception of the contract, the entity would record the premium received in exchange for the obligation to acquire a fixed amount of its own shares in one

7.94 主体回购自身权益工具的合同义务将形成主体的一项金融负债，其金额等于赎回时所需支付金额的现值，即使回购义务取决于交易对方是否行使赎回权利。例如签出看跌期权给予交易对方按固定或可变的价格向主体出售主体自身权益的权利。有关购买少数股东权益的义务问题，也请参见《国际财务报告准则会计实务指引》第24章。

示例2——购买固定数量的自身股票以换取固定金额的现金的签出看跌期权［IAS 32 IE 第30段］

20X5年2月1日，某主体以C5,000元签出了一项看跌期权，如果交易对方行使了该期权，主体有以现金按每股C98元的固定价格购买1,000股其自身股票的义务。该期权将以主体在固定到期日20X6年1月31日收取其自身股票并交付行权价格C98,000元（C98 × 1,000）进行总额结算。

相关信息如下：	每股市场价格 C	期权的公允价值 C
20X5年2月1日	100	5,000
20X5年12月31日	95	4,000
20X6年1月31日	95	3,000

20X5年2月1日该期权行权价格的现值为每股C95元。

从合同开始到结算的会计分录如下所述：

20X5年2月1日	**借**	**贷**
现金	C5,000	
权益		C5,000

在合同开始时，主体应当记录为换取一年后以固定的价格购买固定数量的其自身股票的义务所收到的对价。因为该合同符合权益工具的定义，所

year for a fixed price. As the contract meets the definition of an equity instrument, the premium is credited directly to equity.

	Dr	Cr
Equity	C95, 000	
Liability		C95, 000

Furthermore, at inception of the contract the entity has an obligation to pay C98, 000 in cash in one year's time. Therefore, as stated in the above paragraph, the entity recognises the obligation's present value to pay C98, 000 in one year's time, that is, C95, 000 as a liability.

At 31 December 20X5	**Dr**	**Cr**
Interest expense	C2, 750	
Liability		C2, 750

As the liability needs to be accreted to its final redemption amount of C98, 000, the entity recognises interest expense to 31 December in accordance with the effective interest rate method.

At 31 January 20X6	**Dr**	**Cr**
Interest expense	C250	
Liability		C250

The entity recognises interest expense to 31 January with the result that the liability is stated at its redemption amount of C98, 000.

	Dr	Cr
Liability	C98, 000	
Cash		C98, 000

On the same date, the counterparty exercises the put option as it is in the money (exercise price of C98 per share > market price of C95 per share). The entity settles its obligation under the put option by taking delivery of 1, 000 of its own shares and paying cash of C98, 000 to the counterparty.

以对价按照如上讨论直接贷记权益。

	借	贷
权益	C95,000	
负债		C95,000

此外，在合同开始时主体还有在一年后以现金的形式支付 C98,000 元的义务。因此，如上段所述，主体将在一年后支付 C98,000 元义务的现值，即 C95,000 元，确认为一项负债。

20X5 年 12 月 31 日	借	贷
利息费用	C2,750	
负债		C2,750

由于需要将该项负债增加至最终赎回金额 C98,000，主体按照实际利率法确认截止 12 月 31 日的利息费用。

20X6 年 1 月 31 日	借	贷
利息费用	C250	
负债		C250

主体确认截至 1 月 31 日的利息费用，其结果是该项负债以赎回金额 C98,000 元列报。

	借	贷
负债	C98,000	
现金		C98,000

在同一天，由于看跌期权是价内期权（行权价格每股 C98 元大于市场价格每股 C95 元），交易对方行使了该期权。主体获取 1,000 股其自身股票并向交易对方交付 C98,000 元的现金对该看跌期权的义务进行结算。

If, on the other hand, the contract expires unexercised, the liability of C98,000 is reclassified to equity.

Contracts accounted for as derivative assets or liabilities

7.95 All other contracts on own equity that are not physically settled gross in shares for a fixed sum are treated as derivatives and accounted for as derivative assets or liabilities in accordance with IAS 39. These include contracts that are:

- Settled net in cash (or other financial assets). [IAS 32 para AG 27(c)]. Settled net in cash means that the party with a loss delivers to the party with a gain a cash payment equal to the gain and no shares are exchanged.
- Settled net in the entity's own shares. [IAS 32 para AG 27(c)]. Settled net in shares means that the party with a loss delivers to the party with a gain shares with a current fair value equal to the gain. In other words, the entity's own shares are used as a settlement currency.
- Settled net in cash or net in shares at the option of the entity or the counterparty (see para 7.57).

7.96 The following examples illustrate the accounting treatment discussed above where an entity enters into derivative contracts on an entity's own equity instruments that require settlement either net in cash or net in shares.

Example 1 – Forward purchase contract on own shares settled net in cash or net in shares[IAS 32 paras IE 3, IE 4]

On 1 February 20X5, an entity enters into a forward purchase contract under which it has the obligation to acquire 1,000 of its own shares at a fixed price of C104 per share on 31 January 20X6.

In scenario 1, the contract can only be settled net in cash (no choice by either party).

In scenario 2, the contract can only be settled net in shares (no choice by either party).

For simplicity, it is assumed that no dividends are paid on the underlying

在另一方面，如果合同在未行权的情况下到期，C98,000 元的负债将重新划分为权益。

作为衍生工具资产或负债核算的合同

7.95　所有其他那些不以实物总额结算的以股票换取固定金额的现金的基于自身权益的合同应当视为衍生工具并按照 IAS 39 作为衍生工具资产或负债来进行核算。这包括符合以下条件的合同：

- 以现金（或其他金融资产）净额结算的合同。[IAS 32 AG 第 27（c）段]。以现金净额结算指的是损失一方向利得一方支付等同于利得的现金，不交换任何股票。
- 以主体自身的股票净额结算的合同。[IAS 32 AG 第 27（c）段]。以股票净额结算指的是损失一方向利得一方交付当前公允价值等于利得的股票。换言之，主体自身的股票用作了结算货币。
- 由主体或交易对方选择以现金或股票净额结算的合同（参见第 7.57 段）。

7.96　如下示例说明了上述在主体签订了基于其自身权益工具的要求以现金或股票净额结算的的衍生工具合同的情况下应采用的会计处理。

示例 1——基于自身股票的以现金或股票净额结算的远期购买合同［IAS 32 IE **第** 3、4 **段**］

20X5 年 2 月 1 日，某主体签订了一项远期购买合同，根据该合同其具有在 20X6 年 1 月 31 日按每股 C104 元的固定价格购买 1,000 股其自身股票的义务。

在第一种情况下，该合同只能以现金净额结算（双方均无选择权）。

在第二种情况下，该合同只能以股票净额结算（双方均无选择权）。

为简便起见，假定对标的股票不支付任何股利（即“息差交易回报/持有

shares (that is the 'carry return' is zero) so that the present value of the forward price equals the spot price of the entity's shares when the fair value of the forward contract is zero. The fair value of the forward has been computed as the difference between the market share price and the present value of the fixed forward price.

The following information is given:	**Market price per share**	**Fair value of forward**
	C	**C**
At 1 February 20X5	100	Nil
At 31 December 20X5	110	6, 300
At 31 January 20X6	106	2, 000

The present value of the forward price on 1 February 20X5 is C100 per share.

The accounting entries from inception to settlement of the contract in the two scenarios (settled net in cash or net in shares) are as follows:

At 1 February 20X5

The price per share when the contract is agreed on 1 February 20X5 is C100, which is also the market price of the shares at that date. No entry is required, because the derivative's fair value is zero and no cash is paid or received. This applies whether the forward purchase contract is settled net in cash or net in shares.

At 31 December 20X5	**Dr**	**Cr**
Forward asset	C6, 300	
Gain in profit or loss		C6, 300

On 31 December 20X5, the market price per share has increased to C110 and, as a result, the forward contract's fair value has increased to C6, 300. The increase in the contract's fair value is recognised in profit or loss.

回报”为零)，使得当远期合同的公允价值为零时远期价格的现值等于主体股票的即期价格。该远期合同的公允价值按照股票市场价格和固定远期价格的现值之间的差额计算。

相关信息如下：	每股市场价格	远期的公允价值
	C	C
20X5 年 2 月 1 日	100	0
20X5 年 12 月 31 日	110	6, 300
20X6 年 1 月 31 日	106	2, 000

20X5 年 2 月 1 日，远期价格的现值为每股 C100 元。

在这两种情况下（以现金或股份净额结算），从合同开始到结算的会计分录如下所述：

20X5 年 2 月 1 日

20X5 年 2 月 1 日合同签订时每股价格为 C100 元，即股票在该日的市场价格。不需要作分录，因为该衍生工具的公允价值为零，且没有支付或收取现金。无论该远期购买合同是以现金还是股票净额结算均适用。

20X5 年 12 月 31 日	**借**	**贷**
远期资产	C6, 300	
损益中的利得		C6, 300

20X5 年 12 月 31 日，每股市场价格增加到 C110 元，从而远期合同的公允价值增加到 C6, 300 元。合同公允价值的增加确认为损益。

At 31 January 20X6	Dr	Dr
Loss in profit or loss	C4, 300	
Forward asset		C4, 300

On 31 January 20X6, the market price per share has decreased to C106. The fair value of the forward contract is C2, 000 [1, 000 × (C106 – C104)]. The decrease in the fair value on the forward contract from C6, 300 to C2, 000 is recognised in profit or loss.

Scenario 1 – Settled net in cash	Dr	Cr
Cash	C2, 000	
Forward asset		C2, 000

On the same day, the contract is settled net in cash. The entity has an obligation to deliver C104, 000 in cash, being the settlement amount of the contract, to the counterparty. The counterparty has an obligation to deliver cash equal to the fair value of 1, 000 shares at the date, that is C106, 000 (1, 000 × C106) to the entity. So the counterparty pays the net amount of C2, 000 to the entity.

Scenario 2 – Settled net in shares	Dr	Cr
Equity	C2, 000	
Forward asset		C2, 000

If the contract is settled net in shares, the entity has an obligation to deliver C104, 000 worth of its own shares to the counterparty. The counterparty has an obligation to deliver C106, 000 (1, 000 × C106) worth of the entity's shares to the entity. So the counterparty delivers the net amount of C2, 000 worth of the entity's shares to the entity, that is, 18. 9 shares (C2, 000/C106). The settlement in shares is accounted for as an equity transaction.

20X6 年 1 月 31 日	**借**	**贷**
损益中的损失	C4, 300	
远期资产		C4, 300

20X6 年 1 月 31 日，每股市场价格减少至 C106 元。远期合同的公允价值为 C2, 000 元［1, 000 ×（C106 – C104）］。远期合同公允价值从 C6, 300 元到 C2, 000 元的跌幅确认为损益。

第一种情况——以现金净额结算	**借**	**贷**
现金	C2, 000	
远期资产		C2, 000

在同一天，合同以现金净额进行了结算。主体有义务向交易对方交付 C104, 000 元现金，即合同的结算金额。交易对方有义务向主体交付 1, 000 股股票在该日公允价值的等值现金，即 C106, 000 元（1, 000 ×C 106）。所以交易对方向主体支付净额 C2, 000 元。

第二种情况——以股票净额结算	**借**	**贷**
权益	C2, 000	
远期资产		C2, 000

如果合同是以股票净额结算，主体有义务向交易对方交付价值 C104, 000 元的自身股票。交易对方有义务向主体交付价值 C106, 000 元（1, 000 × C106）的主体股票。所以交易对方向主体交付价值为净额 C2, 000 元的主体股票，即 18. 9 股（C2, 000/C106）。以股票结算作为一项权益交易进行会计处理。

Example 2 – Written call option on own shares settled net in cash or net in shares[IAS 32 paras IE 18, IE 19]

On 1 February 20X5, an entity writes a call option for C5,000 under which it has an obligation to sell 1,000 of its own shares at a fixed price of C102 per share, if the counterparty exercises the call option. The option will be settled on the fixed maturity date of 31 January 20X6.

In scenario 1, the contract can only be settled net in cash (no choice by either party).

In scenario 2, the contract can only be settled net in shares (no choice by either party).

The following information is given:	**Market price per share**	**Fair value of option**
	C	**C**
At 1 February 20X5	100	5,000
At 31 December 20X5	104	3,000
At 31 January 20X6	104	2,000

The accounting entries from inception to settlement of the contract in the two scenarios (settled net in cash or net in shares) are as follows:

At 1 February 20X5	**Dr**	**Cr**
Cash	C5,000	
Call option obligation		C5,000

At inception of the contract, the entity would record the premium received under the contract in both scenarios.

At 31 December 20X5	**Dr**	**Cr**
Call option obligation	C2,000	
Gain in profit or loss		C2,000

示例 2——基于自身股票的以现金或股票净额结算的签出看涨期权［IAS 32 IE 第 18、19 段］

20X5 年 2 月 1 日，某主体以 C5,000 元签出了一项看涨期权，如果交易对方行使了该期权，主体有义务按每股 C102 元的固定价格出售 1,000 股其自身股票。该期权将在固定到期日 20X6 年 1 月 31 日结算。

在第一种情况下，该合同只能以现金进行净额结算（双方均无选择权）。

在第二种情况下，该合同只能以股票进行净额结算（双方均无选择权）。

相关信息如下：	**每股市场价格**	**期权的公允价值**
	C	**C**
20X5 年 2 月 1 日	100	5,000
20X5 年 12 月 31 日	104	3,000
20X6 年 1 月 31 日	104	2,000

在这两种情况下（以现金或股票净额结算），从合同开始到结算的会计分录如下所述：

20X5 年 2 月 1 日	**借**	**贷**
现金	C5,000	
看涨期权义务		C5,000

在合同开始时，主体应当记录根据合同上述两种情况下所收到的对价。

20X5 年 12 月 31 日	**借**	**贷**
看涨期权义务	C2,000	
损益表中的利得		C2,000

On 31 December 20X5, the fair value of the call option obligation has fall to C3, 000. The decrease in the fair value of the obligation is recognised as a gain in profit or loss.

At 31 January 20X6	**Dr**	**Cr**
Call option obligation	C1, 000	
Gain in profit or loss		C1, 000

On 31 January 20X6, the fair value of the call option obligation has fallen further to C2, 000. The decrease in the fair value is recognised as a gain in profit or loss.

Scenario 1 – Settled net in cash	**Dr**	**Cr**
Call option obligation	C2, 000	
Cash		C2, 000

If the contract is settled net in cash, the entity has an obligation to deliver C104, 000 in cash, being the fair value of the 1, 000 shares on 31 January 20X6, to the counterparty. The counterparty has an obligation to deliver cash equal to the option's exercise price of C102, 000 to the entity. So the entity pays the net amount of C2, 000 to the counterparty.

Scenario 2 – Settled net in shares	**Dr**	**Cr**
Call option obligation	C2, 000	
Equity		C2, 000

If, the contract is settled net in shares, the entity has an obligation to deliver C104, 000 worth of its own shares to the counterparty. The counterparty has an obligation to deliver C102, 000 worth of the entity's shares to the entity. So the entity delivers the net amount of C2, 000 worth of its own shares to the counterparty, that is, 19. 2 shares (C2, 000/C104). The settlement in shares is accounted for as an equity transaction.

20X5 年 12 月 31 日，看涨期权义务的公允价值降至 C3,000 元。该义务公允价值的减少在损益中确认为一项利得。

20X6 年 1 月 31 日	**借**	**贷**
看涨期权义务	C1,000	
损益中的利得		C1,000

20X6 年 12 月 31 日，看涨期权义务的公允价值进一步降至 C2,000 元。公允价值的减少在损益中确认为一项利得。

第一种情况——以现金净额结算	**借**	**贷**
看涨期权义务	C2,000	
现金		C2,000

如果合同以现金净额进行结算，主体有义务向交易对方交付 C104,000 元现金，即这 1,000 股股票在 20X6 年 1 月 31 日的公允价值。交易对方有义务向主体交付等于该期权行权价格 C102,000 元的现金。所以主体向交易对方支付净额 C2,000 元。

第二种情况——以股票净额结算	**借**	**贷**
看涨期权义务	C2,000	
权益		C2,000

如果合同是以股票净额结算，主体有义务向交易对方交付价值 C104,000 元的自身股票。交易对方有义务向主体交付价值 C102,000 元的主体股票。所以主体向交易对方交付价值为净额 C2,000 元的自身股票，即 19.2 股（C2,000/C104）。以股票结算作为一项权益交易进行会计处理。

Issuer or holder's settlement options

7.97 The examples above deal with situations where the settlement of the derivative contracts on own equity, either net in cash or net in shares, was dictated by the contractual terms (no choice). Sometimes such derivative contracts may contain settlement options that give either party a choice over how it is settled (for example, the issuer or the holder can choose to settle the contract net in cash, or net in shares or by exchanging shares for cash). As explained in paragraph 7.57 above, when a derivative financial instrument gives one party a choice over how it is settled, it is a financial asset or a financial liability unless all of the settlement alternatives would result in it being an equity instrument. [IAS 32 para 26].

[The next paragraph is 7.99.]

Treatment of interest, dividends, gains and losses

7.99 The general principle of IAS 32 is that the treatment of interest, dividends, losses and gains follows the classification of the related instrument. Therefore, where such items relate to equity instruments, they are included in equity. On the other hand, if they relate to instruments that are classified as financial liabilities, they are included in profit or loss. IAS 32, therefore, requires that:

- Interest, dividends, losses and gains relating to a financial instrument or a component that is a financial liability should be recognised as income or expense in profit or loss.

- Distributions to holders of an equity instrument should be debited by the entity directly to equity, net of any related income tax benefit.

[IAS 32 para 35].

7.100 It follows from the above requirement that dividend payments on preference shares that are classified wholly as liabilities are included in calculating amortised cost and, hence, recognised as expenses in the same way as interest on a bond. They may be presented in the income statement either with interest on other liabilities or as a separate item. The standard notes that in some circumstances, it may be desirable to disclose interest and dividends separately in the income

发行人或持有人的结算选择权

7.97 上述示例讨论了根据合同条款确定的（没有选择权）用现金还是股票对基于自身权益的衍生工具合同进行净额结算的情况。有时这种衍生工具合同可能会包含给予任何一方选择如何进行结算的结算选择权（例如，发行人或持有人可以选择以现金净额、股票净额或是以股票交换现金的方式来结算合同）。如上文第7.57段中所解释的，如果一项衍生金融工具给予某一合同方选择结算方式的权利，则该衍生工具是一项金融资产或金融负债，除非所有的可选结算方式都将使其成为一项权益工具。[IAS 32 第26段]。

[下一段为第7.99段。]

利息、股利、利得和损失的处理

7.99 IAS 32 的基本原则是利息、股利、损失和利得的处理应根据其相关工具的分类而定。因此，在这些项目与权益工具相关的情况下，将计入权益。另一方面，如果它们与划分为金融负债的工具相关，则将计入损益。所以，IAS 32 要求：

- 与金融工具或属于金融负债的组成部分相关的利息、股利、损失和利得，应作为收益或费用计入损益。

- 对权益工具持有人的分配，应在扣除相关的所得税利益后直接借记主体权益。

[IAS 32 第35段]。

7.100 根据以上要求，整体划分为负债的优先股，其股利支付包括在摊余成本的计算中，因此，应将其以与债券利息相同的方式确认为费用。可以将其与其他负债的利息一起或是作为一个单独项目在利润表中进行列报。该准则指出在某些情况下，因为利息和股利在诸如纳税可抵扣等问题上的差别，在利润表中将利息和股利分开披露更为可取。利息和股利的披露应遵循《国际会计准则第1号——财务报表的列报》和《国际财务报告准则第7号——金融工

statement, because of the differences between interest and dividends with respect to matters such as tax deductibility. Disclosure of interest and dividends is subject to the requirements of IAS 1, 'Presentation of financial statements', and IFRS 7, 'Financial instruments: Disclosures'. Disclosures of the tax effects should be made in accordance with IAS 12, 'Income taxes'. [IAS 32 para 40].

7.101 Gains and losses associated with redemptions or refinancings of financial liabilities are recognised in profit or loss. Similarly, gains and losses related to changes in the carrying amount of a financial liability are recognised in profit or loss. This is so even when they relate to an instrument that includes a right to the residual interest in the entity's assets in exchange for cash or another financial asset (for example, units in mutual funds that are puttable – see para 7.19 above). Under IAS 1, the entity presents any gain or loss arising from remeasurement of such an instrument separately on the face of the income statement when it is relevant in explaining the entity's performance. [IAS 32 para 41]. IAS 32 contains examples of income statement presentation where an entity has little or no equity. [IAS 32 paras IE 32 – IE 33].

7.102 Redemptions or refinancings of equity instruments are recognised in equity. Changes in the fair value of an equity instrument are not recognised in the financial statements. [IAS 32 para 36].

7.103 The application of the principle in paragraph 7.99 above to compound financial instruments would require any payments relating to the liability component to be reported in profit or loss and any payments relating to the equity component to be reported in equity. A classic example is mandatorily redeemable preference shares with discretionary dividend payments. Such an instrument is a compound financial instrument, with the liability component being the present value of the redemption amount. The unwinding of the discount on this component is recognised in profit or loss and classified as interest expense. Any dividends paid relate to the equity component and are recognised as a distribution of profit or loss. A similar treatment would apply if the redemption was not mandatory but at the option of the holder, or if the preference shares were mandatorily convertible into a variable number of ordinary shares calculated to equal a fixed amount or an amount based on changes in an underlying variable (for example, a commodity). However, if any unpaid

具：披露》。关于纳税影响的披露应遵循《国际会计准则第 12 号——所得税》。[IAS 32 第 40 段]。

7.101　与金融负债的赎回或再融资相关的利得和损失应确认为损益。类似地，与金融负债账面价值的变动相关的利得和损失，应计入损益，即使该金融负债与一项包含以对主体资产的剩余收益权换取现金或其他金融资产时的权利相关联时（例如，共同基金的可回售单位——参见上文第 7.19 段）。根据 IAS 1，如果有助于反映主体的经营业绩，主体应将由这类工具重新计量而产生的利得或损失在利润表中单独列示。[IAS 32 第 41 段]。IAS 32 包括主体没有或只有很少权益情况下的利润表列报示例。[IAS 32 IE 第 32 – 33 段]。

7.102　权益工具的赎回或再融资在权益中确认。权益工具的公允价值变动不在财务报表中确认。[IAS 32 第 36 段]。

7.103　对复合金融工具运用上文第 7.99 段所述原则时应该要求在损益中报告与负债组成部分相关的任何付款，及在权益中报告与权益组成部分相关的任何付款。其典型示例为具有自主决定股利付款的强制可赎回优先股。这种工具是复合金融工具，其负债部分为赎回金额的折现值。对该部分折现额的转回计入损益并划分为利息费用。与权益部分相关的股利支付应确认为利润分配。如果优先股的赎回不是强制性而是取决于持有人的选择，或该优先股必须转换为可变数量的普通股，其数量刚好使得其价值等于某一固定金额或根据某一基础变量（例如商品）的变化而确定的金额，则应采用类似的会计处理方式。但是，如果赎回时所需支付的金额还包括未支付的股利，则整个工具是一项负债。在这种情况下，所有股利都应计入根据实际利率法进行会计处理的利息费用。[IAS 32 AG 第 37 段]。

dividends are added to the redemption amount, the entire instrument is a liability. In such a case, any dividends are classified as interest expense that will be accounted for in accordance with the effective interest method. [IAS 32 para AG 37].

Example – Premium payable on the cancellation of the conversion option in a convertible bond

An entity has issued a convertible bond, which is classified as a compound instrument (liability host bond and an equity conversion option). The entity decides after issue to cancel the conversion option in order to remove the dilution effect on its share capital. The issuer will have to pay the bondholder a premium to compensate for giving up its conversion rights, which is likely to be greater than the fair value of the conversion option to incentivise the bondholder to accept the change in terms. Provided that the terms of the liability component of the bond remain unchanged, the premium paid to cancel the equity conversion option is a payment for an own equity instrument. The premium paid is, therefore, debited to equity, as for any repurchase of an entity's own equity instruments.

Treatment of transaction costs of equity instruments

7.104 An entity typically incurs various costs in issuing or acquiring its own equity instruments. Those costs might include registration and other regulatory fees, underwriting costs and brokerage fees, amounts paid to lawyers, accountants, investment bankers and other professional advisers, fees and commissions paid to agents, brokers, and dealers, printing costs and stamp duties. Most such costs are transaction costs, that is, incremental costs that are directly attributable to the equity transaction that otherwise would have been avoided had the equity instruments not been issued. Transaction costs arising on the issue of equity instruments, however, do not include indirect costs, such as the costs of management time and administrative overheads, or allocations of internal costs that would have been incurred had the equity instruments not been issued. Nor do they include costs of researching different types of equity instruments or of ascertaining the suitability or feasibility of particular equity instruments. Generally, costs for marketing an IPO, including the 'road show', do not meet the definition of a

示例——取消某项可转换债券的转股权所需支付的对价

某主体发行了一项划分为复合工具的可转换债券（负债主债券和一项转股权）。主体在发行后决定取消该转股权以免除对其股本的稀释作用。发行人将不得不向债券持有人支付一定的对价作为对其放弃转换权的补偿，对价很可能大于该转股权的公允价值，以促使债券持有人接受该条款变更。只要负债部分的条款保持不变，为取消转股权而支付的对价即为对自身权益工具的付款。因此，为重新购入主体自身权益工具而支付的对价将借记权益。

权益工具交易费用的处理

7.104 主体在发行或回购自身权益工具时通常会发生各种费用。这种费用可能包括注册费以及其他监管费，承销费和经纪人佣金，支付给律师、会计师、投资银行和其他专业顾问的费用，支付给代理人、经纪人和经销商的费用和佣金，印刷费用和印花税等。这些费用大部分都是交易费用，即如果未发行这种权益工具就可以避免的直接归属于权益交易的增量费用。但是，因发行权益工具而发生的交易费用并不包括间接费用，例如管理层时间成本和管理费用，或是如果未发行权益工具可能已经发生的的内部费用的分配。交易费用也不包括对不同类型的权益工具所发生的研究成本或确定某个特别的权益工具的适用性或可行性的成本。一般而言，包括“路演”等为首次公开募股进行市场推广活动的费用，不符合交易费用的定义。市场推广费用主要与主体自身的市场推广活动相关。因此在大部分情况下首次公开募股的市场推广费用都不符合可直接归属的定义，因而应将其费用化。

transaction cost. Marketing costs primarily relate to the marketing of the entity itself. Therefore in most situations marketing costs for an IPO do not meet the definition of directly attributable and therefore are expensed through profit or loss.

7. 105 IAS 32 requires that transaction costs of an equity transaction should be accounted for as a deduction from equity, net of any related income tax benefit. [IAS 32 para 35]. This treatment is based on the view that the transaction costs incurred are a necessary part of completing the equity transaction and form an integral part of it. Linking the equity transaction and costs of the transaction reflects the net proceeds received from the transaction in equity. This approach achieves a result which is consistent with paragraph 7. 99 above, which states that a financial instrument's classification in the balance sheet determines whether interest, dividends, losses and gains relating to that instrument are reported in the income statement. As a result, losses relating to a financial instrument classified as the issuer's equity are reported by the issuer as movements in equity.

7. 106 Transaction costs that relate to the issue of a compound financial instrument are allocated to the instrument's liability and equity components in proportion to the allocation of proceeds (see example in para 7. 67). See Chapter 9 for more discussion on transaction costs.

7. 107 Transaction costs that relate jointly to more than one transaction (for example, costs of a concurrent offering of some shares and a stock exchange listing of other shares) are allocated to those transactions using a basis of allocation that is rational and consistent with similar transactions. [IAS 32 para 38]. This situation often arises when an entity undertakes an initial public offering (IPO) of its shares. As a result of the IPO, new shares are issued to investors to raise additional capital and, along with existing shares, subsequently become listed on a stock exchange. Costs incurred in listing existing shares on a stock exchange are not transaction costs relating to the issue of an equity instrument. This is because these costs are simply incurred to make the existing shares more marketable and are not related to the equity instrument's issue. In some situations, the existing shares may be included in a ' secondary offering ' (that is, a sale of shares by existing shareholders as opposed to the company itself). As the cash generated from the sale of secondary shares is given to the selling shareholders, rather than the

7.105 IAS 32 要求权益性交易的交易费用应在扣除相关的所得税利益后直接扣减权益。[IAS 32 第 35 段]。这种处理方法所依据的观点是这些发生的交易费用是完成权益性交易的必要部分且构成了其不可分割的一部分。将权益性交易和交易费用关联在一起反映了从权益交易中所收到的净收入。这种方法所得到的结果与上文第 7.99 段一致，该段内容规定金融工具在资产负债表中的分类决定了与该工具相关的利息、股利、损失和利得是否应在利润表中进行列报。因而与划分为发行人权益的金融工具相关的损失应由发行人列报为权益的变动。

7.106 与发行复合金融工具相关的交易费用应根据发行收入的分配比例分配至该工具的负债和权益部分中（参见的第 7.67 段所述示例）有关交易费用的更多讨论参见第 9 章。

7.107 与多项交易相关的交易费用（例如，同时发行某些股票和申请另一些股票在证券交易所上市的费用）应基于合理的、与其他类似交易一致的方法将其分配至这些交易。[IAS 32 第 38 段]。这种情况经常在主体进行首次公开募股（IPO）时出现。作为首次公开募股的结果，主体向投资人发行新股以筹集更多的资本，并使得这些新股与现有股票一起在证券交易所上市。使现有股票在证券交易所上市所发生的费用并不是与发行权益工具相关的交易费用。这是因为这些费用的发生仅仅是为了使现有的股票更市场化，与权益工具的发行并不相关。在某些情况下，现有股票可能包括在“二次发售”（即，由现有股东而不是由公司本身出售股票）中。由于出售二次发售股票所获取的现金将交至出售股东而非公司手中，所发生的任何费用均不是权益交易费用。因此，应将这些费用计入利润表。另一方面，在首次公开募股时发行新股筹集资本（“初次发售”）所发生的费用是权益工具的交易费用，如上所述，应计入权益。实务中，主体应当确定出可具体归属于新股发行的费用。如果未进行首次公开募股则不会发生的所有募股费用均应根据合理的依据在新股和旧股之

company, any costs incurred are not equity transaction costs. Therefore, these costs should be charged to the income statement. On the other hand, costs incurred in issuing new shares to raise capital ('primary offering') in an IPO are transaction costs of equity instrument and, as explained above, falls to be charged to equity. In practice, entities would need to identify the costs that are specifically attributable to the issue of new shares. All other costs of the IPO that would not have been incurred had the IPO not taken place should be allocated between the new shares and old shares on some reasonable basis, for example, in the ratio of old to new shares. It follows from the above that any costs incurred by the company in a 'secondary offering' of its own shares are not equity transaction costs. Accordingly, those costs should be charged to profit or loss.

7.108 The amount of transaction costs accounted for as a deduction from equity in the period is disclosed separately under IAS 1. The related amount of income taxes recognised directly in equity is included in the aggregate amount of current and deferred income tax credited or charged to equity that is disclosed under IAS 12. [IAS 32 para 39; IAS 12 para 81(a)].

Treasury shares

7.109 When an entity purchases its own shares and holds them in treasury ('treasury shares'), IAS 32 requires the following:

- The amount paid for the treasury shares is deducted from equity. This is because an entity's own equity instruments are not recognised as a financial asset regardless of the reason for which they are acquired. However, where an entity holds its own equity on behalf of others, for example, a financial institution holding its own equity on behalf of a client, there is an agency relationship and as a result those holdings are not included in the entity's balance sheet.
- No gain or loss should be recognised in profit or loss on the purchase, sale, issue or cancellation of an entity's own equity instruments. This is because the acquisition and subsequent resale of treasury shares are transactions with entity's owners rather than a gain or loss to the entity.
- Consideration paid or received for the purchase or sale of an entity's own equity

间进行分配，例如旧股与新股之间的比例。根据上文所述，公司在对其自身股票进行“二次发售”时所发生的任何费用均不属于权益交易费用。因此，应将这些费用计入损益。

7.108　当期作为权益扣减项核算的交易费用金额应根据 IAS 1 进行单独披露。直接在权益中确认的所得税金额应包括在根据 IAS 12 进行披露的贷记或借记权益的当期所得税和递延所得税的总额里。［IAS 32 第 39 段；IAS 12 第 81（a）段］。

库藏股

7.109　当主体购买了其自身股票并将其库藏时（“库藏股”），IAS 32 有如下要求：

- 为库藏股所支付的金额从权益中扣除。这是因为不论其购买的原因，主体自身权益工具不能作为金融资产确认。然而，如果主体是替其他人持有其自身权益，例如金融机构替其客户持有自身权益，由于存在代理关系，因此所持有的自身权益不包括在主体的资产负债表中。

- 在购回、出售、发行或取消主体的自身权益工具时不应在损益中确认任何利得或损失。这是因为库藏股的获取和后续重新出售是与主体所有人的交易而不是主体的利得或损失。

- 在购回、出售主体的自身权益工具时所支付或收取的对价应直接在权益中

instruments should be recognised directly in equity.

[IAS 32 paras 33, AG 36].

7.110 IAS 32 notes that own equity instruments may be acquired and held by the entity or by other members of the consolidated group (that is, the parent and its subsidiaries, but excluding the group's associates and joint ventures). [IAS 32 para 33]. Therefore, the above accounting applies to all interests in own equity instruments held by a company and, in consolidated financial statements, the parent's shares held by subsidiaries. In the latter case, this applies to all such shareholdings, including those held by subsidiaries that carry on a business of dealing in securities. However, in the individual financial statements of a subsidiary that holds shares in its parent, such shares are treated as an asset; that is, 'treasury shares' accounting does not apply as these are not 'own shares' for the subsidiary itself.

Example – Purchase of own shares held in treasury

Entity A (a listed company) has in issue 1,000,000 C1 ordinary shares originally issued at a premium of C9. It buys back 20,000 shares when their market value is C40 per share. The purchase is made out of retained profits and the entity holds the shares in treasury. In this situation, the entity does not reduce its issued share capital, but instead will reduce its retained profits by the consideration paid for the shares (that is, 20,000 × C40 = C800,000), as shown below.

It should be noted that this treatment only applies in the UK and the treatment in other jurisdictions may be different.

确认。

［IAS 32 第 33 段、AG 第 36 段］。

7.110　IAS 32 指出自身权益工具可能由主体或是集团合并范围内的其他成员（即，母公司及其子公司，但是不包括集团的联营和合营）所购回并持有。［IAS 32 第 33 段］。因此，上述会计处理适用于所有公司所持有的自有权益工具，以及在合并财务报表中，子公司所持有的母公司股票。后一情况对所有此类持股都适用，包括那些进行证券交易业务的子公司所持有的股票。但是，在持有母公司股票的子公司的个别财务报表中，这些股票被视为资产，即由于其并非子公司的“自身股票”，“库藏股”会计处理方法并不适用。

示例——购回作为库藏股持有的自身股票

主体 A（一家上市公司）最初以 C9 元的溢价发行了 1,000,000 股 C1 元的普通股。在每股市场价值为 C40 元时购回了 20,000 股。此购买是以未分配利润进行的，且主体将其作为库藏股持有。在这种情况下，主体并不抵减其已发行股本，而是将为股票所支付的对价抵减其未分配利润（即，$20,000 \times C40 = C800,000$），如下所示。

应注意，这种处理方法仅在英国适用，在其他管辖区的处理方法可能不同。

	Before purchase C'000	Purchase C'000	After purchase C'000
Net assets other than cash	20, 000		20, 000
Cash	5, 000	(800)	4, 200
	25, 000	(800)	24, 200
Share capital	1, 000		1, 000
Share premium	9, 000		9, 000
Capital	10, 000		10, 000
Retained profits	15, 000	(800)	14, 200
	25, 000	(800)	24, 200

As can be seen from the above example, the entire consideration paid for the purchase is recognised directly in equity (retained profits).

In the notes to the financial statements, entity A should explain that 20, 000 C1 ordinary shares with an aggregate nominal value of C20, 000 were purchased during the period and are held in treasury and that retained profits have been reduced by C800, 000, being the consideration paid for these shares.

As stated in paragraph 7. 105 above, the costs of an equity transaction should be accounted for as a deduction from equity. [IAS 32 para 35]. Therefore, expenses directly relating to the treasury share purchase should be treated as part of the overall cost of purchase and like the purchase cost itself should be recognised directly in equity (retained profits) and shown in the statement of changes in equity.

	购回前	购回	购回后
	C’000	C’000	C’000
除现金以外的净资产	20, 000		20, 000
现金	5, 000	(800)	4, 200
	25, 000	(800)	24, 200
股本	1, 000		1, 000
股本溢价	9, 000		9, 000
资本	10, 000		10, 000
未分配利润	15, 000	(800)	14, 200
	25, 000	(800)	24, 200

通过以上示例可以看出，购回所支付的所有对价直接在权益（未分配利润）中确认。

在财务报表的注释中，主体 A 应说明合计票面价值为 C20, 000 元的 20, 000 股 C1 元的普通股在本期被购回并作为库藏股持有，未分配利润减少了 C800, 000 元，即为这些股票所支付的对价。

如上文第 7. 105 段中所述，权益性交易的费用应直接扣减权益。[IAS 32 第 35 段]。因此，与库藏股购回直接相关的费用应被视为整体购回成本的一部分，而且就像购回成本一样，应直接在权益（未分配利润）中确认并在权益变动表中体现出来。

Chapter 11 Presentation and disclosure

Content

Presentation of financial instruments 11001
Presentation as current or non-current 11001
Current and non-current assets 11001
Current and non-current liabilities 11003
Offsetting a financial asset and a financial liability 11017
General principle 11017
Legal right of set-off 11019
Intention to settle on a net basis 11021
Simultaneous settlement 11021
Situations where offset is usually inappropriate 11023
Master netting agreements 11025
Disclosure of financial instruments 11029
Scope of IFRS 7 11031
Objectives of IFRS 7 11037
General matters 11039
Classes of financial instruments 11039
Location, level of disclosure and aggregation 11043
Risks arising from financial instruments 11043
Balance sheet disclosures 11045
Financial assets or liabilities at fair value through profit or loss 11051
Other sundry balance sheet disclosure 11059
Re-classification 11059
Derecognition 11067
Collateral 11069
Allowance amount for credit losses 11073
Compound financial instruments with multiple embedded derivatives 11073
Defaults and breaches 11073

第十一章　列报和披露

目　录

金融工具的列报　11002
　列报为流动或非流动　11002
　　流动和非流动资产　11002
　　流动和非流动负债　11004
　抵销金融资产和金融负债　11018
　　一般原则　11018
　　法定抵销权　11020
　　以净额为基础进行结算的意向　11022
　　同时结算　11022
　　通常不适于抵销的情况　11024
　　总互抵协议　11026
金融工具的披露　11030
IFRS 7 的范围　11032
IFRS 7 的目的　11038
一般事宜　11040
　金融工具的类型　11040
　披露和汇总的位置和等级　11044
　金融工具所产生的风险　11044
资产负债表的披露　11046
　以公允价值计量且变动计入损益的金融资产或负债　11052
　其他各种资产负债表披露　11060
　　重分类　11060
　　终止确认　11068
　　抵押物　11070
　　信用损失备抵金额　11074
　　具有多重嵌入衍生工具的复合金融工具　11074
　　拖欠和违约　11074

Income statement and equity disclosures 11075

Items of income, expense, gains or losses 11075

Other disclosures 11081

Accounting policies 11081

Hedge accounting 11085

Fair value 11091

Fair value hierarchy 11095

Financial instrument risk disclosures 11129

Qualitative disclosures 11131

Quantitative disclosures 11137

Credit risk 11145

Collateral and other credit enhancements 11149

Credit quality of financial assets that are neither past due nor impaired 11151

Financial assets that are either past due or impaired 11153

Liquidity risk 11161

Market risk 11187

Sensitivity analysis 11187

Other market risk disclosures 11205

利润表及权益的披露 11076
收益、费用、利得或损失项目 11076
其他披露 11082
会计政策 11082
套期会计 11086
公允价值 11092
公允价值级次 11096
金融工具风险的披露 11130
定性披露 11132
定量披露 11138
信用风险 11146
抵押物和其他信用增级 11150
未逾期也未发生减值的金融资产的信用质量 11152
已逾期或发生减值的金融资产 11154
流动性风险 11162
市场风险 11188
敏感性分析 11188
其他市场风险的披露 11206

Presentation of financial instruments

11.1 The principles for presenting financial and other assets and liabilities, and any related income and expense, are set out in IAS 1, 'Presentation of financial statements'. This standard's requirements are considered in chapter 4 of the Manual of Accounting – IFRS. The paragraphs that follow consider only the presentation of financial assets and liabilities as current or non-current.

Presentation as current or non-current

11.2 IAS 1 states that an entity should present current and non-current assets, and current and non-current liabilities, as separate classifications on the face of the balance sheet, except when a presentation based on liquidity provides information that is reliable and is more relevant. When that exception applies, all assets and liabilities should be presented broadly in order of liquidity. [IAS 1 para 60].

Current and non-current assets

11.3 Where an entity presents assets and liabilities as either current or non-current, it should classify an asset as current when:

- it expects to realise the asset, or intends to sell or consume it in its normal operating cycle;
- it holds the asset primarily for the purpose of trading;
- it expects to realise the asset within 12 months after the reporting period; or
- the asset is cash or a cash equivalent (as defined in IAS 7, 'Cash flow statements'), unless it is restricted from being exchanged or used to settle a liability for at least 12 months after the reporting period.

[IAS 1 para 66].

11.4 Applying the above definition, it could be argued that financial assets classified as held for trading should be presented as current assets. [IAS 1 para 68]. Similarly, trading derivative assets should also be presented as current assets.

金融工具的列报

11.1 《国际会计准则第 1 号——财务报表的列报》（IAS 1）中规定了金融及其他资产和负债以及其相关收入和费用的列报原则。在《会计实务指引——国际财务报告准则》的第 4 章中对该准则的要求进行了讨论。以下各段仅讨论金融资产和负债作为流动或非流动的列报。

列报为流动或非流动

11.2 IAS 1 指出，主体应在其资产负债表中将流动和非流动资产、流动和非流动负债作为单独的类别列报，除非按流动性列报提供的信息是可靠的并且更为相关。当应用这种例外情况时，所有的资产和负债应大体按其流动性顺序列报。[IAS 1 第 60 段]。

流动和非流动资产

11.3 当主体将资产和负债按照流动或非流动列报时，应在下述情况下将资产划分为流动资产：

- 主体预期在其正常经营周期中实现，或打算出售或消耗；
- 主体主要为交易目的而持有该资产；
- 主体预期在报告期后十二个月之内实现该资产；或者
- 该资产是现金或现金等价物（根据《国际会计准则第 7 号——现金流量表》中的定义），除非在报告期后至少十二个月内将该资产交换或用于清偿债务是受到限制的。

[IAS 1 第 66 段]。

11.4 在应用上述定义时，可以说被分类为为交易而持有的金融资产应被列报为流动资产。[IAS 1 第 68 段]。同样，交易性的衍生工具资产也应列报为流动资产。

11.4.1 IAS 1 sets out the requirements for the presentation of an asset or a liability as current or non-current in the balance sheet and paragraph 65 specifically states that the presentation should be in such a format that it provides useful information about the liquidity and solvency of an entity.

11.4.2 Paragraph 68 of IAS 1 clarifies that some rather than all financial assets and liabilities classified as held for trading in accordance with IAS 39 are examples of current assets and liabilities respectively. Non-hedging derivatives are not required to be classified as current simply because they fall within the 'held for trading' category in IAS 39. Rather, the requirements of IAS 1 referred to above should be applied in determining classification. This means that financial assets, including portions of financial assets expected to be realised within 12 months of the balance sheet date, should only be presented as current assets if realisation within 12 months is expected. Otherwise they should be classified as non-current. Financial liabilities should be presented as current if they meet the criteria in paragraph 11.6.

11.4.3 The treatment of hedging derivatives will be similar. Where a portion of a financial asset is expected to be realised within 12 months of the balance sheet date, that portion should be presented as a current asset; the remainder of the financial asset should be shown as a non-current asset. This suggests that hedging derivatives should be split into current and non-current portions. However, as an alternative, the full fair value of hedging derivatives could be classified as current if the hedge relationships are for less than 12 months and as non-current if those relationships are for more than 12 months.

[The next paragraph is 11.6.]

Current and non-current liabilities

11.6 Where an entity presents assets and liabilities as either current or non-current, the entity should classify a liability as current when:

- it expects to settle the liability in its normal operating cycle;
- it holds the liability primarily for the purpose of trading;

11.4.1　IAS 1 规定了在资产负债表中将资产或负债列报为流动或非流动的要求，并且第 65 段特别指出列报的格式应能提供有关主体的流动性和偿债能力的有用信息。

11.4.2　IAS 1 第 68 段澄清，某些（而非所有）按照 IAS 39 划分为为交易而持有的金融资产和金融负债分别是流动资产和流动负债的例子。非套期衍生工具并不仅仅因为其按照 IAS 39 属于“为交易而持有”类别即划分为流动；相反，在确定分类时应运用上文所述 IAS 1 中的要求。这意味着金融资产，包括其预期在资产负债表日后 12 个月内实现的部分，只有预期在 12 个月内实现时才应列报为流动资产，否则其应划分为非流动资产。金融负债如果符合第 11.6 段中所述的条件，则应列报为流动负债。

11.4.3　套期衍生工具的处理方式与此类似。金融资产中预期在资产负债表日后十二个月内实现的部分，应列报为流动资产；而该项金融资产的剩余部分则应列报为非流动资产。这表明套期衍生工具应当分为流动和非流动部分。但是，也可以选择将用于套期关系为十二个月以下的套期衍生工具的全部公允价值划分为流动，而用于套期关系在十二个月以上的划分为非流动。

[下一段为第 11.6 段。]

流动和非流动负债

11.6　当主体将资产和负债按照流动或非流动列报时，应在下述情况下将负债划分为流动负债：

■ 主体预期在其正常经营周期中清偿；

■ 主体主要为交易目的而持有该负债；

- the liability is due to be settled within twelve months after the reporting period; or
- the entity does not have an unconditional right to defer settlement of the liability for at least twelve months after the reporting period.

[IAS 1 para 68].

11.6.1 Under IAS 32, the equity and liability components of financial instruments must be classified separately as financial liabilities, financial assets or equity instruments. [IAS 32 para 28]. The liability component of financial instruments should be classified as current or non-current, depending on the terms of the contract. Similar to financial assets, where a portion of a financial liability (including a hedging derivative) is expected to be settled within 12 months of the balance sheet date, or settlement cannot be deferred for at least 12 months after the balance sheet date, that portion should be presented as a current liability; the remainder should be presented as a non-current liability.

11.6.2 The question arises whether the liability component of a convertible financial instrument should be presented as current or non-current, when the instrument is convertible to equity at any time within the next 12 months, but if not converted, is repayable in cash only beyond 12 months. Such instruments would have an equity component, being the holders' right to convert the instrument into a fixed number of equity instruments of the issuer any time before the maturity date; and a liability component, being the entity's obligation to deliver cash to holders at the maturity date, which is more than one year after the balance sheet date.

11.6.3 The 2009 annual improvements clarified that conversion features that are at the holder's discretion do not impact the classification of the liability component of a convertible instrument. [IAS 1 para 69 (d)]. The liability component of the convertible debt should be classified as non-current when repayable in more than 12 months and the components of an instrument that are classified as equity should be ignored. In the case of a convertible instrument, ignoring the conversion option leaves a debt component that is not re-payable within 12 months. Ignoring any equity components when classifying the liability component reflects that the equity components are not part of the liability for accounting purposes. Any equity components are accounted for in the same way as if they had been issued as separate instruments. It follows that the presentation should be the same as if they

■ 该项负债在报告期后十二个月内到期清偿；或者

■ 主体不能无条件将负债的清偿延期到报告期后至少十二个月。

［IAS 1 第 68 段］。

11.6.1 根据 IAS 32，金融工具的权益和负债组成部分必须被分别划分为金融负债、金融资产或权益工具。［IAS 32 第 28 段］。金融工具的负债组成部分应根据合同的条款划分为流动或非流动负债。与金融资产类似，在金融负债（包括套期衍生工具）的一部分预期在资产负债表日后十二个月内清偿，或清偿不能延期至资产负债表日后至少十二个月的情况下，该部分应列报为流动负债；剩余部分则应列报为非流动负债。

11.6.2 当某项可转换金融工具可以在接下来的十二个月中的任何时间转换为权益，但如果不转换，只有在十二个月之后以现金偿还时，该项工具的负债组成部分应当列报为流动还是非流动负债的问题就出现了。这种工具有一个权益部分，即持有人在到期日之前任何时候将该工具转换为固定数量的发行人权益工具的权利；以及一个负债部分，即主体在到期日向持有人交付现金的义务，该到期日在资产负债表日后一年以上。

11.6.3 2009 年年度改进澄清了按照持有人意愿的转换特征不影响可转换工具负债部分的分类。［IAS 1 第 69（d）段］。在十二个月以后偿还的可转换债务的负债部分应被划分为非流动负债，被划分为权益的工具组成部分不应予以考虑。对于可转换工具，不考虑可转换期权就剩下无需在十二个月内偿还的债务部分。在对负债部分进行分类时不考虑任何权益部分体现出从会计角度权益工具并不是负债的一部分。所有权益部分就像它们是以单独工具的形式发行一样来进行会计处理，因此，列报也应像它们是以单独工具的形式发行一样来进行列报。

had been issued as separate instruments.

11.6.4 In contrast, consider puttable debt that is puttable by the holder within the next 12 months but, if not put, is repayable only beyond 12 months. In this case, the puttable debt should be classified in its entirety as current, irrespective of whether IAS 39 requires the put option to be accounted for as a separated embedded derivative and, if it does, of whether the host debt contract is reported in a separate balance sheet line item from the embedded derivative. This reflects that the put option could cause the entire instrument to be settled in a manner that is regarded as a liability under IAS 32.

11.7 The presentation of financial liabilities as current or non-current would take account of similar considerations to financial assets (see para 11.4 above). However, IAS 1 provides additional guidance for financial liabilities that have been renegotiated or refinanced. Specifically, the standard requires that a financial liability should be presented as current when it is due to be settled within 12 months after the balance sheet date, even if:

- the original term was for a period longer than 12 months; and
- an agreement to refinance, or to reschedule payments, on a long-term basis is completed after the balance sheet date and before the financial statements are authorised for issue.

[IAS 1 para 72].

11.8 The current or non-current classification of financial liabilities is governed by the condition of those liabilities at the balance sheet date. Where rescheduling or refinancing is at the lender's discretion, and it occurs after the balance sheet date, it does not alter the liability's condition at that date. Accordingly, it is regarded as a non-adjusting post balance sheet event and it is not taken into account in determining the current/non-current classification of the debt. On the other hand where the refinancing or rescheduling is at the entity's discretion and the entity can elect to roll over an obligation for at least one year after the balance sheet date, the obligation must be classified as non-current, even if it would otherwise be due within a shorter period. However, if the entity expects to settle the obligation within 12 months, despite having the discretion to refinance for a longer period,

11.6.4　与此相反，考虑一下可回售债务，该债务可由持有人在接下来的十二个月内回售，但若未回售则只能在十二个月以后偿付。在这种情形下，不论 IAS 39 是否要求将该看跌期权作为单独的嵌入衍生工具进行会计处理，也不论主债务合同是否与嵌入衍生工具（若单列）在资产负债表不同项目下进行列报，该可回售债务应整个地被划分为流动负债。这体现了该看跌期权可能导致整个工具以 IAS 32 规定的负债的形式结算。

11.7　在将金融负债列报为流动或非流动时所考虑的因素与列报金融资产时类似（参见上文第 11.4 段）。但是，IAS 1 对进行了重新商定或再融资的金融负债提供了额外的指引。具体而言，该准则要求如果金融负债在资产负债表日后十二个月内清偿，即使满足下列条件，主体仍然应将其列报为流动负债：

- 原始期限超过十二个月；并且
- 在资产负债表日后、财务报表批准报出前，已完成了长期再融资协议或新的付款计划。

[IAS 1 第 72 段]。

11.8　对金融负债的流动或非流动分类是由资产负债表日这些负债的条件确定。在新计划或再融资是由贷款人决定，且发生在资产负债表日后时，并不会改变负债在该日的条件。相应地，应将其视作一项报告期后非调整事项，且在确定债务的流动/非流动分类时不予考虑。另一方面，在主体可以自主决定再融资或新计划，及主体可以选择将义务展期至资产负债表日后至少一年的情况下，即使其本可能在更短时期内到期，也应将该义务划分为非流动负债。但是，如果主体虽然可以自主决定再融资至更长时间，只要其仍预期在十二个月内清偿该义务，则该项债务应被划分为流动负债。[IAS 1 第 73 段]。

then the debt should be classified as current. [IAS 1 para 73].

Example – rolling over bank facilities

A company has entered into a facility arrangement with a bank. It has a committed facility that the bank cannot cancel unilaterally and the scheduled maturity of this facility is 3 years from the balance sheet date. The company has drawn down funds on this facility and these funds are due to be repaid 6 months after the balance sheet date. The company intends to roll over this debt through the three year facility arrangement. How should this borrowing be shown in the company's balance sheet?

Would the answer be different if the facility and existing loan were with different banks?

The borrowing should be shown as non-current. Although the loan is due for repayment within six months of the balance sheet date, the company is entitled to 'rollover' this borrowing into a 'new loan'. The substance is, therefore, that the debt is not repayable until 3 years after the balance sheet date when the committed facility expires. In addition, the entity expects to rollover the debt, so does not expect to repay it within 12 months.

The position would be different if the facility was with a different bank or if the loan was in the form of commercial paper. In the first case, the company would have a loan repayable in six months, but would be entitled to take out a new loan to settle its existing debt. These two loans are separate and the new loan is not, either in substance or in fact, an extension of the existing. Similarly if the loan was in the form of commercial paper, which typically has a maturity of 90 to 180 days, it would be classified as a current liability as it is likely that the back up facility would be provided by a different bank.

11.9 It is common practice for financial institutions to include borrowing covenants in the terms of loans. Under these borrowing covenants a loan which would otherwise be long-term in nature becomes immediately repayable if certain items related to the borrower's financial condition are breached. Typically, these items are measures of liquidity or solvency based on ratios derived from the entity's financial statements. Where the borrower has breached the borrowing covenant by

示例——银行信贷的展期

某公司同一家银行签订了一项信贷安排。该公司拥有一笔银行不能单方决定取消的承诺信贷额度，其规定的到期日为资产负债表日后三年。该公司已经从该笔信贷额度中提取了资金，并应在资产负债表日后六个月内偿还。该公司有意通过该期限为三年的信贷额度将该负债展期。应如何在公司的资产负债表中列示该借款?

如果该项信贷额度和现有贷款是从不同银行获得的，上述问题的答案是否会有所不同?

该借款应列示为非流动负债。尽管该借款应在资产负债表日后六个月偿还，公司有权将其“展期”为一笔“新借款”。因此，其实质是该债务在资产负债表日后三年即承诺信贷到期时才需要偿还。此外，主体预期将该债务展期，即预期不会在十二个月内将其偿付。

如果该信贷额度是同其他银行签订或该贷款是以商业票据的形式签订，那么情况应当有所不同。在第一种情况下，公司应该有一笔在六个月后偿付的贷款，但也有权通过取得新贷款来清偿现有债务。这两项贷款互不相关，新贷款无论从本质上还是在实际上都不是现有贷款的延续。与此类似，如果该贷款是以商业票据的形式签订的，通常其到期日为九十到一百八十天，应当将其划分为流动负债，因为备用的信贷款项很可能是由不同的银行所提供的。

11.9　金融机构在贷款条款中加入借款契约的情况实务上很常见。根据这些借款契约，一项本应是长期的贷款如果在违反了与借款人财务状况相关的某些条款时会变为需立即偿还。典型的条款为基于由主体财务报表所得出的比率对流动性或偿债能力的评估。如果借款人在资产负债表日之前违反了借款契约或令贷款在资产负债表日后十二个月以内到期，但在报告期后、财务报表批准报出之前贷款人已经同意不要求立即偿还该项贷款，则应将贷款人的同

the balance sheet date, or ends less than 12 months from the balance sheet date but the lender agrees, after the balance sheet date but before authorisation of the financial statements, not to require immediate repayment of the loan, the agreement of the lender is regarded as a non-adjusting post balance sheet event. Since, at the year end, the agreement of the lender had not been obtained, the condition of the borrowing at the balance sheet date was that it was immediately repayable and should, therefore, be shown as a current liability. [IAS 1 para 74]. An example of disclosure of a breach of covenant disclosed in an interim report and events subsequent to the interim reporting date is given in Table 11. 1.

Table 11. 1 – Breach of covenant resulting in loans restated as current at period end, post the balance sheet refinancing

First Technology plc – Interim report – 31 October 2005

14. Bank overdrafts and loans

	Six months ended 31st October 2005	Six months ended 31st October 2004	Year ended 30th April 2005
	£'m	£'m	£'m
Bank overdrafts	0. 3	2. 8	1. 0
Bank loans	112. 4	111. 4	105. 3
	112. 7	114. 2	106. 3
Repayable:			
On demand or within one year	112. 7	7. 9	6. 2
In the second year	–	48. 9	47. 0
In the third year	–	8. 1	7. 8
In the forth year	–	8. 1	7. 8
In the fifth year	–	41. 2	37. 5
	112. 7	114. 2	106. 3
Less: Amount due for settlement within 12 months (shown under current liabilities)	(112. 7)	(7. 9)	(6. 2)
Amounts due for settlement after more than 12 months	–	106. 3	100. 1

意视为一项报告期后非调整事项。因为在年末尚未获得贷款人的同意，而该借款在资产负债表日的条件是需立即偿还，因此应作为流动负债列报。[IAS 1 第74段]。表11.1提供了一份中期报告中所披露的违反契约事项及中期报告期后事项的披露示例。

表11.1——违反契约导致贷款在期末重述为流动负债，期后再融资

First Technology plc —— 中期报告 —— 2005年10月31日

14. 银行透支和贷款

	截至2005年10月31日的6个月期间	截至2004年10月31日的6个月期间	截至2005年4月30日的年度
	£'m	£'m	£'m
银行透支	0.3	2.8	1.0
银行贷款	112.4	111.4	105.3
	112.7	114.2	106.3
应偿还金额：			
随时或一年以内	112.7	7.9	6.2
第二年以内	–	48.9	47.0
第三年以内	–	8.1	7.8
第四年以内	–	8.1	7.8
第五年以内	–	41.2	37.5
	112.7	114.2	106.3
减去：应在十二个月内清偿的金额（在流动负债项下列示）	(112.7)	(7.9)	(6.2)
十二个月以后清偿的金额	–	106.3	100.1

Con.

The Group's principal source of debt at 31st October 2005 was a multi-currency syndicated bank loan ('the Facilities') entered into with a group of seven banks in May 2004 in connection with the Group's offer for BWT. The Facilities comprised three tranches: a US$75 million revolving credit facility; a term loan of up to US$75 million and a US$100 million revolving credit facility. The Facilities were repayable between May 2006 and May 2009. The Facilities were unsecured and initially carried interest at a margin of 1.5% over LIBOR (or EURIBOR for amounts advanced in Euros), plus mandatory costs. The applicable margin was variable (ranging from a minimum of 0.875% up to a maximum of 1.75%) according to the ratio of consolidated net borrowings to EBITDA.

The Facilities were subject to three financial covenants, which were tested quarterly. On 17th August 2005, First Technology PLC informed its bankers that it had failed to meet one of these covenants with respect to the test for the period ended 26th July 2005. As a result of the covenant breach, the Facilities technically became repayable on demand.

On 12th December 2005, the Group signed an agreement for a new bank loan ('the new Facility') with its two principal bankers, HSBC Bank plc and The Royal Bank of Scotland plc, the proceeds of which are being used to repay the existing Facilities. The new Facility comprises two tranches: a US$80 million revolving credit facility and a US$140 million term loan, each available until December 2006. Both tranches, under certain circumstances, can be extended at the Company's option for a further twelve months to December 2007. The new Facility carries interest at a margin of 1.5% over LIBOR, plus mandatory costs. The new Facility is unsecured, although certain of First Technology PLC's wholly-owned subsidiaries have given guarantees with respect to First Technology PLC's obligations under the agreement. However, in the event that the offer announced on 19th December, or any other offer, for the entire issued share capital of the Company does not become wholly unconditional or that the Company has not completed an equity issue raising proceeds of at least £40 million and used such amount to repay the new Facility, the Company will be required to give security by 30th September 2006. Any net proceeds of an equity issue must be applied to repay the new Facility. If the amount prepaid is more than £40 million, the Company has the option to extend the new Facility for an additional one year term. Under all circumstances, the Company retains the flexibility to re-finance this new Facility.

In July 2004, First Technology PLC entered into an interest rate swap to fix the rate of interest that it would pay under the US$75 million term loan tranche of the syndicated loan. The interest rate swap fixed for the whole term the rate of interest at 3.605% plus the applicable margin for this element of the Group's debt. This swap is now being used to fix the rate of interest payable under a proportion of the new Facility.

续表

本集团于2005年10月31日的主要债务是与本集团对BWT的收购要约相关的、于2004年5月与七家银行所组成的银行团所签订的一项多货币银团贷款（“贷款项目”）。该贷款项目包括三部分：一项7,500万美元的循环信贷额度；一项最高达7,500万美元的定期贷款以及一项1亿美元的循环信贷额度。贷款项目应于自2006年5月至2009年5月的期间偿还。贷款项目没有担保，且初始利率为LIBOR（对欧元贷款为ERUIBOR）加息差1.5%及强制成本。适用的息差根据合并报表中净借款与扣除利息、税项、折旧和摊销之前的盈利（EBITDA）之间的比值的变动而变动（最低为0.875%，最高可达1.75%）。 贷款项目需遵循三项财务契约，并于每个季度测试一次。于2005年8月17日，First Technology PLC公司通知其银行，称其在对截至2005年7月26日的期间进行测试时未能满足其中的一项契约。由于违背了契约，该贷款项目从技术角度来说成为可被随时要求偿还。 2005年12月12日，本集团同其两家主要银行HSBC Bank plc and The Royal Bank of Scotland plc签订了一项新的银行贷款协议（“新贷款项目”），该贷款的收入将用来清偿现有的贷款项目。新贷款项目包括两部分：一项8,000万美元的循环信贷额度及一项1.4亿美元的定期贷款，两者均在2006年12月前有效。这两部分在特定情况下都能由公司决定延期十二个月至2007年12月。新贷款项目的利率为LIBOR加息差1.5%及强制成本。新贷款项目没有抵押，虽然First Technology PLC公司的某些全资子公司已经对First Technology. PLC公司在该协议下的义务提供了担保。但是，如果于12月19日针对公司发行的全部股本所宣布的要约或其他任何要约并不是完全无条件的或公司未能完成发行股份以筹集至少4,000万英镑的收入并将该金额用于清偿新贷款项目，公司将被要求于2006年9月30日提供抵押品。发行股份所获得的所有净收入必须被用于清偿新贷款项目。如果预先偿付的金额超过4,000万英镑，公司可以选择将新贷款项目的期限再延长一年。在任何情况下，公司均保留对该新贷款项目再融资的灵活选择权。 First Technology PLC公司于2004年7月签订了一项利率互换以固定其就该银团贷款中金额为7,500万美元的定期贷款所应支付的利息的利率。利率互换将整个期间的利率固定为3.605%加集团债务中这一部分所适用的息差。现在此互换用于固定新贷款项目一部分的应付利息的利率。

11.10 However, following a breach of a borrowing covenant, lenders often agree to a period of grace during which the borrower agrees to rectify the breach. The lender agrees not to demand repayment during this time but, if the breach is not rectified, the debt would become immediately repayable at the end of the period of grace. If, before the balance sheet date, the lender has agreed to such a period of grace and that period ends at least 12 months after the balance sheet date, then the liability should be shown as non-current. [IAS 1 para 75]. If the breach of the borrowing covenant occurs after the balance date, then the liability would still be shown as non-current, unless the breach was so serious that the financial statements could no longer be prepared on a going concern basis. However, if the breach occurred before the balance sheet date, but the period of grace was not granted until after the balance sheet date, then the liability would be classified as current. The key to this approach is that the loan's presentation is dictated by the loan's condition as at the balance sheet date. Events after the balance sheet date may give evidence of that condition but they do not change it. This is consistent with IAS 10, 'Events after the balance sheet date'.

11.11 The standard's approach to breaches of borrowing covenants focuses on the legal rights of the entity rather than on the intentions of either of the parties to the loan. In dealing with situations where the entity has the discretion to roll over or refinance loans, the entity's expectations on the timing of settlement play a part in deciding the liability's classification. The liability's classification is, however, unaffected by the entity's intentions in the case of a breach of a loan agreement. If the entity breaches the loan agreement before the balance sheet date and the lender grants a period of grace of more than 12 months from the balance sheet date, then the loan is classified as non-current even if it is the entity's intention to repay the loan within 12 months of the balance sheet date. In many cases, however, the period of grace will be a matter of negotiation between the borrower and the lender and will match the borrower's intentions in any event. In addition, breaches of loan agreements occur most often in entities that are experiencing financial difficulties and these entities are unlikely to wish to repay the loan earlier than required by the lender.

11.12 Although post balance sheet events may not alter the liability's classification, they may require disclosure as a non-adjusting event. IAS 1 paragraph

11.10 但是，在发生借款契约违约后，贷款人经常会同意提供一个宽限期，在此期间借款人同意纠正违约行为。贷款人同意在此期间内不要求清偿，但是如果违约行为未能纠正，则债务在该宽限期结束时即需立即清偿。如果在资产负债表日之前，贷款人同意提供这种宽限期，且该宽限期到资产负债表日后至少十二个月才结束，那么应将该负债列示为非流动负债。[IAS 1 第 75 段]。如果违反借款契约发生在资产负债表日之后，除非该违约非常严重以至于不能以持续经营的方式编制财务报表，否则仍将该负债列示为非流动负债。但是，如果违约发生在资产负债表日之前，但宽限期直到资产负债表日后才被授予，则应将该负债划分为流动负债。这种方法的关键在于贷款的列报情况由贷款在资产负债表日的条件决定。发生在资产负债表日后的事项可能提供有关其状况的证据，但并不能使其发生任何改变。这与《国际会计准则第 10 号——资产负债表日后事项》（“IAS 10”） 的规定一致。

11.11 IAS 1 对违反借款契约的处理方法着重于主体的法定权利而非贷款双方的意向。在主体可以自主决定对贷款进行展期或再融资的情况下，主体预期的清偿时间在确定负债的分类时起一定的作用。但是在违反贷款协议时，负债的分类不受主体的意向影响。如果主体在资产负债表日之前违反了贷款协议，而贷款人授予了资产负债表日后超过十二个月的宽限期，那么即使主体有意在资产负债表日后十二个月之内偿还贷款，该贷款也应被划分为非流动负债。但是在很多情况下，宽限期将由借款人和贷款人双方协商确定，而且无论如何都将与借款人的意向相一致。此外，违反贷款协议的情况常常发生于经历财务困难的主体，而这些主体不太可能愿意在贷款人所要求的日期之前偿还贷款。

11.12 虽然资产负债表日后事项可能并不会改变负债的分类，但是可能需要将其披露为非调整事项。IAS 1 第 76 段指出，对于被划分为流动负债的贷款，

76 states that, in respect of loans classified as current liabilities, the following events must be disclosed as non-adjusting events in accordance with IAS 10, if they occur between the balance sheet date and the date of authorisation of the financial statements:

- Refinancing on a long-term basis.
- Rectification of a breach of a long-term loan agreement.
- The receipt from the lender of a period of grace to rectify a breach of a long-term loan agreement ending at least 12 months after the balance sheet date.

11.13 IAS 1 does not specify any disclosures for non-adjusting post balance sheet events in respect of loans classified as non-current liabilities. However, IAS 10 requires that an entity should disclose the following for each material category of non-adjusting event after the balance sheet date:

- The nature of the event.
- An estimate of its financial effect, or a statement that such an estimate cannot be made.

[IAS 10 para 21].

11.14 Further disclosure of defaults and breaches of loan agreements is required by IFRS 7 (see para 11.61 below).

Offsetting a financial asset and a financial liability

General principle

11.15 A financial asset and a financial liability should be offset when, and only when, both of the following conditions are satisfied:

- The entity currently has a legally enforceable right to set off the recognised amounts.
- The entity intends either to settle on a net basis, or to realise the asset and settle the liability simultaneously.

如果在资产负债表日和财务报表批准报出日之间发生下述事项，则其应根据IAS 10作为非调整事项进行披露：

- 长期再融资。
- 纠正长期贷款协议的违约行为。
- 获得贷款人授予的资产负债表日后至少十二个月的宽限期，以在此期间内纠正长期贷款协议的违约行为。

11.13 IAS 1并未特别规定有关被划分为非流动负债的贷款的非调整资产负债表日后事项的披露。但是，IAS 10要求主体应对每一重要类别的资产负债表日后的非调整事项作如下披露：

- 事项的性质。
- 对财务影响的估计，或不能作出这种估计的说明。

[IAS 10第21段]。

11.14 IFRS 7规定了对贷款协议的拖欠或违约事项的进一步披露（参见下文第11.61段）。

抵销金融资产和金融负债

一般原则

11.15 当且仅当以下两个条件同时满足时，金融资产和金融负债应当互相抵销：

- 主体拥有抵销已确认金额的可实施的法定权利。
- 主体准备以净额为基础进行结算，或同时变现资产和清偿负债。

[IAS 32 para 42].

11.16 Where the above offset conditions are satisfied, the entity has the right to receive or pay a single net amount and intends to do so, it has, in effect, only a single financial asset or financial liability. In that situation, the financial asset and the financial liability are presented on the balance sheet on a net basis. Where the offset conditions are not satisfied, the financial asset and the financial liability are presented separately from each other, consistently with their characteristics as the entity's resources or obligations. [IAS 32 para 43].

11.17 There can be situations where there are transfers of financial assets that do not qualify for derecogntion and in such case the entity has to recognise an associated liability (see chapter 8). Such assets and liabilities can not be offset because offsetting a recognised financial asset and a recognised financial liability and presenting the net amount is different from derecognising that financial asset or financial liability. Derecognising a financial instrument not only results in the removal of the previously recognised item from the balance sheet, but also may result in recognising of a gain or loss. Offsetting does not give rise to recognising a gain or loss. [IAS 32 paras 42, 44]. In other words, in considering presentation of particular items, recognition, derecognition and measurement need to be considered first.

Legal right of set-off

11.18 IAS 32 defines a right of offset as "*a debtor's legal right, by contract or otherwise, to settle or otherwise eliminate all or a portion of an amount due to a creditor by applying against that amount an amount due from the creditor*". Because the right of offset is essentially a legal right, the conditions supporting the right may vary from one legal jurisdiction to another and, therefore, the laws applicable to the relationships between the parties would need to be considered carefully. [IAS 32 para 45]. It follows that instruments such as receivables and payables with the same counterparty would fall to be offset if a legal right of offset is agreed between the parties (and the entity intends to settle net or simultaneously).

［IAS 32 第 42 段］。

11.16　在满足上述抵销条件的情况下，主体有权收取或支付净额并打算这样做时，其实际上只有一项金融资产或金融负债。在该情况下，金融资产和金融负债在资产负债表内以净额列报。在不满足抵销条件的情况下，金融资产和金融负债应彼此分别单独列报，与其作为主体的资源或义务的性质相符合。［IAS 32 第 43 段］。

11.17　有时，金融资产的转让不符合终止确认的条件，在此情况下，主体必须确认一项相关负债（参见第 8 章）。这些资产和负债不能予以抵销，因为抵销已确认金融资产和已确认金融负债并以其净额进行列报与对终止确认金融资产或金融负债是有区别的。终止确认一项金融工具不仅要从资产负债表中消除以前确认的项目，而且还可能会导致利得或损失的确认。抵销不会导致利得或损失的确认。［IAS 32 第 42、44 段］。换言之，在考虑具体项目的列报时，首先要考虑确认、终止确认和计量。

法定抵销权

11.18　IAS 32 将抵销权定义为“*债务人根据合同或其他协议，以应收债权人的金额全部或部分抵销应付债权人的金额的法定权利*”。因为抵销权本质上是一项法定权利，所以支持这种权利的条件可能依法定管辖区的不同而不同，因此，应仔细地考虑对合同各方之间的关系进行规范的法律。［IAS 32 第 45 段］。如果合同各方议定了法定抵销权（且主体准备以净额结算或同时清偿），与同一交易对方所产生的诸如应收款项和应付款项等工具均应当进行抵销。

11.19 In unusual circumstances, a debtor may have a legal right to apply an amount due from a third party against the amount due to a creditor provided that there is an agreement between the three parties that clearly establishes the debtor's right of set-off. [IAS 32 para 45].

Intention to settle on a net basis

11.20 It is clear from the general principle in paragraph 11.15 above that, in order to achieve offset, an entity must have both the right and the intention to do so. It is not sufficient to have one and not the other. Although the existence of an enforceable legal right of offset affects the entity's rights and obligations associated with a financial asset and a financial liability and may affect its exposure to credit and liquidity risk, it is, by itself, not a sufficient basis for offsetting. This is because, in the absence of an intention to exercise the right or to settle simultaneously, the amount and timing of the entity's future cash flows are not affected. However, if, in addition to the legal right, the entity clearly intends to exercise the right or to settle simultaneously, it is, in effect, exposed to a net amount, which reflects the timing of the expected future cash flows and the risks to which those cash flows are exposed. Similarly, an intention by one or both parties to settle on a net basis without the legal right to do so is not sufficient to justify offsetting because the rights and obligations associated with the individual financial asset and financial liability remain unaltered. [IAS 32 para 46].

11.21 An entity's intentions with respect to settlement of particular assets and liabilities may be influenced by its normal business practices, the requirements of the financial markets and other circumstances that may limit the ability to settle net or to settle simultaneously. When an entity has a right of offset, but does not intend to settle net or to realise the asset and settle the liability simultaneously, the effect of the right on the entity's credit risk exposure is disclosed in accordance with paragraph 11.83 below.

Simultaneous settlement

11.22 IAS 32 states that realisation of a financial asset and settlement of a

11.19 在少数情况下，债务人可能拥有以应收第三者的金额来抵销应付债权人的金额的法定权利，前提是三者之间签署的协议明确表示债务人拥有该抵销权。[IAS 32 第45段]。

以净额为基础进行结算的意向

11.20 根据上文第11.15段所述的一般原则可以清楚地看到，为了实现抵销，主体必须既拥有这种权利又具有这种意愿。只有其中之一是不够的。虽然存在的可强制实施的法定抵销权影响到主体与金融资产和金融负债相关的权利和义务，也可能影响到主体所承受的信用风险和流动性风险，但是其本身并不足以构成互相抵销的基础。这是因为，在不打算行使这项权利或不打算同时进行结算时，主体未来现金流量的金额和时间不受影响。但是，如果除该项法定权利以外，主体明确打算行使这项权利或同时进行结算时，那么其实际上所承受的是净额风险，反映了预期未来现金流量的时间以及这些现金流量所承受的风险。类似地，在没有法定权利的情况下，一方或双方以净额为基础进行结算的意向不足以成为抵销的依据，因为与单项金融资产和金融负债相关的权利和义务没有改变。[IAS 32 第46段]。

11.21 主体对特定资产和负债进行结算的意向可能会受到其正常业务活动、金融市场的要求以及其他可能会限制以净额结算或同时结算能力的情况的影响。当主体拥有抵销权但并不打算以净额结算或同时变现资产和清偿负债时，应根据下文第11.83段披露这种权利对主体所承受的信用风险的影响。

同时结算

11.22 IAS 32 指出，金融资产的变现和金融负债的结算只有发生在同一时刻

financial liability are treated as simultaneous only when the transactions occur at the same moment. For example, the operation of a clearing house in an organised financial market or a face-to-face exchange will facilitate simultaneous settlement of two financial instruments. In these circumstances the cash flows are, in effect, equivalent to a single net amount and there is no exposure to credit or liquidity risk. In other circumstances, an entity may settle two instruments by receiving and paying separate amounts, becoming exposed to credit risk for the full amount of the asset or liquidity risk for the full amount of the liability. Such risk exposures, though brief, may be significant and therefore, net presentation is not appropriate. [IAS 32 para 48].

Situations where offset is usually inappropriate

11.23 IAS 32 sets out the following specific situations where the offset criteria in paragraph 11.15 above are not met.

- Several different financial instruments are used to emulate the features of a single financial instrument (a 'synthetic instrument'). For example, a floating rate long-term debt combined with an interest rate swap that involves receiving floating payments and making fixed payments synthesises a fixed rate long-term debt. Each of the individual financial instruments that together constitute a 'synthetic instrument':

  - represents a contractual right or obligation with its own terms and conditions;
  - may be transferred or settled separately;
  - is exposed to risks that may differ from the risks to which other financial instruments are exposed.

  Accordingly, when one financial instrument in a 'synthetic instrument' is an asset and another is a liability, they are not offset and presented on an entity's balance sheet on a net basis unless they meet the criteria for offsetting in paragraph 11.15 above.

- Financial assets and financial liabilities arise from financial instruments having the same primary risk exposure (for example, assets and liabilities within a

才被认为是同时进行的。例如，有组织的金融市场结算机构的运营或面对面交换可以达到两项金融工具的同时结算。在这些情况下，现金流量实际上等于单一的净额，并没有信用风险或流动性风险敞口。在其他情况下，主体可能通过分别收取和支付款项来结算两项工具，使资产全额承受信用风险或负债全额承受流动性风险。这些风险敞口虽然短暂但也可能重大，因此以净额列报是不恰当的。[IAS 32 第 48 段]。

通常不适于抵销的情况

11.23　IAS 32 规定了不符合上文第 11.15 段所述抵销标准的下述具体情况：

- 使用多项不同的金融工具来仿效单项金融工具的特征（“合成工具”）。例如，长期浮动利率债务与收取浮动利息和支付固定利息的利率互换结合在一起即合成了一项长期固定利率债务。构成“合成工具”的每项金融工具均：

  - 代表着其本身条款和条件的合同权利或义务；
  - 可以单独转让或结算；
  - 承受的风险可能与其他金融工具不同。

  因此，当“合成工具”中的一项金融工具是资产而另一项是负债时，除非它们满足上文第 11.15 段的抵销标准，否则不能将它们抵销并在主体的资产负债表中以净额列报。

- 金融工具所形成的金融资产和金融负债具有同样的主要风险敞口（例如，远期合同或其他衍生工具组合中的资产和负债），但涉及不同的合同方。

portfolio of forward contracts or other derivative instruments), but involve different counterparties.

- Financial or other assets are pledged as collateral for non-recourse financial liabilities.
- Financial assets are set aside in trust by a debtor for the purpose of discharging an obligation without those assets having been accepted by the creditor in settlement of the obligation (for example, a sinking fund arrangement).
- Obligations incurred as a result of events giving rise to losses are expected to be recovered from a third party by virtue of a claim made under an insurance contract.

[IAS 32 para 49].

Master netting agreements

11.24 An entity that undertakes a number of financial instrument transactions with a single counterparty may enter into a 'master netting arrangement' with that counterparty. Such an arrangement creates a right of set-off that becomes enforceable and affects the realisation or settlement of individual financial assets and financial liabilities only following a specified event of default or in other circumstances not expected to arise in the normal course of business. These arrangements are commonly used by financial institutions to provide protection against loss in the event of bankruptcy or other circumstances that result in a counterparty being unable to meet its obligations. In the event of default on, or termination of, any one contract, the agreement provides for a single net settlement of all financial instruments covered by the agreement. [IAS 32 para 50].

11.25 Where an entity has entered into such an agreement, the agreement does not provide a basis for offsetting unless both of the criteria in paragraph 11.15 above are satisfied. This is because the entity's right of set off under such an agreement is conditional and enforceable only on the occurrence of some future event, usually a default of the counterparty. To offset a financial asset and a financial liability, an entity must have a currently legally enforceable right to set off the recognised amounts. Thus, such an arrangement does not meet the

- 金融资产或其他资产作为无追索权金融负债的抵押物。

- 债务人为解除某项义务而托管的金融资产，但债权人尚未接受以这些资产清偿该义务（例如，偿债基金协议）。

- 因某些导致损失的事项而产生的义务预计可以通过保险合同向第三方索赔而得以补偿。

[IAS 32 第 49 段]。

总互抵协议

11.24　与同一交易对方进行多项金融工具交易的主体可能与对方订立“总互抵协议”。这种协议形成的抵销权只有在出现特定的违约事件，或在正常经营过程中出现预期不会出现的其他情况时，才可以强制执行并影响单项金融资产和金融负债的变现或结算。这种协议常常被金融机构用于在对方破产或发生其他导致对方无法履行义务的事件时保护金融机构免受损失。在协议涵盖的任何一项合同发生违约或终止时，协议规定对协议所包括的所有金融工具按单一净额进行结算。[IAS 32 第 50 段]。

11.25　在主体签订了这种协议的情况下，只有上文第 11.15 段列示的两个条件同时被满足时这种协议才构成抵销的依据。这是因为主体根据这种协议拥有的抵销权是有条件的，其仅仅在发生某种未来事件（通常是交易对方违约）时，才可以实施。要抵销一项金融资产和一项金融负债，主体必须在当前拥有可实施的抵销已确认金额的法定权利。因此，这种协议不符合抵销的条件。[IAS 32 第 50 段]。

conditions for offsetting. [IAS 32 para 50].

Example – Various arrangements in a group for cash management purposes

Group X comprises various subsidiaries, each of which has a separate bank account with bank B. At any time, some of these accounts have a positive cash balance and others a negative (overdraft) balance. Group X operates the following arrangements for cash management purposes:

- Zero balancing (sometimes referred to as a cash sweep), under which the balances on a number of designated accounts are transferred to a single netting account on a regular basis, including at the balance sheet date. In some cases, the amounts transferred are repaid to the relevant subsidiaries shortly afterwards. This may be agreed contractually or at the choice of group management.

- Notional pooling, under which bank B calculates the net balance on a number of designated accounts with interest being earned or paid on the net amount. There may be a transfer of balances into a netting account, but this is not always at the balance sheet date.

Is Group X able to offset cash and overdraft balances and hence present net balances in its consolidated balance sheet?

If balances are to be presented net, both of the criteria set out in paragraph 11.15 should be satisfied. Group X should have a currently legally enforceable right to set-off, which means that it is enforceable at anytime and not just in stipulated circumstances, such as an event of default or bankruptcy. Also, Group X should demonstrate a clear prospect that there will be future settlement of cash flows with the same counterparty. A notional pooling for the purpose of calculating interest that does not involve settlement of the associated balances will not meet the requirements described in paragraph 11.20 above.

Assuming the agreement with bank B gives group X the necessary legally enforceable right to set off, its position will be as follows:

- Where there is zero balancing at the balance sheet date and no repayment of

示例——集团中有关现金管理的各种安排

集团 X 由多个子公司组成，各子公司均在银行 B 开具单独的银行账户。无论何时，这些账户中都有一些账户现金余额为正而另一些为负（透支）。集团 X 在现金管理方面有如下安排：

- 零余额法（有时称为现金清零），根据这种方法，多个指定账户中的余额会定期地（包括在资产负债表日）被转到一个单独的抵销账户中。在某些情况下，转入的金额在之后会很快地被返还给相应的子公司。这可以通过合同的方式议定或是根据集团管理层的选择而定。

- 名义集合，根据这种方法，银行 B 计算多个指定账户的净余额并根据净额收取或支付利息。可能会有将余额转入抵销账户中的情况，但是这并不一定总是发生在资产负债表日。

集团 X 是否能够抵销现金和透支余额，并在其合并资产负债表中以净余额进行列报？

如果要以净额方式对余额进行列报，则应同时满足第 11.15 段中所列示的两个条件。集团 X 应该在当前拥有可强制执行的法定抵销权，即该项权利可在任何时候实施而不仅仅是在所规定的情况下，例如出现违约或破产事项时。而且，集团 X 还应证明其具有与同一交易对方进行未来现金流结算的明确意愿。不涉及相关余额的结算而仅为计算利息所采用的名义集合法，不满足上文第 11.20 段所述要求。

假定与银行 B 的协议给予集团 X 必需的可强制执行的法定抵销权，其状况将为如下所示：

- 在资产负债表日采用零余额法，且无论是其次日还是之后的任何一天

funding (reversal of cash flows) takes place, either on the following day or any day thereafter, Group X has a single cash balance or overdraft at the balance sheet date and it is presented as such.

- Where there is zero balancing at the balance sheet date, but the amounts transferred are repaid to the relevant subsidiaries shortly afterwards, Group X will not be able to demonstrate 'the intention to settle net' and therefore will not be able to present net balances in its consolidated balance sheet.
- Where there is notional pooling, but no physical transfer of balances to one account, group X will not be able to demonstrate 'the intention to settle net', as the arrangement does not actually involve net cash settlement. Accordingly, the balances should be presented gross.
- Where there is notional pooling and there is regular net cash settlement of the accounts, net presentation is appropriate. This will not be affected by the fact that actual settlement of the net position may not coincide with the balance sheet date, as long as group X can clearly demonstrate the intention to settle net through a regular practice of net cash settlement throughout the year.

Note that arrangements such as those described above can be complex; each arrangement should be viewed in light of its specific facts and circumstances.

11.26 When financial assets and financial liabilities subject to a master netting arrangement are not offset, the effect of the arrangement on an entity's exposure to credit risk is disclosed in accordance with paragraph 11.83 below.

Disclosure of financial instruments

11.27 There have been significant developments in risk management concepts and practices in recent years. New techniques have evolved for measuring and managing exposures to risks arising from financial instruments. This, coupled with the credit and liquidity crisis experienced recently in the financial markets, has increased the need for more relevant information and greater transparency about an

都不进行资金偿付（返还现金流）的情况下，集团 X 在资产负债表日具有单项的现金余额或透支并据此进行列报。

- 在资产负债表日采用零余额法，但是所转移的金额在之后很快被返还给相关子公司的情况下，集团 X 不能够证明其有"以净额为基础进行结算的意向"，因此不能够在其合并资产负债表中以净余额进行列报。

- 在采用名义集合法，但并未实际发生向某一账户中转移余额的情况下，因为此项安排实际上并未涉及净现金结算，集团 X 不能够证明其有"以净额为基础进行结算的意向"。因此其余额应以总额为基础列报。

- 在采用名义集合法且对账户进行定期净现金结算的情况下，以净额为基础进行列报是恰当的。其净头寸的实际结算可能并不是在资产负债表日发生的事实并不对此产生任何影响，只要集团 X 能够通过在全年定期进行净现金结算的方式明确证明其具有以净额为基础进行结算的意愿。

值得注意的是上述安排可能会比较复杂，需根据每项安排的具体事实与情况进行考虑。

11.26　当总互抵协议所涵盖的金融资产和金融负债未抵销时，应根据下文第 11.83 段披露该项协议对主体所承受的信用风险的影响。

金融工具的披露

11.27　近年来在风险管理理念和实践方面有了重大的发展。用以计量和管理金融工具产生的风险敞口的新技术已逐步形成。这同最近金融市场中所经历的信用和流动性危机一起增加了对主体因金融工具所承受的风险敞口和如何来管理这些风险提供更为相关信息以及更高透明度的需求。作为对此的响应，IASB 于 2009 年 3 月发布了一项对 IFRS 7 的修订以加强对公允价值计量（参

entity's exposures arising from financial instruments and how those risks are managed. In response, the IASB published an amendment to IFRS 7 in March 2009 to enhance the disclosure requirements on fair value measurement (see para 11.78) and liquidity risk (see para 11.98.1). Financial statement users and other investors need such information to make more informed judgements about the risk that entities run from the use of financial instruments and their associated returns. IFRS 7 sets out the disclosure requirements for financial instruments.

[The next paragraph is 11.30.]

Scope of IFRS 7

11.30 IFRS 7 applies to all types of financial instruments, except those that are specifically covered by another standard such as interests in subsidiaries, associates and joint ventures, acquirer's interest in contracts for contingent consideration in a business combination, employers' rights and obligations arising from employee benefit plans, share based payments and insurance contracts. IFRS 7's scope is similar to IAS 39. Chapter 3 discusses in detail which instruments are in the scope of IAS 39 and therefore also in IFRS 7's scope. However, although finance leases are mostly outside the scope of IAS 39, they remain within the scope of IFRS 7. Operating leases are not regarded as financial instruments and are not therefore in the scope of either IAS 39 or IFRS 7, except for those individual payments that are currently due and payable. [IAS 32 para AG 9].

11.30.1 Applying IFRS 7 can be challenging for entities that enter into contracts for the purchase, sale or usage of commodities. Commodity contracts that are settled net in cash or through other financial instruments are in IFRS 7's scope; those contracts that meet the 'own use exemption' would be outside IFRS 7's scope, because they are not financial instruments. [IAS 39 para 6]. These terms are discussed in detail in Chapter 3. It is likely for internal reporting purposes that management may exclude 'own use' contracts when assessing the company's exposure to financial risks, such as liquidity risk, credit risk and market risk, or they may treat all commodity contracts in the same way. The onus therefore falls on management to determine how to provide disclosures that capture the complete

见第 11. 78 段）和流动性风险（参见第 11. 98. 1 段）的披露要求。财务报表使用者及其他投资人需要这些信息使其能作出有关主体因使用金融工具而面临的风险及其相关收益作出更切实的判断。IFRS 7 规定了有关金融工具的披露要求。

[下一段为第 11. 30 段。]

IFRS 7 的范围

11. 30　除了那些诸如在子公司、联营和合营中的权益，购买方在业务合并的或有对价合同中的权益，因职工福利计划而产生的雇主权利和义务，以股份为基础的支付和保险合同等由其他准则明确涵盖的工具以外，IFRS 7 适用于所有类型的金融工具。IFRS 7 的范围与 IAS 39 类似。第 3 章中详细讨论了有哪些工具在 IAS 39 的范围内，因而也在 IFRS 7 的范围内。但是，尽管大部分情况融资租赁不在 IAS 39 的范围内，它们仍在 IFRS 7 的范围内。经营租赁不被视为金融工具，因此除了那些目前已经到期并应支付的单独款项外，不在 IAS 39 或 IFRS 7 的范围内。[IAS 32 AG 第 9 段]。

11. 30. 1　对于签订了购买、销售或使用商品合同的主体而言，应用 IFRS 7 可能会面临一些挑战。通过现金或其他金融工具以净额结算的商品合同在 IFRS 7 的范围内；而满足“自用豁免”的合同则不然，因为它们不是金融工具。[IAS 39 第 6 段]。在第 3 章中对这些条款进行了详细的讨论。管理层在内部报告时很可能会在评估公司所承受的诸如流动性风险、信用风险和市场风险等金融风险时将“自用合同”排除在外，或者也可能将所有的商品合同以同样的方式进行处理。因此需要由管理层来决定如何进行披露，以囊括报告主体由于商品合同所面临的全部风险敞口。IFRS 7 并未禁止管理层提供进一步的解释或详细信息来帮助财务报表使用者理解这些披露或提供完整的描述。

exposure of the risks faced by the reporting entity in connection with its commodity contracts. IFRS 7 does not preclude management from providing additional explanations or details to assist users of the financial statements in interpreting the disclosures or in providing a complete picture.

11.30.2 Receivables and payables arising from application of IAS 11, 'Construction contracts', need to be considered carefully in order to determine whether these items are in IFRS 7's scope or not. The amount due from/to customers is generally the net amount of cost incurred plus recognised profits less progress billings and recognised losses. This amount is 'billable' to customers. It, therefore, represents a contractual right to receive cash and is a financial asset in IFRS 7's scope. Progress billings to customers are also receivables in the IFRS 7's scope. On the other hand, advances received from customers are non-financial liabilities (obligation to perform work) and hence are not in the scope of IFRS 7.

11.30.3 In a similar manner, accruals representing a right to receive cash or an obligation to deliver cash are in IFRS 7's scope. For example, an accrual for goods received but not yet invoiced is within the IFRS 7's scope. On the other hand, a pre-paid expense, which is settled by the future delivery of goods or services, is not a financial instrument and is excluded from IFRS 7's scope.

11.30.4 Provisions as defined in IAS 37, 'Provisions, contingent liabilities and contingent assets', are scoped out of IFRS 7 because they are not financial instruments. [IAS 37 para 2; IFRS 7 paras 3-4; IAS 39 para 2(j)]. Financial guarantee contracts may be measured in accordance with IAS 37's principles if the provision is higher than the unamortised premium amount, but they are financial instruments within IAS 39's scope and so are within IFRS 7's scope. Financial guarantee contracts that are considered insurance contracts and measured in accordance with IFRS 4 are outside the scope of IFRS 7. [IFRS 4 para 4(d)].

11.30.5 IFRS 7 applies to both recognised and unrecognised financial instruments, even if the financial instrument may not be recognised under IAS 39. [IFRS 7 para 4, 5]. For example, some loan commitments are outside IAS 39's scope but within IFRS 7's scope because they expose an entity to financial risks, such as credit and liquidity risk. However, the same is not necessarily true for a firm commitment that is designated as a hedged item in a fair value hedge. The

11.30.2 因运用《国际会计准则第11号——建造合同》（“IAS 11”）而产生的应收款和应付款需要仔细的考量以判定这些项目是否在IFRS 7的范围内。应收/应付客户款一般是已发生的成本加上已确认的利润减去进度款和已确认的损失的净额。此金额对客户而言为“可开账单”金额。因此，它代表了一项收取现金的合同权利，是IFRS 7范围内的一项金融资产。对客户的进度款也是IFRS 7范围内的应收款。另一方面，从客户处取得的预收款是非金融负债（施工义务），因此不在IFRS 7的范围内。

11.30.3 类似地，代表了收取现金的权利或交付现金的义务的预提费用在IFRS 7的范围内。例如，对已经收到但尚未开具发票的货物的预提费用在IFRS 7的范围内。与之相反，通过未来交付货物或服务来结算的预付费用不是金融工具，不在IFRS 7的范围内。

11.30.4 《国际会计准则第37号——准备、或有负债和或有资产》（“IAS 37”）中所定义的准备不在IFRS 7的范围内，因为它们不是金融工具。[IAS 37第2段；IFRS 7第3、第4段；IAS 39第2（j）段]。财务担保合同在准备高于未摊销溢价时要根据IAS 37的原则进行计量，但它们是在IAS 39范围内的金融工具，故也在IFRS 7的范围内。被认为是保险合同并按照IFRS 4来计量的财务担保合同不在IFRS 7的范围内。[IFRS 4第4（d）段]。

11.30.5 IFRS 7同时适用于已确认及未确认的金融工具，即使这种金融工具可能不会按照IAS 39进行确认。[IFRS 7第4、第5段]。例如，某些贷款承诺不在IAS 39的范围内但在IFRS 7的范围内，因为它们会使主体承受诸如信用和流动性风险等金融风险。但是，对于在公允价值套期中被指定为被套期项目的确定承诺而言则不然。按照IAS 39中的套期会计规则，确定承诺中归属于套期风险的公允价值的后续累计变动应确认为一项资产或负债。[IAS 39第

subsequent cumulative change in the fair value of the firm commitment attributable to the hedged risk is recognised as an asset or liability under IAS 39's hedge accounting rules. [IAS 39 para 93]. However, this 'firm commitment' asset or liability does not expose the entity to credit or liquidity risk until it becomes a financial asset or liability. The fact that hedge accounting is applied does not mean that the 'firm commitment' asset or liability is a financial instrument or that IFRS 7's disclosure requirements would apply.

11.30.6 There is no scope exemption in IFRS 7 for financial assets and liabilities within the scope of IFRS 5, 'Non-current assets held for sale and discontinued operations'. However, IFRS 5 specifies the disclosures required in respect of non-current assets (or disposal groups) classified as held for sale and discontinued operations. Paragraph 2 of the standard states that the classification and presentation requirements of IFRS 5 apply to all recognised non current assets and to all disposal groups of an entity and paragraph 5(c) specifies that the measurement provisions do not apply to financial assets within IAS 39's scope. A question arises as to whether IFRS 7 disclosures are also required for financial assets and financial liabilities classified as held-for-sale or part of disposal groups. This question was addressed by the IASB in an amendment to IFRS 5 issued in April 2009 and effective for accounting periods starting on or after 1 January 2010. The amendment clarifies that disclosures required by other standards do not apply to non-current assets or disposal groups held for sale unless they are outside the scope of IFRS 5's measurement requirements. [IFRS 5 para 5B(b)]. As financial instruments measured in accordance with IAS 39 are outside the scope of IFRS 5's measurement requirements, IFRS 7 should be applied. See chapter 26 of the IFRS Manual of Accounting.

11.31 Consistent with IAS 32 and IAS 39, the standard applies to all entities, not just those in the financial services sector. This means that it applies to a manufacturing entity whose only financial instruments may be cash, bank loans and overdrafts, trade debtors and creditors as well as to a bank with many and complex financial instruments. It also applies to subsidiaries of a consolidated group, even though in most large groups risks are managed at the consolidated level.

11.31.1 There is no scope exemption for the financial statements of subsidiaries

93 段]。但是，这项“确定承诺”资产或负债在它成为金融资产或负债之前并不会使主体承受信用或流动性风险。采用的套期会计并不意味着该“确定承诺”资产或负债是金融工具或应该适用 IFRS 7 的披露要求。

11.30.6 IFRS 7 的范围规定并未豁免在《国际财务报告准则第 5 号——持有待售非流动资产和终止经营》（“IFRS 5”）范围内的金融资产和负债。但是，IFRS 5 规定了有关被划分为持有待售或终止经营的非流动资产（或处置组）的披露要求。该准则第 2 段中指出 IFRS 5 的分类和列报要求适用于主体的所有已确认的非流动资产和所有处置组，而第 5（c）段中明确有关计量的规定不适用于包括在 IAS 39 范围内的金融资产。这里就产生了一个问题，即是否要求对被划分为持有待售或属于处置组一部分的金融资产和金融负债按照 IFRS 7 作出披露。该问题由 IASB 于 2009 年 4 月针对 IFRS 5 所发布的一项于起始日在 2010 年 1 月 1 日或以后的会计期间生效的修订予以解决。该修订澄清，除非不在 IFRS 5 的计量要求范围内，否则其他准则所要求的披露均不适用于持有待售的非流动资产或处置组。[IFRS 5 第 5B（b）段]。由于按照 IAS 39 计量的金融工具不在 IFRS 5 的计量要求范围内，故应采用 IFRS 7。参见《国际财务报告准则会计实务指引》第 26 章。

11.31 与 IAS 32 和 IAS 39 一样，IFRS 7 适用于所有主体，而不仅仅是那些金融服务领域的主体。这意味着它不仅适用于可能只有现金、银行贷款和透支、应收账款和应付账款等金融工具的生产型主体；也适用于有很多复杂的金融工具的银行。它还适用于某一合并集团的子公司，即使大多数大型集团的风险是在合并层面进行管理的。

11.31.1 对于子公司或者中小型公司的财务报表目前并没有范围豁免。对子

or, as yet, for small and medium-sized companies. The application of IFRS 7 to subsidiaries may present a challenge, as financial risk is often managed at a consolidated or group level.

11.31.2 The 2010 IFRS annual improvements project made several changes to IFRS 7, mostly around the simplification of credit risk and collateral disclosures. The 2010 annual improvements are applicable for periods beginning on or after 1 January 2011, with early application permitted. See paragraph 11.90 onwards.

Objectives of IFRS 7

11.32 IFRS 7's objective is to provide information to users of financial statements about an entity's exposure to risks and how the entity manages those risks. To this end, the standard requires an entity to provide disclosures in its financial statements that enable users to evaluate:

- the significance of financial instruments for the entity's financial position and performance; and
- the nature and extent of risks arising from financial instruments to which the entity is exposed (quantitative disclosure) and how the entity manages those risks (qualitative disclosures).

[IFRS 7 paras 1, 7, 31].

11.33 The first bullet point above covers disclosures about the figures in the balance sheet and the income statement. IFRS 7 requires disclosures of categories of financial instruments and hedging activities. In addition, it requires various disclosures by 'class' of financial instruments (see para 11.39).

11.34 The second bullet point covers disclosure of qualitative and quantitative information about an entity's exposure to risks arising from financial instruments. IFRS 7 expands the qualitative disclosure to include information on the process that an entity uses to manage and measure risk. IFRS 7 introduces new quantitative risk disclosures that should be given 'through the eyes of management', that is, based on information provided internally to key management personnel. Certain minimum

公司应用 IFRS 7 可能会具有挑战性，因为金融风险通常都是在合并或是集团层面进行管理的。

11.31.2　IFRS 2010 年度改进项目对 IFRS 7 做了几处改动，主要简化了信用风险和抵押品的披露。2010 年度改进于起始日在 2011 年 1 月 1 日或以后的期间生效，允许提前实施。参见第 11.90 段及其下文。

IFRS 7 的目的

11.32　IFRS 7 的目的是向财务报表使用者提供有关主体所承受的风险以及主体如何管理这些风险的信息。因此，该准则要求主体在其财务报表中提供披露以使财务报表使用者能对下述事项进行评估：

- 金融工具对主体的财务状况和业绩的重要性；以及
- 主体承受金融工具所产生的风险的性质和程度（定量披露）以及主体如何管理这些风险（定性披露）。

[IFRS 7 第 1、7、31 段]。

11.33　上文第一点中所涵盖的是有关资产负债表和利润表中数字的披露。IFRS 7 要求披露金融工具的类别和套期活动。此外，还要求根据金融工具的“类型”进行各种其他披露（参见第 11.39 段）。

11.34　第二点所涵盖的是有关主体承受金融工具产生风险的定性和定量信息披露。IFRS 7 扩展了定量披露的范围，使其包括主体用来管理和计量风险程序的信息。IFRS 7 介绍了一种应“透过管理层的眼睛”来提供的新定量风险披露，即，披露要基于提供给关键管理人员的内部信息。对“透过管理层的眼睛”所提供的信息未能涵盖的特定最低披露也要求提供。主体被要求就其如何理解、管理和衡量风险与市场进行沟通。

disclosures are also required to the extent they are not already covered by the 'through the eyes of management' information. Entities are required to communicate to the market how they perceive, manage and measure risk.

11.34.1 The 'through the eyes of management' approach brings financial reporting more closely into line with the way management run their businesses. As management's internal measures may not have previously been provided under IFRS or local accounting principles, they could enhance a company's ability to demonstrate the strengths of its control environment, but equally they could expose any flaws. They may also enable the market to better evaluate the strength (or otherwise) of an entity's risk management activities.

11.35 IFRS 7 includes mandatory application guidance that explains how to apply the standard's requirements. It is also accompanied by non-mandatory implementation guidance that describes how an entity might provide the necessary disclosures.

[The next paragraph is 11.39.]

General matters

Classes of financial instruments

11.39 IFRS 7 requires certain disclosures to be given by class of financial instruments, including the following:

- Financial assets not qualifying for derecognition (see para 11.55).
- The reconciliation of an allowance account (see para 11.59).
- The amount of impairment loss for financial assets (see para 11.64).
- Fair values and the methods or assumptions applied in determining those values.
- Specific disclosures relating to credit risk (see para 11.91).

The standard itself does not provide a prescriptive list of classes of financial instruments. However, IFRS 7 states that an entity should take into account the

11.34.1　“透过管理层的眼睛”这一方法能够使财务报告更贴近管理层经营业务的方式。由于管理层的内部考量可能在以前并未按照IFRS或当地会计原则提供，这能够促使公司证明其在控制环境方面优势的能力，但同样也能够暴露缺陷。这还可能使市场更好地对主体风险管理活动的优势（或劣势）进行评估。

11.35　IFRS 7包括需强制执行的实施指南，对如何应用该准则的要求进行了解释；同时还包括非强制性执行的应用指南，对主体可能如何作出必要的披露进行了描述。

[下一段为第11.39段。]

一般事宜

金融工具的类型

11.39　IFRS 7要求根据金融工具的类型作出某些特定的披露，其中包括：

- 不符合终止确认要求的金融资产（参见第11.55段）。
- 备抵账户的调节表（参见第11.59段）。
- 金融资产的减值损失金额（参见第11.64段）。
- 公允价值以及确定该价值时所使用的方法或假设。
- 与信用风险相关的具体披露（参见第11.91段）。

该准则本身并没有提供金融工具类型的标准清单。但是，IFRS 7指出主体应考虑金融工具的特征而且所选择的类型应合乎所披露信息的性质。[IFRS 7第

characteristics of financial instruments and that the classes selected should be appropriate to the nature of information disclosed. [IFRS 7 para 6].

11.40 A 'class' of financial instruments is not the same as a 'category' of financial instruments. Categories are defined in paragraph 9 of IAS 39 as financial assets at fair value through profit or loss (held for trading or designated at initial recognition), held-to-maturity investments, loans and receivables, available-for-sale financial assets, financial liabilities at fair value through profit or loss (held for trading or designated at initial recognition) and financial liabilities measured at amortised cost. [IFRS 7 para 8]. Classes should be determined at a lower level than the measurement categories and reconciled back to the balance sheet. [IFRS 7 para 6]. The level of detail for a class should be determined on an entity specific basis and may be defined for each individual disclosure in a different way. In determining classes of financial instrument, an entity should, at a minimum:

- Distinguish instruments measured at amortised cost from those measured at fair value.
- Treat as a separate class or classes those financial instruments outside IFRS 7's scope. IFRS 7's disclosure requirements would not apply to this class.

[IFRS 7 App B para 2].

11.41 For example, in the case of banks, the category 'loans and receivables' comprises more than one class, unless the loans have similar characteristics. In this situation, it may be appropriate to group financial instruments into the following classes:

- types of customers – for example, commercial loans and loans to individuals; or
- types of loans – for example, mortgages, credit cards, unsecured loans and overdrafts.

However, in some cases, 'loans to clients' can be one class if all the loans have similar characteristics (for example, a savings bank providing only one type of loan to individuals).

11.41.1 'Available-for-sale' assets could be split into bond and equity investment classes. The equity investments could be further subdivided into those

6 段]。

11.40　金融工具的“类型”与金融工具的“类别”并不相同。IAS 39 第 9 段将类别定义为以公允价值计量且变动计入损益的金融资产（为交易而持有或在初始确认时指定）、持有至到期的投资、贷款和应收款项、可供出售的金融资产、以公允价值计量且变动计入损益的金融负债（为交易而持有或在初始确认时指定）以及以摊余成本计量的金融负债。[IFRS 7 第 8 段]。类型应该在比计量类别更低的一个层次确定并能被调节至资产负债表。[IFRS 7 第 6 段]。类型的详细程度应视每个主体的具体情况确定，而且可能对每一个单独的披露有不同的定义。在确定金融工具的类型时，主体至少应当：

- 对以摊余成本计量的金融工具和以公允价值计量的金融工具进行区分。
- 将不在 IFRS 7 范围内的那些金融工具作为单独的一类或几类。对此类型，IFRS 7 的披露要求将不适用。

[IFRS 7 附录二第 2 段]。

11.41　例如，对银行来说，除非贷款具有类似的特征，否则其“贷款和应收款项”这一类别会由多个类型组成。在这种情况下，将金融工具分为如下类型可能比较适合：

- 客户的类型——例如，商业贷款和个人贷款；或
- 贷款的类型——例如，抵押贷款、信用卡、无担保贷款及透支。

但是，在某些情况下，如果所有贷款都具有相似的特征（如储蓄银行仅向个人提供一种贷款），则“对客户的贷款”也可以归为一个类型。

11.41.1　“可供出售”的资产可以被分为债券和权益投资这两个类型。而权益投资可以被进一步分为对上市和非上市的投资。

that are listed and those that are unlisted.

Location, level of disclosure and aggregation

11.42 An entity is permitted to disclose some of the information required by the standard (specifically, the information on the nature and extent of risks arising from financial instruments required by paragraphs 31 to 42) either in the notes or on the face of the balance sheet or on the income statement. [IFRS 7 paras 8, 20]. Some entities might present some of the information required by IFRS 7, such as the nature and extent of risks arising from financial instruments and the entity's approach to managing those risks, alongside the financial statements in a separate management commentary or business review. This is only permissible where the information is incorporated by cross-reference from the financial statements and is made available to users of the financial statements on the same terms as the financial statements and at the same time. [IFRS 7 App B para 6].

11.43 An entity should decide, in the light of its own circumstances, how much detail it should provide, how much emphasis it should place on different aspects of the disclosure requirements and how much aggregation it should undertake to satisfy the standard's requirements. Obviously, a significant amount of judgement is required to display the overall picture without combining information with different characteristics. A balance should be maintained between providing excessive detail that may not assist users of financial statements and obscuring important information as a result of too much aggregation. For example, an entity should not obscure important information by including it amongst a large amount of insignificant detail. Similarly, an entity should not disclose information that is so aggregated that it obscures important differences between individual transactions or associated risks. [IFRS 7 App B para 3].

Risks arising from financial instruments

11.44 IFRS 7 requires a significant amount of qualitative and quantitative disclosure about risks associated with financial instruments. In the context of financial instruments, risk arises from the uncertainty in cash flows, which in turn

披露和汇总的位置和等级

11.42　主体可以在附注或资产负债表或利润表主表中披露该准则所要求的一些信息（具体而言，第31到42段所要求的由金融工具所产生的风险的性质和程度的信息）。[IFRS 7第8、第20段]。有些主体可能将IFRS 7所要求的一些信息，如金融工具所产生的风险的性质和程度和主体管理这些风险的方法，在和财务报表一起的单独的管理层评论或业务回顾中列示。仅当这些信息与财务报表交互参照且该信息可以由财务报表使用者在同一时间以获得财务报表相同的条件获取时，才可以采取这种方式。[IFRS 7附录B第6段]。

11.43　主体应根据其自身环境决定其所提供信息的详细程度、其对披露要求的不同方面的重视程度、以及其为满足该准则的要求进行何种程度的汇总。很明显，在不合并不同特征信息的情况下显示其总体情况需要很大程度的判断。应该在披露过于详细的信息从而无助于财务报表使用者和由于过度汇总而模糊了重要信息这两者间取得平衡。例如，主体不应通过将重要信息置于大量的不重要的详述中而模糊其重要性。同样，主体不应披露过于汇总的信息以致于难以区分单个交易或相关风险间的重要差异。[IFRS 7附录B第3段]。

金融工具所产生的风险

11.44　IFRS 7要求对与金融工具相关的风险进行大量定性和定量的披露。对于金融工具来说，现金流量的不确定性产生风险，反过来又会影响未来现金流量以及金融资产和金融负债的公允价值。与金融工具相关的金融风险种类

affects the future cash flows and fair values of financial assets and liabilities. The following are the types of financial risk that are related to financial instruments:

- Market risk – the risk that the fair value or cash flows of a financial instrument will fluctuate, because of changes in market prices. Market risk embodies not only the potential for loss, but also the potential for gain. It comprises three types of risk as follows:
  - Interest rate risk-the risk that the fair value or future cash flows of a financial instrument will fluctuate because of changes in market interest rates.
  - Currency risk-the risk that the fair value or future cash flows of a financial instrument will fluctuate because of changes in foreign exchange rates.
  - Other price risk-the risk that the fair value or future cash flows of a financial instrument will fluctuate because of changes in market prices (other than those arising from interest rate risk or currency risk), whether those changes are caused by factors specific to the individual financial instrument or its issuer, or factors affecting all similar financial instruments traded in the market.
- Credit risk-the risk that one party to a financial instrument will cause a financial loss for the other party by failing to discharge an obligation.
- Liquidity risk-the risk that an entity will encounter difficulty in meeting obligations associated with financial liabilities.

[IFRS 7 App A].

11.44.1 Operational risk disclosures, on the other hand, are not within IFRS 7's scope.

Balance sheet disclosures

11.45 The carrying amounts of each of the following categories should be disclosed, either on the face of the balance sheet or in the notes:

- Financial assets at fair value through profit or loss, showing separately:

列示如下：

■ 市场风险——金融工具的公允价值或未来现金流量因市场价格变化而波动的风险。市场风险不仅包括潜在损失而且包括潜在利得。它包括如下三种类型的风险：

  ■ 利率风险——金融工具的公允价值或未来现金流量因市场利率变化而波动的风险。

  ■ 货币风险——金融工具的公允价值或未来现金流量因外汇汇率变化而波动的风险。

  ■ 其他价格风险——金融工具的公允价值或未来现金流量因市场价格（不包括利率风险或货币风险引起的价格变动）变化而波动的风险，不论这些变动是由与单项金融工具或其发行人有关的具体因素引起的，还是由与市场内交易的所有类似金融工具有关的因素引起的。

■ 信用风险——金融工具的一方未能履行义务而导致另一方发生财务损失的风险。

■ 流动性风险——主体在履行与金融负债相关的义务时将面临困难的风险。

[IFRS 7 附录 A]。

11.44.1　与此相反，经营风险的披露不在 IFRS 7 的范围之内。

资产负债表的披露

11.45　下述各类别的账面金额应在资产负债表的主表或其附注中披露：

■ 以公允价值计量且变动计入损益的金融资产，并分别披露：

- those designated as such upon initial recognition; and
- those classified as held for trading in accordance with IAS 39.

- Held-to-maturity investments.
- Loans and receivables.
- Available-for-sale financial assets.
- Financial liabilities at fair value through profit or loss, showing separately:
  - those designated as such upon initial recognition; and
  - those classified as held for trading in accordance with IAS 39.
- Financial liabilities measured at amortised cost.

[IFRS 7 para 8].

11.46 Table 11.2 shows the analysis of financial assets and financial liabilities by category.

Table 11.2 – Analysis of financial assets and financial liabilities by class and by categories

Amer Sports Corporation – Annual Report – 31 December 2008

27 Balance sheet values of financial assets and liabilities by measurement categories December 31 2008

EUR million	Financial assets/ liabilities fair value through income statement	Derivative financial instruments used in hedge accounting	Loans and other receivables	Available-for-sale financial assets	Financial liabilities measured at amortized cost	Carrying amount by balance sheet item	Fair value
Non-current financial assets							
Other non-current financial assets			2.7	0.8		3.5	3.5
Derivative financial instruments							
Interest rate derivatives		0.2				0.2	0.2

- ■ 在初始确认时指定为以公允价值计量且变动计入损益的金融资产；以及
- ■ 根据 IAS 39 被划分为为交易而持有的金融资产。

■ 持有至到期的投资。

■ 贷款和应收款项。

■ 可供出售的金融资产。

■ 以公允价值计量且变动计入损益的金融负债，并分别披露：

- ■ 在初始确认时指定为以公允价值计量且变动计入损益的金融负债；以及
- ■ 根据 IAS 39 被划分为为交易而持有的金融负债。

■ 按摊余成本计量的金融负债。

［IFRS 7 第 8 段］。

11.46　表 11.2 列示了按类别分析的金融资产和金融负债。

表 11.2——金融资产和金融负债按类型和类别的分析

Amer Sports Corporation——年报——2008 年 12 月 31 日

27 按照计量类别划分的金融资产和负债的资产负债表金额
2008 年 12 月 31 日

百万欧元	以公允价值计量且变动计入损益表的金融资产/负债	套期会计中使用的衍生金融工具	贷款和其他应收款项	可供出售的金融资产	按摊余成本计量的金融负债	资产负债表项目的账面价值	公允价值
非流动金融资产							
其他非流动金融资产			2.7	0.8		3.5	3.5
衍生金融工具							
利率衍生工具		0.2				0.2	0.2

Con.

Current financial assets							
Accounts receivables			523.4			523.4	523.4
Loan receivables			0.2			0.2	0.2
Other non-interest yielding receivables			49.5			49.5	49.5
Foreign exchange derivatives	3.6	1.5				5.1	5.1
Liquid funds			68.0			68.0	68.0
Balance sheet values by category	3.6	1.7	643.8	0.8	0.0	649.9	649.9
Long-term financial liabilities							
Long-term interest bearing liabilities					218.6	218.6	218.6
Other long-term liabilities					6.5	6.5	6.5
Derivative financial instruments							
Interest rate derivatives		1.8				1.8	1.8
Current financial liabilities							
Current interest – bearing liabilities					437.6	437.6	437.6
Accounts payable					164.8	164.8	164.8
Other current liabilities					172.5	172.5	172.5
Derivative financial instruments							
Foreign exchange derivatives	1.0	3.6				4.6	4.6
Balance sheet values by category	1.0	5.4	0.0	0.0	1,000.0	1,006.4	1,006.4

续表

流动金融资产							
应收账款			523.4			523.4	523.4
应收贷款			0.2			0.2	0.2
其他无息应收账款			49.5			49.5	49.5
外汇衍生工具	3.6	1.5				5.1	5.1
流动资金			68.0			68.0	68.0
按类别分的资产负债表金额	3.6	1.7	643.8	0.8	0.0	649.9	649.9
长期金融负债							
计息的长期负债					218.6	218.6	218.6
其他长期负债					6.5	6.5	6.5
衍生金融工具							
利率衍生工具		1.8				1.8	1.8
流动金融负债							
计息的流动负债					437.6	437.6	437.6
应付账款					164.8	164.8	164.8
其他流动负债					172.5	172.5	172.5
衍生金融工具							
外汇衍生工具	1.0	3.6				4.6	4.6
按类别分的资产负债表金额	1.0	5.4	0.0	0.0	1,000.0	1,006.4	1,006.4

Financial assets or liabilities at fair value through profit or loss

11.47 If the entity has designated a loan or receivable (or group of loans or receivables) as at fair value through profit or loss, it should disclose:

- The maximum exposure to credit risk of the loan or receivable (or group of loans or receivables) at the reporting date (see para 11.88 below).
- The amount by which any related credit derivatives or similar instruments mitigate that maximum exposure to credit risk, for example financial guarantees and credit insurance.
- The amount of change, during the period and cumulatively, in the fair value of the loan or receivable (or group of loans or receivables) that is attributable to changes in the financial asset's credit risk, determined either
  - as the amount of change in its fair value that is not attributable to changes in market conditions that give rise to market risk; or
  - using an alternative method the entity believes more faithfully represents the amount of change in its fair value that is attributable to changes in the asset's credit risk.

  Changes in market conditions that give rise to market risk include changes in an observed (benchmark) interest rate, commodity price, foreign exchange rate or index of prices or rates (see para 11.49 below).
- The amount of the change in the fair value of any related credit derivatives or similar instruments that has occurred during the period and cumulatively since the loan or receivable was designated as at fair value through profit or loss.

[IFRS 7 para 9].

11.48 The disclosures described above apply only to those loans and receivables (or groups of loans and receivables) that have been designated at fair value through profit and loss ('FVTPL'). They do not apply to all loans and receivables or to all assets designated as FVTPL assets. For example, a listed bond asset is not classified as 'loans and receivables', as it is quoted. Therefore, in this case the above disclosures are not required.

以公允价值计量且变动计入损益的金融资产或负债

11.47　如果主体指定一项贷款或应收款项（或一组贷款或应收款项）为以公允价值计量且变动计入损益的金融资产，则其应当披露下述项目：

- 在报告日贷款或应收款项（或一组贷款或应收款项）的最大信用风险敞口（参见下文第11.88段）。
- 任何相关的信用衍生工具或类似工具降低最大信用风险敞口的金额，如财务担保和信用保险。
- 由于金融资产信用风险变化导致的贷款或应收款项（或一组贷款或应收款项）公允价值在本期间和至本期累计的变动金额，该金额根据下述方法确定
  - 按并非由于产生市场风险的市场环境变动导致的公允价值变动的金额确定；或者
  - 使用主体认为能更真实地反映由于资产信用风险变动导致的公允价值变动的其他方法确定。

  产生市场风险的市场环境的变动，包括观察到的（基准）利率、商品价格、外汇汇率及价格或费率指数的变动（参见下文第11.49段）。

- 从贷款或应收款项被指定为以公允价值计量且变动计入损益的金融资产开始，任何相关的信用衍生工具或类似工具在本期间和至本期累计的公允价值变动的金额。

［IFRS 7 第9段］。

11.48　上述披露仅适用于指定为以公允价值计量且变动计入损益的贷款或应收款项（或一组贷款或应收款项）。它们并不适用于所有的贷款或应收款项或所有指定为以公允价值计量且变动计入损益的资产。例如，上市债券资产因为其有市场公开报价不能被划分为“贷款或应收款项”。因此，在这种情况下并不要求进行上述披露。

11.49 Where an entity discloses the information required by the third bullet point in paragraph 11.47, it should also disclose the methods used to comply with the disclosure requirements. However, where the entity believes that this disclosure does not faithfully represent the change in the financial asset's fair value attributable to changes in its credit risk, it should disclose the reasons and the factors it believes are relevant in reaching that conclusion. [IFRS 7 para 11].

11.50 If the entity has designated a financial liability as at fair value through profit or loss, it should disclose:

- The amount of change, during the period and cumulatively, in the financial liability's fair value that is attributable to changes in the credit risk of that liability determined either:
  - as the amount of change in its fair value that is not attributable to changes in market conditions that give rise to market risk; or
  - using an alternative method the entity believes more faithfully represents the amount of change in its fair value that is attributable to changes in the liability's credit risk.

  Changes in market conditions that give rise to market risk include changes in an observed (benchmark) interest rate, the price of another entity's financial instrument, a commodity price, a foreign exchange rate or an index of prices or rates. For contracts that include a unit-linking feature, changes in market conditions include changes in the performance of the related internal or external investment fund (see para 11.52 below).

- The difference between the financial liability's carrying amount and the amount the entity would be contractually required to pay at maturity to the holder of the obligation.

[IFRS 7 para 10].

11.51 As stated in the first bullet point in paragraph 11.50 above, an entity is required to disclose the amount of change in a liability's fair value that is attributable to changes in the liability's credit risk. Although quantifying such changes might be difficult in practice, the IASB concluded that disclosure of such

11.49 当主体披露第 11.47 段中第三点所要求的信息时，它还应披露为遵循这一披露要求而采用的方法。但是，如果主体认为这种披露不能真实地反映由于金融资产信用风险变动导致的公允价值变动，则应披露主体认为得出此结论相关的原因及因素。[IFRS 7 第 11 段]。

11.50 如果主体指定一项金融负债为以公允价值计量且变动计入损益的金融负债，则其应当披露下述项目：

- 由于金融负债信用风险变化导致的金融负债公允价值在本期间和至本期累计的变动金额，该金额根据下述方法确定：

  - 按并非由于产生市场风险的市场环境变动导致的公允价值变动的金额确定；或者
  - 使用主体认为能更真实地反映由于负债信用风险变动导致的公允价值变动的其他方法确定。

  产生市场风险的市场环境的变动，包括所观察到的（基准）利率、其他主体的金融工具的价格、商品价格、外汇汇率及价格或利率指数的变动。对于包含投资连结特征的合同，市场环境的变动包括相关内部或外部投资基金业绩的变化（参见下文第 11.52 段）。

- 金融负债的账面金额和主体按合同约定应当在到期日偿付给债务持有人的金额之间的差额。

[IFRS 7 第 10 段]。

11.51 如上文第 11.50 段第一点所述，要求主体披露由于负债信用风险变化导致的负债公允价值变化的金额。尽管在实务中量化这种变动是困难的，但是 IASB 认为，这些信息的披露对使用者是有用的，并且有助于减轻使用者可能会错误理解信用风险变化对损益的影响的担忧，特别是在缺少信息披露时。因

information would be useful to users and would help alleviate concerns that users may misinterpret the profit or loss changes in credit risk, especially in the absence of disclosures. Consequently, the standard provides a relatively easy method of computing the amount to be disclosed, as illustrated in the example below. The method assumes that the only relevant change in market condition for the liability is a change in the observed benchmark interest rate. Changes in fair value arising from factors other than changes in the instrument's credit risk or changes in interest rates are assumed not to be significant.

Example – Fair value change attributable to changes in a liability's credit risk

On 1 January 20X1, an entity issues a 10 year bond with a par value of C150,000 and an annual fixed coupon rate of 8%, which is consistent with market rates for bonds with similar characteristics. The entity uses LIBOR as its observable (benchmark) interest rate.

The entity assumes a flat yield curve, all changes in interest rates result from a parallel shift in the yield curve, and the changes in LIBOR are the only relevant changes in market conditions. It is also assumed that changes in the fair value arising from factors other than changes in the bond's credit risk or changes in interest rate are not significant.

At the date of inception of the bond, LIBOR was 5%. At the end of the first year, LIBOR has decreased to 4.75%. The bond's fair value is C153,811, consistent with a market interest rate of 7.6% for the bond. The market rate reflects the bond's credit rating at the end of the first year (see below).

The entity estimates the amount of change in the bond's fair value that is not attributable to changes in market conditions that give rise to market risk as follows:

- Calculate the instrument-specific component of the bond's internal rate of return:

  At inception, the internal rate of return for the 10 year bond is 8%. Since LIBOR at inception was 5%, the instrument-specific component of the internal rate of return is 3% (8% – 5%).

此，该准则提供了一个计算所披露金额的相对简单的方法，如下文示例所示。这种方法假定，对负债而言市场环境的唯一相关变化就是可观察的基准利率。假定由工具信用风险变化或利率变化以外的因素导致的公允价值变动不重大。

示例——由于负债的信用风险变化所导致的公允价值变动

20X1 年 1 月 1 日，主体按面值 C150,000 元发行了一笔 10 年期的债券，年固定票面利率为 8%，该利率与具有类似特征债券的市场利率一致。主体采用伦敦同业拆借利率（“LIBOR”）作为可观察的（基准）利率。

主体假定收益率曲线是水平的，利率的所有变动均来自收益率曲线的平行移动，而伦敦同业拆借利率的变动是市场环境唯一相关的变动。且假定由债券的信用风险变化或利率变化以外的因素导致的公允价值变动不重大。

在债券开始日，伦敦同业拆借利率为 5%。在第一年年末，伦敦同业拆借利率下降至 4.75%。债券的公允价值为 C153,811，与债券 7.6% 的市场利率一致。该市场利率反映了债券在第一年年末的信用等级（参见下文）。

对于并非由产生市场风险的市场环境变化导致的债券公允价值变动的金额，主体作出的估计如下：

- 计算债券的内含报酬率中特属于该工具的部分：

  在开始时，该笔 10 年期债券的内含报酬率为 8%。由于开始时伦敦同业拆借利率为 5%，内含报酬率中特属于该工具的部分为 3%（8% - 5%）。

- Determine the discount rate to be used to calculate the present value of the bond at the end of year 1 using the bond's contractual cash flows:

  Since the only relevant change in the market conditions is that LIBOR has decreased to 4.75% at the end of the year, the discount rate for the present value calculation is 7.75% (4.75% +3%).

- Calculate the present value at the end of year 1 using the above discount rate and the bond's contractual cash flows as follows:

		C
PV of C12,000 interest payable for 9 years (year 2 – 10)	$= \frac{12,000 \times [1-(1+0.0775)^{-9}]}{0.0775}$	75,748
PV of C150,000 payable in year 10	$= 150,000 \times (1+0.0775)^{-9}$	76,619
Total PV		152,367

- Calculate the present value at the end of year 1 using the market rate and the bonds contractual cash flows as follows:

		C
PV of C12,000 interest payable for 9 years (year 2 – 10)	$= \frac{12,000 \times [1-(1+0.076)^{-9}]}{0.076}$	76,226
PV of C150,000 payable in year 10	$= 150,000 \times (1+0.076)^{-9}$	77,585
Observed market value of liability		153,811

- Calculate change in fair value that is not attributable to the change in the benchmark interest rate:

	C
Observed market value of bond	153,811
PV of bond as calculated above	152,367
Change in fair value not attributable to changes in the observed benchmark rate	1,444

■ 确定折现率，用以将债券的合同现金流量折现为债券在第一年年末现值：

由于市场环境唯一相关的变动就是伦敦同业拆借利率在年末下降至4.75%，所以计算现值的折现率为7.75%（4.75% +3%）。

■ 用如上折现率以及债券的合同现金流量按以下方式计算第一年年末的现值：

		C
9年（第2年至第10年）应付利息C12,000的现值 =	$\frac{12,000 \times [1-(1+0.0775)^{-9}]}{0.0775}$	75,748
第10年应付款项C150,000的现值 =	$150,000 \times (1+0.0775)^{-9}$	76,619
现值合计		152,367

■ 用市场利率以及债券的合同现金流量按以下方式计算第一年年末的现值：

		C
9年（第2年至第10年）应付利息C12,000的现值 =	$\frac{12,000 \times [1-(1+0.076)^{-9}]}{0.076}$	76,226
第10年应付款项C150,000的现值 =	$150,000 \times (1+0.076)^{-9}$	77,585
可观察的负债市场价值		153,811

■ 计算并非由于基准利率的变动导致的公允价值变化：

	C
可观察的债券市场价值	153,811
如上述计算的债券现值	152,367
并非由于基准利率的变动导致的公允价值变化	1,444

The change in fair value not attributable to changes in the observed benchmark rate is a reasonably proxy for the change in fair value that is attributable to changes in the liability's credit risk, since the difference in present values calculated at 7.75% and 7.6% is assumed to reflect changes in the instrument's credit risk. Thus, the amount to be disclosed is C1,444. [IFRS 7 para IG 11].

11.52 Where an entity discloses the information required by the first bullet point in paragraph 11.50 above, it should also disclose the methods used to comply with the disclosure requirements. However, where the entity believes that the disclosure it has given to comply with the requirements does not faithfully represent the change in the fair value of the financial liability attributable to changes in its credit risk, it should disclose the reasons and the factors it believes are relevant are relevant in reaching that conclusion. [IFRS 7 para 11].

[The next paragraph is 11.54.]

Other sundry balance sheet disclosure

Re-classification

11.54 If the entity has re-classified a financial asset (in accordance with paras 51 – 54 of IAS 39) as one measured:

- at cost or amortised cost, rather than at fair value; or
- at fair value, rather than at cost or amortised cost,

it should disclose the amount re-classified into and out of each category and the reason for that re-classification (see chapter 6). [IFRS 7 para 12].

11.54.1 In addition to the disclosure required by the previous paragraph, if the entity has taken advantage of the amendment to IAS 39 issued in October 2008 (see chapter 6) and has reclassified a financial asset out of the fair value through profit or loss category (in accordance with paras 50B or 50D of IAS 39) or out of the available-for-sale category (in accordance with para 50E of IAS 39), it should disclose the following:

并非由于可观察的基准利率变动导致的公允价值变动是由于负债的信用风险变动导致的公允价值变动的合理替代，因为假定按照 7.75% 所计算的现值与按照 7.6% 所计算的现值之间的差额反映了工具信用风险的变化。因此，所披露的金额为 C1,444 元。[IFRS 7 IG 第 11 段]。

11.52 当主体披露上文第 11.50 段第一点所要求的信息时，它还应披露为遵循披露要求而采用的方法。但是，如果主体认为为遵循要求而作的披露不能真实地反映由于金融负债信用风险变动导致的公允价值变动，则应披露主体认为得出此结论相关的原因及因素。[IFRS 7 第 11 段]。

[下一段为第 11.54 段。]

其他各种资产负债表披露

重分类

11.54 如果主体将一项金融资产（根据 IAS 39 第 51 ~ 54 段规定）重分类为以下述方法计量的金融资产：

- 以成本或摊余成本而不是公允价值计量；或
- 以公允价值而不是成本或摊余成本计量，

则其应披露重分类至和转出每类金融资产的金额以及重分类的原因（参见第 6 章）。[IFRS 7 第 12 段]。

11.54.1 除了上段所要求的披露以外，如果主体利用了于 2008 年 10 月发布的对 IAS 39 的修订（参见第 6 章）并将某一金融资产从以公允价值计量且变动计入损益类别（根据 IAS 39 第 50B 或 50D 段）或可供出售类别（根据 IAS 39 第 50E 段）重分类转出，则其应披露如下信息：

- The amount reclassified into and out of each category.
- For each reporting period until derecognition, the carrying amounts and fair values of all financial assets that have been reclassified in the current and previous reporting periods.
- If a financial asset was reclassified in accordance with paragraph 50B of IAS 39, the rare situation, and the facts and circumstances indicating that the situation was rare.
- For the reporting period when the financial asset was reclassified, the fair value gain or loss on the financial asset recognised in profit or loss or other comprehensive income in that reporting period and in the previous reporting period.
- For each reporting period following the reclassification (including the reporting period in which the financial asset was reclassified) until derecognition of the financial asset, the fair value gain or loss that would have been recognised in profit or loss or other comprehensive income if the financial asset had not been reclassified, and the gain, loss, income and expense recognised in profit or loss.
- The effective interest rate and estimated amounts of cash flows the entity expects to recover, as at the date of reclassification of the financial asset.

[IFRS 7 para 12A].

11.54.2 An example of some of this disclosure is provided in the following table.

Table 11.3.1 – Financial assets reclassified from held for trading category in rare circumstances

Royal Bank of Scotland Plc – 2008 annual report Note 11 – Page 208

As discussed in accounting policies, during 2008 the Group reclassified financial assets from the held-for-trading and available-for-sale categories into the loans and receivables category (as permitted by paragraph 50D of IAS 39 as amended) and from the held-for-trading category into the available-for-sale category (as permitted by paragraph 50B of IAS 39 as amended).

The turbulence in the financial markets during the second half of 2008 was regarded by management as rare circumstances in the context of paragraph 50B of IAS 39 as amended.

■ 重分类至或转出每个类别的金额。

■ 在终止确认前的每个报告期间，在当前和之前报告期间重分类的所有金融资产的账面金额和公允价值。

■ 如果按照 IAS 39 第 50B 段对一项金融资产进行了重分类，该罕见情况以及表明该情况为罕见的事实和情况。

■ 对于金融资产被重分类的报告期间，该金融资产在该报告期间和之前报告期间在损益或其他综合收益确认的公允价值利得或损失。

■ 在该金融资产重分类日到终止确认的每个报告期间（包括金融资产被重分类的报告期间），若该金融资产未被重分类应在损益或其他综合收益确认的公允价值利得或损失，以及在损益中所确认的利得、损失、收益和费用。

■ 在金融资产被重分类之日的实际利率以及主体预期收回的现金流量的估计金额。

[IFRS 7 第 12A 段]。

11.54.2 如下表格中列出了某些披露的示例。

表 11.3.1——在罕见情况下从为交易而持有类别中重分类出去的金融资产

Royal Bank of Scotland Plc——2008 年年报附注 11——第 208 页

如在会计政策中所述，本集团在 2008 年将金融资产从为交易而持有和可供出售的类别重分类至贷款或应收款项类别（如修订的 IAS 39 第 50D 段所允许的），并从为交易而持有类别重分类至可供出售类别（如修订的 IAS 39 第 50B 段所允许的）。

管理层将 2008 年下半年金融市场的动荡视为符合修订的 IAS 39 第 50B 段所述的罕见情况。

The balance sheet values of these assets, the effect of the reclassification on the income statement for the period from the date of reclassification to 31 December 2008 and the gains and losses relating to these assets recorded in the income statement for the years ended 31 December 2008, 2007 and 2006 were as follows:

							2008				2007	2006
	2008 – on reclassification			**31 December 2008**			**After reclassification**					
	Carrying value	**Effective interest rate**	**Expected cash flows**	**Carrying value**	**Fair value**	**Gains/(losses) up to the date of reclassification**	**Income**	**Impairment losses**	**Gains/(losses) in AFS reserves**	**Amount that would have been recognised**	Gains/(losses) recognised in the income statement in prior periods	
	£m	**%**	**£m**	**£m**	**£m**	**£m**	**£m**	**£m**	**£m**	**£m**	£m	£m
Reclassified from HFT to LAR:												
Loans:												
Leveraged finance	**3,602**	**10.15**	**6,083**	**4,304**	**2,523**	**(457)**	**454**	**—**		**(1,206)**	(155)	—
Corporate loans	**5,040**	**6.19**	**7,582**	**5,827**	**4,940**	**(76)**	**198**	**—**		**(681)**	(50)	3
	8,642		**13,665**	**10,131**	**7,463**	**(533)**	**652**	**—**		**(1,887)**	(205)	3
Debt securities:												
CDO of RMBS	**215**	**4.92**	**259**	**236**	**221**	**4**	**5**	**—**		**(11)**	5	6
RMBS	**1,765**	**6.05**	**2,136**	**2,011**	**1,536**	**(115)**	**157**	**—**		**(302)**	(12)	—
CMBS	**1**	**11.11**	**4**	**1**	**1**	**1**	**—**	**—**		**—**	—	—
CLOs	**835**	**6.34**	**1,141**	**952**	**717**	**(22)**	**104**	**—**		**(130)**	(14)	(2)
Other ABS	**2,203**	**5.07**	**3,202**	**2,514**	**2,028**	**(67)**	**129**	**—**		**(338)**	3	(1)
Other	**2,538**	**2.62**	**2,764**	**2,602**	**2,388**	**72**	**3**	**—**		**(166)**	94	476
	7,557		**9,506**	**8,316**	**6,891**	**(127)**	**398**	**—**		**(947)**	76	479
Total	**16,199**		**23,171**	**18,447**	**14,354**	**(660)**	**1,050**	**—**		**(2,834)**	(129)	482

这些资产的账面价值、该重分类对从重分类日到2008年12月31日止期间利润表的影响，以及与这些资产相关的确认在2008年、2007年和2006年各年度利润表中的利得和损失列示如下：

	2008年 – 重分类时			2008年12月31日		2008					2007	2006
							重分类后					
	账面价值	实际利率	预计现金流量	账面价值	公允价值	截止重分类日的利得/(损失)	收益	减值损失	可供出售准备中的利得/(损失)	若未重分类已确认的金额	之前期间利润表中所确认的利得/(损失)	
	百万英镑	%	百万英镑	百万英镑	百万英镑	百万英镑	百万英镑	百万英镑	百万英镑	百万英镑	百万英镑	百万英镑
从为交易而持有重分类至贷款或应收款项：												
贷款：												
杠杆融资	3,602	10.15	6,083	4,304	2,523	(457)	454	—		(1,206)	(155)	—
公司贷款	5,040	6.19	7,582	5,827	4,940	(76)	198	—		(681)	(50)	3
	8,642		13,665	10,131	7,463	(533)	652	—		(1,887)	(205)	3
债权证券：												
住宅房贷担保证券的担保债务凭证	215	4.92	259	236	221	4	5	—		(11)	5	6
住宅房贷担保证券	1,765	6.05	2,136	2,011	1,536	(115)	157	—		(302)	(12)	—
商业房地产抵押贷款支持证券	1	11.11	4	1	1	1	—	—		—	—	—
担保贷款凭证	835	6.34	1,141	952	717	(22)	104	—		(130)	(14)	(2)
其他资产支持证券	2,203	5.07	3,202	2,514	2,028	(67)	129	—		(338)	3	(1)
其他	2,538	2.62	2,764	2,602	2,388	72	3	—		(166)	94	476
	7,557		9,506	8,316	6,891	(127)	398	—		(947)	76	479
合计	16,199		23,171	18,447	14,354	(660)	1,050	—		(2,834)	(129)	482

Con.

Reclassified from HFT to AFS:												
Debt securities:												
CDO of RMBS	6,228	8.14	8,822	5,695	5,695	(1,330)	1,147	(464)	(1,069)	(280)	(400)	—
RMBS	5,205	8.03	8,890	5,171	5,171	(530)	24	—	(162)	(122)	(4)	73
CMBS	32	6.81	85	31	31	(5)	5	—	(3)	2	(4)	—
CLOs	1,457	5.02	1,804	1,288	1,288	(168)	421		(383)	58	(36)	1
Other ABS	2,199	6.02	3,183	1,847	1,847	(356)	(10)	—	(354)	(311)	(42)	72
Other	614	12.55	1,311	698	698	—	130	—	(166)	(5)	(1)	—
	15,735		24,095	14,730	14,730	(2,389)	1,717	(464)	(2,137)	(658)	(487)	146
Reclassified from AFS to LAR:												
Debt securities	704	1.38	772	1,028	968	(12)[1]	6	—	—	(37)[1]	—	—
Total	32,638		48,038	34,205	30,052	(3,061)	2,773	(464)	(2,137)	(3,529)	(616)	628

Note:

[1] Gains/(losses) recognised in the available-for-sale reserve

Amounts included in the consolidated income statement:

	Group		
	2008	2007	2006
	£m	£m	£m
Gains on financial assets/liabilities designated as at fair value through profit or loss	**(901)**	1,074	573
Gains on disposal or settlement of loans and receivables	**4**	3	21

On the initial recognition of financial assets and liabilities valued using valuation techniques incorporating information other than observable market data, any difference between the transaction price and that derived from the valuation technique is deferred. Such amounts are recognised in profit or loss over the life of the transaction; when market data become observable; or when the transaction matures or is closed out as appropriate. At 31 December 2008, net gains of £102 million (2007 – £72 million) were carried forward in the balance sheet. During the year net gains of £89 million (2007 – £67 million) were deferred and £65 million (2007 – £10 million) released to profit or loss.

续表

从为交易而持有重分类至可供出售：												
债权证券：												
住宅房贷担保证券的担保债务凭证	6,228	8.14	8,822	5,695	5,695	(1,330)	1,147	(464)	(1,069)	(280)	(400)	—
担保债务凭证	5,205	8.03	8,890	5,171	5,171	(530)	24	—	(162)	(122)	(4)	73
商业房地产抵押贷款支持证券	32	6.81	85	31	31	(5)	5	—	(3)	2	(4)	—
担保贷款凭证	1,457	5.02	1,804	1,288	1,288	(168)	421		(383)	58	(36)	1
其他资产支持证券	2,199	6.02	3,183	1,847	1,847	(356)	(10)	—	(354)	(311)	(42)	72
其他	614	12.55	1,311	698	698	—	130	—	(166)	(5)	(1)	—
	15,735		24,095	14,730	14,730	(2,389)	1,717	(464)	(2,137)	(658)	(487)	146
从可供出售重分类至贷款或应收款项：												
债权证券	704	1.38	772	1,028	968	(12)[1]	6	—	—	(37)[1]	—	—
合计	32,638		48,038	34,205	30,052	(3,061)	2,773	(464)	(2,137)	(3,529)	(616)	628

注：

[1] 在可供出售准备中确认的利得/(损失)

包括在合并利润表中的金额：

	集团		
	2008	2007	2006
	百万英镑	百万英镑	百万英镑
指定为以公允价值计量且变动计入损益的金融资产/负债的利得	**(901)**	1,074	573
贷款或应收款项的处置或清偿利得	**4**	3	21

在对金融资产和负债进行初始确认时，使用了包含可观察市场数据以外的其他信息的估值技术进行估值，交易价格和使用估值技术所得的价值之间的差异被递延。此金额将在交易的存续期内，当市场数据可观察时或在交易到期或结算时适当地确认为损益。2008 年 12 月 31 日，资产负债表中结转至后期的净利得为 1.02 亿英镑（2007 年 - 7,200 万英镑）。在该年度递延了 8,900 万英镑的净利得（2007 年 - 6,700 万英镑）并向损益中释放了 6,500 万英镑（2007 年 - 1,000 万英镑）。

Derecognition

11.55 An entity may have transferred financial assets in such a way that part or all of the financial assets do not qualify for derecognition (see chapter 8). In that situation, the entity should disclose for each class of such financial assets:

- The nature of the assets.
- The nature of the risks and rewards of ownership to which the entity remains exposed.
- When the entity continues to recognise all of the assets, the carrying amounts of the assets and of the associated liabilities.
- When the entity continues to recognise the assets to the extent of its continuing involvement, the total carrying amount of the original assets, the amount of the assets that the entity continues to recognise and the carrying amount of the associated liabilities.

[IFRS 7 para 13].

Table 11.3.2 – Disclosure in respect of assets transferred but not derecognised

Daimler AG – Annual report – 31 December 2009

13. Receivables from financial services (extract)

Sale of receivables. Based on market conditions and liquidity needs, Daimler may sell portfolios of retail and wholesale receivables to third parties (i. e. special purpose entities). At the time of the sale, Daimler determines whether the legally transferred receivables meet the criteria for derecognition in conformity with the appropriate provisions. If the criteria are not met, the receivables continue to be recognized in the Group's consolidated statement of financial position.

As of December 31, 2009, the carrying amount of receivables from financial services sold but not derecognized for accounting purposes amounted to €1,006 million (2008: €697 million). The associated risks and rewards are similar to those with respect to receivables from financial services that have not been transferred. For information on the related total liabilities associated with these receivables sold but not derecognized, see Note 23.

终止确认

11.55　主体可能以某种方式转让了金融资产，但部分或全部金融资产不符合终止确认的条件（参见第8章）。在这种情况下，对每类这样的金融资产，主体应当披露：

- 资产的性质。
- 主体仍保留的与所有权相关的风险和报酬的性质。
- 在主体仍继续确认全部资产的情况下，资产及相关负债的账面金额。
- 在主体按照继续涉入程度继续确认资产的情况下，原来资产的账面金额总额、主体继续确认的资产金额以及相关负债的账面金额。

[IFRS 7 第13段]。

表11.3.2——转让但未终止确认的资产的相关披露

Daimler AG——年报——2009年12月31日

13. 金融服务应收款（节选）

出售应收款。根据市场条件和流动性需求，Daimler可能将零售或批发应收款组合出售给第三方（如特殊目的实体）。在出售时，Daimler根据相关的要求确定法定转让的应收款是否满足终止确认的条件。如果未满足该条件，则应收款将继续确认在本集团的合并财务状况表中。

于2009年12月31日，为会计目的已出售但未终止确认的应收款的账面金额为10.06亿欧元（2008年：6.97亿欧元）。其相关的风险和报酬与那些未转让的应收款类似。有关已出售但未终止确认应收款相关的负债总额的信息，参见附注23。

Con.

17. Trade receivables (extract)

Sale of receivables. Based on market conditions and liquidity needs, Daimler may sell portfolios of trade receivables to third parties. At the time of the sale, Daimler determines whether the legally transferred receivables meet the criteria for derecognition in conformity with the appropriate provisions. If the criteria are not met, the receivables continue to be recognized in the Group's consolidated statement of financial position.

As of December 31, 2009, the carrying amount of trade receivables sold, but not derecognized for accounting purposes amounted to €38 million (2008: €67 million). For information on the liabilities related to sold but not derecognized receivables, see Note 23.

23. Financing liabilities (extract)

Based on market conditions and liquidity needs, Daimler may sell certain receivables and future lease payments resulting from equipment on operating leases to third parties. As of December 31, 2009, relating to these transactions, liabilities of €1,330 million (2008: €764 million) are accounted for as secured borrowings. The respective liabilities are reported under liabilities from ABS transactions in the amount of €1,292 million (2008: €697 million) and under liabilities to financial institutions in the amount of €38 million (2008: €66 million). In 2008, €1 million was reported under loans, other financing liabilities.

Collateral

11.56 An entity should disclose:

- The carrying amount of financial assets it has pledged as collateral for liabilities or contingent liabilities, including amounts that have been re-classified in circumstances where the transferee has the right to sell or pledge the transferred asset. [IAS 39 para 37(a)].

- The terms and conditions relating to its pledge. [IFRS 7 para 14].

11.57 When an entity holds collateral (of financial or non-financial assets) and is permitted to sell or repledge it in the absence of default by the owner of the collateral, it should disclose:

- The fair value of the collateral held.

续表

17. 应收账款（节选）

出售应收款。根据市场条件和流动性需求，Daimler 可能将应收账款组合出售给第三方。在出售时，Daimler 根据相关的要求确定法定转让的应收款是否满足终止确认的条件。如果未满足该条件，则应收款将继续确认在本集团的合并财务状况表中。

于 2009 年 12 月 31 日，为会计目的已出售但未终止确认的应收账款的账面金额为 3,800 万欧元（2008 年：6,700 万欧元）。有关已出售但未终止确认应收款相关的负债的信息，参见附注 23。

23. 金融负债（节选）

根据市场条件和流动性需求，Daimler 可能将某些应收款和设备经营租赁的未来租赁款出售给第三方。于 2009 年 12 月 31 日，与这些交易相关的、金额为 13.30 亿欧元的负债作为担保借款核算。该负债中金额为 12.92 亿欧元（2008 年：6.97 亿欧元）列报于资产支持证券交易的负债中，金额为 3,800 万欧元（2008 年：6,600 万欧元）列报于对金融机构的负债中。在 2008 年，还有 100 万欧元列报于贷款、其他金融负债中。

抵押物

11.56　主体应当披露：

- 作为负债或或有负债的抵押物的金融资产的账面金额，包括在受让人有权出售或抵押被转让资产的情况下已进行重分类的金额。[IAS 39 第 37（a）段]。

- 与该项抵押相关的条款和条件。[IFRS 7 第 14 段]。

11.57　当主体持有抵押物（金融资产或非金融资产），且可以在抵押物的所有人没有违约的情况下出售或再次抵押这些抵押物时，主体应当披露：

- 所持有抵押物的公允价值。

- The fair value of any such collateral sold or repledged, and whether the entity has an obligation to return it.

- The terms and conditions associated with its use of the collateral.

[IFRS 7 para 15].

11.58 An example of how an entity has disclosed the necessary information about assets pledged and held as collateral is given in Table 11.3.3 below.

Table 11.3.3 – Assets pledged and held as collateral

Deutsche Bank AG – Annual Report – 31 December 2009

[20] Assets Pledged and Received as Collateral

The Group pledges assets primarily for repurchase agreements and securities borrowing agreements which are generally conducted under terms that are usual and customary to standard securitized borrowing contracts. In addition the Group pledges collateral against other borrowing arrangements and for margining purposes on OTC derivative liabilities. The carrying value of the Group's assets pledged as collateral for liabilities or contingent liabilities is as follows.

in €m.	**Dec 31, 2009**	**Dec 31, 2008**[1]
Interest-earning deposits with banks	59	69
Financial assets at fair value through profit or loss	88,663	81,555
Financial assets available for sale	558	517
Loans	19,537	22,534
Other[2]	56	24
Total	**108,873**	**104,699**

[1] Prior year amounts have been adjusted.

[2] Includes Property and equipment pledged as collateral in 2007.

Assets transferred where the transferee has the right to sell or repledge are disclosed on the face of the balance sheet. As of December 31, 2009, and December 31, 2008, these amounts were €80 billion and €69 billion, respectively.

As of December 31, 2009, and December 31, 2008, the Group had received collateral with a fair value of €225 billion and €255 billion, respectively, arising from securities purchased under reverse repurchase agreements, securities borrowed, derivatives transactions,

■ 已出售或再次抵押的抵押物的公允价值，以及主体是否承担将其退回的义务。

■ 与抵押物的使用相关的条款和条件。

[IFRS 7 第 15 段]。

11.58　下表 11.3.3 中给出了主体如何披露有关已抵押和作为抵押物持有的资产必要信息的示例。

表 11.3.3——已抵押和作为抵押物持有的资产

Deutsche Bank AG——年报—— 2009 年 12 月 31 日

[20]——已抵押和获取的抵押物资产

本集团主要为那些根据标准担保借款合同的常规和惯例性条款而签署的回购协议和证券融入协议进行资产抵押。此外，本集团还会为其他借款协议以及柜台交易的衍生工具负债保证金提供抵押物。作为负债或或有负债的抵押物的集团资产账面金额如下。

百万欧元	**2009 年 12 月 31 日**	**2008 年 12 月 31 日[1]**
计息的银行存款	59	69
以公允价值计量且变动		
计入损益的金融资产	88,663	81,555
可供出售的金融资产	558	517
贷款	19,537	22,534
其他[2]	56	24
合计	**108,873**	**104,699**

[1] 以前年度的金额已作调整。

[2] 包括 2007 年被作为抵押物的不动产和设备。

受让人有权出售或再次抵押的被转让资产在资产负债表的主表中披露。在 2009 年 12 月 31 日和 2008 年 12 月 31 日，其金额分别为 800 亿欧元和 690 亿欧元。

于 2009 年 12 月 31 日和 2008 年 12 月 31 日，本集团获取的抵押物公允价值分别为 2,250亿欧元和 2,550 亿欧元，这些抵押物源于买入反售协议所购买的证券、融入证券、衍生工具交易、客户保证金贷款和其他交易。这些交易一般都是在标准的融券活动

Con.

customer margin loans and other transactions. These transactions were generally conducted under terms that are usual and customary for standard secured lending activities and the other transactions described. The Group, as the secured party, has the right to sell or repledge such collateral, subject to the Group returning equivalent securities upon completion of the transaction. As of December 31, 2009, and 2008, the Group had resold or repledged €200 billion and €232 billion, respectively. This was primarily to cover short sales, securities loaned and securities sold under repurchase agreements.

Allowance amount for credit losses

11.59 When financial assets are impaired by credit losses and the entity records the impairment in a separate account (for example, an allowance account used to record individual impairments or a similar account used to record a collective impairment of assets) rather than directly reducing the asset's carrying amount, it should disclose a reconciliation of changes in that account during the period for each class of financial assets. [IFRS 7 para 16].

Compound financial instruments with multiple embedded derivatives

11.60 If an entity has issued an instrument that contains both a liability and an equity component (see chapter 7) and the instrument has multiple embedded derivatives whose values are interdependent (such as a callable convertible debt instrument), it should disclose the existence of those features. [IFRS 7 para 17].

Defaults and breaches

11.61 An entity is required to disclose information on defaults and breaches of loans payable (that is, financial liabilities other than short-term trade payables on normal credit terms) and other loan agreements. Such disclosures provide relevant information about the entity's creditworthiness and its prospects for obtaining future loans. Any defaults or breaches may affect the liability's classification as current or non-current in accordance with IAS 1 (see para 11.9 above) and may also require disclosure if the liability is considered as capital by the entity's management. [IAS

续表

和其他上述所提及交易的常规和惯例性条款下所进行的。本集团作为被担保方,在本集团交易完成时返还等价证券的情况下,有权出售或再次抵押这些抵押物。于 2009 年 12 月 31 日及 2008 年 12 月 31 日,本集团再次出售或再次抵押的金额分别为 2,000 亿欧元和 2,320 亿欧元。这主要是为了卖空、融出的证券以及按照回购协议出售证券。

信用损失备抵金额

11.59　在金融资产因信用风险而发生减值且主体用单独的账户（例如用来记录单项减值的备抵账户或用来记录资产总体减值的类似账户）记录减值金额，而不是直接减少资产的账面金额的情况下，对于每类金融资产，主体应披露本期该账户变动的调节表。[IFRS 7 第 16 段]。

具有多重嵌入衍生工具的复合金融工具

11.60　如果某主体发行了一项既包括负债部分又包括权益部分的工具（参见第 7 章），而该工具具有价值相互关联的多重嵌入衍生工具（例如可赎回的可转换债务工具），则主体应当披露这些特征的存在。[IFRS 7 第 17 段]。

拖欠和违约

11.61　主体被要求披露有关应付贷款（即，除基于正常信用条款的短期贸易应付款之外的金融负债）及其他贷款协议的拖欠和违约信息。这种披露提供了有关主体的信誉以及其获取未来贷款的前景的相关信息。任何拖欠或违约行为均可能会影响负债根据 IAS 1 所作的流动或非流动分类（参见上文第 11.9 段）；如果管理层将该负债视为资本，也会要求额外披露。[IAS 1 第 135（e）段]。

1 para 135(e)].

11.62 For loans payable recognised at the reporting date, an entity should disclose:

- Details of any defaults during the period of principal, interest, sinking fund, or redemption terms of those loans payable.
- The carrying amount of the loans payable in default at the reporting date.
- Whether the default was remedied, or the terms of the loans payable were renegotiated, before the financial statements were authorised for issue.

[IFRS 7 para 18].

11.63 If, during the period, there were breaches of loan agreement terms other than those described in the above paragraph, an entity should disclose the same information as above if those breaches permitted the lender to demand accelerated repayment, unless the breaches were remedied, or the loan's terms were renegotiated, on or before the reporting date. [IFRS 7 para 19].

11.63.1 The above requirements would apply if the terms were renegotiated after the balance sheet date but before the signing of the financial statements. However, the disclosure need not include short-term trade payables on normal credit terms as these do not meet the definition in the standard of loans payable. [IFRS 7 App A].

Income statement and equity disclosures

Items of income, expense, gains or losses

11.64 An entity should disclose the following items of income, expense, gains or losses, either on the face of the financial statements or in the notes:

- Net gains or net losses on:
  - Financial assets or financial liabilities at fair value through profit or loss, showing separately those on financial assets or financial liabilities designated as such upon initial recognition and those on financial assets or financial liabilities that are classified as held-for-trading in accordance with IAS 39. Where these financial instruments accrue interest income or expense, the standard allows an accounting

11.62 对于在报告日确认的应付贷款，主体应当披露：

- 应付贷款的本金、利息、偿债基金或赎回条款在本期内发生拖欠的详细情况。
- 在报告日拖欠应付贷款的账面金额。
- 在财务报表批准报出之前，拖欠情况是否已得到补救，或者应付贷款的条款是否已重新商定。

[IFRS 7 第 18 段]。

11.63 如果本期内存在除上段已述情况之外的贷款协议条款的违约情况，且这种违约允许贷款人要求对贷款进行加速偿还，除非在报告日或之前违约情况已得到补救或贷款条款已重新商定，则主体应当披露与上述相同的信息。[IFRS 7 第 19 段]。

11.63.1 如果条款是在资产负债表日后但签署财务报表之前重新商定，则适用于上述要求。但是，该披露并不需要包括基于正常信用条款的短期应付贸易账款，因为它们不符合准则中应付贷款的定义。[IFRS 7 附录 A]。

利润表及权益的披露

收益、费用、利得或损失项目

11.64 主体应当在财务报表的主表或其附注中披露下述收益、费用、利得或损失项目：

- 下列金融工具的利得或损失净额：
  - 以公允价值计量且变动计入损益的金融资产或金融负债，分别披露初始确认时指定为以公允价值计量且变动计入损益的金融资产或金融负债和根据 IAS 39 划分为为交易而持有的金融资产或金融负债。在这些金融工具会产生利息收入或费用的情况下，该准则允许在如何对其进行披露方面选择会计政策。利息收入、利息费用和股利收入可以作为这些金融工

policy choice on how to disclose these. The interest income, interest expense and dividend income can be reported as part of net gains or net losses on these financial instruments or can be disclosed separately as part of interest income and expenses. [IFRS 7 App B5(e)]. In addition, it is possible to adopt one treatment for interest income and expense and a different treatment for dividend income as no such prohibition exists in IFRS 7. However, different treatments cannot be adopted for interest income and interest expense.

Note that if the dividend income is significant, regardless of how it is disclosed here, it will also need to be disclosed separately in the notes. [IAS 18 para 35(b)(v)].

- Available-for-sale financial assets, showing separately the amount of gain or loss recognised directly in other comprehensive income during the period and the amount reclassified from equity and recognised in profit or loss for the period.
- Held-to-maturity investments.
- Loans and receivables.
- Financial liabilities measured at amortised cost.

- Total interest income and total interest expense (calculated using the effective interest method) for financial assets or financial liabilities that are not at fair value through profit or loss.
- Fee income and expense (other than amounts included in determining the effective interest rate) arising from:
  - Financial assets or financial liabilities that are not at fair value through profit or loss.
  - Trust and other fiduciary activities that result in the holding or investing of assets on behalf of individuals, trusts, retirement benefit plans and other institutions.
- Interest income on impaired financial assets accrued in accordance with paragraph AG93 of IAS 39, which requires an entity to continue to recognise interest income using the rate of interest used to discount the future cash flows for the purposes of measuring the impairment loss (see chapter 9).

具利得净额或损失净额的一部分列报，也可以单独作为利息收入和费用的一部分披露。[IFRS 7 附录 B5（e）]。此外，IFRS 7 并未禁止对利息收入和费用选择一种处理方法而对股利收入选择另一种处理方法。但是，不能对利息收入和利息费用采用不同的处理方法。

值得注意的是如果股利收入很重大，无论在此采用何种披露方法，都需要在附注中单独披露。[IAS 18 第 35（b）（v）段]。

- 可供出售的金融资产，分别披露本期确认为其他综合收益的和本期从权益重分类转入损益的利得或损失的金额。

- 持有至到期的投资。
- 贷款和应收款项。
- 以摊余成本计量的金融负债。

■ 对于不是以公允价值计量且变动计入损益的金融资产或金融负债，其利息收入总额和利息费用总额（使用实际利率法计算）。

■ 下列事项所产生的手续费收入和费用（不含计算实际利率时所包括的金额）：

- 不是以公允价值计量且变动计入损益的金融资产或金融负债。

- 信托或其他托管活动，这些活动导致主体代表个人、信托人、退休福利计划和其他机构持有资产或进行资产投资。

■ 主体按照 IAS 39 AG 第 93 段计提的已减值金融资产的利息收入，该段要求主体采用将未来现金流量折现以计量减值损失时所用的利率来继续确认利息收入（参见第 9 章）。

■ The amount of any impairment loss for each class of financial asset.

[IFRS 7 para 20].

11.65 Certain of the disclosure requirements described above are illustrated in Table 11.4.

Table 11.4 – Items of income, expense, gains or losses
EADS N. V. – Annual Report – 31 December 2009
35. Information about financial instruments (extract)
E) NET GAINS OR LOSSES

EADS net gains or (losses) recognised in profit or loss in 2009 and 2008 respectively are as follows:

(in €m)	**2009**	2008
Financial assets or financial liabilities at fair value through profit or loss:		
> Held for trading	**(100)**	(149)
> Designated on initial recognition	**12**	64
Available-for-sale-financial assets:		
> Result before taxes removed from OCI and recognised in profit or loss	**0**	6
Net income from equity securities	**133**	313
Loans and receivables	**(179)**	(160)
Financial liabilities measured at amortised cost	**83**	79

Interest income from financial assets or financial liabilities through profit or loss is included in net gains and losses.

Net gains and losses of loans and receivables contain among others results from currency adjustments from foreign operations and impairment losses.

The following net gains and (losses) are recognised directly in equity in 2009 and 2008:

(in €m)	**2009**	2008
Available-for-sale-financial assets:		
> Unrealised net gains and (losses) recognised directly in OCI	**162**	6

F) TOTAL INTEREST INCOME AND TOTAL INTEREST EXPENSES

In 2009, the total interest income amounts to €344 million for financial assets which are not measured at fair value through profit or loss. For financial liabilities which are not measured at fair value through profit or loss € –503 million are recognised as total interest expenses. Both amounts are calculated by using the effective interest method.

■ 每类金融资产的减值损失金额。

[IFRS 7 第 20 段]。

11.65　表 11.4 中举例说明了上文所述的某些披露要求。

表 11.4——收益、费用、利得或损失项目
EADS N. V. ——年报——2009 年 12 月 31 日
35. 金融工具相关信息（节选）
E）利得或损失净额

EADS 分别于 2009 年和 2008 年确认在损益中的利得或损失净额如下：

(百万欧元)	**2009**	2008
以公允价值计量且变动计入损益的金融资产或金融负债：		
＞为交易而持有	**(100)**	(149)
＞初始确认时指定	**12**	64
可供出售的金融资产：		
＞从其他综合收益中转出并确认为		
损益的税前结果	**0**	6
权益证券净收益	**133**	313
贷款和应收款项	**(179)**	(160)
按摊余成本计量的金融负债	**83**	79

以公允价值计量且变动计入损益的金融资产或金融负债的利息收入包括在利得和损失净额中。

贷款和应收款项的利得和损失净额中包含境外经营外币调整的结果和减值损失等项。

以下利得和（损失）净额于 2009 年和 2008 年直接确认为权益：

(百万欧元)	**2009**	2008
可供出售的金融资产：		
＞直接确认为其他综合收益的		
未实现利得和（损失）净额	**162**	6

F）利息收入总额和利息费用总额

2009 年度，非以公允价值计量且变动计入损益的金融资产的利息收入总额为 3.44 亿欧元。非以公允价值计量且变动计入损益的金融负债的利息费用总额为负 5.03 亿欧元。两个金额都是采用实际利率法计算得出的。

G) IMPAIRMENT LOSSES

The following impairment losses on financial assets are recognised in profit or loss in 2009 and 2008 respectively:

(in €m)	**2009**	2008
Available-for-sale financial assets	**(12)**	(23)
Loans and receivables	**(76)**	(114)
Other[1]	**(3)**	(36)
Total	**(91)**	(173)

[1] Concerns finance lease receivables.

Other disclosures

Accounting policies

11.66 IAS 1 requires an entity to disclose, in the summary of significant accounting policies, the measurement basis (or bases) used in preparing the financial statements and the other accounting policies used that are relevant to an understanding of the financial statements. [IAS 1 para 108; IFRS 7 para 21]. For financial instruments such disclosure may include:

- For financial assets or financial liabilities designated as at fair value through profit or loss:
  - The nature of the financial assets or financial liabilities the entity has designated as at fair value through profit or loss.
  - The criteria for so designating such financial assets or financial liabilities on initial recognition.
  - How the entity has satisfied the conditions for such designation, including, where appropriate, a narrative description of the circumstances underlying the

G）减值损失

以下金融资产的减值损失分别于2009年和2008年确认为损益：

（百万欧元）	**2009**	**2008**
可供出售的金融资产	**（12）**	（23）
贷款和应收款项	**（76）**	（114）
其他[(1)]	**（3）**	（36）
总计	**（91）**	（173）

(1) 指融资租赁应收款。

其他披露

会计政策

11.66　IAS 1要求主体在重要会计政策概述中披露其编制财务报表时所采用的计量基础和运用的与理解财务报表相关的其他会计政策。[IAS 1第108段；IFRS 7第21段]。就金融工具而言，这些披露可能包括：

- 对指定为以公允价值计量且变动计入损益的金融资产或金融负债而言：
  - 主体指定为以公允价值计量且变动计入损益的金融资产或金融负债的性质。
  - 在初始确认时，指定这些金融资产或金融负债的标准。
  - 主体如何满足这些指定的适用条件，包括例如对导致计量或确认不一致出现的情况所作的简要描述，或对以公允价值计量且变动计入损益的指

measurement or recognition inconsistency that would otherwise arise, or how designation at fair value through profit or loss is consistent with the entity's documented risk management or investment strategy.

- The criteria for designating financial assets as available for sale.
- Whether regular way purchases and sales of financial assets are accounted for at trade date or at settlement date (see chapter 9).
- When an allowance account is used to reduce the carrying amount of financial assets impaired by credit losses:
  - The criteria for determining when the carrying amount of impaired financial assets is reduced directly (or, in the case of a reversal of a write-down, increased directly) and when the allowance account is used.
  - The criteria for writing off amounts charged to the allowance account against the carrying amount of impaired financial assets.
- How net gains or net losses on each category of financial instrument are determined, for example, whether the net gains or net losses on items at fair value through profit or loss include interest or dividend income.
- The criteria the entity uses to determine that there is objective evidence that an impairment loss has occurred.
- When the terms of financial assets that would otherwise be past due or impaired have been renegotiated, the accounting policy for financial assets that are the subject of renegotiated terms.

[IFRS 7 App B para 5].

11.67 IAS 1 also requires entities to disclose, in the summary of significant accounting policies or other notes, the judgements, apart from those involving estimations, that management has made in the process of applying the entity's accounting policies and that have the most significant effect on the amounts recognised in the financial statements. [IAS 1 para 122].

定是如何同主体书面记录的风险管理或投资策略保持一致的简要描述。

- 将金融资产指定为可供出售的标准。
- 金融资产的常规购买和出售是在交易日还是结算日进行会计处理（参见第9章）。
- 当使用备抵账户以减少由于信用损失而发生减值的金融资产账面金额时：
  - 用于确定何时直接减少（或者，对于减值损失转回，直接增加）发生减值的金融资产的账面金额，以及何时使用备抵账户的标准。
  - 从备抵账户冲销发生减值的金融资产账面金额的标准。
- 每种类别的金融工具的净利得或净损失是如何确定的，例如，以公允价值计量且变动计入损益项目的净利得或净损失是否包括利息或股利收入。
- 主体确定存在客观证明表明发生减值损失的标准。
- 本已逾期或发生减值的金融资产的条款被重新商定时，作为重新商定条款对象的金融资产的会计政策。

［IFRS 7 附录 B 第 5 段］。

11.67　除涉及的估计外，IAS 1 还要求对管理层在运用会计政策过程中所做的、对财务报表中确认的金额最具有重大影响的判断，主体应在重大会计政策概述或其他附注中进行披露。［IAS 1 第 122 段］。

Hedge accounting

11.68 An entity should disclose the following separately for each type of hedge described in IAS 39 (that is, fair value hedges, cash flow hedges and hedges of net investments in foreign operations).

- A description of each type of hedge.
- A description of the financial instruments designated as hedging instruments and their fair values at the reporting date.
- The nature of the risks being hedged.

[IFRS 7 para 22].

11.69 In addition, for cash flow hedges, an entity should disclose:

- The periods when the cash flows are expected to occur and when they are expected to affect profit or loss.
- A description of any forecast transaction for which hedge accounting had previously been used, but which is no longer expected to occur.
- The amount that was recognised in other comprehensive income during the period.
- The amount that was reclassified from equity and included in profit or loss for the period, showing the amount included in each line item in the income statement. This would also apply to hedging instruments with a short maturity that have been acquired and have matured within the same accounting period. As a practical expedient it is common for entities to recognise the gains and losses on such instruments directly in the income statement rather than to recognise the gains and losses initially in the hedging reserve and then recycle to the income statement. Although the accounting entries net off in the same accounting period, there should still be disclosure of the amounts that would have been recycled.
- The amount that was reclassified from equity during the period and included in the initial cost or other carrying amount of a non-financial asset or non-financial liability whose acquisition or incurrence was a hedged highly probable forecast

套期会计

11.68 对于 IAS 39 所述的每种类型的套期（即公允价值套期、现金流量套期和境外经营净投资套期），主体应当分别进行如下披露。

■ 每类套期的描述。

■ 被指定为套期工具的金融工具的描述及这些金融工具在报告日的公允价值。

■ 被套期风险的性质。

［IFRS 7 第 22 段］。

11.69 对于现金流量套期主体还应披露：

■ 预期将发生现金流量的期间以及预期其将影响损益的期间。

■ 对之前已使用了套期会计，但预期将不再发生的预期交易的描述。

■ 本期在其他综合收益中确认的金额。

■ 本期从权益中重分类转入损益中的金额，分别列示包括在利润表每个单列项目下的金额。这对于期限较短、在同一会计期间购买并到期的套期工具同样适用。作为实务中的权宜之计，主体常常会将这些工具的利得和损失直接在利润表中确认，而不是将其首先确认为套期准备而后再转出至利润表。虽然会计分录在同一会计期间可以相互抵销，但仍应该对本应转出的金额进行披露。

■ 本期从权益中重分类出来并计入非金融资产或非金融负债的初始成本或其他账面金额中的金额，这些非金融资产或非金融负债的取得或发生是一个很可能发生的、被套期的预期交易。

transaction.

[IFRS 7 para 23].

11.70 An entity should disclose separately:

- In fair value hedges, gains or losses on:
  - The hedging instrument.
  - The hedged item attributable to the hedged risk.

  The requirement here relates to the current reporting period only and not to a disclosure on a cumulative basis (since the inception of the hedge designation).

- The ineffectiveness recognised in profit or loss that arises from cash flow hedges.
- The ineffectiveness recognised in profit or loss that arises from hedges of net investments in foreign operations.

[IFRS 7 para 24].

11.71 Disclosure of information on fair value hedges, cash flow hedges and hedges of net investments is given in Table 11.5 below.

Table 11.5 – Income statement, hedge ineffectiveness, fair value hedges, amounts recycled from equity, interest

National Grid Plc – Annual Report – 31 March 2010

5. Finance income and costs

	2010 £m	2009 £m	2008 £m
Interest income and similar income			
Expected return on pension and other post-retirement benefit plan assets	981	1,236	1,064
Interest income on financial instruments:			
Interest income from bank deposits and other financial assets	18	60	209
Interest receivable on finance leases	–	1	2

［IFRS 7 第 23 段］。

11.70　主体应当单独披露：

- 在公允价值套期中的如下利得或损失：
  - 套期工具的利得或损失。
  - 由于被套期风险导致的被套期项目的利得或损失。

    此要求仅针对当前报告期间，与累计（自套期指定开始之时起）披露无关。

- 现金流量套期产生的、在损益中确认的无效套期部分。

- 境外经营净投资套期产生的在损益中确认的无效套期部分。

［IFRS 7 第 24 段］。

11.71　下表 11.5 中列举了公允价值套期、现金流量套期和净投资套期的信息披露。

表 11．5——利润表、套期无效性、公允价值套期、从权益中转出的金额、利息

National Grid Plc——年报——2010 年 3 月 31 日

5. 财务收入和成本

	2010	**2009**	**2008**
	百万英镑	**百万英镑**	**百万英镑**
利息收入及类似收益			
养老金和其他退休后福利			
计划资产的预期回报	981	1, 236	1, 064
金融工具的利息收入：			
银行存款和其他金融资产的利息收入	18	60	209
融资租赁的应收利息	–	1	2

Con.

Gains transferred from equity on disposal of available-for-sale investments	6	18	–
Interest income and similar income	**1,005**	**1,315**	**1,275**
Interest expense and other finance costs			
Interest on pension and other post-retirement benefit plan obligations	(1,193)	(1,250)	(1,001)
Interest expense on financial liabilities held at amortised cost:			
Interest on bank loans and overdrafts	(80)	(136)	(71)
Interest on other borrowings	(938)	(1,135)	(990)
Interest on finance leases	–	(14)	(11)
Interest on derivatives	22	5	(46)
Unwinding of discounts on provisions	(70)	(68)	(45)
Less: Interest capitalised[(i)]	99	133	119
Interest expense and other finance costs before exceptional items and remeasurements	**(2,160)**	**(2,465)**	**(2,045)**
Exceptional items			
Exceptional debt redemption costs	(33)	–	–
Remeasurements			
Net gains/(losses) on derivative financial instruments included in remeasurements [(ii)]:			
Ineffectiveness on derivatives designated as fair value hedges[(iii)]	67	(34)	1
Ineffectiveness on derivatives designated as cash flow hedges	(5)	(18)	13
Ineffectiveness on derivatives designated as net investment hedges	(19)	(2)	14
On undesignated forward rate risk relating to derivatives designated as net investment hedges	51	112	(53)
On derivatives not designated as hedges or ineligible for hedge accounting	(13)	(140)	18
Financial element of remeasurements on commodity contracts	(1)	(2)	(9)
	80	(84)	(16)
Interest expense and other finance costs	(2,113)	(2,549)	(2,061)
Net finance costs	(1,108)	(1,234)	(786)

续表

因处置可供出售的投资而从权益中转出的利得	6	18	–
利息收入及类似收益	**1,005**	**1,315**	**1,275**
利息费用和其他财务成本			
养老金和其他退休后福利计划义务的利息	(1,193)	(1,250)	(1,001)
以摊余成本持有的金融负债的利息费用：			
银行贷款和透支的利息	(80)	(136)	(71)
其他借款的利息	(938)	(1,135)	(990)
融资租赁的利息	–	(14)	(11)
衍生工具的利息	22	5	(46)
预计负债折现的释放	(70)	(68)	(45)
减：资本化利息(i)	99	133	119
不含异常项目和重新计量的利息费用和其他财务成本	**(2,160)**	**(2,465)**	**(2,045)**
异常项目			
异常的债务赎回成本	(33)	–	–
重新计量			
包括在重新计量中的衍生金融工具的净利得/(损失)(ii)：			
指定为公允价值套期的衍生工具的无效套期部分(iii)	67	(34)	1
指定为现金流量套期的衍生工具的无效套期部分	(5)	(18)	13
指定为净投资套期的衍生工具的无效套期部分	(19)	(2)	14
指定为净投资套期的衍生工具相关的未指定远期汇率风险部分	51	112	(53)
未指定为套期或不符合套期会计的衍生工具部分	(13)	(140)	18
商品合同中重新计量的金融要素	(1)	(2)	(9)
	80	(84)	(16)
利息费用和其他财务成本	(2,113)	(2,549)	(2,061)
财务成本净值	(1,108)	(1,234)	(786)

Con.

Comprising:			
Interest income and similar income	1,005	1,315	1,275
Interest expense and other finance costs:			
Before exceptional items and remeasurements	(2,160)	(2,465)	(2,045)
Exceptional items and remeasurements	47	(84)	(16)
After exceptional items and remeasurements	(2,113)	(2,549)	(2,061)
	(1,108)	(1,234)	(786)

(i) Interest on funding attributable to assets in the course of construction was capitalised during the year at a rate of 2.8% (2009: 5.7%; 2008: 6.3%).

(ii) Includes a net foreign exchange gain on financing activities of £334m (2009: £1,500m loss; 2008: £885m loss) offset by foreign exchange gains and losses on derivative financial instruments measured at fair value.

(iii) Includes a net loss on instruments designated as fair value hedges of £90m (2009: £382m gain; 2008: £87m gain) offset by a net gain of £157m (2009: £416m loss; 2008: £86m loss) arising from fair value adjustments to the carrying value of debt.

Fair value

11.72 Except as set out in paragraph 11.76 below, for each class of financial assets and financial liabilities (see para 11.39 above), an entity should disclose the fair value of that class of assets and liabilities in a way that permits it to be compared with its carrying amount. [IFRS 7 para 25].

11.72.1 Where an entity has issued a convertible bond and has under IAS 32 accounted for it as a compound instrument, the equity component will not need to be fair valued. This is because the above requirement is only for financial assets and financial liabilities and the equity component does not meet the definition of a financial asset or a financial liability.

11.73 In disclosing fair values, an entity should group financial assets and

续表

包括：			
利息收入及类似收益	1,005	1,315	1,275
利息费用和其他财务成本：			
不含异常项目和重新计量	(2,160)	(2,465)	(2,045)
异常项目和重新计量	47	(84)	(16)
含异常项目和重新计量	(2,113)	(2,549)	(2,061)
	(1,108)	(1,234)	(786)

(i) 可归于建造过程中的资产的资金利息在当年按 2.8% 的利率进行了资本化（2009：5.7%；2008：6.3%）。

(ii) 包括融资活动净外汇利得 3.34 亿英镑（2009：损失 15 亿英镑；2008：损失 8.85 亿英镑）并抵销了以公允价值计量的衍生金融工具的外汇利得和损失。

(iii) 包括指定为公允价值套期的工具的净损失 9,000 万英镑（2009：利得 3.82 亿英镑；2008：利得 8,700 万英镑；）并抵销将负债账面金额调至公允价值的利得 1.57 亿英镑（2007：损失 4.16 亿英镑；2008：损失 8,600 万英镑）。

公允价值

11.72　除下文第 11.76 段所列示的情况外，对每一类型的金融资产和金融负债而言（参见上文第 11.39 段），主体应以能与其账面金额对比的方式披露该类资产和负债的公允价值。[IFRS 7 第 25 段]。

11.72.1　在主体已经发行了一项可转换债券并已按照 IAS 32 将其作为一项复合工具核算的情况下，无需对权益部分进行公允价值评估。这是因为上述要求仅适用于金融资产和金融负债，而权益部分不符合金融资产或金融负债的定义。

11.73　在披露公允价值时，主体应对金融资产和金融负债按类型进行汇总，

financial liabilities into classes, but should offset them only to the extent that their carrying amounts are offset in the balance sheet. [IFRS 7 para 26].

11.74 An entity should disclose, for each class of financial instruments measured at fair value, the methods and, when a valuation technique is used, the assumptions applied in determining fair values of each class of financial asset or financial liability. For example, if applicable, an entity should disclose information about the assumptions relating to pre-payment rates, rates of estimated credit losses and interest rates or discount rates. If there has been a change in valuation technique, the entity should disclose that change and the reasons for making it. [IFRS 7 para 27].

11.75 If the market for a financial instrument is not active, its fair value is established using a valuation technique. [IAS 39 paras AG 74 – 79]. The best evidence of fair value at initial recognition is the transaction price (that is, the fair value of the consideration given or received), unless the fair value of that instrument is evidenced by comparison with other observable current market transactions in the same instrument (that is, without modification or repackaging) or based on a valuation technique whose variables include only data from observable markets as described in paragraph AG 76 of IAS 39. There could be a difference between the fair value at initial recognition and the amount that would be determined at that date using the valuation technique. If such a difference exists, an entity should disclose, by class of financial instrument:

- Its accounting policy for recognising that difference in profit or loss to reflect a change in factors (including time) that market participants would consider in setting a price. [IAS 39 para AG 76A].

- The aggregate difference yet to be recognised in profit or loss at the beginning and end of the period, and a reconciliation of changes in the balance of this difference.

[IFRS 7 para 28].

11.76 Disclosure of fair values is not required:

- When the carrying amount is a reasonable approximation of fair value-for

但只有那些账面金额在资产负债表中相互抵销的金融资产和金融负债才能按抵销后的公允价值披露。[IFRS 7 第 26 段]。

11.74 对于以公允价值计量的每类金融工具，主体应当披露确定每类金融资产或金融负债的公允价值所使用的方法，以及当采用了估值技术时所应用的假设。例如，如果适用，主体应当披露与提前还款率、预计信用损失率和利率或折现率相关的假设。如果所用的估值技术有所变动，主体应当披露该项变动及其原因。[IFRS 7 第 27 段]。

11.75 如果金融工具的市场不存在活跃市场，则应采用估值技术确定其公允价值。[IAS 39 AG 第 74 – 79 段]。初始确认时公允价值的最好证据是交易价格（即支付或收到的对价的公允价值），除非如 IAS 39 AG 第 76 段所述，与相同工具（即未经修正或重新包装）的其他可观察现行市场交易的比较、或基于仅以可观察市场数据为变量的估值技术，可以证明该工具的公允价值。初始确认时的公允价值和在该日采用估值技术确定的金额之间可能存在差额。如这一差额存在，主体应按照金融工具的类型披露：

- 在损益中确认这一差额时所采用的会计政策，以反映市场参与者定价时所考虑的因素（包括时间）的变动。[IAS 39 AG 第 76A 段]。

- 期初和期末尚待在损益中确认的总差额及该差额余额的变动。

[IFRS 7 第 28 段]。

11.76 在如下情况时不要求披露公允价值：

- 账面金额合理接近公允价值——例如，短期应收账款和应付账款等金融工

example, for financial instruments such as short-term trade receivables and payables.

- For an investment in equity instruments that do not have a quoted market price in an active market, or derivatives linked to such equity instruments, that are measured at cost in accordance with IAS 39, because their fair value cannot be measured reliably.
- For a contract containing a discretionary participation feature (as described in IFRS 4) if the fair value of that feature cannot be measured reliably.

[IFRS 7 para 29].

11.77 In the cases described in the second and third bullet points above, an entity should disclose information to help users of the financial statements make their own judgements about the extent of possible differences between the carrying amount of those financial assets or financial liabilities and their fair value, including:

- The fact that fair value information has not been disclosed for these instruments because their fair value cannot be measured reliably.
- A description of the financial instruments, their carrying amount and an explanation of why fair value cannot be measured reliably.
- Information about the market for the instruments.
- Information about whether and how the entity intends to dispose of the financial instruments.
- If financial instruments whose fair value previously could not be reliably measured are derecognised, that fact, their carrying amount at the time of derecognition and the amount of gain or loss recognised.

[IFRS 7 para 30].

Fair value hierarchy

11.78 The IASB amended IFRS 7 in March 2009 to enhance the disclosure requirements regarding financial instruments measured at fair value. In order to

具。

■ 对于在活跃市场上没有公开报价的权益工具投资，或与这种权益工具挂钩的衍生工具，其由于公允价值无法可靠地计量而按照 IAS 39 以成本计量。

■ 不能可靠地计量其所包含的相机参与分红特征（如 IFRS 4 所述）的公允价值的合同。

[IFRS 7 第 29 段]。

11.77　在上文第二点和第三点所述情况下，主体应当披露下述信息，以帮助财务报表使用者对金融资产或金融负债的账面金额与其公允价值之间可能的差异程度进行判断：

■ 由于工具的公允价值无法可靠地计量而未披露这些工具公允价值信息的事实。

■ 对金融工具的描述、其账面金额以及对公允价值无法可靠计量的解释。

■ 此类工具的市场信息。

■ 有关主体是否有意及如何处置这些金融工具的信息。

■ 如果之前公允价值无法可靠计量的金融工具已经被终止确认，则应披露这一事实、终止确认时的账面金额和确认的利得或损失金额。

[IFRS 7 第 30 段]。

公允价值级次

11.78　IASB 于 2009 年 3 月对 IFRS 7 进行了修订以加强有关以公允价值计量的金融工具的披露要求。为了提高主体间的可比性并进一步促进国际财务报告

increase comparability between entities and take one further step towards IFRS and US GAAP convergence, the IASB introduced a requirement to make disclosures according to a 'fair value hierarchy' similar to that required under US GAAP by SFAS 157, 'Fair value measurements'. This is different from the current fair value measurement hierarchy implicitly included in IAS 39. The amendment to IFRS 7 does not change these requirements.

11.78.1 As noted above, the amendment to IFRS 7 enhances the disclosure requirements regarding financial instruments measured at fair value. Unlike SFAS 157, it does not apply to items measured at fair value that are not financial instruments. Also, it does not apply to financial instruments measured at amortised cost (for example, held-to-maturity investments, or loans and receivables).

11.78.2 The hierarchy has three levels that reflect the significance of the inputs used in measuring fair value. These are as follows:

- Quoted prices (unadjusted) in active markets for identical assets or liabilities (Level 1).
- Inputs other than quoted prices included within level 1 that are observable for the asset or liability, either directly (that is, as prices) or indirectly (that is, derived from prices) (Level 2).
- Inputs for the asset or liability that are not based on observable market data (unobservable inputs) (Level 3).

[IFRS 7 para 27A].

11.78.3 The level in the fair value hierarchy within which a financial instrument is categorised in its entirety is determined on the basis of the lowest level input that is significant to the fair value measurement. For this purpose, the significance of an input is assessed against the fair value measurement in its entirety. [IFRS 7 para 27A].

11.78.4 Assessing the significance of a particular input to the fair value measurement in its entirety requires judgement, considering factors specific to the asset or liability. In assessing the significance of unobservable inputs to a financial

准则和美国公认会计准则的趋同，IASB 引入了一项与美国公认会计准则《财务会计准则公告第 157 号—公允价值计量》（“SFAS 157”）要求相似的“公允价值级次”披露要求。这与当前 IAS 39 中所暗含的公允价值计量的级次不同。IFRS 7 的修订并未改变这些要求。

11.78.1　如上文所述，IFRS 7 的修订中加强了对以公允价值计量的金融工具的披露要求。与 SFAS 157 不同，它并不适用于以公允价值计量的非金融工具项目。同时，它不适用于以摊余成本计量的金融工具（例如，持有至到期的投资，或贷款和应收款项）。

11.78.2　该级次具有三个层次，反映了计量公允价值时所使用的输入值的重要性。这三个层次如下所述：

■ 相同资产或负债在活跃市场中的报价（未经调整的）（第一层次）。

■ 除第一层次所包含的可观察市场报价之外的、对资产或负债所使用的直接（即价格）或间接（即从价格中衍生出）的输入值（第二层次）。

■ 资产或负债使用的、非基于可观察市场数据的输入值（不可观察输入值）（第三层次）。

[IFRS 7 第 27A 段]。

11.78.3　应基于对公允价值计量具有重要性的输入值的最低层次确定一项金融工具整体所应归入的公允价值级次中的层次。为此，输入值的重要性应针对公允价值计量整体而言进行评价。[IFRS 7 第 27A 段]。

11.78.4　在评价特定输入值对于公允价值计量整体的重要性时，需要考虑资产或负债的特定因素来进行判断。在评价不可观察输入值对于金融工具公允价值的重要性时，主体应当：

instrument's fair value, an entity should:

- consider the sensitivity of the instrument's overall value to changes in the data; and
- re-assess the likelihood of variability in the data over the instrument's life.

For example, if an interest rate swap with a ten-year life has an observable yield curve for nine years, provided that the extrapolation of the yield curve to ten years is not significant to the fair value measurement of the swap in its entirety, the fair value measurement is considered to be at level 2 in the hierarchy.

11.78.5 Only instruments traded on an exchange or an active index/market can fall within level 1 of the hierarchy. Generally, for a price to qualify as level 1, reporting entities should be able to obtain the price from multiple sources. A market is active for a financial instrument if quotes are regularly available and do not represent forced transactions (see chapter 9). The price quote may be a level 2 or level 3 input where there are few transactions for the instrument, where the price is not current, or where price quotations vary substantially either over time or among market makers, or for which little information is released publicly.

11.78.5.1 Whether or not an instrument is considered to have a 'price quoted in an active market' for the purposes of the fair value hierarchy is a different assessment from whether it is considered 'quoted in an active market' for the purposes of IAS 39 and the assessment of whether it can be classified as a loan or receivable. In writing the basis of conclusions to IFRS 7 the board acknowledged that some financial instruments that for measurement purposes are considered to have an active market in accordance with paragraphs AG 71 - AG73 of IAS 39 might be in level 2 for disclosure purposes in the fair value hierarchy. [IFRS 7 BC para 39D].

11.78.6 Many reporting entities obtain information from pricing services, broker pricing information and similar sources, for use as inputs in their fair value measurements. The information provided by these sources could be at any level in the fair value hierarchy, depending on the source of the information for a particular security. However, if the information forms an input to a valuation technique that

■ 考虑工具的整体价值对于数据变化的敏感性；以及

■ 在工具的持有期间，持续评价数据发生变动的可能性。

例如，如果有一个10年期的利率互换，相应可观察的收益率曲线为9年，在将其外推为10年期收益率曲线对此利率互换整体的公允价值计量没有重大影响的情况下，该公允价值计量应归入级次中的第二层次。

11.78.5 只有在交易所或活跃指数/市场上进行交易的工具才能归入级次中的第一层次。一般而言，作为符合第一层次要求的价格，报告主体应当能够通过多种途径获得。对于金融工具而言，如果能经常获取报价并且不代表强制交易，该市场即为活跃市场（参见第9章）。在有关工具的交易很少、价格不是当前价格、或报价随时间或因不同的做市商有重大的波动、或公开发布信息很少的情况下，这种报价可能是第二层次或第三层次。

11.78.5.1 公允价值级次中评价一个工具是否被认为有“活跃市场报价”与在IAS 39下是否被认为“在活跃市场有报价”以及是否能被划分为贷款或应收款的评价是不同的。在编写IFRS 7的结论基础时，理事会承认某些按照IAS 39 AG第71-73段从计量的角度来说被认为有活跃市场的金融工具可能在披露公允价值级次中属于第二层次。[IFRS 7 BC第39D段]。

11.78.6 许多报告主体都通过定价服务商、经纪商定价信息或类似来源取得信息，用作其公允价值计量的输入值。取决于某一特定证券的信息来源，所提供的信息可能是公允价值级次中任何层次的信息。但是，如果该信息作为估值技术的输入值，则排除了划分为第一层次的可能。层次的确定取决于估值所用的输入值，而非估值方法或模型的复杂程度——即，估值模型的使用不

would preclude classification at level 1, the level is determined on the basis of the valuation inputs, not on the methodology or complexity of the model-that is, the use of a model does not automatically result in a level 3 fair value measurement. For example, a standard valuation model using only observable inputs is likely to result in a measurement that is classified as level 2. However, to the extent that adjustments or interpolations are made by management to level 2 inputs in an otherwise standard model, the measurement may fall into level 3, depending on whether the adjusted inputs are significant to the measurement. Furthermore, if a reporting entity uses a valuation model that is proprietary and relies on unobservable inputs, the resulting fair value measurement is likely to be categorised as level 3.

11.78.7 The US standard (SFAS 157) provides examples of inputs and where they would typically lie in the hierarchy. In view of the similarity between SFAS 157 and the amended IFRS 7, the following examples from the former may be relevant.

- As noted in paragraph 11.78.2, level 2 inputs are inputs other than quoted prices included within level 1 that are observable for the asset or liability, either directly (that is, as prices) or indirectly (that is, derived from prices). Examples of level 2 inputs for particular assets and liabilities include the following:

  - Receive-fixed, pay-variable interest rate swap based on the LIBOR swap rate. A level 2 input would include the LIBOR swap rate if that rate is observable at commonly quoted intervals for the swap's full term. However, other inputs will also need to be considered. For example, if credit is a component of the valuation for the pay and receive leg of the swap, its observability and significance to the measurement will need to be evaluated.

  - Three-year option on exchange-traded shares. A level 2 input would include the implied volatility for the shares derived through extrapolation to year three if prices for one-and two-year options on the shares are observable, and the extrapolated implied volatility of a three-year option is corroborated by observable market data for substantially the option's full term. In that case,

会自动导致归入第三层次的公允价值计量。例如，一个仅使用可观察输入值的标准估值模型，很可能导致计量被划分为第二层次。但是，根据管理层对一个标准模型中的第二层次的输入值进行调整或内推的程度，该计量可能会归为第三层次，这取决于经调整的输入值对计量是否重要。此外，如果报告主体使用了专有的估值模型且依赖于不可观察的输入值，所得到的公允价值计量很可能会被划分为第三层次。

11.78.7　美国准则（SFAS 157）中给出了输入值及其一般所属级次的示例。考虑到 SFAS 157 和修订的 IFRS 7 之间的相似性，前者中的如下示例可能是相关的。

- 如第 11.78.2 段所述，第二层次的输入值为除第一层次所包含的可观察市场报价之外的、对资产或负债所使用的直接（即价格）或间接（即从价格中衍生出）的输入值。特定资产和负债的第二层次输入值示例包括：

  - 基于伦敦同业拆借利率互换利率的按固定利率收取利息、按浮动利率支付利息的利率互换。如果伦敦同业拆借利率互换利率在该互换整个存续期内的常见报价间隔中是可观察的，则第二层次输入值即包括该互换利率。但是，还应考虑其他输入值。例如，如果信用是互换的付款和收款分支估值的一个组成部分，则需要评价其可观察性及对计量的重要性。

  - 基于在交易所交易的股票的三年期权。如果基于该股票的一年和两年期权的价格是可观察的，而且三年期权的外推隐含波动率在期权几乎整个存续期可以得到可观察市场数据的佐证，则第二层次的输入值包括该股票通过外推至第三年所得到的隐含波动率。在这种情况下，假如其与一年和两年隐含波动率之间的相关性已经建立，该隐含波动率可以从基于该股

the implied volatility could be derived by extrapolating from the implied volatility of the one-and two-year options on the shares and corroborated by the implied volatility for three-year options on comparable entities' shares, provided that correlation with the one- and two-year implied volatilities is established.

- Equity investment. A level 2 input would include a valuation multiple (for example, a multiple of earnings or revenue or a similar performance measure) derived from observable market data, for example, multiples derived from prices in observed transactions involving comparable businesses, considering operational, market, financial, and non-financial factors.

- As noted in paragraph 11.78.2, level 3 inputs are inputs that are not based on observable market data. They are inputs that reflect the reporting entity's own views about the assumptions market participants would use in pricing the asset or liability (including assumptions about risk), developed based on the best information available in the circumstances. Assumptions about risk include the risk inherent in a particular valuation technique used to measure fair value (such as a pricing model) and/or the risk inherent in the inputs to the valuation technique. Examples of level 3 inputs for particular assets and liabilities include the following:

  - Long-dated currency swap. A level 3 input would include interest rates in a specified currency that are not observable and cannot be corroborated by observable market data at commonly quoted intervals or otherwise for substantially the full term of the currency swap. The interest rates in a currency swap are the swap rates calculated from the respective countries' yield curves.

  - Three-year option on exchange-traded shares. A level 3 input would include historical volatility, that is, the volatility for the shares derived from the shares' historical prices. Historical volatility typically does not represent current market participant expectations about future volatility, even if it is the only information available to price an option.

  - Equity investment. A level 3 input would include a financial forecast (for

票的一年和两年期权的隐含波动率外推得出，并得到基于类似主体股票的三年期权隐含波动率的佐证。

■ 权益投资。第二层次的输入值包括从可观察市场数据得到的估值倍数（如收益或收入或类似业绩衡量指标的倍数），例如，从考虑到经营、市场、金融和非金融因素的类似业务的可观察交易价格所得到的倍数。

■ 如第11.78.2段所述，第三层次的输入值为非基于可观察市场数据的输入值。这些输入值反映报告主体对市场参与者在对资产或负债进行定价时应该使用的假设（包括对风险的假设）、根据当前情形下可用的最佳信息而得出的自身观点。有关风险的假设包括用来计量公允价值的特定估值技术（例如定价模型）的固有风险和/或估值技术输入值的固有风险。特定资产和负债第三层次输入值的示例包括：

■ 长期的货币互换合同。第三层次的输入值应该包括某种不可观察的、而且不能够得到通常的报价间隔或在货币互换基本整个存续期内的可观察市场数据经佐证的具体货币的利率。货币互换的利率是从相应国家的收益率曲线计算得到的互换率。

■ 基于在交易所交易的股票的三年期权。第三层次的输入值应该包括历史波动率，即从股票的历史价格中所得出的股票波动率。历史波动性一般不能代表市场参与者对未来波动率的期望值，即使它是对某项期权定价的唯一可用信息。

■ 权益投资。如果没有信息表明市场参与者将采用不同的假设，第三层次的

example, of cash flows or earnings) developed using the reporting entity's own data if there is no information that indicates that market participants would use different assumptions.

11.78.8 For each class of financial instruments measured at fair value, an entity should disclose the following (the quantitative disclosures should be presented in tabular format, unless another format is more appropriate):

- The level in the fair value hierarchy into which the fair value measurements are categorised in their entirety, segregating fair value measurements in accordance with the levels defined in paragraph 11.78.2 above.

- Any significant transfers between level 1 and level 2 of the fair value hierarchy and the reasons for those transfers. Transfers into each level should be disclosed and discussed separately from transfers out of each level. Significance should be judged with respect to profit or loss and total assets or total liabilities.

- For fair value measurements in level 3 of the fair value hierarchy, a reconciliation from the beginning balances to the ending balances, disclosing separately changes during the period attributable to the following:

  - Total gains or losses for the period recognised in profit or loss and a description of where they are presented in the statement of comprehensive income or the separate income statement (if presented).

  - Total gains or losses recognised in other comprehensive income.

  - Purchases, sales, issues and settlements (each type of movement disclosed separately).

  - Transfers into or out of level 3 (for example, transfers attributable to changes in the observability of market data) and the reasons for those transfers. For significant transfers, transfers into level 3 should be disclosed and discussed separately from transfers out of level 3.

- The amount of total gains or losses for the period included in profit or loss resulting from level 3 financial instruments that are attributable to those assets and liabilities held at the end of the reporting period and a description of where

输入值应该包括使用报告主体自身数据所得到的财务预测（例如现金流量或收益预测）。

11.78.8 对于以公允价值计量的每一类金融工具而言，主体应当进行如下披露（除非其他形式更为适合，定量披露应以表格形式呈列）：

- 公允价值计量整体被归入的公允价值级次的层次，以及根据上文第11.78.2段所定义的层次将公允价值计量进行拆分。

- 任何第一层次和第二层次之间的重大转移及其原因。转入每一层次与转出每一层次的情况应单独披露并讨论。重大与否应根据损益和资产总额或负债总额进行判断。

- 对于公允价值级次第三层次的公允价值计量，期初余额至期末余额的变动表，并单独披露当期由于下述情形产生的变动：

  - 当期确认为损益的利得或损失合计以及这些利得或损失在综合收益表或单独利润表（如列报）中何处列报的描述。

  - 在其他综合收益中所确认的利得或损失合计。

  - 购买、出售、发行和清偿（每种类型的变动均需单独披露）。

  - 转入或转出第三层次（例如由于市场数据的可观察性变化而发生的转移）及其原因。对于重大的转移，转入第三层次与转出第三层次的情况应单独披露并讨论。

- 由第三层次的金融工具产生的、与报告期末仍持有的这些金融资产和金融负债相关的、包括在损益中的利得或损失总额，以及这些利得或损失在综合收益表或单独利润表（如列报）中何处列报的描述。

those gains or losses are presented in the statement of comprehensive income or the separate income statement (if presented).

- For fair value measurements in level 3, if changing one or more of the inputs to reasonably possible alternative assumptions would change fair value significantly, the entity should state that fact and disclose the effect of those changes. The entity should disclose how the effect of a change to a reasonably possible alternative assumption was calculated. Significance should be judged with respect to profit or loss, and total assets or total liabilities, or, when changes in fair value are recognised in other comprehensive income, total equity.

11.78.9 The disclosures described in the previous paragraph are required in financial statements for annual periods beginning on or after 1 January 2009. However, in the first year of application, an entity need not provide comparative information. [IFRS 7 para 44G].

11.78.10 In June 2010 the IASB released an exposure draft on 'Measurement uncertainty analysis disclosure for fair value measurements'. This exposure draft is a limited expansion of previous disclosure proposals around Level 3 fair value measurements which were included in the 'Fair value measurement' exposure draft issued in May 2009. The new exposure draft proposes that disclosures of measurement uncertainty of Level 3 fair values should reflect the interdependencies between unobservable inputs into the valuations.

11.78.11 Examples of the fair value hierarchy are provided in Tables 11.6.1 and 11.6.2. Table 11.6.1 also gives the Level 3 reconciliations and sensitivity analysis required by IFRS 7. It should be noted that the example does not reproduce the company's description of the control framework for financial instruments carried at fair value, its detailed description of valuation techniques used, details of risk related adjustments, model related adjustments and credit risk adjustment methodology.

■ 对于第三层次的公允价值计量，如果在合理可能备选的假设下变更一个或数个输入值将导致公允价值发生重大变化的，主体应当描述该事实及披露这些变更的影响。主体应当披露合理可能备选假设的变更的影响是如何计算的。重大与否应根据损益和资产总额或负债总额，或当公允价值变化确认为其他综合收益时、根据权益总额进行判断。

11.78.9 上段所述披露需在起始日于2009年1月1日或之后开始的年度期间的财务报表中实施。但是，在第一年使用时，主体不需要提供比较信息。[IFRS 7第44G段]。

11.78.10 IASB于2010年6月发布了征求意见稿《公允价值计量的计量不确定性分析披露》。该征求意见稿是对之前包括在2009年5月发布的《公允价值计量》征求意见稿中第三层次公允价值计量披露建议的有限扩展。新征求意见稿建议，对第三层次公允价值计量不确定性的披露应当反映估值中不可观察输入值之间的相互依赖性。

11.78.11 公允价值级次的示例参见表11.6.1和表11.6.2。表11.6.1还列出了IFRS 7所要求的第三层次调节表和敏感性分析。值得注意的是该示例并未重列该公司对以公允价值计量的金融工具的控制框架描述、所采用的估值技术的具体描述、以及风险相关调整、模型相关调整和信用风险调整方法的详情。

Table 11. 6. 1 – Fair value disclosures relating to financial assets and liabilities

HSBC Holdings plc – Annual report – 31 December 2009

Fair values of financial instruments (extract)

(*Audited*)

Fair value valuation bases

The table below provides an analysis of the various bases described above which have been deployed for valuing financial assets and financial liabilities measured at fair value in the consolidated financial statements.

The movement in the balances of assets and liabilities measured at fair value with significant unobservable inputs was mainly attributable to a decrease in the fair value of derivative assets, loans held for securitisation and the disposal of securities in other portfolios. At 31 December 2009, financial instruments measured at fair value using a valuation technique with significant unobservable inputs represented 2 per cent of total assets and liabilities measured at fair value (2008: 2 per cent).

Bases of valuing financial assets and liabilities measured at fair value

	Quoted market price	Using observable inputs	With significant unobservable inputs	
	Level 1	**Level 2**	**Level 3**	**Total**
At 31 December 2009				
Assets				
Trading assets	**272,509**	**142,452**	**6,420**	**421,381**
Financial assets designated at fair value	**24,184**	**11,773**	**1,224**	**37,181**
Derivatives	**1,961**	**244,472**	**4,453**	**250,886**
Financial investments: available for sale	**163,149**	**178,168**	**10,214**	**351,531**
Liabilities				
Trading liabilities	**119,544**	**139,812**	**8,774**	**268,130**
Financial liabilities designated at fair value	**27,553**	**52,032**	**507**	**80,092**
Derivatives	**1,843**	**240,611**	**5,192**	**247,646**
At 31 December 2008				
Assets				
Trading assets	234,399	185,369	7,561	427,329

表 11.6.1——金融资产和负债相关的公允价值披露

HSBC Holdings plc——年报——2009 年 12 月 31 日

金融工具的公允价值（节选）

（已审计）

公允价值估值基础

下表提供了对合并财务报表中以公允价值计量的金融资产和金融负债进行估值所使用的如上所述的各种基础的分析。

以基于重大不可观察输入值的、按公允价值计量的资产和负债余额的变动主要由衍生工具资产和为证券化而持有的贷款的公允价值下跌及处置其他组合中的证券所致。于 2009 年 12 月 31 日，以使用重大不可观察输入值的估值技术得到的公允价值计量的金融工具占以公允价值计量的资产和负债总额的 2%（2008 年：2%）。

以公允价值计量的金融资产和负债的估值基础

	市场报价	使用可观察输入值	使用重大不可观察输入值	
	第一层次	第二层次	第三层次	总计
2009 年 12 月 31 日				
资产				
交易性资产	**272,509**	**142,452**	**6,420**	**421,381**
指定为公允价值计量的金融资产	**24,184**	**11,773**	**1,224**	**37,181**
衍生工具	**1,961**	**244,472**	**4,453**	**250,886**
金融投资：				
可供出售	**163,149**	**178,168**	**10,214**	**351,531**
负债				
交易性负债	**119,544**	**139,812**	**8,774**	**268,130**
指定为公允价值计量的金融负债	**27,553**	**52,032**	**507**	**80,092**
衍生工具	**1,843**	**240,611**	**5,192**	**247,646**
2008 年 12 月 31 日				
资产				
交易性资产	234,399	185,369	7,561	427,329

Con.

Financial assets designated at fair value	14,590	13,483	460	28,533
Derivatives	8,495	476,498	9,883	494,876
Financial investments: available for sale	103,949	173,157	9,116	286,222
Liabilities				
Trading liabilities	105,584	135,559	6,509	247,652
Financial liabilities designated at fair value	23,311	51,276	–	74,587
Derivatives	9,896	473,359	3,805	487,060

Financial instruments measured at fair value using a valuation technique with significant unobservable inputs – Level 3

	Assets				Liabilities		
	Available for sale US$m	Held for trading US$m	Designated at fair value through profit and loss US$m	Derivatives US$m	Held for trading US$m	Designated at fair value through profit and loss US$m	Derivatives US$m
At 31 December 2009							
Private equity investments	**2,949**	**197**	**345**	–	–	–	–
Asset – backed securities	**4,270**	**944**	–	–	–	–	–
Leveraged finance	–	**73**	–	–	–	–	**25**
Loans held for securitisation	–	**1,395**	–	–	–	–	–
Structured notes	–	**196**	–	–	**5,055**	–	–
Derivatives with monolines	–	–	–	**1,305**	–	–	–
Other derivatives	–	–	–	**3,148**	–	–	**5,167**
Other portfolios	**2,995**	**3,615**	**879**	–	**3,719**	**507**	–
	10,214	**6,420**	**1,224**	**4,453**	**8,774**	**507**	**5,192**
At 31 December 2008							
Private equity investments	2,698	54	225	–	–	–	–
Asset – backed securities	4,264	882	–	95	–	–	565
Leveraged finance	–	266	–	–	–	–	33
Loans held for securitisation	–	2,133	–	–	–	–	–
Structured notes	–	87	–	–	5,294	–	–
Derivatives with monolines	–	–	–	2,441	–	–	–
Other derivatives	–	–	–	7,347	–	–	3,207
Other portfolios	2,163	4,139	235	–	1,215	–	–
	9,116	7,561	460	9,883	6,509	–	3,805

At 31 December 2009, available-for-sale ABSs valued using a valuation technique with significant unobservable inputs principally comprised commercial property-related securities, leveraged finance-related securities and Alt-A securities with no particular concentration in any one category. Assets in other portfolios valued using a valuation technique with significant unobservable inputs were principally holdings in an Asian bond portfolio where the credit spreads are not directly observable.

续表

指定为公允价值计量的金融资产	14,590	13,483	460	28,533
衍生工具	8,495	476,498	9,883	494,876
金融投资:可供出售	103,949	173,157	9,116	286,222
负债				
交易性负债	105,584	135,559	6,509	247,652
指定为公允价值计量的金融负债	23,311	51,276	–	74,587
衍生工具	9,896	473,359	3,805	487,060

以使用重大不可观察输入值的估值技术得到的公允价值计量的金融工具——第三层次

	资产				负债		
	可供出售	为交易而持有	指定为以公允价值计量且变动计入损益	衍生工具	为交易而持有	指定为以公允价值计量且变动计入损益	衍生工具
	百万美元	百万美元	百万美元	百万美元	百万美元	百万美元	百万美元
2009 年 12 月 31 日							
无公开报价的权益投资	**2,949**	**197**	**345**	–	–	–	–
资产支持证券	**4,270**	**944**	–	–	–	–	–
杠杆融资	–	**73**	–	–	–	–	**25**
为证券化而持有的贷款	–	**1,395**	–	–	–	–	–
结构性票据	–	**196**	–	–	**5,055**	–	–
专业险种衍生工具	–	–	–	**1,305**	–	–	–
其他衍生工具	–	–	–	**3,148**	–	–	**5,167**
其他组合	**2,995**	**3,615**	**879**	–	**3,719**	**507**	–
	10,214	**6,420**	**1,224**	**4,453**	**8,774**	**507**	**5,192**
2008 年 12 月 31 日							
无公开报价的权益投资	2,698	54	225	–	–	–	–
资产支持证券	4,264	882	–	95	–	–	565
杠杆融资	–	266	–	–	–	–	33
为证券化而持有的贷款	–	2,133	–	–	–	–	–
结构性票据	–	87	–	–	5,294	–	–
专业险种衍生工具	–	–	–	2,441	–	–	–
其他衍生工具	–	–	–	7,347	–	–	3,207
其他组合	2,163	4,139	235	–	1,215	–	–
	9,116	7,561	460	9,883	6,509	–	3,805

于 2009 年 12 月 31 日，以使用重大不可观察输入值的估值技术进行估值的可供出售资产支持证券主要包括未特别集中于某一类别的商用不动产相关的证券、杠杆融资相关的证券和 Alt-A 证券。其他组合中以使用重大不可观察输入值的估值技术进行估值的资产主要是一项信贷息差不可被直接观察到的亚洲债券组合。

Con.

Trading assets valued using a valuation technique with significant unobservable inputs principally comprised ABSs, loans held for securitisation and other portfolios. The ABSs are classified in Level 3 as a result of the unobservability of the underlying price of the assets. Loans held for securitisations are valued using a proprietary model which utilises inputs relating to the credit spread of the obligor. Other portfolios include holdings in various bonds, preference shares and debentures where the unobservability relates to the prices of the underlying securities. The decrease during the year was due to a reduction in the fair value of loans held for securitisation and disposals of positions within other portfolios.

Derivative products with monolines valued using techniques with unobservable inputs decreased during the year as a result of a decrease in exposure to the monoline counterparties, primarily as a result of decreasing credit spreads and from commutations undertaken. The primary unobservable input relates to the probability of default of the counterparty. Further details of the transactions with monoline counterparties are shown on page 163.

Derivative products valued using valuation techniques with significant unobservable inputs included certain correlation products, such as foreign exchange basket options, equity basket options, foreign exchange-interest rate hybrid transactions and long-dated option transactions. Examples of the latter are equity options, interest rate and foreign exchange options and certain credit derivatives. Credit derivatives include certain tranched CDS transactions. The decrease in Level 3 derivative assets during the year was mainly due to a decrease in the fair value of structured credit transactions.

Trading liabilities valued using a valuation technique with significant unobservable inputs principally comprised equity-linked structured notes which are issued by HSBC and provide the counterparty with a return that is linked to the performance of certain equity securities, and other portfolios. The notes are classified as Level 3 due to the unobservability of parameters such as long-dated equity volatilities and correlations between equity prices, between equity prices and interest rates and between interest rates and foreign exchange rates. The movement in Level 3 trading liabilities during the year was primarily due to the issue of new equity derivative linked structures classified in other portfolios, partially offset by transfers out of Level 3 as a result of increased observability of long-dated volatilities.

The increase in derivative liabilities valued using a valuation technique with significant unobservable inputs was primarily attributable to the transfer into Level 3 of swaps linked to securitisation structures whose valuation utilises inputs relating to the prepayment rates for the underlying asset pools which are unobservable. This was partially offset by transfers out of structured interest rate and equity derivatives due to increased observability of longdated swaptions and equity volatilities.

续表

以使用含重大不可观察输入值的估值技术进行估值的交易性资产主要包括资产支持证券、为证券化而持有的贷款和其他组合。资产支持证券由于资产的基础价格不可观察而被划分为第三层次。为证券化而持有的贷款采用了包括债权人信贷息差相关输入值的专有模型进行估值。其他组合包括持有的各种债券、优先股股票和信用债券，这些证券的价格不可观察。当年的减少是由于为证券化而持有的贷款的公允价值下跌以及处置其他组合中的头寸所致。
以使用不可观察输入值的技术进行估值的专业险种衍生工具产品在当年的减少是由于信贷息差的降低和所进行的交换导致的对专业险种保险公司交易对方的敞口减少所致。主要的不可观察输入值是交易对方违约的可能性。和专业险种保险公司交易对方交易的进一步详情见第 163 页。
以使用重大不可观察输入值的估值技术进行估值的衍生工具产品包括某些相关性产品，诸如外汇组合期权，权益组合期权，外汇利率混合交易以及长期期权交易。后者的例子如权益期权，利率和外汇期权以及某些信用衍生工具。信用衍生工具包括某些级次的信用违约掉期交易。当年第三层次衍生工具资产的减少主要是由结构性信用交易的公允价值下跌所致。
以使用重大不可观察输入值的估值技术进行估值的交易性负债主要包括由 HSBC 发行并提供交易对方与某些权益证券业绩回报挂钩的权益连结票据和其他组合。该票据由于诸如长期权益波动率和权益价格间、权益价格和利率以及利率和汇率间的相关性等参数的不可观察性而被划分为第三层次。当年第三层次交易性负债的变动主要是由于新发行了分类为其他组合的权益连结衍生工具的结构性产品，并被因长期波动率的可观察性增加而被转出第三层次的金额部分抵销。
以使用重大不可观察输入值的估值技术进行估值的衍生工具负债的增长主要由其估值采用了不可观察的标的资产池提前偿付率而转入第三层次的连结证券化结构性产品所致。此增长被长期利率互换期权和权益波动率的可观察性增加而被转出第三层次的结构性利率和权益衍生工具部分抵销。

Con.

Reconciliation of fair value measurements in Level 3 of the fair value hierarchy

The following table provides a reconciliation of the movement between opening and closing balances of Level 3 financial instruments, measured at fair value using a valuation technique with significant unobservable inputs:

Movement in Level 3 financial instruments

	Assets				Liabilities		
	Available for sale US$m	Held for trading US$m	Designated at fair value through profit and loss US$m	Derivatives US$m	Held for trading US$m	Designated at fair value through profit and loss US$m	Derivatives US$m
At 1 January 2009	9,116	7,561	460	9,883	6,509	–	3,805
Total gains/(losses) recognised in profit or loss	(260)	(730)	97	(5,275)	(107)	(3)	(1,372)
Total gains recognised in other comprehensive income	617	85	–	119	301	10	94
Purchases	1,785	1,598	260	–	22	–	–
New issuances	–	–	–	–	2,522	500	–
Sales	(806)	(2,166)	(13)	–	–	–	–
Settlements	(1,059)	(295)	(6)	(104)	(1,266)	–	(206)
Transfers out	(3,043)	(1,077)	–	(1,057)	(537)	–	(620)
Transfers in	3,864	1,444	426	887	1,330	–	3,491
At 31 December 2009	10,214	6,420	1,224	4,453	8,774	507	5,192
Total gains/(losses) recognised in profit or loss relating to those assets and liabilities held on 31 December 2009	(371)	(596)	98	(3,753)	(136)	(3)	(135)

For available-for-sale securities, the unobservability of valuations of asset-backed (particularly Alt-A and leveraged finance-related) securities and the Asian bond portfolio discussed on page 173 resulted in assets in these categories being transferred or purchased into Level 3 during 2009. Transfers out of Level 3 were primarily in respect of commercial property related ABSs due to certain valuations in these asset categories becoming observable during 2009.

For trading assets, transfers into Level 3 arose principally on ABSs, fixed income securities and a syndicated loan position where valuations for the specific instruments were not observable. Transfers out also related principally to ABSs and fixed income securities as valuations for specific instruments became observable. Purchases relate primarily to the unwind of certain ABS total return swap funding transactions, in which HSBC's market risk position did not change, but securities were purchased in place of the derivative transactions.

续表

公允价值级次第三层次的公允价值计量调节表

下表提供了以使用重大不可观察输入值的估值技术的公允价值计量的第三层次金融工具从期初到期末余额变动的调节表：

第三层次金融工具变动

	资产				负债		
	可供出售	为交易而持有	指定为以公允价值计量且变动计入损益	衍生工具	为交易而持有	指定为以公允价值计量且变动计入损益	衍生工具
	百万美元	百万美元	百万美元	百万美元	百万美元	百万美元	百万美元
2009 年 1 月 1 日	9,116	7,561	460	9,883	6,509	–	3,805
确认为损益的利得/(损失)总额	(260)	(730)	97	(5,275)	(107)	(3)	(1,372)
确认为其他综合收益的利得总额	617	85	–	119	301	10	94
购买	1,785	1,598	260	–	22	–	–
新发行	–	–	–	–	2,522	500	–
出售	(806)	(2,166)	(13)	–	–	–	–
结算	(1,059)	(295)	(6)	(104)	(1,266)	–	(206)
转出	(3,043)	(1,077)	–	(1,057)	(537)	–	(620)
转入	3,864	1,444	426	887	1,330	–	3,491
2009 年 12 月 31 日	10,214	6,420	1,224	4,453	8,774	507	5,192
与2009 年 12 月 31 日持有的资产和负债相关的确认为损益的利得/(损失)总额	(371)	(596)	98	(3,753)	(136)	(3)	(135)

对于可供出售的证券，于第 173 页讨论的资产支持（主要是 Alt-A 和杠杆融资相关的）证券和亚洲债券组合估值的不可观察性导致了 2009 年该类别的资产转入或购买时被分类为第三层次。从第三层次转出主要是由于在 2009 年商业住房相关的资产支持证券类别的某些估值变得可观察。

对于交易性资产，转入第三层次主要由于资产支持证券，固定收入证券和一个银团贷款头寸这些特定工具的估值不可观察。从第三层次转出也主要由于资产支持证券和固定收入证券这些特定工具的估值变为可观察。采购主要和某些资产支持证券总回报互换融资交易的解除相关，HSBC 的市场风险头寸没有变化，但是为替代衍生工具交易而购入了证券。

Con.

For derivative assets, transfers out of Level 3 were driven by decreases in residual maturity of longer-dated equity options to below the observability boundary, movement in equity prices leading to previously out-of-the money or in-the-money options becoming closer to at-the-money options, and some increased observability of long-dated swaption and foreign exchange volatilities. Transfers in were largely driven by the unobservability of prepayment rates on swaps linked to third-party securitisations.

For held-for-trading liabilities, transfers into Level 3 were primarily due to a reduction in the observability of volatilities and gap risk parameters on embedded derivatives within issued structured notes. Transfers out of Level 3 were driven by similar factors as derivative assets, also relating to embedded derivatives within issued structured notes.

For derivative liabilities, the unobservability of prepayment rates on securitisation swaps was the main reason for transfers into Level 3. Transfers out of Level 3 were driven by similar factors as derivative assets.

During 2009, there were no significant transfers between Levels 1 and 2.

For assets and liabilities classified as held for trading, realised and unrealised gains and losses are presented in the income statement under 'Trading income excluding net interest income'.

Fair value changes on long term debt designated at fair value and related derivatives are presented in the income statement under 'Changes in fair value of long-term debt issued and related derivatives'. The income statement line item 'Net income/(expense) from other financial instruments designated at fair value' captures fair value movements on all other financial instruments designated at fair value and related derivatives.

Realised gains and losses from available-for-sale securities are presented under 'Gains less losses of financial investments' in the income statement while unrealised gains and losses are presented in 'Fair value gains/(losses) within 'Available-for-sale investments' in other comprehensive income/(expense).

Effect of changes in significant unobservable assumptions to reasonably possible alternatives

As discussed above, the fair value of financial instruments are, in certain circumstances, measured using valuation techniques that incorporate assumptions that are not evidenced by prices from observable current market transactions in the same instrument and are not based on observable market data. The following table shows the sensitivity of these fair values to reasonably possible alternative assumptions:

续表

对于衍生工具资产，从第三层次转出是由长期权益期权的剩余期限降至可观察界内，权益价格的变动使得之前的价外或价内期权变得更接近于平价期权，以及某些长期互换期权和外汇波动率的可观察性增加导致。转入主要是由与第三方证券化相关的互换的提前还款率的不可观察性造成。

对于为交易而持有的负债，转入第三层次主要是由于发行的结构性票据中的嵌入衍生工具的波动率和缺口风险参数的可观察性降低所致。从第三层次转出是由衍生工具资产——仍是所发行的结构性票据中的嵌入衍生工具的类似的因素导致。

对于衍生工具负债，证券化互换的提前还款率的不可观察是转入第三层次的主要原因。从第三层次转出是由和衍生工具资产类似的因素导致。

在 2009 年，第一层次和第二层次之间没有重大转移。

对于划分为交易而持有的资产和负债，已实现和未实现的利得和损失在利润表的“扣除利息净收入的交易收益”中列报。

指定为公允价值的长期债务和相关衍生工具的公允价值变动在利润表的“发行的长期债务和相关衍生工具的公允价值变动”中列报。利润表的“指定为公允价值的其他金融工具的净收入/（费用）”包括了所有其他指定为公允价值的金融工具和相关衍生工具的公允价值变动。

可供出售证券的已实现利得和损失列报在利润表的“金融投资的利得减损失”中，而未实现利得和损失列报在其他综合收益/（费用）的“可供出售投资的公允价值利得/（损失）”中。

重大不可观察假设的合理可能备选的变动影响

如上文所述，在某些情况下，金融工具的公允价值是采用了包括无法被同一工具的可观察当前市场交易的价格所证实、且并非基于可观察市场数据的假设的估值技术来计量的。下表列示了这些公允价值对合理可能备选假设的敏感性分析：

Con.

Sensitivity of fair values to reasonably possible alternative assumptions

	Reflected in profit or loss		Reflected in equity	
	Favourable changes US$m	**Unfavourable changes US$m**	**Favourable changes US$m**	**Unfavourable changes US$m**
At 31 December 2009				
Derivatives, trading assets and trading liabilities[23]	**984**	**(577)**	–	–
Financial assets and liabilities designated at fair value	**102**	**(98)**	–	–
Financial investments: available for sale	–	–	**1,161**	**(1,157)**
At 31 December 2008				
Derivatives, trading assets and trading liabilities[23]	1,266	(703)	–	–
Financial assets and liabilities designated at fair value	30	(30)	–	–
Financial investments: available for sale	–	–	984	(1,005)

For footnote, see page 195.

The decrease in the effect of changes in significant unobservable inputs in relation to derivatives, trading assets and trading liabilities during the year primarily reflected the decreased sensitivity to the assumptions for the derivative portfolios. The increase in the effect of changes in significant unobservable inputs for available-for-sale assets arose from the increase in private equity holdings in Level 3 and from increased sensitivity to the assumptions for ABSs.

Sensitivity of fair values to reasonably possible alternative assumptions by Level* 3 *instrument type

	Reflected in profit or loss		Reflected in equity	
	Favourable changes US$m	**Unfavourable changes US$m**	**Favourable changes US$m**	**Unfavourable changes US$m**
At 31 December 2009				
Private equity Investments	**54**	**(54)**	**302**	**(299)**
Asset-backed securities	**41**	**(41)**	**734**	**(735)**
Leveraged finance	**1**	**(1)**	–	–
Loans held for securitization	16	(16)	–	–
Structured notes	**3**	**(3)**	–	–
Derivatives with monolines	**333**	**(25)**	–	–
Other derivatives	**309**	**(332)**	–	–
Other portfolios	**329**	**(203)**	**125**	**(123)**

续表

公允价值对合理可能备选假设的敏感性分析

	在损益中体现		在权益中体现	
	有利变动	不利变动	有利变动	不利变动
	百万美元	百万美元	百万美元	百万美元
2009 年 12 月 31 日				
衍生工具、交易性资产和交易性负债[23]	984	(577)	–	–
指定为公允价值的金融资产和负债	102	(98)	–	–
金融投资:可供出售	–	–	1,161	(1,157)
2008 年 12 月 31 日				
衍生工具、交易性资产和交易性负债[23]	1,266	(703)	–	–
指定为公允价值的金融资产和负债	30	(30)	–	–
金融投资：可供出售	–	–	984	(1,005)

附注参见第195 页。

当年关于衍生工具、交易性资产和交易性负债的重大不可观察输入值的变动影响的减少主要体现为衍生工具组合假设的敏感性下降。关于可供出售资产的重大不可观察输入值的变动影响的增长产生于第三层次中所持有的没有活跃市场的权益以及资产支持证券假设的敏感性上升。

第三层次工具的公允价值对合理可能备选假设的敏感性分析

	在损益中体现		在权益中体现	
	有利变动	不利变动	有利变动	不利变动
	百万美元	百万美元	百万美元	百万美元
2009 年 12 月 31 日				
没有公开报价的权益投资	**54**	**(54)**	**302**	**(299)**
资产支持证券	**41**	**(41)**	**734**	**(735)**
杠杆融资	**1**	**(1)**	–	–
为证券化而持有的贷款	**16**	**(16)**	–	–
结构性票据	**3**	**(3)**	–	–
专业险种衍生工具	**333**	**(25)**	–	–
其他衍生工具	**309**	**(332)**	–	–
其他组合	**329**	**(203)**	**125**	**(123)**

Con.

At 31 December 2008				
Private equity Investments	28	(28)	234	(261)
Asset-backed securities	90	(91)	667	(660)
Leveraged finance	2	(2)	–	–
Loans held for securitization	41	(41)	–	–
Structured notes	8	(8)	–	–
Derivatives with Monolines	341	(250)	–	–
Other derivatives	652	(224)	–	–
Other portfolios	134	(89)	83	(84)

Favourable and unfavourable changes are determined on the basis of changes in the value of the instrument as a result of varying the levels of the unobservable parameters using statistical techniques. When parameters are not amenable to statistical analysis, quantification of uncertainty is judgemental.

When the fair value of a financial instrument is affected by more than one unobservable assumption, the above table reflects the most favourable or most unfavourable change from varying the assumptions individually.

In respect of private equity investments, the valuations are assessed on an asset by asset basis using a valuation methodology appropriate to the specific investment, in line with industry guidelines. In many of the methodologies, the principal assumption is the valuation multiple to be applied to the main financial indicators. This may be determined with reference to multiples for comparable listed companies and includes discounts for marketability.

For ABSs whose prices are unobservable, models are used to generate the expected value of the asset. The principal assumptions in these models are based on benchmark information about prepayment speeds, default rates, loss severities and the historical performance of the underlying assets. The models used are calibrated by using securities for which external market information is available.

For leveraged finance, loans held for securitisation and derivatives with monolines the principal assumption concerns the appropriate value to be attributed to the counterparty credit risk. This requires estimation of exposure at default, probability of default and recovery in the event of default. For loan transactions, assessment of exposure at default is straightforward. For derivative transactions, a future exposure profile is generated on the basis of current market data. Probabilities of default and recovery levels are estimated using market evidence, which may include financial information, historical experience, CDS spreads and consensus recovery levels. In the absence of such evidence, management's best estimate is used.

For structured notes and other derivatives, principal assumptions concern the value to be attributed to future volatility of asset values and the future correlation between asset values. These principal assumptions include credit volatilities and correlations used in the valuation of structured credit derivatives (including leveraged credit derivatives). For such unobservable assumptions, estimates are based on available market data, which may include the use of a proxy method to derive a volatility or a correlation from comparable assets for which market.

续表

2008 年 12 月 31 日				
没有公开报价的权益投资	28	（28）	234	（261）
资产支持证券	90	（91）	667	（660）
杠杆融资	2	（2）	–	–
为证券化而持有的贷款	41	（41）	–	–
结构性票据	8	（8）	–	–
专业险种衍生工具	341	（250）	–	–
其他衍生工具	652	（224）	–	–
其他组合	134	（89）	83	（84）

有利和不利的变动是在工具由于采用统计技术改变不可观察参数的水平而导致价值变动的基础上确定的。当参数不适用于统计分析时，量化不确定性需要实施判断。

当金融工具的公允价值受多个不可观察的假设影响时，上表体现的是单个假设变动所导致的最有利或最不利的变动。

对于没有公开报价的权益投资，估值是以单个资产为基础，采用适合该具体投资、符合行业指引的估值方法来确定的。大多数方法的主要假设是适用于主要财务指标的估值倍数。这可能会参照可比上市公司的倍数而确定并包括可销售性的折扣。

对于价格不可观察的资产支持证券，采用了模型以得到资产的预期价值。这些模型的主要假设是基于提前付款速度、违约率、损失严重性的基准信息和标的资产的历史业绩。所采用的模型使用了有外部市场信息的证券进行校正。

对于杠杆融资，为证券化而持有的贷款和专业险种衍生工具，主要的假设在于确定交易对方信用风险的合适价值。这需要估计违约敞口，违约可能性及违约情况下的可回收金额。对于贷款交易，对违约敞口的估计较简单。对于衍生工具交易，未来风险系基于当前市场数据得出。违约可能性及回收水平是采用可能包括财务信息、历史经验、信用违约互换的息差和一致的回收水平等市场证据来估计的。当没有这样的证据时，则使用管理层的最佳估计。

对于结构性票据和其他衍生工具，主要的假设在于归属于资产价值未来波动性的价值和资产价值未来相关性。这些主要假设包括用于结构性信用衍生工具（包括杠杆信用衍生工具）估值的信用波动性和相关性。对于这些不可观察的假设，估计基于可得到的市场数据可能包括采用替代方法从市场上可比资产得到波动性或相关性等。

Table 11. 6. 2 -Fair value hierarchy

Centrica plc – Annual report – 31 December 2009

(Note: comparatives have not been included in this example)

9. Fair value of financial instruments (extract)

Fair value hierarchy

Financial assets and financial liabilities measured at fair value are classified into one of three categories:

Level 1

Fair value is determined using observable inputs that reflect unadjusted quoted market prices for identical assets and liabilities, for example exchange-traded commodity contracts valued using close-of-day settlement prices. The adjusted market price used for financial assets held by the Group is the current bid price.

Level 2

Fair value is determined using significant inputs that may be either directly observable inputs or unobservable inputs that are corroborated by market data, for example over-the-counter energy contracts within the active period valued using broker quotes or third-party pricing services and foreign exchange or interest rate derivatives valued using quotes corroborated with market data.

Level 3

Fair value is determined using significant unobservable inputs that are not corroborated by market data and may be used with internally-developed methodologies that result in management's best estimate of fair value, for example energy contracts within the inactive period valued using in-house valuation techniques.

The fair value hierarchy of financial assets and liabilities measured at fair value as at 31 December 2009 was as follows:

	Level 1	Level 2	Level 3	Total
	£m	£m	£m	£m
Financial assets				
Derivative financial instruments:				
Energy derivatives	46	550	64	660
Interest rate derivatives	–	72	–	72
Foreign exchange derivatives	2	74	–	76
Treasury gilts designated at fair value through profit and loss	104	–	–	104

表 11.6.2　——公允价值级次

Centrica plc——年报——2009 年 12 月 31 日

（注：此示例未包括比较数字）

9. 金融工具的公允价值（节选）

公允价值级次

以公允价值计量的金融资产和金融负债被划分为三个种类：

第一层次

公允价值是按照反映相同资产或负债在活跃市场中未经调整的报价的可观察输入值确定，如在交易所交易的商品合同采用日收盘的结算价格。本集团持有的金融资产使用的调整的市场价格是当前买入价。

第二层次

公允价值是采用直接可观察的输入值，或者是可以被市场数据佐证的不可观察输入值这两种重大输入值确定的，如买卖双方直接交易的能源合同在活跃期间采用经纪人报价或第三方报价服务估值，以及外汇或利率衍生工具采用被市场数据佐证的报价估值。

第三层次

公允价值是采用无法被市场数据佐证的，和可能用于内部研发的方法得到管理层对公允价值的最佳估计的重大不可观察输入值确定，如非活跃期间的能源合同采用内部估值技术评估。

于 2009 年 12 月 31 日以公允价值计量的金融资产和负债的公允价值级次如下所示：

	第一层次 百万英镑	第二层次 百万英镑	第三层次 百万英镑	总计 百万英镑
金融资产				
衍生金融工具：				
能源衍生工具	46	550	64	660
利率衍生工具	–	72	–	72
外汇衍生工具	2	74	–	76
指定为以公允价值计量且变动计入损益的国库券	104	–	–	104

Con.

Debt instruments	62	56	–	118
Equity instruments	17	–	11	28
Total financial assets	231	752	75	1,058
Financial liabilities				
Derivative financial instruments:				
Energy derivatives	(198)	(1,954)	(490)	(2,642)
Interest rate derivatives	–	(15)	–	(15)
Foreign exchange derivatives	–	(93)	–	(93)
Total financial liabilities	(198)	(2,062)	(490)	(2,750)

There were no significant transfers out of Level 1 into Level 2 and out of Level 2 into Level 1 during 2009.

The reconciliation of the Level 3 fair value measurements during the period is as follows:

	Equity instruments	**Energy derivatives**	**2009**
	£m	**£m**	**£m**
Level 3 financial assets			
1 January	3	399	402
Total realised and unrealised losses recognised in profit or loss	–	(247)	(247)
Transfers from Level 3 to Level 2	–	(88)	(88)
Acquisitions	8	–	8
31 December	11	64	75
Total gains for the period for Level 3 financial assets held at the end of the reporting period	–	64	64

Gains or losses for the period (above) are presented in the Income Statement and Statement of Other Comprehensive Income as follows:

	Exceptional items and certain re-measurements	**Other comprehensive income**	**Total**
	£m	**£m**	**£m**
Total losses for the period	(247)	–	(247)
Total gains for the period for assets held at the end of the reporting period	64	–	64

续表

债权工具	62	56	–	118
权益工具	17	–	11	28
金融资产总计	231	752	75	1,058
金融负债				
衍生金融工具：				
能源衍生工具	(198)	(1,954)	(490)	(2,642)
利率衍生工具	–	(15)	–	(15)
外汇衍生工具	–	(93)	–	(93)
金融负债总计	(198)	(2,062)	(490)	(2,750)

在2009年，无从第一层次到第二层次以及从第二层次到第一层次的重大转移。

当期第三层次的公允价值计量的变动表如下：

	能源工具	**能源衍生工具**	**2009**
	百万英镑	**百万英镑**	**百万英镑**
第三层次金融资产			
1月1日	3	399	402
确认在损益中的已实现和未实现损失总计	–	(247)	(247)
从第三层次转入第二层次	–	(88)	(88)
购买	8	–	8
12月31日	11	64	75
报告期末持有的第三层次金融资产的当期利得总额	–	64	64

当期利得或损失（参见上文）在利润表和其他综合收益表中列报如下：

	例外项目及某些重新计量	**其他综合收益**	**总计**
	百万英镑	**百万英镑**	**百万英镑**
当期损失总额	(247)	–	(247)
报告期末持有资产的当期利得总额	64	–	64

Con.

	Energy derivatives	2009
	£m	£m
Level 3 financial liabilities		
1 January	(568)	(568)
Total realised and unrealised losses:		
recognised in profit or loss	(54)	(54)
Recognised in other comprehensive income	(9)	(9)
Transfers from Level 3 to Level 2	141	141
31 December	(490)	(490)
Total losses for the period for Level 3 financial liabilities held at the end of the reporting period	(490)	(490)

Losses for the period (above) are presented in the Income Statement and Statement of Other Comprehensive Income as follows:

	Exceptional items and certain re-measurements	Other comprehensive income	Total
	£m	£m	£m
Total losses for the period	(54)	(9)	(63)
Total losses for the period for liabilities held at the end of the reporting period	(484)	(6)	(490)

The impacts of reasonably possible changes to assumed gas, power, coal, emissions and oil prices on the net fair value of the Group's fair value measurements categorised as Level 3 are as follows:

Energy price	**2009 Reasonably possible change in variable**
UK gas (p/therm)	+/ −10
UK power (£/MWh)	+/ −5
UK coal (US$/tonne)	+/ −20
UK emissions (€/tonne)	+/ −3
UK oil (US$/bbl)	+/ −19

	2009
Increase/(decrease) in fair value	**£m**
UK energy prices – increase/(decrease)	**17/(17)**

续表

	能源衍生工具 百万英镑	2009 百万英镑
第三层次金融负债		
1月1日	(568)	(568)
已实现和未实现损失总计：		
确认为损益	(54)	(54)
确认为其他综合收益	(9)	(9)
从第三层次转入第二层次	141	141
12月31日	(490)	(490)
报告期末持有的第三层次金融负债的当期损失总额	(490)	(490)

当期损失（参见上文）在利润表和其他综合收益表中列报如下：

	例外项目及某些重新计量 百万英镑	其他综合收益 百万英镑	总计 百万英镑
当期损失总额	(54)	(9)	(63)
报告期末持有负债的当期损失总额	(484)	(6)	(490)

煤气、电力、煤炭、排放以及石油价格的合理可能变动对本集团划分为第三层次的公允价值计量的公允价值净值的影响如下：

能源价格	**2009 变量的合理可能变动**
英国煤气（便士每度）	+/−10
英国电力（英镑每兆瓦时）	+/−5
英国煤炭（美元每吨）	+/−20
英国排放（欧元每吨）	+/−3
英国石油（美元每桶）	+/−19

公允价值的增加/(减少)	**2009 百万英镑**
英国能源价格 – 增加/(减少)	17/(17)

Con.

The impacts disclosed above result from changing the assumptions used for fair valuing energy contracts in relation to gas, power, emissions, coal and oil prices to reasonably possible alternative assumptions at the balance sheet date. The fair value impacts only concern those contracts entered into which are within the scope of IAS 39 and are marked-to-market based on valuation models using assumptions that are not currently observable in an active market. The sensitivity analysis provided is hypothetical only and should be used with caution, as the impacts provided are not necessarily indicative of the actual impacts that would be experienced because the Group's actual exposure to market rates is constantly changing as the Group's portfolio of energy contracts changes. Changes in fair values based on a variation in a market variable cannot be extrapolated as the relationship between the change in market variable and the change in fair value may not be linear.

Financial instrument risk disclosures

11.79 An entity should disclose information that enables users of its financial statements to evaluate the nature and extent of risks arising from financial instruments to which the entity is exposed at the reporting date. [IFRS 7 para 31].

11.80 The disclosures described from paragraph 11.83 onwards focus on the risks that arise from financial instruments and how they have been managed. These risks typically include, but are not limited to, credit risk, liquidity risk and market risk as discussed in paragraph 11.44 above. [IFRS 7 para 32].

11.81 When an entity uses several methods to manage a risk exposure, it should disclose information using the method or methods that provide the most relevant and reliable information. [IFRS 7 App B para 7].

11.82 The disclosures should be given either in the financial statements or incorporated by cross-reference from the financial statements to some other statement, such as a management commentary or risk report, that is available to users of the financial statements on the same terms as the financial statements and at the same time. Without the information incorporated by cross-reference, the financial statements are incomplete. [IFRS 7 App B para 6].

续表

上文披露的影响是运用评估能源合同公允价值中有关煤气、电力、排放、煤炭和石油价格于资产负债表日的合理可能备选假设时所致。对公允价值的影响仅限于那些在 IAS 39 范围内的、且使用基于当前不可在活跃市场观察的假设的估值模型的、以公允价值计量的合同。所提供的敏感性分析仅仅是假设且应当谨慎使用，因为本集团能源合同组合的变动、本集团对市场费率的敞口实时发生变动，因此所披露的影响不一定是应该发生的实际影响的指示。由于市场变量变化和公允价值变动并非线性关系，基于市场变量变化的公允价值变动无法推算。

金融工具风险的披露

11.79　主体应当披露信息，以帮助其财务报表使用者评估在报告日金融工具所产生的风险的性质和程度。[IFRS 7 第 31 段]。

11.80　从 11.83 段开始各段所述的披露要求是针对金融工具所产生的风险以及主体如何管理这些风险的。具有代表性的风险包括但不限于，如上文第 11.44 段中所讨论的信用风险、流动性风险和市场风险。[IFRS 7 第 32 段]。

11.81　当主体使用几种方法管理风险敞口时，主体应当披露为提供最相关和最可靠的信息所使用的一种或多种方法的信息。[IFRS 7 附录 B 第 7 段]。

11.82　该披露应当在财务报表中提供，或者包括在财务报表和一些其他报表的交互参照中，例如管理层评论或风险报告，而财务报表使用者在同一时间可以以获得财务报表相同的条件获得这些文件。如果未能通过交互参照提供这些信息，财务报表是不完整的。[IFRS 7 附录 B 第 6 段]。

Qualitative disclosures

11.83 For each type of risk arising from financial instruments, an entity should disclose:

- The exposures to risk and how they arise.

  Information about risk exposures might describe exposures both gross and net of risk transfer and other risk-mitigating transactions.

- Its objectives, policies and processes for managing the risk and the methods used to measure the risk. This might include, but is not limited to:

  - The structure and organisation of the entity's risk management functions, including a discussion of independence and accountability.
  - The scope and nature of the entity's risk reporting or measurement systems.
  - The entity's policies for hedging or mitigating risk, including its policies and procedures for taking collateral.
  - The entity's processes for monitoring the continuing effectiveness of such hedges or mitigating devices.
  - The entity's policies and procedures for avoiding excessive concentrations of risk.

- Any changes in the above for the period.

  Entities should disclose the reasons for the change. Such changes may result from changes in exposure to risk or from changes in the way those exposures are managed.

[IFRS 7 paras 33, IG 15 – 16].

11.84 An example of a company that has included the above disclosure requirements in its risk management policy is given in Table 11.8 below. Note that the disclosures precede the effective date of the revised IAS 1 and thus the titles of the performance statements referred to are before the new titles introduced by IAS 1.

定性披露

11.83　对金融工具所产生的每种类型的风险，主体应当披露：

- 风险敞口和风险是如何产生的。

  风险敞口的信息可以描述风险转移的总额和净额以及其他分散风险的交易。

- 其管理风险的目标、政策和程序与计量风险的方法。这可能包括但不限于：

  - 主体风险管理职能的结构和组织形式，包括对其独立性和受托责任的描述。
  - 主体的风险报告或计量系统的范围和性质。
  - 主体对风险进行套期或分散风险的政策，包括接受抵押物的政策和程序。
  - 主体对这种套期或分散风险的方法的持续有效性进行管理的程序。
  - 主体避免风险过度集中的政策和程序。

- 本期上述各项目的任何变化。

  主体应当披露变化的原因。这些变化可能是风险敞口改变或管理风险敞口的方法改变的结果。

[IFRS 7 第 33 段、IG 第 15－16 段]。

11.84　下表 11.8 中列出了在风险管理政策中包括了上述披露要求的公司示例。值得注意的是，这些披露早于修订后 IAS 1 的生效日，因此所用的业绩报表名称不是 IAS 1 所引入的新名称。

Table 11. 8 – Risk management policy

Diageo plc – Annual Report – 30 June 2009

Risk Management

This section on risk management forms part of the audited financial statements.

The group's funding, liquidity and exposure to interest rate and foreign exchange rate risks are managed by the group's treasury department. The treasury department uses a combination of derivative and conventional financial instruments to manage these underlying risks.

Treasury operations are conducted within a framework of board-approved policies and guidelines, which are recommended and subsequently monitored by the finance committee. This committee is described in the corporate governance report. These policies and guidelines include benchmark exposure and/or hedge cover levels for key areas of treasury risk. The benchmarks, hedge cover and overall appropriateness of Diageo's risk management policies are reviewed by the board following, for example, significant business, strategic or accounting changes. The framework provides for limited defined levels of flexibility in execution to allow for the optimal application of the board-approved strategies. Transactions giving rise to exposures away from the defined benchmark levels arising on the application of this flexibility are separately monitored on a daily basis using value at risk analysis. These derivative financial instruments are carried at fair value and gains or losses are taken to the income statement as they arise. At 30 June 2009 gains and losses on these transactions were not material.

The finance committee receives monthly reports on the activities of the treasury department, including any exposures away from the defined benchmarks.

Currency risk

The group publishes its consolidated financial statements in sterling and conducts business in many foreign currencies. As a result, it is subject to foreign currency exchange risk due to exchange rate movements, which will affect the group's transaction costs and the translation of the results and underlying net assets of its foreign operations. Where hedge accounting is applied, hedges are documented and tested for hedge effectiveness on an ongoing basis. Diageo expects hedges entered into to continue to be effective and therefore does not expect the impact of ineffectiveness on the income statement to be material.

表 11.8——风险管理政策

Diageo plc 公司——年度报告——2009 年 6 月 30 日

风险管理

此风险管理部分构成已审计的财务报表的一部分。

集团的资金筹措、流动性和利率和外汇汇率风险敞口由集团的财务部门管理。财务部门采用衍生工具和传统金融工具相结合的方式来对这些潜在风险进行管理。

资金运作是在董事会批准的政策和指南框架范围之内进行的，这些政策和指南由其财务委员会建议并进行随后的监控。在公司治理报告中对该委员会进行了描述。这些政策和指南包括资金风险主要方面的基准敞口和/或套期保值涵盖的水平。在出现如商业、战略或会计等重大变更后，将由董事会对 Diageo 公司的风险管理政策的基准值、套期保值涵盖值和整体适宜性进行审查。框架提供执行中设定的有限灵活度，使董事会所批准的策略得以最好的实施。对因采用这种灵活度而出现规定基准值以外的敞口的交易采用风险价值分析每天单独监控。这些衍生金融工具以公允价值计量，其利得或损失在发生时计入利润表。在 2009 年 6 月 30 日这些交易的利得或损失并不重大。

财政委员会收取财务部门的工作月报，包括规定基准值以外的任何敞口。

货币风险

本集团以英镑列报其合并财务报表，并以多种外币从事业务。因此，它将因为外汇汇率的变动而承受外汇风险的影响，这将影响到公司的交易成本及其境外经营的结果和相应净资产的折算。在采用套期会计的情况下，将持续地记录套期以及测试套期有效性。Diageo 预期所进行的套期持续有效，因此预计无效性不会对损益表有重大影响。

Con.

Hedge of net investment in foreign operations

The group hedges a substantial portion of its exposure to fluctuations on the translation into sterling of its foreign operations by designating net borrowings held in foreign currencies and by using foreign currency swaps and forwards. Where a liquid foreign exchange market exists, the group's policy approved by the board is to seek to hedge currency exposure on its net investment in foreign operations within the following percentage bands: 80% to 100% for US dollars, 80% to 100% for euros and 50% to 100% for other significant currencies.

Exchange differences arising on the retranslation of foreign currency borrowings (including foreign currency swaps and forwards), to the extent that they are in an effective hedge relationship, are recognised in the statement of recognised income and expense to match exchange differences on net investments in foreign operations. Exchange differences on foreign currency borrowings not in a hedge relationship and any ineffectiveness are taken to the income statement.

Transaction exposure hedging

For currencies in which there is an active market, the group's policy approved by the board is to seek to hedge between 60% and 100% of forecast transactional foreign exchange rate risk, for up to a maximum of 21 months forward, using forward foreign currency exchange contracts with coverage levels increasing nearer to the forecast transaction date. The effective portion of the gain or loss on the hedge is recognised in the statement of recognised income and expense and recycled into the income statement at the same time as the underlying hedged transaction affects the income statement. Any ineffectiveness is taken to the income statement.

Hedge of foreign currency debt

The group uses cross currency interest rate swaps to hedge the forward foreign currency risk associated with certain foreign currency denominated bonds. The effective portion of the gain or loss on the hedge is recognised in the statement of recognised income and expense and recycled into the income statement at the same time as the underlying hedged transaction affects the income statement. Any ineffectiveness is taken to the income statement.

Interest rate risk

The group has an exposure to interest rate risk, arising principally on changes in US dollar, euro and sterling interest rates. To manage interest rate risk, the group manages its proportion of fixed to floating rate borrowings within limits approved by the board,

续表

境外经营净投资套期

集团通过指定外币净借款及使用外汇互换和远期对其大部分境外经营折算为英镑时波动的敞口进行了套期。在存在某一流动外汇市场的情况下，本集团经董事会批准的政策是争取在如下百分比段中对其境外经营净投资的外币敞口进行套期：美元 80% 到 100%、欧元 80% 到 100%、其他重要货币 50% 到 100%。

对于由外币借款的重新折算（包括外汇互换和远期）产生的汇兑差额，如果它们是处于有效的套期关系中，则将在已确认收益和费用表中确认，与境外经营净投资的汇兑差额相匹配。不属于套期关系的外币借款汇兑差额以及任何无效部分均计入利润表。

交易敞口套期

对于具有活跃市场的货币，本集团经董事会批准的政策是争取对 60% 到 100% 的预期交易外汇汇率风险进行套期，期限最长为 21 个月，采用远期外汇合同将涵盖程度增加并更接近预期交易日。套期利得或损失的有效部分在已确认收益和费用表中确认，并在相关被套期交易影响利润表的同时转至利润表。任何无效部分计入利润表。

外币债务套期

本集团使用交叉货币利率互换对特定以外币计价的债券的远期外汇风险进行套期。套期利得或损失的有效部分在已确认收益和费用表中确认，并在相关被套期交易影响利润表的同时转至利润表。任何无效部分计入利润表。

利率风险

集团的利率风险敞口，主要产生于美元、欧元和英镑利率的变动。为了对利率风险进行管理，本集团主要通过发行固定和浮动利率条款的债务和商业票据以及采用利率衍生工具将其固定利率对浮动利率借款的比例控制在董事会所批准的限值内。这些措施

Con.

primarily through issuing fixed and floating rate term debt and commercial paper, and by utilising interest rate derivatives. These practices serve to reduce the volatility of the group's reported financial performance. To facilitate operational efficiency and effective hedge accounting, the group's policy is to maintain fixed rate borrowings within a band of 40% to 60% of projected net borrowings, and the overall net borrowings portfolio is managed according to a duration measure. The board approved template specifies different duration guidelines and fixed/floating amortisation periods (time taken for the fixed element of debt to reduce to zero) depending on different interest rate environments. The majority of Diageo's existing interest rate hedges are designated as hedges. Designated hedges are expected to be effective.

Liquidity risk

Liquidity risk is the risk that an entity will encounter difficulty in meeting obligations associated with financial liabilities that are settled by delivering cash or other financial assets. The group's policy with regard to the expected maturity profile of borrowings of group financing companies is to limit the amount of such borrowings maturing within 12 months to 50% of gross borrowings less money market demand deposits and the level of commercial paper to 30% of gross borrowings less money market demand deposits. In addition, it is group policy to maintain backstop facility terms from relationship banks to support commercial paper obligations.

Quantitative disclosures

11.85 For each type of risk arising from financial instruments, an entity should disclose:

- Summary quantitative data about its exposure to that risk at the reporting date. This disclosure should be based on the information provided internally to the entity's key management personnel (as defined in IAS 24, 'Related party disclosures'), for example, the entity's board of directors or chief executive officer. An entity with two distinct operations (for example, a retail division and a manufacturing division) may be monitored by management separately as two divisions. All disclosures should normally be provided on a consolidated basis. However, those disclosures that are based on management reporting could be presented separately for both the divisions as that is the way management monitors the financial risks, unless there were material transactions between the divisions, in which case separate disclosures could be misleading.

续表

旨在降低本集团所报告的财务业绩的波动性。为促进操作的效率和有效的套期会计，本集团的政策是将固定利率借款维持在计划净借款的40%到60%的范围内，并根据到期日对净借款总体进行管理。董事会所批准的模版根据不同的利率环境规定了不同的到期日指南和固定/浮动摊销期间（债务的固定成分降为零所需要的时间）。Diageo现有的大部分利率套期都是指定为套期的。所指定的套期均预期有效。
流动性风险
流动性风险是主体通过交付现金和其他金融资产履行相关金融负债结算的义务时将面临困难的风险。本集团对集团融资公司借款预期到期日情况的政策为将12个月内到期的借款金额限制在总借款减去货币市场需求存款后的50%，将商业票据的水平限制在总借款减去货币市场需求存款后的30%。此外，集团的政策还旨在与有关系的银行维持后续贷款额度以支持商业票据业务。

定量披露

11.85　对金融工具所产生的每种类型的风险，主体应当披露：

■ 报告日关于风险敞口的概括性定量信息。这一披露应基于主体内部向关键管理人员（如《国际会计准则第24号——关联方披露》所定义的），例如主体的董事会或首席执行官。对于具有两种截然不同的经营业务（例如，一个零售分部和一个生产分部）的主体，管理层可以将其作为两个分部分别进行监控。正常情况下所有披露均应在合并层面作出。但是，根据管理层报告所作出的披露可以对两个分部进行单独列报，因为管理层正是以这种方式对其金融风险进行监控，除非是两个分部之间有重大的交易，在这种情况下单独披露可能具有误导性。

- The disclosures described in paragraphs 11. 86 to 11. 118, to the extent not provided in the previous bullet point, unless the risk is not material. [IFRS 7 para 34 (b)]. These, in other words, are IFRS 7's minimum disclosure requirements, regardless of whether management uses this information to manage the entity's risks. In terms of determining whether a risk is material consider the following example. An entity invests in a foreign currency bond maturing in one year and simultaneously enters into an foreign currency forward contract with a corresponding maturity to offset the foreign currency risk. In this case, the materiality of the foreign currency risk on the bond is assessed without the foreign currency forward contract. The bond and the forward are dissimilar items and, therefore, the materiality assessment of the foreign currency risk is performed without considering the forward contract. If it is established that the foreign currency risk is material, the disclosure required in the sensitivity analysis (see para 11. 106) is based on the net foreign currency exposure; that after offsetting the foreign currency bond against the forward contract. The same approach would apply for the assessment of credit risk, liquidity risk and other market risk.

- Concentrations of risk if not apparent from the previous two bullet points (see para 11. 86 below).

[IFRS 7 para 34].

11. 86 Concentrations of risk arise from financial instruments that have similar characteristics and are affected similarly by changes in economic or other conditions. The identification of concentrations of risk requires judgement taking into account the entity's circumstances. Disclosure of concentrations of risk should include:

- A description of how management determines concentrations (see para 11. 87 below).

- A description of the shared characteristic that identifies each concentration (for example, counterparty, geographical area, currency or market).

- The amount of the risk exposure associated with all financial instruments sharing that characteristic.

[IFRS 7 App B para 8].

■ 第 11. 86 段到 11. 118 段所述披露，以上段中未提供的信息为限，除非风险是不重要的。[IFRS 7 第 34（b）段]。换言之，这些是 IFRS 7 的最低披露要求，无论管理层是否使用这些信息来管理主体的风险。就确定某项风险是否重大而言，请参考如下示例。某主体投资于某项一年到期的外币债券，同时签订了一个具有相应到期日的外汇远期合同以抵销其外汇风险。在这种情况下，评估债券外汇风险的重要性时不应考虑该项外汇远期合同。该项债券和该项远期合同不是类似的项目，因此在评估外汇风险的重要性时不应考虑该远期合同。如果确定外汇风险为重大，在敏感性分析（参见第 11. 106 段）中所要求的披露将根据外币债券抵销了远期合同之后的净外汇敞口而定。同样的方法在对信用风险、流动性风险及其他市场风险进行评估时也适用。

■ 风险集中信息，如果上述两段披露的信息不明显（参见下文第 11. 86 段）。

[IFRS 7 第 34 段]。

11. 86　风险集中来自具有类似特征的金融工具并且受类似经济或其他环境变化的影响。风险集中的识别要求考虑主体对环境的判断。风险集中的披露应包括：

■ 管理层如何确定集中的描述（参见下文第 11. 87 段）。

■ 识别每种集中（例如交易对方、地理区域、货币或市场）的共有特征的描述。

■ 与共有该特征的所有金融工具相关的风险敞口金额。

[IFRS 7 附录 B 第 8 段]。

11.87 Concentrations of credit risk may arise from:

■ Industry sectors.

Thus, if an entity's counterparties are concentrated in one or more industry sectors (such as retail or wholesale), it would disclose separately exposure to risks arising from each concentration of counterparties.

■ Credit rating or other measure of credit quality.

Thus, if an entity's counterparties are concentrated in one or more credit qualities (such as secured loans or unsecured loans) or in one or more credit ratings (such as investment grade or speculative grade), it would disclose separately exposure to risks arising from each concentration of counterparties.

■ Geographical distribution.

Thus, if an entity's counterparties are concentrated in one or more geographical markets (such as Asia or Europe) it would disclose separately exposure to risks arising from each concentration of counterparties.

■ A limited number of individual counterparties or groups of closely related counterparties.

[IFRS 7 para IG18].

11.88 Similar principles apply to identifying concentrations of other risks, including liquidity risk and market risk. For example, concentrations of liquidity risk may arise from the repayment terms of financial liabilities, sources of borrowing facilities or reliance on a particular market in which to realise liquid assets. Concentrations of foreign exchange risk may arise if an entity has a significant net open position in a single foreign currency, or aggregate net open positions in several currencies that tend to move together. [IFRS 7 para IG18].

11.89 If the quantitative data disclosed as at the reporting date are unrepresentative of an entity's exposure to risk during the period, an entity should provide further information that is representative. [IFRS 7 para 35]. To meet this requirement, an entity might disclose the highest, lowest and average amount of

11.87 信用风险集中可能来自于：

■ 行业部门。

因此，如果主体的交易对方集中于一个或多个行业部门（例如零售业或批发业），主体应分别披露交易对方每个集中点所产生的风险敞口。

■ 信用评级或信用质量的其他计量方法。

因此，如果主体的交易对方集中于一种或多种信用质量（例如担保贷款或无担保贷款），或集中于一个或多个信用等级（例如投资级别或投机级别），主体应分别披露交易对方的每个集中点所产生的风险敞口。

■ 地理分布。

因此，如果主体的交易对方集中于一个或多个地区市场（例如亚洲或欧洲），主体应分别披露交易对方的每个集中点所产生的风险敞口。

■ 有限数量的单个交易对方或密切相关的交易对方组群。

[IFRS 7 IG 第 18 段]。

11.88 类似原则适用于对其他风险集中的识别，包括流动性风险和市场风险。例如，流动性风险集中可能来自于金融负债的偿还条款、融资额度的来源或对变现流动资产特定市场的依赖度。外币风险集中可能来自于主体有单一外币的重大未平仓头寸，或几种倾向于共同波动的外币合计未平仓头寸。[IFRS 7 IG 第 18 段]。

11.89 如果在报告日披露的定量信息不能代表主体在本期的风险敞口，主体应提供能代表其风险敞口的进一步信息。[IFRS 7 第 35 段]。为满足这一要求，主体可以披露其在本期内的风险敞口的最高、最低和平均金额。例如，通常如果主体对某一特定货币具有很大的风险敞口，但在年末时这一情况得以缓解，

risk to which it was exposed during the period. For example, if an entity typically has a large exposure to a particular currency, but at year-end unwinds the position, the entity might disclose a graph showing the exposure at various times during the period, or disclose the highest, lowest and average exposures. [IFRS 7 para IG20]. In addition consider the following examples:

Example 1 – Year end credit risk exposure unrepresentative due to seasonal fluctuations

Entity Y is producing seeds for the agricultural industry. The main season for planting is the spring. 75% of entity Y's markets are in the northern hemisphere; 25% are in the southern hemisphere. Entity Y's account receivables are approximately C400 million in June and C100 million in December. Entity Y has a December year end. Does entity Y have to disclose additional information about its exposure to credit risk on the receivables that is representative of its exposure to risk during the year?

In this case, the December year end exposure to credit risk is unrepresentative of the entity's exposure during the period. Entity Y should provide further information that is representative, such as a description (with amounts) of how the exposures vary during the year, or the average (or highest) exposure to credit risk during the year.

Example 2 – Year end credit risk exposure unrepresentative due to a major acquisition

On 30 November 20X6, entity A (€ functional currency) acquires a major competitor. Due to the acquisition, the US$ denominated receivables increased from $100 million to $300 million and variable interest rate debt doubled from €200 million to €400 million compared to the balances as at 30 June 20X6. Entity A has a December year end. The balances as of 31 December 20X6 are considered to be representative of the next year(s). Does entity A have to disclose additional information that is representative of its exposure to risk during the year?

In this scenario, entity A should disclose additional information because the quantitative data as at 31 December 20X6 is not representative of the financial

则主体可以用图表披露其在期间内不同时间的风险敞口，或披露最高、最低和平均风险敞口。[IFRS 7 IG 第 20 段]。此外，请参考如下示例：

示例 1——因季节性波动而令年末信用风险敞口不具代表性

主体 Y 生产农用种子。主要播种季节为春季。主体 Y 75% 的市场位于北半球；25% 的市场位于南半球。主体 Y 在 6 月的应收账款约为 C4.00 亿，在 12 月为 C1.00 亿。主体 Y 的会计年末为 12 月。主体 Y 是否必须就能够代表其在本年度中风险敞口的应收账款的信用风险敞口披露额外的信息?

在这种情况下，12 月年末时的信用风险敞口并不能够代表主体在当期的敞口。主体 Y 应提供具有代表性的进一步信息，例如敞口在年度中是如何变化的描述（及金额），或本年度中信用风险的平均（或最高）敞口。

示例 2——因一项重大收购而令年末信用风险敞口不具代表性

于 20X6 年 11 月 30 日，主体 A（功能货币为€）收购了一个主要竞争对手。由于此项收购，与 20X6 年 6 月 30 日的余额相比，其以美元计价的应收账款从 1.00 亿美元上升至 3.00 亿美元，而浮动利率债务翻了一倍，从 2.00 亿欧元增加至 4.00 亿欧元。主体 A 的会计年末为 12 月。20X6 年 12 月 31 日的余额被认为是能够代表以后年度的情况。主体 A 是否必须披露能够代表其本年度中风险敞口的额外信息?

在这种情况下，主体 A 应披露额外信息，因为 20X6 年 12 月 31 日的定量数据并不能够代表 20X6 年这一财务期间的情况。仅仅说明该数据不具有

period 20X6. A mere statement that the data is not representative is not sufficient. To meet IFRS 7's requirement the entity might disclose the highest, lowest and average amount of risk to which it was exposed during the period. However, a full high/low/average analysis might not be required if the exposure at the year end is representative for future periods and if sufficient explanations of the facts and circumstances are provided.

Credit risk

11.90 Activities that give rise to credit risk include, but are not limited to:

- Granting loans and receivables to customers and placing deposits with other entities. In these cases, the maximum exposure to credit risk is the carrying amount of the related financial assets.
- Entering into derivative contracts (for example, foreign exchange contracts, interest rate swaps and credit derivatives). When the resulting asset is measured at fair value, the maximum exposure to credit risk at the reporting date will equal the carrying amount.
- Granting financial guarantees. In this case, the maximum exposure to credit risk is the maximum amount the entity could have to pay if the guarantee is called on, which may be significantly greater than the amount recognised as a liability.
- Making a loan commitment that is irrevocable over the life of the facility or is revocable only in response to a material adverse change. If the issuer cannot settle the loan commitment net in cash or another financial instrument, the maximum credit exposure is the commitment's full amount. This is because it is uncertain whether the amount of any undrawn portion may be drawn upon in the future. This may be significantly greater than the amount recognised as a liability.

[IFRS 7 App B para 10].

11.91 IFRS 7 requires an entity to disclose information about its exposure to credit risk by class of financial instrument. Financial instruments in the same class share economic characteristics with respect to the risk being disclosed (in this case,

代表性并不足够。为满足 IFRS 7 的要求，主体可以披露其在本期最高、最低和平均风险敞口。但是，如果年末的敞口能够代表未来期间且如果有关事实和情况的充分解释已提供，可以不要求进行完全的高/低/平均分析。

信用风险

11.90　导致信用风险的行为，包括但不限于：

- 向客户发放贷款和应收款以及存放在其他主体的存款。在这种情况下，对信用风险的最大敞口是相关金融资产的账面金额。

- 签订衍生工具合同（例如，外汇合同、利率互换和信用衍生工具）。当由此产生的资产以公允价值计量时，报告日信用风险的最大敞口等于账面金额。

- 提供财务担保。在这种情况下，信用风险的最大敞口是担保被要求履行时主体所必须支付的最大金额，这一金额可能显著大于已作为负债确认的金额。

- 就融资额度提供期内不可撤销的或只有当重大不利变化出现时才可撤销的贷款承诺。如果发行人不能以现金或其他金融工具对贷款承诺进行净额结算，其最大风险敞口是承诺的全部金额。这是因为任何未用的额度在未来的使用具有不确定性。这一金额可能显著大于已作为负债确认的金额。

[IFRS 7 附录 B 第 10 段]。

11.91　IFRS 7 要求按金融工具的类型披露其信用风险敞口的信息。同一类型金融工具具有所披露风险（这里指信用风险）的共同经济特征。例如，主体可以确定住宅抵押、无担保消费贷款和商业贷款各自具有不同的经济特征。主

credit risk) . For example, an entity might determine that residential mortgages, unsecured consumer loans, and commercial loans each have different economic characteristics. The information an entity should disclose by class of financial instrument is as follows:

- The amount that best represents its maximum exposure to credit risk at the reporting date without taking account of any collateral held or other credit enhancements (for example, netting agreements that do not qualify for offset in accordance with IAS 32 – see para 11.26 above). The 2010 annual improvements clarified that this disclosure is not required for financial instruments whose carrying amount best represents the maximum exposure to credit risk. This amendment applies to annual periods beginning on or after 1 January 2011 and early application is permitted.

- In respect of the amount disclosed above, a description of collateral held as security and other credit enhancements (see para 11.93 below).

- Information about the credit quality of financial assets that are neither past due nor impaired (see para 11.95 below).

- The carrying amount of financial assets that would otherwise be past due or impaired whose terms have been renegotiated. This disclosure should be given only in the year when the renegotiation took place, that is, in the year in which the asset's contractual terms were changed. In subsequent years the asset is considered based on the new (renegotiated) terms and disclosure would only be required if renegotiated again. The disclosure of the carrying amount of financial assets which would have otherwise been past due but have been renegotiated has been removed by the changes to IFRS 7 as part of the 2010 annual improvements. These amendments apply to annual periods beginning on or after 1 January 2011 and early application is permitted.

[IFRS 7 para 36, IG21].

11.91.1 The above disclosures do not apply to an entity's holdings of equity investments. This is because the definition of equity in IAS 32 requires that the issuer has no obligation to pay cash or transfer other assets. Therefore, such equity investments are subject to price risk, not credit risk. The only exception is where

体应按金融工具的类型披露的信息如下：

■ 在不考虑任何所持有的抵押物或其他信用增级（例如，根据 IAS 32 不符合相互抵销条件的净额结算协议——参见上文第 11.26 段）的情况下，在报告日最能代表其最大风险敞口的金额。2010 年年度改进澄清了当账面金额是最大信用风险敞口的最好代表时，该金融资产无需进行该项披露。该修订于起始日在 2011 年 1 月 1 日或以后的年度期间生效，允许提前实施。

■ 对于如上所披露的金额，对持有的抵押物和其他信用增级的描述（参见下文第 11.93 段）。

■ 有关未逾期也未发生减值的金融资产的信用质量的信息（参见下文第 11.95 段）。

■ 相关条款已重新商定否则可能已逾期或发生减值的金融资产的账面金额。该披露只应在进行重新商定的年度，即在资产的合同条款被变更的那一年做出。在之后的年度里该资产被认为是根据新（重新商定的）条款，只有在再次重新商定时才要求进行披露。对于相关条款已重新商定否则可能已逾期或发生减值的金融资产的账面金额的披露已被 2010 年年度改进对 IFRS 7 的部分变动中删除。该修订于起始日在 2011 年 1 月 1 日或以后的年度期间生效，允许提前实施。

[IFRS 7 第 36 段，IG 第 21 段]。

11.91.1　上述披露不适用于主体持有的权益投资。这是因为 IAS 32 对权益的定义要求发行人没有支付现金或转移其他资产的义务。因此，这种权益投资会受到价格风险而不是信用风险的影响。其唯一的例外是在这种金融资产发生减值的情况下，它们将要求作出第 11.96 段第二点所讨论的披露。

such financial assets have been impaired. They will then require the disclosure discussed in second bullet of paragraph 11. 96.

11. 91. 2 In respect of the first bullet point in paragraph 11. 91 above, the amount that best represents the entity's maximum exposure to credit risk relating to financial assets is typically the gross carrying amount, net of:

- any amounts offset in accordance with IAS 32 (see para 11. 15 above); and
- any impairment losses recognised in accordance with IAS 39.

[IFRS 7 App B para 9].

[The next paragraph is 11. 93.]

Collateral and other credit enhancements

11. 93 In respect of the second bullet point in paragraph 11. 91 above, an entity's description about collateral held as security and other credit enhancements might include:

- The policies and processes for valuing and managing collateral and other credit enhancements obtained.
- A description of the main types of collateral and other credit enhancements (examples of the latter being guarantees, credit derivatives and netting agreements that do not qualify for offset in accordance with IAS 32).
- The main types of counterparties to collateral and other credit enhancements and their creditworthiness.
- Information about risk concentrations within the collateral or other credit enhancements.

[IFRS 7 para IG22].

11. 94 When an entity obtains financial or non-financial assets during the period by taking possession of collateral it holds as security or calling on other credit enhancements, and such assets meet the recognition criteria in other IFRSs, an entity should disclose:

11.91.2　对于上文第 11.91 段第一点，最能代表主体由于金融资产产生的最大信用风险敞口的金额通常是总账面金额减去：

- 根据 IAS 32 抵销的任何金额（参见上文第 11.15 段）；以及
- 根据 IAS 39 确认的任何减值损失。

［IFRS 7 附录 B 第 9 段］。

［下一段为第 11.93 段］。

抵押物和其他信用增级

11.93　对于上文第 11.91 段第二点，主体作持有的抵押物和其他信用增级的描述可能包括：

- 对抵押物和已取得的其他信用增级进行估值和管理的政策和程序。
- 对抵押物和其他信用增级的主要类型的描述（其他信用增级的类型例如担保、信用衍生工具和根据 IAS 32 不符合抵销条件的净额结算协议）。
- 抵押物和其他信用增级的交易对方的主要类型和信誉。
- 有关抵押物或其他信用增级风险集中的信息。

［IFRS 7 IG 第 22 段］。

11.94　当主体在本期内通过占有其持有的的抵押物或要求其他信用增级而取得金融资产或非金融资产，并且这些资产满足其他 IFRS 的确认要求时，主体应当披露：

- The nature and carrying amount of the assets obtained.
- When the assets are not readily convertible into cash, its policies for disposing of such assets or for using them in its operations.

[IFRS 7 para 38].

The 2010 annual improvements to IFRS 7 clarified that these disclosures are required only for foreclosed collateral at the balance sheet date. This amendment applies to annual periods beginning on or after 1 January 2011 and early application is permitted.

Credit quality of financial assets that are neither past due nor impaired

11.95 In respect of the third bullet point in paragraph 11.91, information about credit quality of financial assets that are neither past due nor impaired might include:

- An analysis of credit exposures using an external or internal credit rating system.

  Where an entity manages its credit exposures using an external credit rating system, an entity might disclose information about:

  - The carrying amounts of credit exposures for each external credit rating.
  - The rating agencies used.
  - The amount of an entity's rated and unrated credit exposures.
  - The relationship between internal and external ratings.

  Where an entity manages its credit exposures using an internal credit rating system, an entity might disclose information about:

  - The internal credit ratings process.
  - The amounts of credit exposures for each internal credit rating.
  - The relationship between internal and external ratings.

- The nature of the counterparty.

■ 所取得资产的性质和账面金额。

■ 当资产不易转换为现金时，其处置这些资产或拟将其用于经营活动的政策。

[IFRS 7 第 38 段]。

2010 年年度改进中对 IFRS 7 的改动澄清了这些披露要求仅针对于资产负债表日没收的抵押物。该修订于起始日在 2011 年 1 月 1 日或以后的年度期间生效，允许提前实施。

未逾期也未发生减值的金融资产的信用质量

11.95　对于第 11.91 段第三点，有关未逾期也未发生减值的金融资产的信用质量的信息包括：

■ 采用外部或内部的信用评级系统所进行的信用风险敞口分析。

　在主体采用外部信用评级系统对其信用风险敞口进行管理的情况下，主体可以披露以下信息：

　■ 每个外部信用级别的信用风险敞口的账面金额。

　■ 所用的评级机构。

　■ 主体已评级和未评级的信用风险敞口金额。

　■ 内部评级和外部评级之间的关系。

　在主体采用内部信用评级系统对其信用风险敞口进行管理的情况下，主体可以披露以下信息：

　■ 内部信用评级的程序。

　■ 每个内部信用级别的信用风险敞口金额。

　■ 内部评级和外部评级之间的关系。

■ 交易对方的性质。

- Historical information about counterparty default rates.

- Any other information used to assess credit quality.

[IFRS 7 paras IG23-25].

Financial assets that are either past due or impaired

11.96 A financial asset is past due when the counterparty has failed to make a payment when contractually due. As an example, an entity enters into a lending agreement that requires interest to be paid every month. On the first day of the next month, if interest has not been paid, the whole loan is past due, not just the interest. Past due does not mean that a counterparty will never pay, but it can trigger various actions such as renegotiation, enforcement of covenants, or legal proceedings. [IFRS 7 para IG26]. An entity should disclose by class of financial asset:

- An analysis of the age of financial assets that are past due as at the reporting date but not impaired. The purpose of this disclosure is to provide users of the financial statements with information about those financial assets that are more likely to become impaired and to help users to estimate the level of future impairment losses. Thus, the entire balance which relates to the amount past due should be disclosed, rather than only the amount that is past due, as this is the amount that would be disclosed as the amount of the impaired financial assets if impairment crystallises.

  Other associated balances due from the same debtor are not included if the debtor has not yet failed to make a payment on these balances when contractually due.

  In preparing such an age analysis of financial assets, an entity uses its judgement to determine an appropriate number of time bands. For example, an entity might determine that the following time bands are appropriate:

  - Not more than three months.

  - More than three months and not more than six months.

■ 有关交易对方违约率的历史信息。

■ 用于评估信用质量的任何其他信息。

[IFRS 7 IG 第 23 -25 段]。

已逾期或发生减值的金融资产

11.96 当交易对方在合同到期时无法进行偿付，则金融资产已逾期。例如，主体签订了一项借款协议，要求每月支付利息。在下一月的第一天，如果尚未支付利息，则整个贷款而不仅仅是利息已逾期。已逾期并不意味着交易对方永远不会支付，但是它可能引发诸如重新商定、契约执行或法律诉讼等各种行动。[IFRS 7 IG 第 26 段]。主体应按金融资产的类型进行如下披露：

■ 对在报告日已逾期但未发生减值的金融资产的账龄分析。此项披露的目的是为财务报表使用者提供那些更可能发生减值的金融资产的信息，并有助于使用者估计未来减值损失的水平。因此，需要披露与已逾期金额相关的全部余额，而不仅仅是已逾期金额，因为这将是如果减值明确时被披露为减值金融资产的金额。

如果应收同一债务人的其他相关余额在合同到期时并未无法支付，则不包括这些余额。

在编制金融资产的这种账龄分析时，主体运用其判断来确定合理数量的时间段。例如主体可以确定下述时间段是合适的：

■ 3 个月以内。

■ 3 个月至 6 个月。

  - More than six months and not more than one year.
  - More than one year.
- An analysis of financial assets that are individually determined to be impaired as at the reporting date, including the factors the entity considered in determining that they are impaired. These disclosures are not only given in the year of impairment, but also in each subsequent reporting period during which the fair value of a financial asset is below its historical cost and, therefore, considered 'impaired'. Such an analysis might include:
  - The carrying amount, before deducting any impairment loss.
  - The amount of any related impairment loss.
  - The nature and fair value of collateral available and other credit enhancements obtained. The collateral disclosure requirement has been removed as part of the 2010 annual improvements to IFRS 7. These are applicable for periods starting on or after 1 January 2011, with early application permitted.

This is the only disclosure relating to credit risk that must be made in respect of an entity's equity investments (see para 11.91.1).

Example – Assessment of receivables individually determined to be impaired

Entity M has C300m of receivables which it has analysed as follows:

- C120m has been assessed individually for impairment and are considered to be impaired.
- C40m represents a collection of insignificant receivables that are individually determined to be impaired, but the impairment calculation is performed on the whole C40m amount for efficiency purposes.
- C140m represents a portfolio of receivables for which there is observable data indicating that there is a measurable decrease in the estimated future cash flows, although the decrease cannot be identified with individual balances.

Of these, only the first two amounts have been individually assessed for

■ 6 个月至 1 年。

■ 1 年以上。

■ 对在报告日按单项确认减值的金融资产的分析，包括主体在确定其减值时所考虑的因素。这些披露不仅需要在减值年度时作出，而且还需要在金融资产的公允价值低于其历史成本因而被认为“已减值”的每个之后的报告期间作出。这种分析可能包括：

■ 扣减任何减值损失之前的账面金额。

■ 任何相关减值损失的金额。

■ 可用抵押物和已取得的其他信用增级的性质和公允价值。对抵押物的披露要求已在 2010 年年度改进中被删除。该修订于起始日在 2011 年 1 月 1 日或以后的年度期间生效，允许提前实施。

这是主体的权益投资与信用风险相关的、所必须作出的唯一披露（参见第 11.91.1 段）。

示例——对按单项确认已减值的应收款的评估

主体 M 有 C3 亿元的应收账款并分析如下：

■ 对 C1.2 亿元的应收款按单项进行减值评估并认为已发生减值。

■ C4 千万元代表了一系列的按单项确定已发生减值的不重要应收款，但是为提高效率对整个 C4 千万元的金额进行了减值计算。

■ C1.40 亿元代表了一个应收账款组合，有可观察的数据表明估计的未来现金流有可计量的下跌，虽然该下跌无法通过单项余额来确定。

在这些项目中，只有前两项金额按单项进行了减值评价，因此也应要求

impairment and so would require disclosure under IFRS 7. [IFRS 7 para 36 (b)]. Disclosure would not be required in respect of the third bullet, as the receivables have been assessed on a portfolio basis rather than individually. In respect of each of the amounts disclosed above, a description of collateral held by the entity as security and other credit enhancements and unless impracticable, an estimate of their fair value (see para 11.93 above).

[IFRS 7 paras 37, IG28-29].

11.97 An example of a company that has given credit risk disclosures (qualitative and quantitative) for a class of its financial assets (trade receivables) is given in Table 11.9.

Table 11.9 – Trade and other receivables

Adidas AG – Annual report – 31 December 2009

Financial Risks (extract)

Credit risks

A credit risk arises if a customer or other counterparty to a financial instrument fails to meet its contractual obligations. The adidas Group is exposed to credit risk from its operating activities and from certain financing activities. Credit risks arise principally from accounts receivable and to a lesser extent from other contractual financial obligations such as other financial assets, short-term bank deposits and derivative financial instruments see Note 28. Without taking into account any collateral or other credit enhancements, the carrying amount of financial assets represents the maximum exposure to credit risk.

At the end of 2009, there was no relevant concentration of credit risk by type of customer or geography. Instead, our credit risk exposure is mainly influenced by individual customer characteristics. Under the Group's credit policy, new customers are analysed for creditworthiness before standard payment and delivery terms and conditions are offered. This review utilises external ratings from credit agencies. Tolerance limits for accounts receivable are also established for each customer. Then both creditworthiness and accounts receivable limits are monitored on an ongoing basis. Customers that fail to meet the Group's minimum creditworthiness are in general allowed to purchase products only on a prepayment basis. Other activities to mitigate credit risks, which are employed on a selective basis only, include credit insurances, accounts receivable sales without recourse and bank guarantees as well as retention of title clauses.

遵循 IFRS 7 进行披露。[IFRS 7 第 36（b）段]。对于第三点则不要求进行披露，因为该应收账款是以组合为基础而不是按单项进行评价的。对于如上所披露的每项金额，应当披露对持有的抵押物和其他信用增级的描述以及，除非不切实可行，对其公允价值的估计（参见上文第 11.93 段）。

[IFRS 7 第 37 段、IG 第 28、第 29 段]。

11.97　表 11.9 中给出了一公司对其一类金融资产（交易应收账款）进行信用风险披露（定量和定性）的示例。

表 11.9——交易及其他应收款

Adidas AG——年报——2009 年 12 月 31 日

金融风险（节选）

信用风险

如果客户或金融工具的其他交易对方未能履行其合同义务即会产生信用风险。adidas 集团因其经营活动以及某些融资活动而面临信用风险。信用风险主要产生于应收账款，其次则是诸如其他金融资产、短期银行存款和衍生金融工具等其他合同金融义务——参见附注 28。在不考虑任何抵押物或其他信用增级的情况下，金融资产的账面金额代表了最大信用风险敞口。

在 2009 年年末，没有对客户类型或地理位置的信用风险集中。相反，我们的信用风险敞口主要受各个客户特征的影响。根据集团的信用政策，在提供标准的付款和交货条款与条件之前会对新客户的信誉进行分析。此项审查会采用信用机构的外部评级。还会为每个客户确定应收账款的限值。之后将对信誉和应收账款限值进行持续监控。不能满足集团的最低信誉要求的客户只能以预付款的形式购买产品。仅在一定的选择基础上使用的其他规避信用风险的措施包括信用保险、不带追索权的出售应收账款、银行担保以及保留所有权条款。

The Group utilises allowance accounts for impairments that represent our estimate of incurred credit losses with respect to accounts receivable. The allowance consists of two components:

(1) an allowance based on historical experience of unexpected losses established for all receivables dependent on the ageing structure of receivables past due date, and
(2) a specific allowance that relates to individually assessed risk for each specific customer-irrespective of ageing.

At the end of 2009, no Group customer accounted for more than 10% of accounts receivable. Nevertheless the negative impact of the deterioration of the global economy on consumer confidence and spending is not expected to be reversed significantly in 2010 in view of the still very challenging economic environment. As a consequence, we believe that our overall credit risk level from customers, particularly smaller retailers, remains high in several markets see Economic and Sector Development. Therefore, our estimate of the likelihood and potential financial impact of credit risks from customers remains medium.

Credit risks from other financial contractual relationships include items such as other financial assets, short-term bank deposits and derivative financial instruments. The adidas Group Treasury department arranges currency and interest rate hedges, and invests cash, with major banks of a high credit standing throughout the world. adidas Group companies are authorised to work with banks rated "BBB +" or higher.

Only in exceptional cases are subsidiaries authorised to work with banks rated lower than "BBB +". To limit risk in these cases, restrictions are clearly stipulated such as maximum cash deposit levels. In addition, the credit default swap premiums of our partner banks are monitored on a weekly basis. In the event that the defined threshold is exceeded, credit balances are shifted to banks compliant with the limit. During 2009, the credit default swap premiums for many banks declined from their highs in the aftermath of the financial turmoil in 2008, mainly as a result of governmental intervention worldwide. This development indicates a slight decrease of the associated risks.

Although financial market conditions stabilised in 2009, we continue to believe that the likelihood and potential financial impact of credit risks from these assets is medium. Nevertheless, we believe our risk concentration is limited due to the broad distribution of our investment business with more than 24 banks. At December 31, 2009, no bank accounted for more than 19% of our investment business and the average concentration, including subsidiaries' short-term deposits in local banks, was 1%. This leads to a maximum exposure of €158 million in the event of default of any single bank. Furthermore, we held derivatives with a positive fair market value in the amount of €55 million. The maximum exposure to any single bank resulting from these assets amounted to €4 million and the average concentration was 3%.

集团使用减值备抵账户来体现我们对应收账款已发生的信用损失的估计。该备抵由两部分组成：

(1) 根据已逾期应收账款的账龄结构而为所有应收账款根据意外损失的历史经验而确定的备抵，和
(2) 不论账龄如何对每个具体客户的风险进行单独评价的专项备抵。

在2009年年末，没有集团客户占应收账款的10%以上。然而，鉴于仍然非常具有挑战性的经济环境，全球经济环境恶化对消费者信心和花销的负面影响在2010年并未显著消除。因此，我们相信我们客户的总体信用风险水平，尤其是较小的零售商，在一些市场仍然较高（参见经济和分部发展）。因此，我们对客户信用风险的可能性和潜在财务影响的估计仍为中等。

其他金融合同关系的信用风险包括诸如其他金融资产、短期银行存款和衍生金融工具等项目。adidas集团财务部在全球和具有高信用等级的主要银行进行货币和利率套期，并投资现金。adidas集团各公司被授权和等级在“BBB+”或以上的银行交易。

子公司只有在例外的情况下才被授权和等级在“BBB+”以下的银行交易。在这种情况下为规避风险,规定了诸如最高现金存款水平等限制。此外,对我们合作银行的信用违约互换贴水进行每周监控。在超过了所规定的限值之后,则将信用余额转移到符合此限值的银行。在2009年,主要由于全球政府干预所致,很多银行的信用违约互换贴水均从2008年金融混乱造成的高点下降。这表明了相关风险的略微下降。

尽管金融市场的情况在2009年已趋于稳定，我们仍然认为这些资产信用风险的可能性和潜在金融影响还是中级。虽然如此，我们相信我们的风险集中是有限的，因为我们的投资业务广泛分布于超过24家银行。于2009年12月31日，没有一家银行在我们的投资业务中所占份额超过19%，而其平均集中度，包括子公司在当地银行的短期存款，仅为1%。这在任何一家银行违约时将导致1.58亿欧元的最大敞口。此外，我们持有的衍生工具具有5,500万欧元的正公允市场价值。由这些资产导致的对任何一家银行的最大敞口为400万欧元，平均集中度为3%。

7 Accounts receivable

Accounts receivable consist mainly of the currencies US dollar, euro and Japanese yen and are as follows:

ACCOUNTS RECEIVABLE

€ in millions	Dec. 31, 2009	Dec. 31, 2008
Accounts receivable, gross	1,553	1,743
Less: allowance for doubtful accounts	124	119
Accounts receivable, net	**1,429**	**1,624**

Movement in allowances for doubtful accounts

€ in millions	2009	2008
Allowances at January 1	119	111
Additions	68	49
Additions – Ashworth, Inc. acquisition	–	4
Reversals	(29)	(22)
Write-offs charged against the allowance accounts	(34)	(21)
Currency translation differences	0	(2)
Other changes	0	0
Allowances at December 31	124	119

Accounts receivable past due but not impaired

€ in millions	past due 1–30 days	past due 31–60 days	past due 61–90 days	past due 91–180 days	past due more than 180 days
Dec. 31, 2009	**115**	**57**	**10**	**6**	**5**
Dec. 31, 2008	163	77	20	10	10

With respect to accounts receivable past due but not impaired, based on credit history and current credit ratings, there are no indications that customers will not be able to meet their obligations.

Further, no indications of default are recognisable for accounts receivable that are neither past due nor impaired.

Liquidity risk

11.98 Summary quantitative data about an entity's exposure to liquidity risk should be disclosed on the basis of the information provided internally to key management personnel. An entity should explain how those data are determined. If the outflows of cash (or another financial asset) included in those data could either:

7 应收账款

应收账款主要由美元、欧元、日元组成，如下所述：

应收账款

以百万欧元为单位	2009 年 12 月 31 日	2008 年 12 月 31 日
应收账款，总额	1,553	1,743
减去：坏账备抵	124	119
应收账款，净额	**1,429**	**1,624**

坏账备抵的变动

以百万欧元为单位	2009	2008
1 月 1 日的备抵	119	111
新增	68	49
新增——收购 Ashworth 公司	–	4
转回	(29)	(22)
对备抵账户的核销	(34)	(21)
货币折算差额	0	(2)
其他变动	0	0
12 月 31 日的备抵	124	119

已逾期但未发生减值的应收账款

以百万欧元为单位	已逾期 1 – 30 天	已逾期 31 – 60 天	已逾期 61 – 90 天	已逾期 91 – 180 天	已逾期 180 天以上
2009 年 12 月 31 日	**115**	**57**	**10**	**6**	**5**
2008 年 12 月 31 日	163	77	20	10	10

对于已逾期但未发生减值的应收账款，根据信用历史和当前信用评级，没有迹象表明客户不能履行其义务。

此外，对既未逾期又未发生减值的应收账款无应确认的违约迹象。

流动性风险

11.98　有关主体流动性风险敞口的汇总定量数据应根据向关键管理人员提供的内部信息来披露。主体应解释如何确定这些数据。如果这些数据中所包含的现金（或其他金融资产）流出：

- occur significantly earlier than indicated in the data; or
- be for significantly different amounts from those indicated in the data (for example, for a derivative that is included in the data on a net settlement basis, but for which the counterparty has the option to require gross settlement).

the entity should state that fact and provide quantitative information that enables users of its financial statements to evaluate the extent of liquidity risk, unless that information is included in the maturity analyses described in paragraph 11.99 below. [IFRS 7 App B para 10A]. An example of a cash outflow that could occur significantly earlier than indicated in the data could be a bond that is callable by the issuer in, say, two years but has a remaining contractual maturity of, say, ten years.

11.98.1 The amendment to IFRS 7 modified the minimum disclosure requirements related to liquidity risk. An entity should disclose:

- A maturity analysis for non-derivative financial liabilities (including issued financial guarantee contracts) that shows the remaining contractual maturities.
- A maturity analysis for derivative financial liabilities. The maturity analysis should include the remaining contractual maturities for those derivative financial liabilities for which contractual maturities are essential for an understanding of the timing of the cash flows.
- A description of how it manages the liquidity risk inherent in the above.

[IFRS 7 para 39].

11.98.2 This information can be summarised in one or several maturity analysis tables. It should be clear for the users of the financial statements whether the disclosure is based on contractual maturities or expected maturities and whether the financial liabilities are derivatives or non-derivatives.

11.99 In preparing the contractual maturity analyses described in paragraph 11.98.1, an entity uses its judgement to determine an appropriate number of time bands. For example, an entity might determine that the following time bands are appropriate:

- Not later than one month.
- Later than one month and not later than three months.

■ 发生可能较既定时间大幅提前；或

■ 可能与数据中所列示的金额存在重大差异（例如，数据中所包含的以净额为基础结算但交易对方有权要求以总额结算的衍生工具）。

主体应说明该情况并提供能够使财务报表使用者对流动性风险的程度进行评估的定量信息，除非这种信息包含在下文第 11.99 段中所述的到期日分析中。[IFRS 7 附录 B 第 10A 段]。现金流出可能较既定时间大幅提前的例子有虽然 10 年后才到期，但发行人有权在，比如说，2 年内赎回的债券。

11.98.1　IFRS 7 的修订修改了与流动性风险相关的最低披露要求。主体应披露：

■ 对非衍生工具金融负债（包括签出的财务担保合同）的到期日分析，列示其剩余的合同约定到期日。

■ 对衍生金融负债的到期日分析。对于那些合同约定到期日对了解现金流动的时间是必要的衍生金融负债，该到期日分析应包括其剩余的合同约定到期日。

■ 对主体如何管理上述内在的流动性风险的描述。

[IFRS 7 第 39 段]。

11.98.2　此项信息可以在一个或多个到期日分析表中汇总出来。财务报表使用者应能够明确知道这种披露是以合同到期日还是以预计到期日为基础以及金融负债是衍生工具还是非衍生工具。

11.99　在编制第 11.98.1 段所述合同到期日分析时，主体运用其判断来确定合理数量的时间段。例如主体可以确定下述时间段是合适的：

■ 一个月以内。

■ 一个月至三个月。

■ Later than three months and not later than one year.

■ Later than one year and not later than five years.

[IFRS 7 App B para 11].

11.100 For the maturity analyses based on contractual cash flows, when a counterparty has a choice of when an amount is paid, the liability is included on the basis of the earliest date on which the entity can be required to pay. For example, financial liabilities that an entity can be required to repay on demand (for example, demand deposits) are included in the earliest time band. [IFRS 7 App B para 11C (a)].

11.101 When an entity is committed to make amounts available in instalments, each instalment is allocated to the earliest period in which the entity can be required to pay. For example, an undrawn loan commitment is included in the time band containing the earliest date it can be drawn down. [IFRS 7 App B para 11C(b)].

11.101.1 When an entity has issued a financial guarantee contract, the maximum amount of the guarantee is allocated to the earliest period in which the guarantee could be called. [IFRS 7 App B para 11C(c)].

11.101.2 The maximum amount of an undrawn loan commitment should also be included in the maturity analysis, allocated to the earliest period in which the commitment could be called. Once a loan is drawn down, it will be included in the maturity analysis as a non-derivative financial liability.

11.102 The amounts disclosed in the maturity analyses on a contractual basis are the contractual undiscounted cash flows (including principal and interest payments). For example:

■ Gross finance lease obligations (before deducting finance charges).

■ Prices specified in forward agreements to purchase financial assets for cash.

■ Net amounts for pay-floating receive-fixed interest rate swaps for which net cash flows are exchanged.

■ Contractual amounts to be exchanged in a derivative financial instrument (for example, a currency swap) for which gross cash flows are exchanged.

■ 三个月至一年。

■ 一年至五年。

[IFRS 7 附录 B 第 11 段]。

11.100　对于基于合同约定现金流量的到期日分析，当交易对方对何时支付金额有选择权时，该负债根据主体可能被要求支付的最早日期纳入。例如，主体可能被随时要求偿还的金融负债（例如，活期存款）应包括在最早的时间段内。[IFRS 7 附录 B 第 11C（a）段]。

11.101　当主体承诺分期支付款项时，每一分期支付款应被分配至主体可能被要求支付的最早期间。例如，未使用的贷款承诺应归入到其可以使用的最早日期的时间段内。[IFRS 7 附录 B 第 11C（b）段]。

11.101.1　当主体签出了一项财务担保合同时，其最大担保金额应分配至该项担保可被要求执行的最早期间。[IFRS 7 附录 B 第 11C（c）段]。

11.101.2　未使用的贷款承诺的最大金额也应包括在到期日分析中，并归入到该承诺可以被使用的最早期间。贷款一旦被贷出，即将作为一项非衍生金融负债纳入到期日分析中。

11.102　基于合同的到期日分析中披露的金额是未经折现的合同约定现金流量（包括本金和利息）。例如：

■ 融资租赁债务总额（扣减融资费用以前）。

■ 以现金购买金融资产的远期协议中指定的价格。

■ 以净现金流量结算的支付浮动利率、收取固定利率的利率互换的净额。

■ 以总现金流量结算的衍生金融工具（例如货币互换）所需交换的合同金额。

■ Gross loan commitments.

[IFRS 7 App B para 11D].

11.102.1 The undiscounted cash flows described above differ from the amounts included in the balance sheet, which are based on discounted cash flows. There is no specific requirement to reconcile the amounts disclosed in the maturity analysis to the amounts included in the balance sheet.

11.103 When the amount payable is not fixed, the amount disclosed in the maturity analyses is determined by reference to the conditions existing at the end of the reporting period. For example, when the amount payable varies with changes in an index, the amount disclosed may be based on the level of the index at the end of the period. [IFRS 7 App B para 11D]. For floating rate financial liabilities and foreign currency denominated instruments, the use of forward interest rates and forward foreign exchange rates may be conceptually preferable, but the use of a spot rate at the end of the period is also acceptable. Whichever approach is adopted (that is, current/spot rate or forward rate at the reporting date), it should be applied consistently.

11.104 As noted in paragraph 11.98.1, the contractual cash flows of derivative financial liabilities for which contractual maturities are essential for an understanding of the cash flows should be included in maturity analysis. For example, this would be the case for the following:

■ An interest rate swap with a remaining maturity of five years in a cash flow hedge of a variable rate financial asset or liability.

■ All loan commitments.

[IFRS 7 App B para 11B].

11.104.1 Other derivatives are included in a separate maturity analysis on the basis on which they are managed. It may be expected that contractual maturities are essential for an understanding of the timing of cash flows for derivatives, unless the facts and circumstances indicate another basis is appropriate. For example, contractual maturities would not be essential for an understanding of the derivatives in a trading portfolio that are expected to be settled before contractual maturity on a net basis. Disclosure of fair values of such derivatives on an expected maturity basis would, therefore, be appropriate.

■ 贷款承诺总额。

［IFRS 7 附录 B 第 11D 段］。

11.102.1　上文提及的未经折现的现金流与资产负债表中的金额不同，后者是基于折现后的现金流。准则没有将到期日分析中所披露的金额调节至资产负债表中金额的具体要求。

11.103　当应付金额不固定时，在到期日分析中所披露的金额根据报告期末存在的情况确定。例如，当应付金额随着指数的变化而变化时，披露的金额可以基于报告期末指数的水平确定。［IFRS 7 附录 B 第 11D 段］。对于浮动利率的金融负债和以外币计价的工具，使用远期利率和远期外汇汇率从概念上讲可能更好一些，但使用期末时的即期利率或汇率也可以接受。无论使用哪种方法（即报告日的当前/即期利率或远期利率），均应一致地使用。

11.104　如第 11.98.1 段所述，对于那些合同到期日对了解现金流动的时间是必要的衍生金融负债，其合同现金流应当包括在到期日分析中。例如，在下述情况下即应如此：

■ 在浮动利率的金融资产或负债的现金流套期中还有五年剩余期限的利率互换。

■ 所有贷款承诺。

［IFRS 7 附录 B 第 11B 段］。

11.104.1　其他衍生工具根据其被管理的情况而被纳入到单独的到期日分析中。可以预期，合同到期日对于了解衍生工具的现金流时间是必要的，除非事实情况表明采用另一种基础更为适合。例如，对于在交易组合中，预期在合同到期日之前按净额结算的衍生工具来说，合同到期日对于了解该衍生工具来说并非必要。因此，根据预计到期日对这种衍生工具的公允价值进行披露应该是合适的。

11.104.1.1 An entity should disclosure a maturity analysis of financial assets it holds for managing liquidity risk (for example, financial assets that are readily saleable or expected to generate cash inflows to meet cash outflows on financial liabilities), if that information is necessary to enable users of its financial statements to evaluate the nature and extent of liquidity risk. [IFRS 7 App B para 11E].

11.104.1.2 IFRS 7 gives as an example of an amount included in the maturity analysis on a contractual undiscounted basis the amounts exchanged in a gross-settled derivative contract. The standard refers only to a maturity analysis for derivative financial liabilities, so it would appear that only disclosure of gross cash outflows (that is, the pay leg) in respect of derivative financial liabilities is required. However, it may be more helpful to also disclose the cash inflows (that is, the receive leg). As explained in paragraph 11.104.1.1, IFRS 7 requires disclosure of a maturity analysis for financial assets where that information is necessary to enable users of financial statements to evaluate the nature and extent of liquidity risk. By analogy, we consider that disclosure of the receive leg in a gross-settled derivative financial liability will also often be necessary for an understanding of liquidity risk. A maturity analysis of derivative financial assets may also be required.

11.104.1.3 A similar analysis to the previous paragraph applies in the case of gross-settled commodity contracts. Where such a contract falls within IAS 39's scope, the associated cash outflows should be included in the maturity analysis where the contract is a financial liability at the reporting date (that is, it has a negative fair value) and where it will result in a cash outflow (rather than physical outflows of commodities). It may be helpful to disclose the contractual cash outflows of all commodity contracts, including those with both positive and negative fair values at the balance sheet date. Alternatively, it may be more meaningful to disclose gross-settled commodity contracts in a separate table showing both the cash inflows/outflows and the associated commodity outflows/inflows for all contracts. If this additional disclosure is given, an entity might cross-reference the cash outflows to the maturity analysis. Whichever of these alternative methods of presentation is adopted, the basis of preparation and measurement should be explained.

11.104.1.3.1 The liquidity risk disclosures for derivative financial liabilities can be summarised as follows:

11.104.1.1 如果对财务报表使用者能够评估流动性风险的性质和范围是必需的，主体应当披露其为管理流动性风险而持有的金融资产（如随时可出售或预期获取现金流入以满足金融负债现金流出的金融资产）的到期日分析。［IFRS 7 附录 B 第11E 段］。

11.104.1.2 IFRS 7 给出了以总额结算的衍生工具合同中所交换金额以未经折现的基础纳入到期日分析的示例。该准则仅提及衍生金融负债的到期日分析，所以看上去对于衍生金融负债而言只要求披露现金流出总额（即，支付部分）。但是，同时披露现金流入（即，收款部分）可能会更有帮助。如第11.104.1.1 段所解释的，如果对财务报表使用者能够评估流动性风险的性质和范围是必需的，IFRS 7 要求披露金融资产的到期日分析。以此类推，我们认为披露以总额结算的衍生金融负债的收款部分对于了解流动性风险经常是必需的。可能还会需要披露衍生金融资产的到期日分析。

11.104.1.3 与上段所述类似的分析对于以总额结算的商品合同也适用。当这种合同在 IAS 39 范围内时，如果该合同在报告日是一项金融负债（即，其公允价值为负），且它将导致现金流出（而不是交付实物商品），相关现金流出应被纳入到期日分析中。披露所有商品合同的合同现金流出，包括在资产负债表日时有正公允价值和负公允价值的合同，可能会有所帮助。或者，在单独的表格中披露以总额结算的商品合同，显示所有合同的现金流入/流出及相关商品流出/流入出情况可能更有意义。如果作出了这种额外披露，主体可以将现金流出和到期日分析做交叉参考。无论采用了哪种可选的列报方法，均应对其编制和计量基础进行解释。

11.104.1.3.1 对衍生金融负债流动性风险的披露汇总如下：

	Gross settled derivatives	Net settled derivatives
Contractual maturity is essential to understanding	• Disclose pay leg based on contractual maturity. • Disclose receive leg.	• Disclose net cash flows based on contractual maturity.
Contractual maturity is not essential to understanding	Disclose how the risk is managed. For example, an entity might disclose: • Cash flows based on contractual maturities – pay and receive leg. • Fair value in the relevant time band (based on expected maturity (i. e. expected settlement date); contractual maturity or in the on demand category).	Disclose how risk is managed. For example, an entity might disclose: • Net cash flows based on contractual maturity. • Fair value in the relevant time band (based on expected maturity (i. e. expected settlement date); contractual maturity or in the on demand category).

11.104.1.4 For the purpose of the maturity analysis, embedded derivatives included in hybrid (combined) financial instruments should not be separated. A hybrid instrument should be included in the maturity analysis for non-derivative financial liabilities. [IFRS 7 App B para 11A].

11.104.1.5 Contracts settled in own shares that are not equity instruments of the issuer (for example, a contract that requires an entity to issue a fixed number of its own shares for a variable amount of cash upon the holder's request) are not in the scope of the maturity analysis, as the entity will issue own shares to meet the above obligation and does not, therefore, have an obligation to deliver cash or another financial asset. An obligation to deliver own shares does not give rise to liquidity risk as defined by IFRS 7. [IFRS 7 para BC58A (a)].

11.104.1.6 The factors that an entity might consider in providing a description of how it manages liquidity risk include, but are not limited to, whether the entity:

- Has committed borrowing facilities (for example, commercial paper facilities) or other lines of credit (for example, stand-by credit facilities) that it can access to meet liquidity needs.

	以总额结算的衍生工具	以净额结算的衍生工具
合同到期日对了解（现金流出）是必需的	• 按照合同到期日披露支付部分。 • 披露收款部分。	• 按照合同到期日披露净现金流。
合同到期日对了解（现金流出）不是必需的	披露风险是如何管理的。例如，主体可以： • 按照合同到期日披露现金流—支付和收款部分。 • 披露相关时间段（按照预计到期日（如预计结算日）、合同到期日或随时结算类别）的公允价值。	披露风险是如何管理的。例如，主体可以： • 按照合同到期日披露净现金流。 • 披露相关时间段（按照预计到期日（如预计结算日）、合同到期日或随时结算类别）的公允价值。

11.104.1.4　在到期日分析中，不应将包含在混合（组合）金融工具中的嵌入衍生工具分离出来。混合工具应被纳入非衍生金融负债的到期日分析里。[IFRS 7 附录 B 第 11A 段]。

11.104.1.5　虽然不作为发行人权益工具但是以其自身股票结算的合同（例如要求主体在持有人行权时发行固定数量的自身股份以换取可变金额的现金的合同）不在到期日分析的范围内，因为主体将发行自身股票来履行上述义务，因此不具有交付现金或其他金融资产的义务。交付自身股票的义务不形成 IFRS 7 中所定义的流动性风险。[IFRS 7 BC 第 58A（a）段]。

11.104.1.6　主体在提供有关如何管理流动性风险的描述时可以考虑的因素包括，但不限于，主体是否：

■ 持有已承诺的借款额度（如商业票据额度）或其他可以获取以满足流动性需求的信用额度（如备用信用额度）。

- Holds deposits at central banks to meet liquidity needs.
- Has very diverse funding sources.
- Has significant concentrations of liquidity risk in either its assets or its funding sources.
- Has internal control processes and contingency plans for managing liquidity risk.
- Has instruments that include accelerated repayment terms (for example, on the downgrade of the entity's credit rating).
- Has instruments that could require the posting of collateral (for example, margin calls for derivatives).
- Has instruments that allow the entity to choose whether it settles its financial liabilities by delivering cash (or another financial asset) or by delivering its own shares.
- Has instruments that are subject to master netting agreements.

[IFRS 7 App B para 11F].

11.104.1.7 Collateral requirements on financial instruments can pose a significant liquidity risk. For example, an entity with a derivative liability may be required to post cash collateral on the derivative should the liability exceed certain limits. As a result, if collateral calls pose significant liquidity risk, entities should provide quantitative disclosures of their collateral arrangements as those cash flows could occur earlier than the contractual maturity (see also para 11.98).

[The next paragraph is 11.104.1.9]

11.104.1.9 Financial institutions typically use financial assets to manage their liquidity risk. A maturity analysis of financial assets is likely to be necessary to enable users of financial statements to evaluate the nature and extent of liquidity risk. However, the disclosure requirements are not only relevant for financial institutions. Certain other types of entities with significant trading activities (such as energy companies) may hold financial assets to manage liquidity risk. Where such activities are a significant part of the entity's business, a maturity analysis of financial assets may be required.

■ 持有可满足流动性需求的中央银行存款。

■ 具有非常多样化的资金来源。

■ 其资产或资金来源方面有重大的流动性风险集中。

■ 有用于管理流动性风险的内部控制流程或应急计划。

■ 持有包括加速偿付条款的工具（如在主体的信用等级被降级时）。

■ 持有可以要求提供抵押物的工具（如衍生工具的保证金追缴）。

■ 持有允许主体选择通过交付现金（或其他金融资产）还是交付其自身股票来结算其金融负债的工具。

■ 持有遵循总互抵协议的工具。

[IFRS 7 附录 B 第 11F 段]。

11.104.1.7　对金融工具抵押物的要求可能导致重大的流动性风险。例如，有衍生工具负债的主体在负债超过了某特定限值时可能会被要求为衍生工具提供现金抵押物。因此，如果提供抵押物的要求带来重大的流动性风险，主体应对其抵押物协议进行定量披露，因为这些现金流可能早于合同到期日发生（亦参见第 11.98 段）。

[下一段为第 11.104.1.9 段]。

11.104.1.9　金融机构一般会用金融资产来管理其流动性风险。金融资产的到期日分析很可能对财务报表使用者评估流动性风险的性质和范围是必需的。但是，该披露要求并不仅仅与金融机构相关。具有大量交易活动的某些其他类型的主体（如能源公司）可能会持有金融资产来管理流动性风险。在这种活动占主体业务很大部分的情况下，可能要求披露金融资产的到期日分析。

11. 104. 1. 10 Where an entity presents a maturity analysis of financial assets, it should be prepared on the basis of information provided internally to key management personnel. It may be based either on contractual or expected maturity dates, depending on how the risk is managed. Alternatively, the analysis could be presented on a net basis (that is, fair value).

[The next paragraph is 11. 104. 3.]

11. 104. 3 The examples that follow illustrate how a maturity analysis may be prepared on a contractual basis for some typical financial instruments.

Example 1 – Floating rate notes

On 31 December 20X6 entity A issued two-year, US$ 30m floating rate notes that pay interest of 6m LIBOR plus 2%. The notes mature on 31 December 20X8.

Principal is redeemable at maturity. The carrying amount at the balance sheet date is US$ 30m (C21. 6m).

The functional currency of the entity is C (currency units).

The spot rate at the balance sheet date is US$ = C0. 72

The 6 month LIBOR at the balance sheet date is 5% per annum.

Scenario 1 – Contractual cash flows of the notes (using spot rates at the balance sheet date)

	30 Jun 20X7	**31 Dec 20X7**	**30 Jun 20X8**	**31 Dec 20X8**	**Total**
Principal (US$)	–	–	–	30,000	**30,000**
Interest payments (LIBOR +2%)	1,050	1,050	1,050	1,050	**4,200**
Total (in US$)	**1,050**	**1,050**	**1,050**	**31,050**	**34,200**
US/C spot rate as at 31 Dec 20X6	0. 72	0. 72	0. 72	0. 72	0. 72
Total cash flows (in C)	**756**	**756**	**756**	**22,356**	**24,624**

11.104.1.10 当主体列报金融资产的到期日分析时，其应根据提供给关键管理人员的内部信息来编制。到期日分析可基于合同到期日或预计到期日，取决于如何对风险进行管理。或者，该分析可以按净额（即公允价值）为基础列报。

[下一段为第 11.104.3 段]。

11.104.3 如下示例说明了如何根据合同编制一些典型金融工具的到期日分析。

示例 1——浮动利率票据

主体 A 于 20X6 年 12 月 31 日发行了两年期、支付 6 个月的伦敦同业拆借利率加 2% 的利息、3,000 万美元的浮动利率票据。该票据到期日为 20X8 年 12 月 31 日。

本金于到期日赎回。其在资产负债表日的账面金额为 3,000 万美元（C2,160 万元）。

主体的功能货币为 C（货币单位）。

资产负债表日的即期汇率为 US$ = 0.72C。

资产负债表日的 6 个月的伦敦同业拆借利率为每年 5%。

第一种情况——票据的合同现金流（采用资产负债表日的即期利率）

	20X7 年 6 月 30 日	**20X7 年 12 月 31 日**	**20X8 年 6 月 30 日**	**20X8 年 12 月 31 日**	**合计**
本金(美元)	-	-	-	30,000	**30,000**
利息付款(伦敦同业拆借利率 +2%)	1,050	1,050	1,050	1,050	**4,200**
合计(美元)	**1,050**	**1,050**	**1,050**	**31,050**	**34,200**
20X6 年 12 月 31 日的美元兑 C 的即期汇率	0.72	0.72	0.72	0.72	0.72
现金流合计(C)	**756**	**756**	**756**	**22,356**	**24,624**

Scenario 2 – Contractual cash flows of the notes (using forward rates available at the balance sheet date)

6m LIBOR yield curve	5.25%	5.50%	5.75%	5.40%	
6m LIBOR yield curve + 2% per annum	7.25%	7.50%	7.75%	7.40%	
	30 Jun 20X7	**31 Dec 20X7**	**30 Jun 20X8**	**31 Dec 20X8**	**Total**
Principal (US$)	–	–	–	30,000	**30,000**
Interest payments (LIBOR + 2%)	1,088	1,125	1,163	1,110	**4,486**
Total (in US$)	**1,088**	**1,125**	**1,163**	**31,110**	**34,486**
US/C forward rate as at 31 Dec 20X6	0.75	0.78	0.79	0.76	
Total cash flows (in C)	**816**	**878**	**919**	**23,644**	**26,257**

Liquidity analysis

Solution 1 (based on spot rates)

Financial liabilities as at 31 Dec 20X6	**Less than 1 month**	**Between 1 and 3M**	**Between 3M and 1Y**	**Between 1 and 5Y**	**Over 5Y**	**Balance sheet amounts**
Floating rate notes	–	–	1.512	23,112	–	21,600

Alternative answer based on forward rates

Financial liabilities as at 31 Dec 20X6	**Less than 1 month**	**Between 1 and 3 months**	**Between 3 months and 1 year**	**Between 1 and 5 years**	**Over 5 years**	**Balance sheet amounts**
Floating rate notes	–	–	1,694	24,563	–	21,600

第二种情况——票据的合同现金流(采用资产负债表日的远期利率)

6个月的伦敦同业拆借利率收益率曲线	5.25%	5.50%	5.75%	5.40%	
6个月的伦敦同业拆借利率收益率曲线+每年2%	7.25%	7.50%	7.75%	7.40%	
	20X7年6月30日	**20X7年12月31日**	**20X8年6月30日**	**20X8年12月31日**	**合计**
本金(美元)	-	-	-	30,000	**30,000**
利息付款(伦敦同业拆借利率+2%)	1,088	1,125	1,163	1,110	**4,486**
合计(美元)	**1,088**	**1,125**	**1,163**	**31,110**	**34,486**
20X6年12月31日的美元兑C的远期汇率	0.75	0.78	0.79	0.76	
现金流合计(C)	**816**	**878**	**919**	**23,644**	**26,257**

流动性分析

解决方法1(基于即期利率)

20X6年12月31日的金融负债	**一个月以内**	**一至三个月**	**三个月至一年**	**一至五年**	**五年以上**	**资产负债表金额**
浮动利率票据	-	-	1.512	23,112	-	21,600

基于远期利率的可选答案

20X6年12月31日的金融负债	**一个月以内**	**一至三个月**	**三个月至一年**	**一至五年**	**五年以上**	**资产负债表金额**
浮动利率票据	-	-	1,694	24,563	-	21,600

Either the spot rate or the forward rate could be used for the interest rate cash outflow calculation. The forward rate would be based on a yield curve (which will show by how much LIBOR is expected to move each quarter/six months).

Both alternatives are acceptable provided they are properly disclosed and applied consistently.

The sum of all the amounts in the maturity analysis does not reconcile to the balance sheet amount. This is because the liquidity analysis is based on the undiscounted cash flows.

Example 2 – Interest rate swap

Entity A entered into a two-year interest rate swap, notional value C10m, under which fixed interest of 5% per annum is received quarterly and actual 3 month LIBOR is paid. The contract is settled on a net basis. The swap has a negative fair value of C0.071m at the balance sheet date.

Estimated cash flows on the swap (C'000)

	31 Mar 20X7	**30 Jun 20X7**	**30 Sept 20X7**	**31 Dec 20X7**	**31 Mar 20X8**	**30 Jun 20X8**	**30 Sept 20X8**	**31 Dec 20X8**	**Total**
Fixed leg (receives fixed)	125	125	125	125	125	125	125	125	
Variable leg (pays 3 month LIBOR)	-110	-122	-136	-150	-155	-160	-172	-186	
Undiscounted net cash flows	15	3	-11	-25	-30	-35	-47	-61	-191
Discounted cashflows	13	2	-7	-14	-14	-15	-17	-19	-71

Only derivatives with a negative fair value (financial liabilities) at the balance sheet date should be included in the liquidity analysis. The cash flows to be included are those undiscounted cash flows that result in an outflow for the entity at each reporting date. While the standard only requires the gross cash outflows

在计算利息现金流出既可以使用即期利率也可以使用远期利率。远期利率将根据收益率曲线（显示伦敦同业拆借利率每个季度或每 6 个月预期变动多少）而定。

两种选择均可接受，只要进行适当的披露并一致地应用。

到期日分析中所有金额的合计与资产负债表金额并不一致。这是因为流动性分析是根据未经折现的现金流编制的。

示例 2——利率互换

主体 A 签订了一个两年期的利率互换，名义价值为 C1,000 万元，并于每季度按 5% 的年利率收取固定利息并按实际 3 个月的伦敦同业拆借利率支付利息。该合同以净额结算。该互换在资产负债表日的公允价值为负 C71,000 元。

该互换合同的估计现金流（C 千元）

	20X7年3月31日	20X7年6月30日	20X7年9月30日	20X7年12月31日	20X8年3月31日	20X8年6月30日	20X8年9月30日	20X8年12月31日	合计
固定部分(收取固定利息)	125	125	125	125	125	125	125	125	
浮动部分(支付3个月的伦敦同业拆借利率)	-110	-122	-136	-150	-155	-160	-172	-186	
未经折现的净现金流	15	3	-11	-25	-30	-35	-47	-61	-191
折现的现金流	13	2	-7	-14	-14	-15	-17	-19	-71

只有在资产负债表日公允价值为负数的衍生工具（金融负债）才应被纳入流动性分析。要披露的现金流是在每个报告日导致主体产生现金流出的未经折现的现金流。尽管该准则只要求在到期日分析中披露总现金流出（即支付部分），对于以总额结算的衍生工具，单独披露相应的现金流入（即收

(that is, the pay leg) to be included in the maturity analysis, separate disclosure of the corresponding inflows (that is, the receive leg) might make the information more meaningful in the case of gross settled derivatives.

Liquidity analysis (based on forward rates)

Financial liabilities as at 31 Dec 20X6

	Less than 1 month	Between 1 and 3M months	Between 3 months and 1 year	Between 1 and 5 years	Over 5 years	Balance sheet amounts
Interest rate swaps		15	-33	-173		-71

11.104.4 For some instruments, such as perpetual bonds and written put options, it is difficult to determine how, if at all, to include amounts in the maturity analysis. In the case of perpetual bonds, where the debtor/issuer has a call option to redeem the bond, the debtor/issuer has discretion over the repayment of the principal. Until the option is exercised, the bond's contractual terms are that it is a non-redeemable perpetual bond. Once the call option is exercised, the bond's contractual terms are changed and the bond has a maturity date. If the call option was not exercised, then the undiscounted cash flows would be paid in perpetuity. This raises the question of what amount should be shown in the last time band. The standard does not deal explicitly with such a situation so a number of alternative approaches could be applied. One would be to include the principal amount in the last time band. Another option would be not to include any cash flows in the last time band, but disclose the principal amount in time band entitled 'no maturity'. Whatever form of disclosure is chosen, this is an area where it will be important to provide a clear narrative description of the instrument's terms.

[The next paragpragh is 11.104.6.]

11.104.6 The inclusion of an 'out of the money' written put option (financial liability) in the maturity analysis will depend on whether the option is settled net or gross. If the option is out of the money and net settled, no liability is required to be disclosed in the maturity table, because there is no obligation to make a

款部分）可能会使该信息更有意义。

流动性分析（基于远期利率）

20X6 年 12 月 31 日的金融负债

	一个月以内	一至三个月	三个月至一年	一至五年	五年以上	资产负债表金额
利率互换		15	-33	-173		-71

11.104.4　对于某些工具，例如永续债券和签出看跌期权，很难、有时甚至无法确定如何披露到期日分析中的金额。对于永续债券，在债务人/发行人拥有可以赎回债券的看涨期权的情况下，债务人/发行人可自主决定本金的偿还。在该期权被行权之前，根据债券的合同条款其是一项不可赎回的永续债券。期权一旦被行权，债券的合同条款发生了变化，该债券有了到期日。如果未行使该项看涨期权，那么未经折现的现金流将永久地支付。这就产生了一个问题，在最后一个时间段内应披露多大的金额。对这种情况准则并未明确规定，因此可以采用多种可选方法。其中一种方法就是将本金的金额计入到最后一个时间段。另一种选择就是不在最后一个时间段内纳入任何现金流，但是在定义为“无到期日”的时间段内披露本金的金额。无论选择哪种披露方式，重要的是对工具的条款提供清楚的简要描述。

[下一段为第 11.104.6 段]。

11.104.6　在到期日分析中是否纳入“价外”签出看跌期权（金融负债）将取决于该期权是以净额还是总额结算。如果期权是价外期权且以净额结算，则在到期日表格中没有需要披露的负债，因为根据资产负债表日所存在的条件没有进行支付的义务。[IFRS 7 附录 B 第 11D 段]。但是，对于以总额结算的

payment based on the conditions existing at the balance sheet date. [IFRS 7 App B para 11D]. However, for gross settled derivatives where the counterparty can force the issuer to make a payment, the pay leg is disclosed in the liquidity table in the earliest time bucket irrespective of whether the instrument is in or out of the money. An American style option should be disclosed in the earliest time band, a European style option depending on the exercise date.

11.104.7 A narrative disclosure should explain that written options have been included based on their intrinsic value and that the amount actually payable in the future may vary if the conditions change. This is supported by paragraph 10A(b) of appendix B to IFRS 7, which states that an explanation is required if the outflows of cash included in the maturity analysis could be significantly different from those disclosed in the contractual maturity table.

11.105 An entity that has provided a disclosure of its liquidity risk is shown in Table 11.10. This company does not have financial guarantees or loan commitments. Such features are more common in banks, although certain industrial companies, particularly in the construction industry do issue financial guarantees and companies in the motor industry often have lending facilities for customers. Note that the examples below include only certain of the potentially extensive disclosures that IFRS 7 requires.

Table 11.10 – Liquidity risk

Givaudan Plc – Annual report – 31 December 2009

4.2.6 Liquidity risk

Prudent liquidity risk management implies maintaining sufficient cash and marketable securities, the availability of funds through an adequate amount of committed credit facilities and the ability to close out market positions. Due to the dynamic nature of the underlying businesses, Group Treasury maintains flexibility in funding by maintaining availability under committed and uncommitted credit lines.

Group Treasury monitors and manages cash at the Group level and defines the maximum cash level at affiliate level. If necessary, inter-company loans within the Group provide for short-term cash needs; excess local cash is repatriated in the most appropriate manner.

衍生工具，在交易对方可以强制发行人付款的情况下，无论该工具是价内还是价外，支付部分应在流动性表格的最早时间段中披露。美式期权应在最早时间段中披露，而欧式期权则应根据行权日确定。

11.104.7 需要提供叙述式披露解释签出期权是基于内在价值披露，如果条件变化，将来实际应付的金额可能会改变。IFRS 7 附录 B 第 10A（b）段也支持了这一点，该段规定如果到期日分析中所含的现金流出可能与在合同到期日表格中所披露的现金流出显著不同，则要求进行解释。

11.105 表 11.10 中所示为主体对流动性风险的披露。该公司没有财务担保或贷款承诺。这些情况在银行更加常用，尽管一些工业公司，尤其是在建造行业的公司的确会签出财务担保，而汽车行业的公司通常会有给客户的借款额度。值得注意的是以下示例仅仅涵盖了 IFRS 7 所要求的某些可能的详尽披露。

表 11.10——流动性风险

Givaudan Plc——年报——2009 年 12 月 31 日

4.2.6 流动性风险

谨慎的流动性风险管理意味着维持足够的现金和可销售证券、通过足额的承诺信用额度提供可使用的资金以及结算市场头寸的能力。因为所涉及业务的动态特性，本集团资金部通过维持可使用的已承诺和未承诺信用额度的方式来保证资金来源的灵活性。

本集团资金部在集团层面对现金进行监控和管理并规定了附属企业层面的最高现金水平。如需要，可以通过集团内公司间贷款来满足短期现金需求；当地多余的现金以最合适的方式上缴。

Con.

The following table analyses the Group's remaining contractual maturity for financial liabilities and derivative financial instruments. The table has been drawn up based on the undiscounted cash flows of financial liabilities based on the earliest date on which the Group is obliged to pay. The table includes both interest and principal cash flows:

2009 in millions of Swiss francs	**Up to 6 months**	**6 – 12 months**	**1 – 5 years**	**Over 5 years**	**Total**
Short-term debt (excluding bank overdraft)	(74)				(74)
Accounts payable-trade and others	(294)				(294)
Net settled derivative financial instruments	(11)	(9)	(35)	1	(54)
Gross settled derivative financial instruments-outflows	(1,372)				(1,372)
Gross settled derivative financial instruments-inflows	1,377				1,377
Long-term debt	(32)	(27)	(2,337)	(115)	(2,511)
Balance as at 31 December	**(406)**	**(36)**	**(2,372)**	**(114)**	**(2,928)**

2008 in millions of Swiss francs	**Up to 6 months**	**6 – 12 months**	**1 – 5 years**	**Over 5 years**	**Total**
Short-term debt (excluding bank overdraft)	(245)				(245)
Accounts payable-trade and others	(314)				(314)
Net settled derivative financial instruments	(11)	(12)	(37)		(60)
Gross settled derivative financial instruments-outflows	(981)				(981)
Gross settled derivative financial instruments-inflows	1,012				1,012
Long-term debt	(67)	(31)	(2,571)	(258)	(2,927)
Balance as at 31 December	**(606)**	**(43)**	**(2,608)**	**(258)**	**(3,515)**

续表

下表分析了本集团金融负债和衍生金融工具的剩余合同到期日。此表格是根据集团金融负债被要求付款最早日期的未经折现的现金流编制的。本表格中既包括利息又包括本金的现金流：

2009 年以百万瑞士法郎为单位	**六个月以内**	**六至十二个月**	**一至五年**	**五年以上**	**合计**
短期债务（银行透支除外）	(74)				(74)
应付账款 – 交易性及其他	(294)				(294)
以净额结算的衍生金融工具	(11)	(9)	(35)	1	(54)
以总额结算的衍生金融工具 – 流出	(1,372)				(1,372)
以总额结算的衍生金融工具 – 流入	1,377				1,377
长期债务	(32)	(27)	(2,337)	(115)	(2,511)
12 月 31 日余额	**(406)**	**(36)**	**(2,372)**	**(114)**	**(2,928)**
2008 年，以百万瑞士法郎为单位	**六个月以内**	**六至十二个月**	**一至五年**	**五年以上**	**合计**
短期债务（银行透支除外）	(245)				(245)
应付账款 – 交易性及其他	(314)				(314)
以净额结算的衍生金融工具	(11)	(12)	(37)		(60)
以总额结算的衍生金融工具 – 流出	(981)				(981)
以总额结算的衍生金融工具 – 流入	1,012				1,012
长期债务	(67)	(31)	(2,571)	(258)	(2,927)
12 月 31 日余额	**(606)**	**(43)**	**(2,608)**	**(258)**	**(3,515)**

Market risk

Sensitivity analysis

11.106 Unless an entity complies with paragraph 11.114 below, it should disclose:

- A sensitivity analysis for each type of market risk to which the entity is exposed at the reporting date, showing how profit or loss and equity would have been affected by changes in the relevant risk variable that were reasonably possible at that date. The sensitivity analysis should show the effect of changes over the period until the entity next presents these disclosures, which usually is its next annual report. [IFRS 7 App B para 19(b)]. Note that the standard requires this disclosure based on reasonably possible changes and not on a 'worst case scenario' or 'stress test'. Risk variables that are relevant to disclosing market risk include, but are not limited to:
  - The yield curve of market interest rates. It may be necessary to consider both parallel and non-parallel shifts in the yield curve.
  - Foreign exchange rates.
  - Prices of equity instruments.
  - Market prices of commodities.
- The methods and assumptions used in preparing the sensitivity analysis.
- Changes from the previous period in the methods and assumptions used and the reasons for such changes.

[IFRS 7 para 40, IG 32].

11.107 In providing the sensitivity analysis for each type of market risk, an entity should decide how it aggregates information to display the overall picture without combining information with different characteristics about exposures to risks from significantly different economic environments. Entities are not required to disclose the effect for each change within a range of reasonably possible changes

市场风险

敏感性分析

11.106　除非主体符合下文第 11.114 段的要求，否则应当披露：

- 主体在报告日所面临的各类市场风险的敏感性分析，反映在该日相关风险变量发生合理、可能的变动时将对主体损益和权益产生的影响。敏感性分析将体现截止到主体下一次提供此类披露的期间（通常为直到下一个年度报告期）的变动影响。[IFRS 7 附录 B 第 19（b）段]。值得注意的是本准则要求这种披露基于合理、可能的变动而非“最坏的情况”或“压力测试”。与披露市场风险相关的风险变量包括，但不限于：
  - 市场利率的收益率曲线。考虑收益率曲线的平行或非平行移动可能是必要的。
  - 外汇汇率。
  - 权益工具的价格。
  - 商品的市场价格。
- 编制敏感性分析所使用的方法和假设。
- 于前一期相比，所使用的方法和假设的变化及这些变化的原因。

[IFRS 7 第 40 段，IG 第 32 段]。

11.107　在对每种类型的市场风险提供敏感性分析时，主体应决定如何合并信息以显示其总体情况，从而不混合来自重大不同经济环境的风险的不同特征的信息。不要求主体披露相关风险变量在合理、可能的变动范围内的每一变动的影响。披露在合理、可能范围内变动的影响已足够。[IFRS 7 附录 B 第 18 段]。例如，对金融工具进行交易的主体可以分开披露为交易而持有的和不是

of the relevant risk variable. Disclosure of the effects of the changes at the limits of the reasonably possible range would be sufficient. [IFRS 7 App B paras 18]. For example, an entity that trades financial instruments might disclose this information separately for financial instruments held for trading and those not held for trading. Similarly, an entity would not aggregate its exposure to market risks from areas of hyperinflation with its exposure to the same market risks from areas of very low inflation. Conversely, if an entity has exposure to only one type of market risk in only one economic environment, it would not show disaggregated information. [IFRS 7 App B para 17].

11.107.1 In addition, where there are changes in volatility, an entity should not restate the prior year disclosures. For example, where the reasonable possible change in an exchange rate changes from 5 per cent in the prior year to 8 per cent in the current year, the prior year disclosures should not be restated. An entity could, however, present additional sensitivity information for the comparative period.

11.108 For the purposes of disclosing the effect on profit or loss and equity of reasonably possible changes in the relevant risk variable, for example interest rate risk, as required by the first bullet point of paragraph 11.106 above, an entity might show separately the effect of a change in market rates on:

- Interest income and expense.
- Other line items of profit or loss (such as trading gains and losses).
- When applicable, equity.

[IFRS 7 para IG34].

11.109 An entity might disclose a sensitivity analysis for interest rate risk for each currency in which the entity has material exposures to interest rate risk. Similarly, a sensitivity analysis is disclosed for each currency to which an entity has significant exposure. [IFRS 7 paras IG34, App B para 24].

11.109.1 This disclosure would also be relevant to those instruments where an entity has effectively hedged the interest rate risk, as illustrated in the following example.

为交易而持有的金融工具。类似地，主体不应将来自恶性通货膨胀地区的市场风险敞口和低通货膨胀地区的类似市场风险敞口进行合并。与此相反，如果主体仅在单一经济环境中存在唯一一种类型的市场风险敞口，主体不应将信息分开披露。[IFRS 7 附录 B 第 17 段]。

11.107.1　此外，在波动性有变动的情况下，主体不应重述上一年度的披露。例如，在汇率的合理可能变化从上一年度的 5% 变为当前年度的 8% 的情况下，上一年度的披露不应重述。但是，主体可以为比较期列报额外的敏感性信息。

11.108　如上文第 11.106 段第一点所要求的，为了披露相关风险变量的合理可能变动对损益和权益的影响，例如利率风险，主体可以分别列示市场利率变化对下列事项的影响：

- 利息收入和费用。
- 其他损益项目（例如交易利得和损失）。
- 权益（如果适用的话）。

[IFRS 7 IG 第 34 段]。

11.109　主体可以对其具有重大利率风险敞口的每一种货币披露其利率风险的敏感性分析。类似地，对主体具有重大风险敞口的每一种货币均应披露敏感性分析。[IFRS 7 IG 第 34 段，附录 B 第 24 段]。

11.109.1　这种披露还应该与主体对利率风险进行了有效套期的工具相关，如下文示例所示：

Example – A bond hedged for variable interest rate risk

An entity hedges its exposure to variable interest rate risk on an issued bond. The hedge is designated as a cash flow hedge. The bond and the hedging instrument (interest rate swap) have a five-year remaining life. The variable leg of the swap exactly matches the variable interest of the bond (causing no ineffectiveness).

The high effectiveness of the hedge does not necessarily mean that there would be no impact on equity or profit or loss due to changes in interest rate risk. The accounting for a cash flow hedge means that the fair value movement related to the effective part of the hedging instrument is included in other comprehensive income. Amounts deferred in other comprehensive income are recycled in profit or loss when the hedged transaction occurs. Hence, reasonably possible movements in the interest rate risk exposure have an impact on both profit or loss and equity.

At the same time, reasonably possible movements in the interest rate risk exposure on the outstanding bond would impact profit or loss, as the bond was a recognised financial liability at the balance sheet date.

If the effects of recycling and ineffectiveness are not material, the entity could consider the following disclosure as an approximation for the sensitivity analysis: "*The movements related to the bond and the swap's variable leg are not reflected as they offset each other. The movements related to the remaining fair value exposure on the swap's fixed leg are shown in the equity part of the analysis*".

11.110 It should be noted that for the purposes of disclosing a sensitivity analysis for foreign currency risk, translation related risk is not taken into account. This is because foreign currency risk can only arise on financial instruments that are denominated in a currency other than the functional currency in which they are measured. [IFRS 7 App B para 23]. Translation exposures arise from financial and non-financial items held by an entity (for example, a subsidiary) with a functional currency different from the group's presentation currency. Therefore, translation-related risks are not taken into consideration for the purpose of the

示例——浮动利率风险已套期的债券

某主体对一其所发行债券的浮动利率风险敞口进行了套期。该项套期被指定为现金流量套期。该债券和套期工具（利率互换）仍有五年期限。互换合同的浮动部分与债券的浮动利息完全匹配（因而没有无效性）。

套期的高度有效并不一定意味着利率风险的变化不会对权益或损益造成任何影响。现金流量套期的会计处理指的是与套期工具的有效部分相关的公允价值变动计入其他综合收益。当被套期交易发生时，递延至其他综合收益的金额会转入损益。因此，利率风险敞口的合理、可能变动对损益和权益都会有影响。

同时，由于该债券在资产负债表日是一项已确认的金融负债，其利率风险敞口的合理、可能变动会对损益产生影响。

如果转入损益和无效性的影响并不重大，主体可以考虑进行如下披露作为敏感性分析：“*债券和互换浮动部分的变动并未披露，因为它们可以相互抵销。和互换固定部分剩余公允价值敞口相关的变动在分析中的权益部分列示。*”

11.110　值得注意的是在披露外汇风险的敏感性分析时，不应将与折算相关的风险考虑在内。这是因为外汇风险只能产生于以功能货币之外的其他货币计量的金融工具。[IFRS 7 附录 B 第 23 段]。折算风险产生于功能货币与集团的列报货币不同的主体（如子公司）所持有的金融和非金融项目。因此，在外汇风险的敏感性分析中并不考虑与折算相关的风险。这也包括准权益贷款（作为境外经营净投资一部分的公司间外币贷款）。另一方面，在敏感性分析中应包括被用作折算风险套期的所有贷款或衍生工具。以外币计价的公司间应收款和应付款，因为即使它们会在合并资产负债表中抵销，但是根据 IAS

sensitivity analysis for foreign currency risks. This also includes quasi-equity loans (foreign currency inter-company loans that are part of the net investment in a foreign operation). On the other hand, any loans or derivatives used as hedges of translation risk should be included within the sensitivity analysis. Also, foreign currency denominated inter-company receivables and payables would be included because, even though they cancel in the consolidated balance sheet, the effect on profit or loss of their revaluation under IAS 21 is not fully eliminated. Although they cannot be included within the analysis of foreign currency risks, additional translation risks can, however, be separately disclosed. This may be appropriate where an entity manages its translation risks together with its foreign currency transaction risks (for example, where a forward contract hedges movements in the retranslation of a foreign operation).

11.110.1 In the same way that translation exposures may have an impact on equity but are not included in the sensitivity analysis, there are other items that may be exposed to market price risk, but which are not necessarily included. For example, consider instruments that expose an entity to changes in its own share price. These include entities that have issued warrants with a foreign currency exercise price, those that have issued convertible debt that fails the 'fixed for fixed' requirement in IAS 32 and those that have issued share based compensation awards that are classified as liabilities. In the first two cases, the entity should disclose information about the effect of reasonably possible changes in its share price on its profit or loss and equity. This is because the first two instruments are in the scope of IAS 39 and, therefore, in the scope of IFRS 7. The third instrument, although classified as a liability, is outside the scope of IAS 39 as it is accounted for under IFRS 2. It, therefore, also falls outside the IFRS 7's scope.

11.111 Because the factors affecting market risk vary depending on the specific circumstances of each entity, the appropriate range to be considered in providing a sensitivity analysis of market risk varies for each entity and for each type of market risk. [IFRS 7 para IG35].

11.112 However, an entity is not required to determine what the profit or loss for the period would have been if relevant risk variables had been different. Instead, it should disclose the effect on profit or loss and equity at the balance sheet date,

21 对其进行重估对损益的影响并不能完全抵销。尽管折算风险不能被纳入外币风险的分析，额外的折算风险仍可以单独披露。当主体将折算风险与外币交易风险一起管理时（如用远期合同对境外经营重新折算的变动进行套期），这样披露可能是合适的。

11.110.1 正如折算风险可能会影响权益但并未包括在敏感性分析里，还有其他一些可能面临市场价格风险但并不一定需要包括的项目。例如，使主体面临其自身股票价格风险的工具。这包括那些发行了具有外币行权价格的认股权的主体、那些发行了不符合 IAS 32“固定换固定”要求的可转换债务的主体、以及那些发行了被划分为负债的以股份为基础的薪酬的主体。在前两种情况下，主体应披露其股份价格的合理可能变化对损益和权益的影响的信息。这是因为前两种工具在 IAS 39 的范围内，因此也在 IFRS 7 的范围内。第三种工具虽然被划分为负债，但因为其按照 IFRS 2 进行会计处理，并不在 IAS 39 的范围内，因此，它也不在 IFRS 7 的范围内。

11.111 由于影响市场风险的因素的变化取决于每个主体所处的特定环境，因此，在提供市场风险的敏感性分析时，应考虑的合理范围对各个主体和各个类型的市场风险是不同的。[IFRS 7 IG 第 35 段]。

11.112 但是，不要求主体在相关的风险变量不同的情况下确定当期的损益应该是多少。相反，主体应披露假定相关风险变量在资产负债表日发生了合理可能的变化并且应用于该日已存在的风险敞口，对损益和资产负债表日的权

assuming that a reasonably possible change in the relevant risk variable had occurred at the balance sheet date and had been applied to the risk exposures in existence at that date. For example, if an entity has a floating rate liability at the end of the year, the entity would disclose the effect on profit or loss (that is, interest expense) for the current year if interest rates had varied by reasonably possible amounts. [IFRS 7 App B para 18(a)].

11.113 Furthermore, an entity is not required to disclose the effect on profit or loss and equity for each change within a range of reasonably possible changes of the relevant risk variable. Disclosure of the effects of the changes at the limits of the reasonably possible range would be sufficient. [IFRS 7 App B para 18(b)].

11.114 If an entity prepares a sensitivity analysis, such as value-at-risk (VaR), that reflects interdependencies between risk variables (for example, interest rates and exchange rates) and uses it to manage financial risks, it may use that sensitivity analysis in place of the analysis described above. However, a precondition for disclosing sensitivity in such a format (VaR) is that the company uses VaR in managing its financial risks. It cannot choose just to apply VaR for disclosures purposes but continue to manage each risk variable separately. In addition, it is likely that outstanding intercompany foreign currency receivables and payables at the year end are not considered in the VaR model. If this is the case, the entity will need to prepare additional sensitivity disclosures for these amounts (see para 11.110 above). The entity should also disclose:

- an explanation of the method used in preparing such a sensitivity analysis, and of the main parameters and assumptions underlying the data provided; and
- an explanation of the objective of the method used and of limitations that may result in the information not fully reflecting the fair value of the assets and liabilities involved.

[IFRS 7 para 41].

11.114.1 In view of the requirement for VaR to be used in managing financial risk, IFRS 7 recognises that the measure used may not reflect the full potential risk over the next reporting period. [IFRS 7 App B para 20]. For example, an entity may use a 10 day VaR, or a measure that recognises only the potential for loss and

益的影响。例如，如果主体在年末拥有浮动利率负债，则主体应披露如果利率发生了合理可能金额的变动对当年损益（即利息费用）的影响。[IFRS 7 附录 B 第 18（a）段]。

11.113　此外，不要求主体披露相关风险变量在合理可能的变化范围内的每一变动对损益和权益的影响。披露在合理可能范围内变动的影响已足够。[IFRS 7 附录 B 第 18（b）段]。

11.114　如果主体采用风险价值法（“VaR”）编制的敏感性分析能够反映风险变量（例如利率和汇率）之间的关联性，并将之用于管理财务风险，则可使用这种敏感性分析取代上文所指定的分析。但是，以这种形式（VaR）进行敏感性披露的一个前提条件就是公司在管理财务风险时使用风险价值法。它不能选择仅采用风险价值法进行披露但继续单独管理各个风险变量。此外，在风险价值法模型中很可能不会考虑年末尚未支付的公司间的外币应收和应付款。如果是这种情况，主体将需要为这些金额进行其他的敏感性披露（参见上文第 11.110 段）。主体还应披露：

- 对用于该敏感性分析的方法，以及所提供的数据所依据的主要参数和假设的说明；以及
- 对所使用方法的目的、以及可能导致信息不能充分反映所涉及资产和负债公允价值的局限性的说明。

[IFRS 7 第 41 段]。

11.114.1　对于要求使用风险价值法对金融风险进行管理，IFRS 7 承认所用的方法可能无法反映下一报告期间的全部潜在风险。[IFRS 7 附录 B 第 20 段]。例如，主体可以使用 10 天 VaR，或仅计量潜在损失而不计量潜在利得。

not the potential for gain.

11. 115 An example of a company that has provided an analysis of market risk sensitivity and how it manages its market risk is provided in Table 11. 11. 1 (Note the company had no equity investments and, therefore, price risk sensitivity has not been disclosed.) An example of a company providing a price risk sensitivity is provided in Table 11. 11. 2.

Table 11. 11. 1 – Disclosure of market risk management and sensitivity

Glaxosmithkline plc – Annual report – 31 December 2008

Interest rate risk management

The policy on interest rate risk management requires the minimum amount of net borrowings at fixed rates to increase with the ratio of forecast interest payable to trading profit. The fixed to floating ratio is reviewed monthly by the TMG.

We use an interest rate swap to redenominate one of our external borrowings into the interest rate coupon required by GSK. The duration of this swap matches the duration of the principal instrument. Interest rate derivative instruments are accounted for as fair value or cash flow hedges of the relevant assets or liabilities.

Foreign exchange risk management

Foreign currency transaction exposure arising on internal and external trade flows is not hedged. The exposure of overseas operating subsidiaries to transaction risk is minimised by matching local currency income with local currency costs. For this purpose, our internal trading transactions are matched centrally and we manage intercompany payment terms to reduce risk. Exceptional foreign currency cash flows are hedged selectively under the management of Corporate Treasury.

We manage the short-term cash surpluses or borrowing requirements of subsidiary companies centrally using forward contracts to hedge future repayments back into the originating currency.

We seek to denominate borrowings in the currencies of our principal assets and cash flows. These are primarily denominated in US dollars, Euros and Sterling. Certain borrowings are swapped into other currencies as required.

Borrowings denominated in, or swapped into, foreign currencies that match investments in overseas Group assets are treated as a hedge against the relevant assets. Forward contracts are also used in major currencies to reduce our exposure to our investment in overseas Group assets (see 'Net Investment Hedges' section of this note for further details). The TMG review the ratio of borrowings to assets for major currencies monthly.

11.115　表 11.11.1 中列出了一个公司披露对市场风险的敏感性分析及其如何管理市场风险的示例。（值得注意的是该公司并没有权益投资，因此未披露价格风险的敏感性。）表 11.11.2 中列出了一个公司披露的价格风险敏感性分析。

表 11.11.1——市场风险管理及敏感性的披露

Glaxosmithkline plc——年报——2008 年 12 月 31 日

利率风险管理

利率风险管理的政策要求固定利率借款净额的最低金额需随预计应付利息对交易利润的比率的提高而提高。TMG 每月对固定利率对浮动利率借款的比率进行审查。

我们使用了一个利率互换将我们外部借款之一的借款改为 GSK 所要求的固定利率。该互换的期间与主要工具的期间相符。利率衍生工具相关资产或负债按照公允价值或现金流量套期核算。

外汇风险管理

因内部和外部交易流产生的外汇交易敞口并未被套期。境外经营子公司的外币风险敞口通过匹配当地货币收入与当地货币费用的方式得到最大程度的降低。为此，我们的内部交易被集中地匹配并且我们对公司间付款的条款进行管理以降低风险。在公司资金部的管理下有选择地对特殊外币现金流量进行套期保值。

通过使用远期合同将未来付款转换至原币种的方式，我们对子公司的短期现金结余或借款需求进行集中管理。

我们旨在以我们的主要资产和现金流量的货币来对借款计价。借款主要以美元、欧元和英镑计价。根据要求特定的借款被转换为其他货币。

与境外集团资产的投资相匹配的外币计价或已被转换为这种外币的借款被用于对相关资产的套期。对于主要货币还使用了远期合同来降低我们对境外集团资产的投资的风险敞口（进一步详细信息参见本附注“净投资套期”部分）。TMG 每月对主要货币的借款与资产比率进行审查。

Con.

Sensitivity analysis

The sensitivity analysis has been prepared on the assumption that the amount of net debt, the ratio of fixed to floating interest rates of the debt and derivatives portfolio and the proportion of financial instruments in foreign currencies are all constant and on the basis of the hedge designations in place at 31st December. Financial instruments affected by market risk include borrowings, deposits and derivative financial instruments. The following analyses are intended to illustrate the sensitivity of such financial instruments to changes in relevant foreign exchange and interest rates.

Foreign exchange sensitivity

The table below shows the Group's sensitivity to foreign exchange rates on its US dollar, Euro and Yen financial instruments excluding obligations under finance leases and certain non-derivative financial instruments not in net debt and which do not present a material exposure. These three currencies are the major currencies in which GSK's financial instruments are denominated. GSK has considered movements in these currencies over the last three years and has concluded that a 20% movement in rates is a reasonable benchmark. In this table, financial instruments are only considered sensitive to foreign exchange rates where they are not in the functional currency of the entity that holds them. Intercompany loans which are fully hedged to maturity with a currency swap have been excluded from this analysis.

	2008		2007	
	Increase/ (decrease) in income £m	**Reduction in equity £m**	Increase/ (decrease) in income £m	Reduction in equity £m
20% appreciation (2007 – 10% appreciation) of the US dollar	**210**	**991**	38	580
20% appreciation (2007 – 10% appreciation) of the Euro	**(20)**	**1,760**	(10)	709
20% appreciation (2007 – 10% appreciation) of the Yen	**1**	**52**	–	15

A 20% (2007 – 10%) depreciation of the stated currencies would have an equal and opposite effect. The movements in the income statement relate primarily to hedging instruments for US dollar legal provisions, trade payables and trade receivables. Whilst these are economic hedges, the provisions are not financial instruments and therefore are not included in the table above. The sensitivity of these hedging instruments would be insignificant if the provisions were included. The movements in equity relate to foreign

续表

敏感性分析

敏感性分析是在假设债务净额、债务和衍生工具组合的固定浮动利率比以及以外币计价的金融工具的比例均保持恒定且 12 月 31 日的套期指定已存在的基础上编制的。受市场风险影响的金融工具包括借款、存款及衍生金融工具。以下分析旨在说明这些金融工具对相关外汇汇率和利率变动的敏感性。

外汇敏感性

下表列示了集团对除融资租赁的债务和特定非债务净额且不具有重要风险敞口的非衍生金融工具之外的美元、欧元和日元金融工具的外汇汇率的敏感性。这三种货币是 GSK 金融工具的主要计价货币。GSK 考虑了这些货币在过去三年中的变动情况，并得出结论认为其合理的基准为汇率变动 20%。在此表中，只有在金融工具不以持有主体的功能货币计价的情况下才认为它们对外汇汇率具有敏感性。此项分析中未包括通过货币互换对直至到期日完全套期保值的公司间贷款。

	2008		2007	
	收益的增加／（减少）百万英镑	**权益减少百万英镑**	收益的增加／（减少）百万英镑	权益减少百万英镑
美元增值 20%（2007 年 – 增值 10%）	**210**	**991**	38	580
欧元增值 20%（2007 年 – 增值 10%）	**（20）**	**1,760**	（10）	709
日元增值 20%（2007 年 – 增值 10%）	**1**	**52**	–	15

所述货币贬值20%（2007 年 – 10%）将具有等量的反向影响。利润表中的变动主要与美元的法务预计负债、应付账款和应收账款的套期工具相关。尽管这些是经济套期，但预计负债不属于金融工具，因此并未被包括在上表中。如果包括了预计负债，则这些套期工具的敏感性应该不重要。权益的变动与用来对以美元、欧元和日元计价的集团资产进行套期保值的外汇情况相关。因此，货币互换的贬值将导致集团资产出现相应的增值。金融工具以外的集团资产对外汇的敏感性未包括在上表中。

Con.

exchange positions used to hedge Group assets denominated in US dollar, Euro and Yen. Therefore, a depreciation on the currency swap would give rise to a corresponding appreciation on the Group asset. Foreign exchange sensitivity on Group assets other than financial instruments is not included above.

The table below shows the Group's sensitivity to interest rates on its floating rate Sterling, US dollar and Euro financial instruments, being the currencies in which GSK has historically issued debt and held investments. GSK has considered movements in these interest rates over the last three years and has concluded that a 2% increase is a reasonable benchmark. Debt with a maturity of less than one year is floating rate for this calculation. A 2% movement in interest rates is not deemed to have a material effect on equity.

	2008 Increase/ (decrease) in income	2007 Increase/ (decrease) in income
2% increase (2007 – 1% increase) in Sterling interest rates	**16**	1
2% increase (2007 – 1% increase) in US dollar interest rates	**13**	(16)
2% increase (2007 – 1% increase) in Euro interest rates	**4**	3

A 2% (2007 – 1%) decrease in these interest rates would have an equal and opposite effect, with the exception of US dollar, where interest rates could not be decreased by 2% as they are currently less than 0.5%. The maximum decrease in income would therefore be limited to £1 million. Interest rate movements on obligations under finance leases, foreign currency and interest rate derivatives, trade payables, trade receivables and other financial instruments not in net debt do not present a material exposure to the Group's balance sheet based on a 2% increase or decrease in these interest rates.

Table 11.11.2 – Disclosure of price risk management and sensitivity

Henderson Group plc – Annual report – 31 December 2009

28. Financial risk management (extract)

Financial risk management objectives and policies

Financial assets principally comprise investments in equity securities, short-term investments, trade and other receivables, and cash and cash equivalents. Financial liabilities

续表

下表列示了集团对浮动利率的英镑、美元和欧元金融工具的利率敏感性，这些货币是GSK在过去发行债务和进行投资时所用货币。GSK考虑了这些利率在过去三年中的变动情况，并得出结论认为其合理的基准为增长2%。在本计算中将期限为一年以下的债务视为浮动利率债务。利率2%的变动不被认为会对权益产生重大的影响。

	2008 收益的增加/（减少）	2007 收益的增加/（减少）
英镑利率增加2%（2007 – 增加1%）	**16**	1
美元利率增加2%（2007 – 增加1%）	**13**	(16)
欧元利率增加2%（2007 – 增加1%）	**4**	3

这些利率减少2%（2007 – 1%）将具有等量的反向影响，而美元除外，因为其利率目前已经在0.5%以下所以不能减少2%。因此收益最大减少量将不超过一百万英镑。基于利率增加或减少2%，融资租赁的债务、外汇和利率衍生工具、应付账款、应收账款和其他以及并非债务净额的金融工具的利率变动并不会对集团的资产负债表造成重大的风险敞口。

表11.11.2——价格风险管理和敏感性披露

Henderson Group plc——年报——2009年12月31日

28. 金融风险管理（节选）

金融风险管理的目标和政策

金融资产主要包括对权益证券的投资、短期投资、交易和其他应收款、及现金和现金等价物。金融负债包括为融资而借入的借款、某些准备及交易和其他应付款。金融工

Con.

comprise borrowings for financing purposes, certain provisions and trade and other payables. The main risks arising from financial instruments are price risk, interest rate risk, liquidity risk, foreign currency risk and credit risk. Each of these risks is discussed in detail below. The Group monitors financial risks on a consolidated basis and intra-Group balances are settled when it is deemed appropriate for both parties to the transaction. The Company is not exposed to material financial risk and separate disclosures for the Company have not been included.

The Group has designed a framework to manage the risks of its business and to ensure that the Directors have in place risk management practices appropriate for a listed company. The management of risk within the Group is governed by the Board and overseen by the Audit Committee.

28.1 Price risk

Price risk is the risk that a decline in the value of assets adversely impacts on the profitability of the Group.

The Group is exposed to price risk in respect of seed capital investments in Henderson funds (available-for-sale financial assets). Seed capital investments vary in duration, depending on the nature of the investment, with a typical range of less than one year for Listed Asset products and between three and five years for Private Equity and Property funds. The total market value of seed capital investments at 31 December 2009 was £41.7m (2008: £57.2m). In 2008, the Group also had a corporate investment in BP of £18.7m which has been disposed of in full during 2009.

Management monitors exposures to price risk on an ongoing basis. Significant movements in investment values are monitored on a daily basis. Where appropriate, management will hedge price risk, but there were no such hedges in place at 31 December 2009.

A fall in the value of an investment which is significant or prolonged is considered to be objective evidence of impairment under IAS 39. In such an event, an investment is written down to its fair value and cumulative amounts previously recognised in equity, in respect of market value and unhedged foreign exchange movements on the investment, are recognised in the consolidated income statement as an impairment charge.

	2009		**2008**	
Price risk sensitivities	**Consolidated Income statement £m**	**Other comprehensive income £m**	**Consolidated Income statement £m**	**Other comprehensive income £m**
Market value movement +/−10%	–	4.2	–	7.6

续表

具产生的主要风险为价格风险、利率风险、流动性风险、外币风险和信用风险。每项风险都在下文做了详细讨论。本集团以合并的基础监控金融风险，集团内部余额在交易双方都认为合适时结算。本公司并未承受重大的金融风险，故未包括对公司的单独披露。

本集团已经筹划了框架以管理其业务风险的并向其董事确保有适合于上市公司的风险管理实务。本集团的风险管理由董事会进行并受到审计委员会的监督。

28.1 价格风险

价格风险是资产价值下跌对本集团营利性产生负面影响的风险。

本集团由于对 Henderson 基金的种子资本投资而承受价格风险。取决于投资的性质，种子资本投资的期限不同，一般来说上市资产产品少于一年，而私募股权和财富基金为三至五年。2009 年 12 月 31 日种子资本投资的总市场价值为 4,170 万英镑（2008：5,720 万英镑）。本集团于 2008 年还持有 1,870 万英镑的对 BP 公司的投资，该投资已于 2009 年全额处置。

管理层持续监控其价格风险敞口。投资价值的重大变动每日监控。如果合适，管理层会对价格风险进行套期，但于 2009 年 12 月 31 日并没有这样的套期。

按照 IAS 39，投资价值的重大或长期下跌被认为是减值的客观证据。在那种情况下，投资被减记至其公允价值，之前由于市场价值和投资未套期的外汇变动而在权益中确认的金额作为减值损失确认在合并利润表中。

	2009		**2008**	
价格风险敏感性	**合并利润表 百万英镑**	**其他综合收益 百万英镑**	**合并利润表 百万英镑**	**其他综合收益 百万英镑**
市场价值变动 +/-10%	-	4.2	-	7.6

Other market risk disclosures

11.116 When the sensitivity analyses disclosed in accordance with paragraph 11.106 above are unrepresentative of a risk inherent in a financial instrument (for example because the year-end exposure does not reflect the exposure during the year), the entity should disclose that fact and the reason it believes the sensitivity analyses are unrepresentative. [IFRS 7 para 42].

11.117 As noted above, the sensitivity analysis might be unrepresentative of a risk inherent in a financial instrument where the year end exposure does not reflect the exposure during the year. Other circumstances include the following:

- A financial instrument contains terms and conditions whose effects are not apparent from the sensitivity analysis, for example options that remain out of (or in) the money for the chosen change in the risk variable. In such a situation, additional disclosure might include:
  - the terms and conditions of the financial instrument (for example, the options);
  - the effect on profit or loss if the term or condition were met (that is, if the options were exercised); and
  - a description of how the risk is hedged.
- Financial assets are illiquid, for example, when there is a low volume of transactions in similar assets and an entity finds it difficult to find a counterparty. In such a situation, additional disclosure might include the reasons for the lack of liquidity and how the entity hedges the risk.
- An entity has a large holding of a financial assets that, if sold in its entirety, would be sold at a discount or premium to the quoted market price for a smaller holding. In such a situation, additional disclosure might include:
  - The nature of the security (for example, entity name).
  - The extent of holding (for example, 15 per cent of the issued shares).
  - The effect on profit or loss.

其他市场风险的披露

11. 116　当根据上文第 11. 106 段披露的敏感性分析不能代表金融工具的内在风险时（例如，由于年末的风险敞口不能反映当年的风险敞口），主体应当披露该事实以及其认为敏感性分析不具代表性的原因。[IFRS 7 第 42 段]。

11. 117　如上所述，在年末的风险敞口不能反映当年的风险敞口的情况下，敏感性分析可能不能代表金融工具的内在风险。其他情况包括：

- 从敏感性分析来看，金融工具包含的条款与条件的影响并不明显时，例如，在风险变量所选的变化值中保持价外（或价内）的期权。在这种情况下，额外的披露可能包括：
  - 金融工具（例如期权）的条款与条件；
  - 如果这些条款与条件被满足的话（即如果行权的话）对损益的影响；以及
  - 有关如何对风险进行套期保值的描述。
- 金融资产的流动性较弱，例如，当类似资产的交易量较低以及主体发现很难找到交易对方时。在这种情况下，额外的披露可能包括缺乏流动性的原因和主体如何对风险进行套期保值。
- 主体持有大量的金融资产，如果将其全部出售，需按持少量该资产时的市场报价的折价或溢价出售。在这种情况下，额外的披露可能包括：
  - 证券的性质（如主体名称）。
  - 持股比例（如发行股票的 15%）。
  - 对损益的影响。

■ How the entity hedges the risk.

[IFRS 7 para IG37 – 40].

11.118 An entity should provide sensitivity analyses for the whole of its business, but may provide different types of sensitivity analysis for different classes of financial instruments. [IFRS 7 App B para 21].

11.119 The sensitivity of profit or loss (that arises, for example, from instruments classified as at fair value through profit or loss and impairments of available-for-sale financial assets) is disclosed separately from the sensitivity of equity (that arises, for example, from instruments classified as available for sale). [IFRS 7 App B para 27]. For example, where the fair value of a non-monetary available-for-sale asset is close to the impairment threshold, an entity should distinguish between profit or loss and equity effects, taking into consideration its impairment policy. In cases where the asset is already impaired, the downward shift (due to the impairment) should be shown as affecting the profit or loss while the upward shift should be shown as affecting equity.

11.120 Financial instruments that an entity classifies as equity instruments are not remeasured. Neither profit or loss nor equity will be affected by the equity price risk of those instruments. Accordingly, no sensitivity analysis is required. [IFRS 7 App B para 28].

■ 主体如何对风险进行套期保值。

[IFRS 7 IG 第 37 - 40 段]。

11.118　主体应提供其全部业务的敏感性分析，但是对不同类型的金融工具可以提供不同类型的敏感性分析。[IFRS 7 附录 B 第 21 段]。

11.119　损益（例如，由划分为以公允价值计量且变动计入损益的金融工具或可供出售的金融资产的减值所导致的）的敏感性分析应与权益（例如由划分为可供出售的工具所导致的）的敏感性分析分开来进行单独披露。[IFRS 7 附录 B 第 27 段]。例如，在非货币性、可供出售的资产的公允价值接近减值临界值的情况下，主体应考虑其减值政策将对损益和权益的影响区分开来。对于资产已经减值的情况，应将向下的变动（因减值）显示为影响损益而将向上的变动显示为影响权益。

11.120　主体已划分为权益工具的金融工具不再重新计量。这些工具的权益价格风险既不影响损益也不影响权益。因而不要求进行敏感性分析。[IFRS 7 附录 B 第 28 段]。

PwC Assurance Service Contacts
联系普华永道审计业务部

北京 Beijing
梁伟坚 Thomas Leung
电话 Tel：+86（10）6533 2838
电子邮件 Email：thomas. w. leung@ cn. pwc. com

重庆 Chongqing
李松波 Bobby Lee
电话 Tel：+86（23）6393 7388
电子邮件 Email：bobby. lee@ cn. pwc. com

大连 Dalian
关兆文 Dorman Kwan
电话 Tel：+86（411）8379 1666
电子邮件 Email：dorman. kwan@ cn. pwc. com

广州 Guangzhou
张展豪 Albert Cheung
电话 Tel：+86（755）8261 8833
电子邮件 Email：albert. cheung@ cn. pwc. com

杭州 Hangzhou
潘振翔 Steve Pan
电话 Tel：+86（21）2323 2626
电子邮件 Email：steve. pan@ cn. pwc. com

南京 Nanjing
钱进 Jevens Qian
电话 Tel：+86（21）2323 3579
电子邮件 Email：jevens. qian@ cn. pwc. com

宁波 Ningbo
徐 宏 Toby Xu
电话 Tel：+86（21）2323 3399
电子邮件 Email：toby. xu@ cn. pwc. com

青岛 Qingdao
张国俊 Kevin Zhang
电话 Tel：+86（532）8089 1818
电子邮件 Email：kevin. zhang@ cn. pwc. com

上海 Shanghai
李丹 Daniel Li
电话 Tel：+86（21）2323 3388
电子邮件 Email：daniel. li@ cn. pwc. com

深圳 Shenzhen
张展豪 Albert Cheung
电话 Tel：+86（755）8261 8833
电子邮件 Email：albert. cheung@ cn. pwc. com

新加坡 Singapore
Yeoh Oon Jin
电话 Tel：+65 6236 3108
电子邮件 Email：oon. jin. yeoh@ sg. pwc. com

苏州 Suzhou
杨志勤 Zhiqin Yang
电话 Tel：+86（21）2323 3555
电子邮件 Email：zhiqin. yang@ cn. pwc. com

台湾 Taiwan
周建宏 Joseph Chou
电话 Tel：+886 2 2729 6666 * 26693
电子邮件 Email：joseph. chou@ tw. pwc. com

天津 Tianjin
郑广安 Kwong On Cheng
电话 Tel：+86（22）2318 3003
电子邮件 Email：kwong. on. cheng@ cn. pwc. com

西安 Xi'an
林兆荣 Benny Lam
电话 Tel：+86（29）8720 3838
电子邮件 Email：benny. s. lam@ cn. pwc. com

厦门 Xiamen
张祚诚 Douglas Chang
电话 Tel：+86（592）210 7888 * 1616
电子邮件 Email：douglas. dc. chang@ cn. pwc. com

PwC Accounting Consulting Services Contacts
联系普华永道会计咨询服务

黄家勇 Wilfred Wong
电话 Tel：+852 2289 1322
电子邮件 Email：wilfred. wong@ hk. pwc. com

金以文 Yvonne Kam
电话 Tel：+86（21）2323 3267
电子邮件 Email：yvonne. kam@ cn. pwc. com

陈保郎 Baolang Chen
电话 Tel：+86（21）2323 2555
电子邮件 Email：baolang. chen@ cn. pwc. com

陈燕华 Tracy Chen
电话 Tel：+86（21）2323 3070
电子邮件 Email：tracy. yh. chen@ cn. pwc. com

PwC China, Hong Kong, Taiwan and Singapore office locations and contacts
普华永道在中国大陆、香港、台湾及新加坡的事务所

北京 Beijing
中国北京市
朝阳区东三环中路7号
北京财富中心写字楼A座26楼
邮政编码 100020
26/F Office Tower A
Beijing Fortune Plaza
7 Dongsanhuan Zhong Road
Chaoyang District
Beijing 100020, PRC
电话 Tel: +86 (10) 6533 8888
传真 Fax: +86 (10) 6533 8800

重庆 Chongqing
中国重庆市渝中区邹容路68号
大都会商厦19楼1905室
邮政编码 400010
Room 1905
19/F Metropolitan Tower
68 Zou Rong Road
Chongqing 400010, PRC
电话 Tel: +86 (23) 6393 7888
传真 Fax: +86 (23) 6393 7200

大连 Dalian
中国大连市西岗区中山路147号
森茂大厦8楼
邮政编码 116011
8/F Senmao Building
147 Zhongshan Road
Xigang District
Dalian 116011, PRC
电话 Tel: +86 (411) 8379 1888
传真 Fax: +86 (411) 8379 1800

广州 Guangzhou
中国广州市天河区珠江新城
珠江西路10号
普华永道中心18楼
邮政编码 510623
18/F PricewaterhouseCoopers Center
10 Zhujiang Xi Road
Pearl River New City
Tianhe District
Guangzhou 510623, PRC
电话 Tel: +86 (20) 3819 2000
传真 Fax: +86 (20) 3819 2100

杭州 Hangzhou
中国杭州市下城区环城北路208号
坤和中心3205室
邮政编码 310006
Room 3205, Canhigh Center
208 Huancheng Road North
Xiacheng District
Hangzhou 310006, PRC
电话: +86 (571) 2807 6388
传真: +86 (571) 2807 6300

香港 Hong Kong
中国香港中环太子大厦22楼
22/F Prince's Building
Central
Hong Kong, PRC
电话 Tel: +852 2289 8888
传真 Fax: +852 2810 9888

澳门 Macau
中国澳门苏亚利斯博士大马路 323 号
中国银行大厦 29 楼
29/F Bank of China Building
323 Avenida Doutor Mario Soares
Macau, PRC
电话 Tel: +853 8799 5111
传真 Fax: +853 8799 5222

青岛 Qingdao
中国青岛市
香港中路 59 号
青岛国际金融中心 4601 室
邮政编码 266071
4601 Qingdao International
Finance Center
59 Hong Kong Middle Road
Qingdao 266071, PRC
电话 Tel: +86 (532) 8089 1888
传真 Fax: +86 (532) 8089 1800

南京 Nanjing
中国南京市鼓楼区中央路 201 号
南京国际广场南塔 12A 层 01 室
邮政编码 210009
Room 12A01, South Tower
Nanjing International Center
201 Zhongyang Road
Gulou District
Nanjing 210009, PRC
电话 Tel: +86 (25) 6608 6288
传真 Fax: +86 (25) 6608 6210

上海 Shanghai
中国上海市卢湾区湖滨路 202 号
企业天地 2 号楼
普华永道中心 11 楼
邮政编码 200021
11/F PricewaterhouseCoopes Center
2 Corporate Avenue
202 Hu Bin Road
Luwan District
Shanghai 200021, PRC
电话 Tel: +86 (21) 2323 8888
传真 Fax: +86 (21) 2323 8800

宁波 Ningbo
中国宁波市江东区民安东路 268 号
宁波国际金融服务中心 E 座 1203 室
邮政编码 315040
Room 1203, Tower E
Ningbo International Financial Center
268 Min An Road East
Jiangdong District
Ningbo 315040, PRC
电话 Tel: +86 (574) 8187 1788
传真 Fax: +86 (574) 8187 1700

深圳 Shenzhen
中国深圳市深南东路 5002 号
信兴广场地王商业中心 38 楼
邮政编码 518008
38/F Shun Hing Square
Di Wang Commercial Centre
5002 Shennan Road East
Shenzhen 518008, PRC
电话 Tel: +86 (755) 8261 8888
传真 Fax: +86 (755) 8261 8800

苏州 Suzhou
中国苏州市
苏州工业园区
旺墩路188号
建屋大厦1501室
邮政编码215028
Room 1501, Genway Tower
188 Wang Dun Road
Suzhou Industrial Park
Suzhou 215028, PRC
电话 Tel: +86 (512) 6273 1888
传真 Fax: +86 (512) 6273 1800

台湾 Taiwan
中国台北市信义区110
基隆路一段333号27楼
27/F, International Trade Building
333 Keelung Road, Section 1
Taipei, Taiwan 110, PRC
电话 Tel: +886 2 27296666
传真 Fax: +886 2 27576371 或 27576372

天津 Tianjin
中国天津市和平区
南京路189号
津汇广场2座36楼
邮政编码300051
36/F The Exchange Tower Two
189 Nanjing Road
Heping District
Tianjin 300051, PRC
电话 Tel: +86 (22) 2318 3333
传真 Fax: +86 (22) 2318 3300

厦门 Xiamen
中国厦门市
思明区鹭江道8号
国际银行大厦11楼B室
邮政编码361001
Unit B, 11/F
International Plaza
8 Lujiang Road
Siming District
Xiamen 361001, PRC
电话 Tel: +86 (592) 210 7888
传真 Fax: +86 (592) 210 8800

西安 Xi'an
中国西安市南大街30号
中大国际大厦728室
邮政编码710002
Room 728, Zhongda International Mansion
30 Nan Da Street
Xi'an 710002, PRC
电话 Tel: +86 (29) 8720 3336
传真 Fax: +86 (29) 8720 3335

新加坡 Singapore
新加坡048424邮区
PWC大厦
克罗士街8号17楼
8 Cross Street # 17 - 00
PWC Building
Singapore 048424
电话 Tel: +65 6236 3388
传真 Fax: +65 6236 3300

如欲了解更多资讯，敬请登陆公司网站：
For more information, please visit our websites at:
pwccn. com
pwchk. com

图书在版编目（CIP）数据

国际财务报告准则实务指引——金融工具：汉、英/陈燕华等编译．—北京：中国财政经济出版社，2011.9

（普华永道国际财务报告准则实务指引金融工具系列 1）

ISBN 978－7－5095－2983－6

Ⅰ.①国…　Ⅱ.①陈…　Ⅲ.①会计准则－世界－汉、英　Ⅳ.①F233.1

中国版本图书馆 CIP 数据核字（2011）第 131980 号

责任编辑：李　磊　　　　　　　　责任校对：徐艳丽

中国财政经济出版社出版

URL：http：//www.cfeph.cn

E－mail：cfeph@cfeph.cn

社址：北京市海淀区阜成路甲 28 号　邮政编码：100142

发行处电话：88190406　财经书店电话：64033436

涿州市新华印刷有限公司印刷　各地新华书店经销

787×1092 毫米　16 开　36.5 印张　616 000 字

2011 年 9 月第 1 版　2011 年 9 月涿州第 1 次印刷

定价：86.00 元

ISBN 978－7－5095－2983－6/F·2527

（图书出现印装问题，本社负责调换）

本社质量投诉电话：010－88190744